Conceptual **Frameworks**
for Giftedness and Talent Development

Conceptual Frameworks
for Giftedness and Talent Development

Enduring Theories and Comprehensive Models in Gifted Education

Edited by **TRACY L. CROSS, PH.D., AND PAULA OLSZEWSKI-KUBILIUS, PH.D.**

Routledge
Taylor & Francis Group
NEW YORK AND LONDON

First published in 2020 by Prufrock Press Inc.

Published in 2021 by Routledge
605 Third Avenue, New York, NY 10017
2 Park Square, Milton Park, Abingdon, Oxon OX14 4RN

Routledge is an imprint of the Taylor & Francis Group, an informa business.

Copyright © 2020, Taylor & Francis Group

Cover and layout design by Allegra Denbo

All rights reserved. No part of this book may be reprinted or reproduced or utilised in any form or by any electronic, mechanical, or other means, now known or hereafter invented, including photocopying and recording, or in any information storage or retrieval system, without permission in writing from the publishers.

Notice:
Product or corporate names may be trademarks or registered trademarks, and are used only for identification and explanation without intent to infringe.

Library of Congress Cataloging-in-Publication Data

Names: Cross, Tracy L., editor. | Olszewski-Kubilius, Paula, 1954-
Title: Conceptual frameworks for giftedness and talent development :
   enduring theories and comprehensive models in gifted education / edited
   by Tracy L. Cross & Paula Olszewski-Kubilius.
Description: Waco, TX : Prufrock Press Inc., 2020. | Includes
   bibliographical references. | Summary: ""Conceptual Frameworks for
   Giftedness and Talent Development" explores current and enduring
   theories and comprehensive models of giftedness and talent
   development"-- Provided by publisher.
Identifiers: LCCN 2020025955 (print) | LCCN 2020025956 (ebook) | ISBN
   9781646320486 (paperback)
Subjects: LCSH: Gifted children--Education.
Classification: LCC LC3993 .C596 2020 (print) | LCC LC3993 (ebook) | DDC
   371.95--dc23
LC record available at https://lccn.loc.gov/2020025955
LC ebook record available at https://lccn.loc.gov/2020025956

ISBN: 978-1-0321-4476-4 (hbk)
ISBN: 978-1-6463-2048-6 (pbk)

DOI: 10.4324/9781003233787

Table of Contents

FOREWORD   vii
DON AMBROSE

CHAPTER 1   **Evolving Complexity Theory of Talent Development**   1
A Developmental Systems Approach
DAVID YUN DAI

CHAPTER 2   **The Talent Development Megamodel**   29
RENA F. SUBOTNIK, PAULA OLSZEWSKI-KUBILIUS, AND FRANK C. WORRELL

CHAPTER 3   **Toward a Science of Expertise**   55
Obstacles, Implications, and Applications
DAVID Z. HAMBRICK AND BROOKE N. MACNAMARA

CHAPTER 4   **Tannenbaum's Psychosocial Conception of Giftedness**   93
LANNIE KANEVSKY

CHAPTER 5   **The Three-Ring Conception of Giftedness and the Schoolwide Enrichment Model**   145
A Talent Development Approach for All Students
JOSEPH S. RENZULLI AND SALLY M. REIS

CHAPTER 6   **Nonuniversal Theory and the Development of Gifts and Talents**   181
DAVID HENRY FELDMAN

CHAPTER 7   **Transformational Giftedness**   203
ROBERT J. STERNBERG

CHAPTER 8   **The Talent Search Model for Identifying and Developing Academic Talent**   235
LINDA E. BRODY

CHAPTER 9	**An Enhanced School-Based Conception of Giftedness** TRACY L. CROSS AND JENNIFER RIEDL CROSS	**265**
CHAPTER 10	**Advanced Academics** A Model for Gifted Education Without Gifted Students SCOTT J. PETERS AND JAMES H. BORLAND	**289**
CHAPTER 11	**Giftedness as IQ** JOHN D. WASSERMAN	**317**
CHAPTER 12	**Charting a Course for the Future** PAULA OLSZEWSKI-KUBILIUS AND TRACY L. CROSS	**357**

ABOUT THE EDITORS — **365**

ABOUT THE AUTHORS — **367**

FOREWORD

DON AMBROSE

THIS book is a major contribution to the field of gifted studies. It draws from the deep, extensive, impressive knowledge bases of leading thinkers in the field. The group of contributing authors includes highly accomplished, pioneering researchers and theorists. In the past, their work has done much to enrich ideas about the nature and purposes of gifted education, and their contributions to this volume continue along those lines.

Every important project needs outstanding leaders. Fortunately, this book project was initiated and led by two of the most impressive scholars in the field, Tracy L. Cross and Paula Olszewski-Kubilius. Having collaborated with both of them on a variety of projects I can attest to their extraordinary, cutting-edge knowledge and innovative inclinations. In addition, both Tracy and Paula are excellent examples of Robert Sternberg's WICS construct (wisdom, intelligence, and creativity synthesized; see Sternberg, 2003, 2005, 2017). Although creative and intelligent leaders can achieve significant results when they bring forth large-scale projects, they can cause harm inadvertently or even intentionally if they lack the wisdom element, which enables an individual to engage in ethical actions that are beneficial to all stakeholders to the extent possible. But when the leaders of a project have WICS going for them, the prospects for strong, positive, influential results are very good. Due to their extraordinary WICS, Tracy and Paula did much to achieve strong, positive, influential results through this book project.

Aside from the impressive nature of the scholars who developed and contributed to this volume, a number of other features of the project underlie its importance. First, clarifying the nature of giftedness and talent will improve educational and counseling experiences for bright young people whose needs are often misinterpreted or ignored. This volume provides some of that important clarification.

Second, the highly complex macroproblems and macro-opportunities arising from 21st-century socioeconomic, technological, cultural, and ideological turbulence demand an evolutionary leap forward in problem-solving abilities and ethical awareness (Ambrose, 2019; Ambrose & Sternberg, 2016a, 2016b). Without that leap forward, the prospects for human thriving and even survival over the long term are rather dim. This project provides some of the basis for that evolutionary leap.

Third, it might seem paradoxical that a field devoted to the discovery and development of lofty abilities has experienced such difficulty in determining exactly what giftedness is. Much of this paradox arises from the field's structure and dynamics fitting into a fragmented, porous, contested pattern instead of being unified, insular, and firmly policed (see Ambrose et al., 2010). A field aligning with the first of these patterns is fragmented and contested because it includes an array of diverse, often competing theoretical perspectives, and it is porous because it either invites or cannot resist invasion by constructs from other fields. Conversely, a field fitting the second pattern is unified around a single, dominant theory so conceptions that deviate from the theory are immediately rejected by the field's gatekeepers. And constructs from foreign disciplines are not allowed to intrude on, and mess up, the seemingly precise conceptual terrain (Bender & Schorske, 1997).

Each of these patterns presents advantages and disadvantages to scholars and other professionals who want to move their field forward, but the second pattern poses an especially damaging disadvantage. It forces virtually everyone in the field to oversimplify the important concepts they are grappling with to the point where major distortions occur. An example is neoclassical economics, which revolves around the theory that humans are rational actors making perfectly rational decisions based on complete information sets for entirely selfish purposes. Arguably, economic phenomena are far too complex to be captured within this theoretical model, so the conceptual distortions have been extreme, and the consequences have been devastating. Those consequences include the establishment of an extremely unfair economic system that pushes virtually all of the rewards up into the overstuffed pockets of a very small, increasingly corrupt elite while robbing the vast majority of economic security (Ambrose, 2012; Kotz, 2015; Madrick, 2014; Piketty, 2013/2014; Stiglitz, 2010, 2017; Temin & Vines, 2013). To the extent that many of those elite, economic actors are gifted individuals, this represents the effects of extremely harmful, unethical giftedness and dark creativity (for details about dark creativity, see Cropley et al., 2010; Gutworth et al., 2016; Majid al-Rifaie et al., 2016). These harmful effects magnify the importance and urgency of clarifying the conceptual terrain in the field of gifted studies, which this volume was well-designed to address.

Due to the high stakes for gifted young people, and arguably for society as a whole, the field of gifted studies can't afford to revolve around a simplified, dominant theory as it would if it were a unified, insular, firmly policed field. But it also can't abide the excessive ambiguity and uncertainty it suffers from being a fragmented, porous, contested field. A nuanced approach is needed so the field of gifted studies can straddle these two problematic patterns. This book goes a long way toward constructing that nuance. The editors and contributors do much to achieve this because their approach was set up to synthesize the various theories and models of giftedness and gifted education to the extent possible. Moreover, they work diligently to achieve these syntheses at all levels of analysis, from research to theory to practical application. They integrate the intellectual and social-emotional aspects of the gifted individual with the nature of educational, counseling, and mentorship environments. Importantly, they also go beyond these aspects of individual and educational dynamics to incorporate thoughtful analyses of the various large-scale contextual influences that shape the lives of gifted young people. Reading the final, synthesis chapter of the volume, authored by the editors, will give a panoramic view of the ways in which the collaborators in this project brought together all of these pieces of the gifted studies puzzle to provide a highly informative big-picture framework. The remainder of this foreword includes brief reactions to just a few of those puzzle pieces.

Attention to Complexity and Context

The aforementioned connections between theory, research, and practice can help to generate more attention to complexity and context in the field. For example, in Chapter 5, Joseph S. Renzulli and Sally M. Reis argue for syntheses of work in the field through all of these levels of analysis, and they show how the Schoolwide Enrichment Model (SEM) establishes an effective framework for those syntheses. They also argue that gifted education must become more sensitive to changing world conditions, such as the rapid evolution of technology and its effects on employment and the economy. As an example, they show how the SEM addresses the demands of 21st-century contexts.

Providing an overview of work pertaining to the talent development paradigm, Linda E. Brody (Chapter 8) illustrates much of the complexity that is dealt with in the field. She shows how the Talent Search model recognizes and addresses the complex diversity that educators of the gifted confront when they work with young people who present very different cognitive strengths, talents, motivational dynamics, and social-emotional issues.

Robert J. Sternberg (Chapter 7) addresses big-picture contextual issues in his portrayal of transformational giftedness. He warns the field about falling prey to short-range vision and ignoring the need for attention to the enormous problems humanity faces in the decades to come. He explores a range of these problems while showing how wisdom must be a key component of gifted programming. Anything short of this will limit the effectiveness of the field, the life prospects for bright young people, and even the long-term viability of life on Earth. Lannie Kanevsky (Chapter 4) also highlights the influences of large-scale contexts by employing Abraham Tannenbaum's explorations of the long-term development of giftedness as shaped by sociocultural forces.

Another important trend in the field magnifying contextual issues is the vibrant research trajectory focusing on domain-specific expertise. Rena

F. Subotnik, Paula Olszewski-Kubilius, and Frank C. Worrell are the most prominent explorers in this area, and Chapter 2 in this volume is a valuable extension of their work on this aspect of talent development. By emphasizing the importance of talent development within domains, they push attention out toward a wide variety of arenas for human endeavor, each of which features its own unique set of requirements for success. Taken together, all of these domains represent contexts that must be explored in more depth and detail. In Chapter 9 in this volume, Tracy L. Cross and Jennifer Riedl Cross also provide helpful elaboration on the nature of domain-specific development within school settings. In addition, the strengthening focus on contextual influences on the gifted and talented could go for naught if insufficient attention is paid to the structure and dynamics of schools, and the sociocontextual pressures that constrain them. Fortunately, Cross and Cross also provide detailed analyses of these contexts in their chapter.

For decades, scholars of gifted education have recognized that students who are not from White privileged backgrounds face daunting barriers when it comes to identification and inclusion in gifted programs (e.g., Ford, 2010, 2013; Ford et al., 2018; Frasier, 1987; Moore et al., 2005). Interdisciplinary inquiry shows that social problems in societies enlarge and strengthen these barriers. For example, in highly unequal societies, the social problems are far more severe than in more egalitarian contexts, and the United States is an extremely unequal context (Cabieses et al., 2016; Wilkinson & Pickett, 2010, 2019). Those not born into substantial privilege have to grapple with severe, chronic stress that magnifies the impact of social problems, such as mental illness, drug and alcohol abuse, violence, mass incarceration, lack of opportunity, suppression of social mobility, and mistrust. Due to the fact that gifted education tends to be reserved for those who demonstrate very high potential, the field must take responsibility for ensuring that these severe contextual barriers don't contaminate and distort identification procedures. Attention to the pernicious effects of inequality show up throughout this volume. For example, Scott J. Peters and James H. Borland (Chapter 10) illustrate how gifted education itself can inadvertently aggravate socioeconomic stratification.

Battling Sterile Certainty

The prominent mathematician William Byers (2007, 2011) used the term *sterile certainty* to show how excessive, simplistic assumptions about the accuracy of mechanistic precision in mathematical work cause people to ignore important phenomena that feature ambiguity, aesthetic appeal, and messy inner complexity. Fortunately, contributing authors in this volume recognize and address the problem of sterile certainty in gifted education. For example, some highlight the problem of underrepresentation by using talent discovery and development to go beyond the sterile certainty of traditional, quantitative identification procedures. This extends the reach of gifted education processes out toward many more young people than would otherwise be the case (see Chapters 1, 6, 9, and 11).

Additional examples of resistance to sterile certainty come from chapters that make strong cases against other forms of excessive mechanistic reductionism in the field. For example, in Chapter 10, Peters and Borland question the traditional, dominant notions of giftedness and gifted programs. In other movements away from sterile certainty, the volume features some major initiatives in the field deemphasizing the mechanistic identification of giftedness in favor of talent development and recognition of domain-specific expertise (see Chapter 2 by Subotnik, Olszewski-Kubilius, & Worrell, and Chapter 6 by David Henry Feldman). These works include some impressive efforts to synthesize theoretical perspectives in the field. One also might interpret the chapter on the Talent Development Megamodel (see Chapter 2) as working against sterile certainty because it encourages readers to consider domain-specific talent development instead of focusing too much on giftedness as a trait of the individual. Arguably, portrayals of giftedness as a heritable trait have been excessively certain and somewhat sterile in years past.

John D. Wasserman (Chapter 11) develops an extensive, in-depth analysis of the strengths and limitations of intelligence measures in his chapter. His recommendation that educators consider intelligence testing as a tool that can be used and misused, and that needs continual refinement as the field's knowledge base grows over time, can align well with the warnings about sterile certainty provided by others in this volume.

In Chapter 3, David Z. Hambrick and Brooke N. Macnamara combat another potentially pernicious and resilient form of sterile certainty—scientific authoritarianism, which entails advocacy of a theoretical view using antiscientific tactics, at the expense of scientific progress. They tackle the problem of dogmatism, which arises when individuals or groups fall prey to any blend of narrow-minded, shortsighted, superficial, or rigid thinking about a phenomenon (see Ambrose & Sternberg, 2012; Ambrose et al., 2012). They explore the relevance of attention to domains and social justice. In addition, Sternberg's (Chapter 7) analysis of the pseudo-quantitative precision in gifted education is another strong argument against scientific authoritarianism in the field.

In her use of Tannenbaum's analyses of giftedness as a launching pad for interpretation of current work in the field, Kanevsky (Chapter 4) also effectively attacks the problem of sterile certainty. For example, while recognizing the value of general intelligence, she discusses some of its inbuilt biases and distortions that arise from socioeconomic, cultural, and linguistic differences. Fortunately, her chapter is a good example of the holistic, conceptual synthesizing that scholars need to engage in to capture the essence of the highly complex phenomena that abound in the field.

I have always been a fan of interdisciplinary work, and there are many prominent thinkers who agree with its importance. One example is a past National Science Foundation president who argued that international, interdisciplinary collaboration is the new way of doing science (Suresh, 2013). Fortunately, interdisciplinary work is featured in this volume. For example, David Yun Dai (Chapter 1) uses complexity theory to establish an innovative, holistic model of talent development. The study of complex adaptive systems represents a creative way to portray giftedness as non-static, ever-evolving, and context sensitive. Chapter 3 by Hambrick and Macnamara incorporates important insights from philosophy and sociology as well as some other fields. Sternberg (see Chapter 7) pulls together descriptions from socioeconomic and ideological phenomena that were revealed by an array of disciplines in the social sciences and natural sciences.

I could go on much longer extolling the virtues of arguments put forth in the various chapters in this volume; however, a foreword to a book shouldn't turn into another of its chapters. Consequently, I must stop here. Suffice it to say that this book is a must read for those who want to understand the ways in which gifted studies should evolve in the years to come. I extend my admiration and appreciation to the impressive scholars who contributed to this project.

—Don Ambrose

References

Ambrose, D. (2012). The not-so-invisible hand of economics and its impact on conceptions and manifestations of high ability. In D. Ambrose, R. J. Sternberg, & B. Sriraman (Eds.), *Confronting dogmatism in gifted education* (pp. 97–114). Routledge.

Ambrose, D. (2019). The erosion of democracy: Can we muster enough wisdom to stop it? In R. J. Sternberg, H. Nusbaum, & J. Glück (Eds.), *Applying wisdom to contemporary world problems* (pp. 21–50). Palgrave-Macmillan.

Ambrose, D., & Sternberg, R. J. (Eds.). (2012). *How dogmatic beliefs harm creativity and higher-level thinking.* Routledge.

Ambrose, D., & Sternberg, R. J. (Eds.). (2016a). *Creative intelligence in the 21st century: Grappling with enormous problems and huge opportunities.* Sense.

Ambrose, D., & Sternberg, R. J. (Eds.). (2016b). *Giftedness and talent in the 21st century: Adapting to the turbulence of globalization.* Sense.

Ambrose, D., Sternberg, R. J., & Sriraman, B. (Eds.). (2012). *Confronting dogmatism in gifted education.* Routledge.

Ambrose, D., VanTassel-Baska, J., Coleman, L. J., & Cross, T. L. (2010). Unified, insular, firmly policed or fractured, porous, contested, gifted education? *Journal for the Education of the Gifted, 33*(4), 453–478. https://doi.org/10.1177/016235321003300402

Bender, T., & Schorske, C. E. (Eds.). (1997). *American academic culture in transformation: Fifty years, four disciplines.* Princeton University Press.

Byers, W. (2007). *How mathematicians think: Using ambiguity, contradiction, and paradox to create mathematics.* Princeton University Press.

Byers, W. (2011). *The blind spot: Science and the crisis of uncertainty.* Princeton University Press.

Cabieses, B., Pickett, K. E., & Wilkinson, R. G. (2016). The impact of socioeconomic inequality on children's health and well-being. In J. Komlos & I. R. Kelly (Eds.), *The Oxford handbook of economics and human biology* (pp. 244–265). Oxford University Press,.

Cropley, D. H., Cropley, A. J., Kaufman, J. C., & Runco, M. A. (Eds.). (2010). *The dark side of creativity.* Cambridge University Press.

Ford, D. Y. (2010). *Reversing underachievement among gifted Black students: Theory, research, and practice* (2nd ed.). Prufrock Press.

Ford, D. Y. (2013). *Recruiting and retaining culturally different students in gifted education*. Prufrock Press.

Ford, D. Y., Dickson, K. T., Davis, J. L., Scott, M. T., & Grantham, T. C. (2018). A culturally responsive equity-based Bill of Rights for gifted students of color. *Gifted Child Today, 41*(3), 125–129. https://doi.org/10.1177/1076217518769698

Frasier, M. M. (1987). The identification of gifted Black students: Developing new perspectives. *Journal for the Education of the Gifted, 10*(3), 155–180.

Gutworth, M. B., Cushenbery, L., & Hunter, S. T. (2016). Creativity for deliberate harm: Malevolent creativity and social information processing theory. *Journal of Creative Behavior, 52*(4), 305–322. https://doi.org/10.1002/jocb.155

Kotz, D. M. (2015). *The rise and fall of neoliberal capitalism*. Harvard University Press.

Madrick, J. (2014). *Seven bad ideas: How mainstream economists have damaged America and the world*. Knopf.

Majid al-Rifaie, M., Cropley, A., Cropley, D., & Bishop, M. (2016). On evil and computational creativity. *Connection Science, 28*(2), 171–193. https://doi.org/10.1080/09540091.2016.1151862

Moore, J. L., III, Ford, D. Y., & Milner, H. R. (2005). Underachievement among gifted students of color: Implications for educators. *Theory Into Practice, 44*(2), 167–177. https://doi.org/10.1207/s15430421tip4402_11

Piketty, T. (2014). *Capital in the twenty-first century* (A. Goldhammer, Trans.). Harvard University Press. (Original work published 2013)

Sternberg, R. J. (2003). *Wisdom, intelligence, and creativity synthesized*. Cambridge University Press.

Sternberg, R. J. (2005). WICS: A model of giftedness in leadership. *Roeper Review, 28*(1), 37–44. https://doi.org/10.1080/02783190509554335

Sternberg, R. J. (2017). ACCEL: A new model for identifying the gifted. *Roeper Review, 39*(3), 152–169. https://doi.org/10.1080/02783193.2017.1318658

Stiglitz, J. E. (2010). *Freefall: America, free markets, and the sinking of the world economy*. Norton.

Stiglitz, J. E. (2017). *Globalization and its discontents revisited: Globalization in the era of Trump*. Norton.

Suresh, S. (2013, October). To tap the world's vast and growing potential for new ideas, we need new rules. *Scientific American, 309*(4), 60. https://www.scientificamerican.com/article/to-tap-the-vast-and-growing-potential-for-new-ideas-we-need-new-rules

Temin, P., & Vines, D. (2013). *The leaderless economy: Why the world economic system fell apart and how to fix it*. Princeton University Press.

Wilkinson, R. G., & Pickett, K. E. (2010). *The spirit level: Why great equality makes societies stronger*. Bloomsbury.

Wilkinson, R. G., & Pickett, K. E. (2019). *The inner level: How more equal societies reduce stress, restore sanity and improve everyone's well-being*. Penguin.

CHAPTER 1

Evolving Complexity Theory of Talent Development

A Developmental Systems Approach

DAVID YUN DAI

> The stimulations which the organism tends toward are those which heighten its vitality, which give it pleasure, and those from which it draws back are those whose effect upon it is the contrary—the damaging, the painful ones.
>
> —James Baldwin

> Cognitive functions come into existence and differentiate due to the constant challenges and adaptation tasks that the social world entails ... human cognition (including its highest form, creativity) is fundamentally culturally and symbolically mediated.
>
> —Jaan Valsiner

2 Conceptual **Frameworks** for Giftedness and Talent Development

This chapter presents a new theory of talent development, Evolving Complexity Theory (ECT), in the context of the changing theoretical directions as well as the landscape of gifted education. I argue that talent development provides a broader psychosocial basis for gifted and talented education than the concept of giftedness can afford. In this chapter, I first offer rationale for developing a developmental systems theory of talent development. I then discuss three essential dimensions of a developmental system and explicate how structural and functional changes in talent development (structural regularities) occur as the result of person-environmental interaction (process regularities) and are manifested as contextual-contextual emergence of new properties and new organizational principles. Finally, I discuss the policy and practical implications of ECT, and compare it with existing talent development models to demonstrate how a developmental systems theory can help solve some critical issues regarding the nature and nurture of human potential.

Talent development is a theoretical movement in the field of giftedness and gifted education. It is not new and can be traced back as early as the 1950s (e.g., Witty, 1958; see also Borland, 2014, on the Talented Youth Project), but it is gaining momentum at the policy and practical level worldwide (e.g., the Talent Support model in Europe; Csermely, 2015). It poses challenges to a long-standing tradition in gifted education, the Gifted Child Paradigm (Dai, 2011; Dai & Chen, 2013; Subotnik et al., 2011). The ongoing "paradigm shift" is predicated on a profound change in the understanding of human potential and ability. First, the field of gifted education no longer espouses a static, fixed capacity view of human potential in general and intelligence in particular. Instead, it now sees human exceptional competence as diverse and pluralistic, dynamically shaped through developmental interaction with environmental opportunities and challenges (Dai, 2016). Second, the field has gone beyond a purely cognitive view of "giftedness" in espousing a broader scope of what constitutes giftedness, encompassing a range of endogenous and exogenous forces (Dai & Renzulli, 2008; Dai & Sternberg, 2004). Talent development, in this sense, provides a broader psychosocial basis for gifted education than what the notion of "giftedness" can afford. Evolving Complexity Theory is developed in this context to provide a new theoretical model of talent development that reflects this trend and can be used to guide educational policy and practice.

Motivation for a New Theory of Talent Development

More than 10 years ago, I started to think of giftedness not as a static quality but as contextually bound, dynamically shaped through person-environment interaction, and temporally emergent—hence the Contextual, Emergent, Dynamic Model of Giftedness and Talent Development (Dai & Renzulli, 2008), which I dubbed "giftedness in the making" (Dai, 2010, p. 196). At the core of this conceptualization is the assumption of exceptional competence as part of a relational developmental system, which is by nature interactive, dynamic, and complex (Overton, 2014; Molenaar et al., 2014). Over the years, my work has been guided by this developmental perspective, now better articulated as a developmental science framework (Cairns et al., 1996), featuring prominently developmental systems theory. The result is a theory of talent development that specifies the process of talent development from its initially more or less nebulous state to an increasingly differentiated and integrated state with emergent new properties and organizational principles for its further development—a process that can best be described as that of *evolving complexity*, hence Evolving Complexity Theory (Dai, 2017).

There are strategic and methodological considerations for theorizing about talent development. One can use the traditional, reductionist approach, tracing development of exceptional human competence back to basic components, endogenous as well as exogenous (e.g., Gagné, 1985, 2005; Tannenbaum, 1983). However, a component theory, in its way of simplifying the realities, does not explicate how these components interact at the system level and how the developing system evolves over time as a whole (see Ziegler & Phillipson, 2012, for a critique). In addition, component models take a reductionist approach that lends itself easily to dichotomizing the role of nature and nurture, even polarizing debates on their respective role (e.g., Ericsson et al., 2005, vs. Gagné, 2009), when, as a matter of fact, nature and nurture never work alone developmentally without some interaction and reciprocation of each other (Gottlieb, 1998; Horowitz, 2000).

A developmental systems approach takes a more integrative approach to the nature-nurture problem: how nature is nurtured (i.e., epigenesis, bidirectional interaction; Gottlieb, 1998), how nurture reveals nature (e.g., gene-environment interactions and differential intervention outcomes; Baltes, 1998), and how nurture surpasses or transcends nature (e.g., structural and functional changes at neural, cognitive, and behavioral levels as a result of systematic training; Schlaug, 2001). The developmental systems approach treats *emergence* (i.e., the emergence of new structural and functional properties, including competence, through development) as a fundamental tenet of human development, avoiding any radical reductionist explanation of gifts and talents as static and genetically predetermined (Dai, 2005). In short, a truly developmental theory of talent is by nature nonreductionist and organismic; that is, treating the organization of the person as a whole with higher order organizational properties (e.g., increasingly purposive, self-directed behavior) and principles (e.g., adaptive value, cultural distinction) not reducible to lower level components and operational rules. The notion of evolving complexity reflects this fundamental organization principle in human development. More specifically, ECT adheres to the following four tenets of dynamic systems (Lewis, 2000): (a) producing true novelty such that new forms or structures (e.g., giftedness, talent, creativity) spontaneously appear; (b) becoming more complex (differentiated and integrated) over time, fine-tuned to environments and transformed via "proximal processes"; (c) going through phase transitions in which new properties emerge, creating new dynamics and new levels of organized complexity, resulting in a more effective system; and (d) extrinsically sensitive (adaptive) and intrinsically robust (stable). Thus talent development is indeterminate but principled.

How ECT Explicates Structural, Process, and Temporal Regularities

Originally conceptualized as contextual, emergent, and dynamic (Dai & Renzulli, 2008), talent development is cast in a three-dimensional conceptual framework shown in Figure 1.1. The vertical dimension represents the person-environment interface, the horizontal dimension represents a life-span temporal progression, and the diagonal dimension represents the increasingly differentiated and integrated personhood (i.e., individuality) *contextually and temporally emergent* from the person-environment transactions at particularly developmental junctures. The three dimensions intersect to form a basic unit of analysis: person-in-context, meaning that the person is investigated and understood as a developing agent

FIGURE 1.1
A Schematic Representation of Three Critical Dimensions of Human Functioning and Development

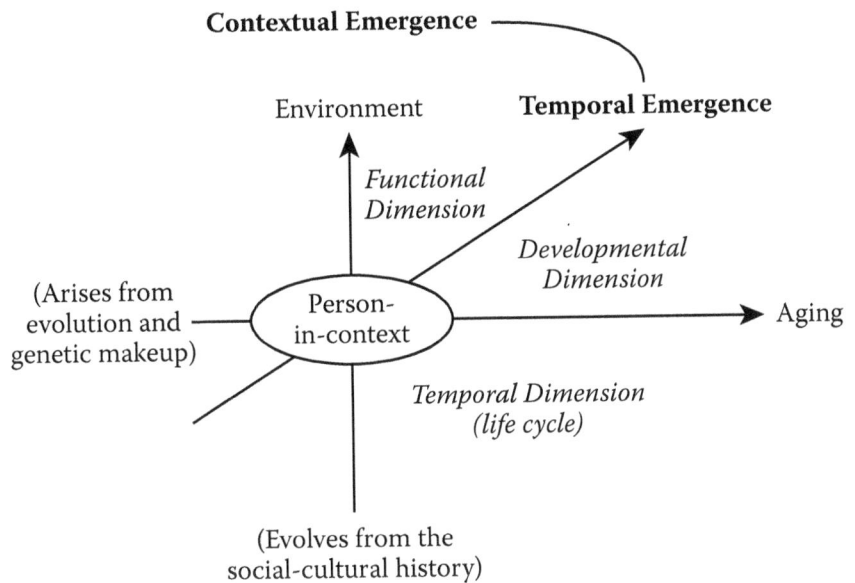

Note. The oval indicates a unit of analysis that intersects the three dimensions. The arrows signify the dynamic nature and directionality of the three dimensions. Adapted from "Snowflakes, Living Systems, and the Mystery of Giftedness," by D. Y. Dai and J. S. Renzulli, 2008, *Gifted Child Quarterly*, 52(2), p. 115 (https://doi.org/10.1177/0016986208315732). Copyright 2008 by SAGE.

interacting with specific social-cultural contexts at a specific developmental juncture, with a particular timescale of the course of action. Based on this three-dimensional conceptual foundation, a theory of talent development needs to explicate:

- *what develops or evolves* in terms of structural and functional changes of the person in competence and selfhood (i.e., structural regularities);
- *how the person evolves* as the result of specific ways of interacting with a particular task and social environments (process regularities); and

- *when and for how long these processes take place* (i.e., the developmental timing and duration of specific processes; temporal regularities).

In short, the three regularities address the issue of *what, how, and when* in an integrated manner. Methods of empirical observations have to honor the contextual, dynamic, and emergent principle reflected in Figure 1.1 (e.g., observations of proximal processes with time-intensive and relation-intensive methods; Hilpert & Marchand, 2018). Through this developmental lens, one can simply see talent development as a prolonged process of human adaptation resulting in outstanding human accomplishments, which either stretches human limits in terms of extraordinary skilled performance (e.g., in sports and performing arts) or makes eminent creative contributions that significantly improve human conditions (e.g., philosophy, science, literature, art, and technology). In short, talent development represents the highest form of human development in terms of demonstrating what humans can accomplish at the individual (ontogenetic) as well as species (phylogenetic) level. In the following section, structural, process, and temporal regularities of talent development is discussed, respectively, against the framework presented in Figure 1.1.

Structural Regularities: Evolving Complexity of the Developing Person Over Time

A major assumption underlying ECT is that the person is an open, dynamic, and adaptive system, undergoing changes in oneself in multiple ways while interacting with the world and exercising agency. Developmental changes occur in a structurally predictable manner, "from a state of relative globality and lack of differentiation to a state of increasing differentiation, articulation, and hierarchical integration" (Werner, 1957, p. 126). For ECT, this "increasing differentiation and hierarchical integration" is captured through a multilevel analytic framework presented in Figure 1.2, which shows how the evolving complexity of the developing person builds up through development (Dai, 2010).

At Level I are *aptitudes and dispositions* in foundational domains. Aptitudes are more of an ability construct, and dispositions more of a personality one. They are stable traits developed and calibrated in early years of life with certain facilitative social-cultural environments (e.g., exposure

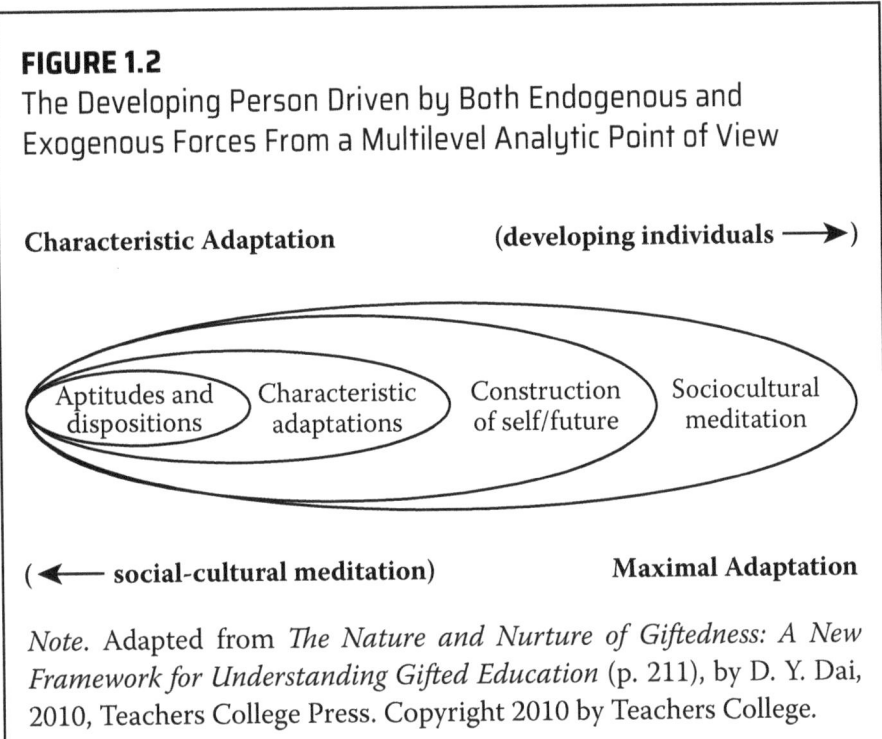

FIGURE 1.2
The Developing Person Driven by Both Endogenous and Exogenous Forces From a Multilevel Analytic Point of View

Note. Adapted from *The Nature and Nurture of Giftedness: A New Framework for Understanding Gifted Education* (p. 211), by D. Y. Dai, 2010, Teachers College Press. Copyright 2010 by Teachers College.

to chess, or early musical experiences). ECT identifies five basic functional domains of human activity: *expressive* (expressing oneself through imaginative play and artistic means, such as writing, drawing, acting, singing, and dancing), *technical* (making tools and gadgets to enhance effectiveness and efficiency), *intellectual* (reasoning, understanding, explaining, and theorizing using mathematics, logic, visual-spatial imaging, or literary means), *social* (achieving practical purposes through effective communication, negotiation, collaboration, and leadership), and *psychomotor* (executing and coordinating body movements to accomplish complex physical tasks as in the case of most competitive and extreme sports and complex surgical operations). These foundational effectivities help human beings survive and thrive, and thus hold a fundamental adaptive value. Aptitudes and dispositions facilitate development of effectivities in these foundational domains. Thus, one might identify a child or adolescent's profile of aptitudes and dispositions vis-à-vis affordances and constraints of a wide range of cultural activities, including but not confined to formal education (Lohman, 2005). ECT also identifies aptitudes that mainly exert regulatory power, similar to the metacomponent in the triarchic theory of intelligence (Sternberg, 1985). For example, one exercises metacognitive control to backtrack and fine-tune one's performance (Feltovich et al., 2006). In addition, dispositions refer to a set of "nonintellective" personal characteristics that have action potency, such as openness to experience, curiosity, passion, conscientiousness, and perseverance, which have a direct bearing on developmental potential.

A particular profile of aptitudes and dispositions can be conducive to a science or art career trajectory (Feist, 2006; Lubinski, 2010). However, one can develop many "effectivities" that are discrete: differentiated and not integrated. It is *characteristic adaptation* (CA; i.e., characteristic ways the person seeks certain developmental opportunities to carves out a distinct developmental niche; Wachs, 2000) that dynamically shapes the self-organization of effectivities into a talent trajectory in cultural domains (Csikszentmihalyi, 1996). In other words, CA represents a higher level self-organization of personal adaptation compared to the first-order personal properties reflected in aptitudes and dispositions as a heterogeneous set. The most powerful evidence for such self-organization comes from research conducted by Lubinski, Benbow, and their colleagues, indicating that directions and trajectories of talent development are shaped by distinct combinations of mathematical, verbal, and spatial abilities (e.g., Wai et al., 2009), coupled with distinct interests (Lubinski & Benbow, 2006). Characteristic adaptation is predicated on the assumption that "human lives vary with respect to a wide range of motivational, social-cognitive, and developmental adaptations, contextualized in time, place, and/or social role" (McAdams & Pals, 2006, p. 208). Compared to trait-level aptitudes and dispositions, CA is a more holistic, organismic construct, more contextually and dynamically situated in specific social contexts.

Beyond CA in development, Level III captures a unique human tendency to purposefully initiate and sustain a particular line of talent development. I label it *construction of self and future* to highlight its purposive (top-down), proactive, and deliberate nature in self-engendered changes, which is responsible for the emergence of *maximal adaptation* (MA) to certain task environments, as compared to the more situational, spontaneous, self-organized (bottom-up) nature of CA. Edelman (1995) emphasized the nonreductionist, contextually emergent nature of this developmental property: "By selfhood, I mean not just the individuality that emerges from genetics and immunology but personal individuality that emerges from developmental and social interactions" (p. 201). The notion of *construction of self and future* highlights the functional significance of maintaining a particular line of personal undertaking regardless of how facilitative or adverse situational conditions may be.

Finally, at Level IV, as shown in Figure 1.2, is the most inclusive level of analysis. It is all-encompassing in the sense that all structural and functional changes in Levels I–III can be understood in a broader context to reveal the social-cultural mediation of these developmental changes (Valsiner, 1989). As the two arrows indicate, as the developing person makes adaptive efforts vis-à-vis developmental opportunities and challenges, the cultural meaning and significance of a particular personal endeavor is increasingly integrated into the core of their individuality. Together, this four-level analytic framework reveals the main endogenous and exogenous forces propelling the development of individuality, of which talent is just a manifestation.

Structural regularities, defined as increasing differentiation and integration, have an external dimension. From a population viewpoint, different individuals, given their unique experiences as well as developmental potential, will become more and more different from each other, due not only to their profiles of aptitudes and dispositions, but also to their characteristic adaptation and more purposive life choices and commitments in particular social-cultural contexts. In other words, structural regularities so defined also capture properties of the *social distribution of talent*: Some individuals may be more prone to becoming engineers, and others artists, given a range of opportunities and choices; some become regional major players, and others international-caliber players. In addition, structural regularities, indicative of structural and functional changes that can be qualitative as well as quantitative, also highlight the continuity and discontinuity of individual development. In the early phase of development, individual differences in aptitudes and dispositions may be quantitative in nature (i.e., the difference found is a matter of degree). However, when cumulative changes in advantages and inclinations build up to a critical point, not only does intrapersonal developmental discontinuity take place (hence phase transition), but also interindividual differences in talent become a matter of kind (see Dai, 2010, Chapter 4, for detailed discussion). Implications of such developmental changes are profound in terms of the universal-unique continuum (Feldman, 2003). Talented individuals show increasingly qualitative differences, especially with respect to their knowledge base, skill sets, and ways of thinking; they develop a modus operandi that is highly tuned into a particular set of task constraints (hence its domain specificity; Feltovich et al., 2006).

In sum, *structural regularities* specify the nature of evolving complexity through increasing differentiation and integration; the concept of structural regularities elucidates the nature of talent in the context of individual development. More specifically, structural regularities help delineate diverse patterns of developmental changes in behavioral, cognitive, and psychosocial functions indicative of niche potential and talent trajectories and pathways that are discernable in cross-sectional and longitudinal data. What leads to these structural and functional changes in real-time transactional interaction between the developing person and dynamic environments? Evolving Complexity Theory postulate specific psychosocial mechanisms underlying CA and the transition to MA.

Process Regularities: Processes Undergirding Characteristic and Maximal Adaptation

Talent development is fundamentally a cultural phenomenon, not a natural one (Csikszentmihalyi & Robinson, 1986). Almost all talent domains, including those as basic as linguistic systems and mathematics (let alone science and art), are invented cultural artifacts and *biologically secondary* (Geary, 1995); that is, they are not innately built into, or hardwired through, people's genetic codes. In order to understanding the genesis of talent as well as specific talent trajectories and pathways, talent-related developmental changes have to be situated in social-cultural contexts and understood as contextually emergent through real-time person-environment interaction, what Bronfenbrenner and Ceci (1994) called *proximal processes*:

> Human development takes place through processes of progressively more complex reciprocal interaction between an active, evolving biopsychological human organism and the persons, objects, and symbols in its immediate environment. To be effective, the interaction must occur on a fairly regular basis over extended periods of time. Such enduring forms of interaction in the immediate environment are referred to as *proximal processes*. (p. 572)

Accordingly, ECT uses a push-sustain metaphor to characterize mechanisms underlying the developing person's transactional experiences that propel talent development (see Figure 1.3). The arrow represents the developing person, with all of their endogenous power, interacting with two kinds of exogenous forces: environmental press (opportunities and challenges) on the one hand, and sociocultural support (resources, tools, and values) on the other. That ECT starts with environmental press, rather than with a

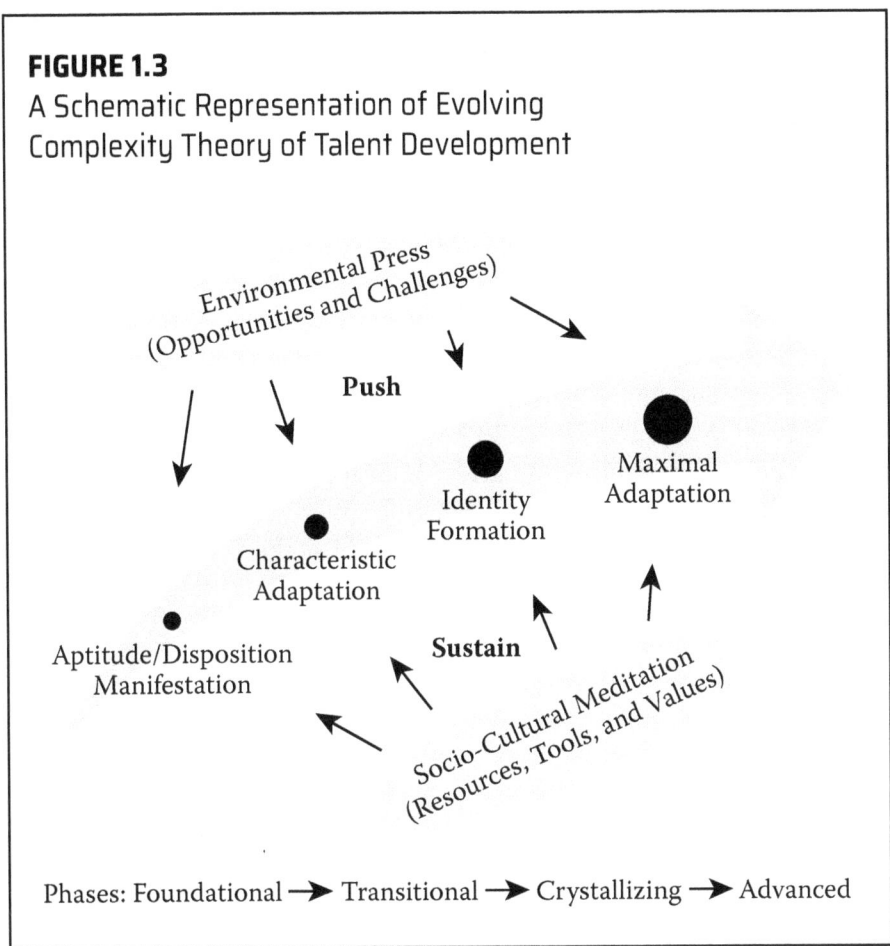

FIGURE 1.3
A Schematic Representation of Evolving Complexity Theory of Talent Development

"talent" or "gift," distinguishes it from trait theories of gifts and talents (e.g., Gagné, 2005). Environmental press refers to a situation that evokes a need within the organism that has adaptive consequences (Murray, 1938). To use the language of ecological psychology, environmental press *affords* certain opportunities to learn, develop, control, enjoy, and achieve certain personal ambitions; at the same time, however, it sets constraints and conditions (i.e., challenges) that need to be met in order to materialize the affordances in question. The nature of such person-environmental transaction determines, first and foremost, that a talent is not innate (e.g., there is not a set of genes dedicated to music) but the result of self-organized, self-directed adaptive responses to environmental opportunities and challenges. I use the "push-sustain" metaphor to denote this need-evoking, action-sustaining process.

As a first approximation, ECT assumes that individuals in their lifetime go through a progressive course of learning and talent development experiences in the order of informal learning experiences (e.g., those facilitated at home or initiated by oneself), followed by formal education, advanced training, and ultimately cutting-edge work in particular domains. Educators can roughly view the long-term process of talent development as characterized by the emergence of CA, followed by a graduate transition to MA. This is not to say that MA does not exist in early phases of development. Rather, as well-established in both the personality and educational psychology literature, in loosely structured environments typical in early stages of human development, developing persons tend to follow their own "agendas" and pursue their own interests while interacting with formal and informal learning environments (see the arrow indicating one's CA in Figure 1.2). As a result, individual differences in CA are more likely to show through (Ackerman, 2013; Buss, 1989). In contrast, MA is the norm in regimented cultural environments characterizing most advanced training and development, and all professional work (as suggested by the backward arrow in Figure 1.2). The turning point from CA to MA is a change from avocational interests and vocational commitments. To further specify the developmental process in terms of the emergence of CA and MA, ECT postulates four phases of talent development. To use music for illustration, demonstrating music-related aptitudes and dispositions (Foundational Phase) is one thing, and pursuing a musical interest (Transitional Phase) is another; becoming a musician (Crystallizing Phase) is one thing, and sustained effort to perfect one's music skills and exploring a new form or personal style of musical expression (Advanced Phase) is another (Subotnik & Jarvin, 2005). The game changes, so to speak, as the person moves to a later phase of talent development. Table 1.1 shows different developmental tasks involved, affect (endogenous), and social conditions and expectations (exogenous) that sustain these tasks. For ECT, the development of effectivities in foundational domains through self-organization of aptitudes and dispositions in formative years (Phase 1) prepares one for CA (Phase 2), and the development of identity and commitment through construction of self and future (Phase 3; see Figure 1.2) leads to a phase transition to MA (Phase 4). Of central importance to ECT is what drives the emergence of CA and the transition to MA, respectively.

The push-sustain mechanisms for CA and MA are quite different. For CA, the push comes from the development of autonomy and the adaptive pressure of "niche picking," and increasing cultural expectations for individual competence and effectiveness. What underlies CA endogenously is a set

TABLE 1.1
Four Phases of Talent Development (TD) and the Nature of Talent, Affect, and Social Conditions and Processes at Each Stage

Phase of Talent Development	Developmental Tasks That Initiate and Sustain TD	The Nature of Affect That Sustains TD	Social Conditions That Sustain TD
The Advanced Phase MA	Doing cutting-edge work and developing a personal niche	Vision/ perseverance	Institutionalized standards and norms; modus operandi
The Crystallizing Phase	Making commitment to a line of serious work	Identity/ commitment	Serious participation; mentorship
The Transitional Phase CA	Exploration/ expansion of a personal action space	Interest/ self-efficacy; selective affinity	Autonomy support; opportunity structure
The Foundational Phase	Developing basic effectivities; demonstrating aptitudes/ dispositions	Agency/ willpower	Typical/optimal condition; evocative interaction

Note. CA = characteristic adaptation; MA = maximal adaptation.

of cognitive, affective-conative, and social factors: *ease of learning, comparative advantage*, and *selective affinity* that indicates the overall goodness of fit with a particular task and social environment. To be sure, signs of such fit could be shown in formative years, but the mind of a developing child is not well differentiated and integrated in the Foundational Phase; what sustains CA exogenously is a set of facilitative and supporting factors or the opportunity structure that favors specific selections of course of action or development. In contrast, for MA, the push comes from increasingly difficult tasks or cognitive demands, for which even having "natural talent" is not sufficient. It also comes, more socially, from cultural and institutional expectations for excellence and rigor. What prompts and sustains MA is the development of identity and commitment (in Crystallizing Phase; Dai et al., 2015) and dedicated effort for self-improvement (staying at the edge of chaos; Dai & Renzulli, 2008) endogenously, and often indispensable pedagogical, technical, and institutional support exogenously. Given the complex interaction of these endogenous and exogenous factors, ECT is a distinct interaction-dominant rather than component-dominant model of talent development (Hilpert & Marchand, 2018), as it sees talent development as involving a *relational developmental system* with interacting components (cognitive, affective-conative, and social), and new emergent properties and organizational principles (CA and MA) at a system level, irreducible to lower level explanations (i.e., lower level components and operations).

Temporal Regularities: The Timing and Duration of Transactional Experiences

Structural and process regularities in talent development are always intertwined with the issue of timing and duration of specific developmental changes involved. For example, structurally, hierarchical integration in terms of emergent CA cannot occur very early when a child does not gain sufficient autonomy psychologically and socially to seek out developmental opportunities or choose a particular course of action, no matter how "talented" they are. By the same token, the duration of specific *proximal processes* may be essential to sustain a line of talent development, or it will discontinue for life. Temporal regularities, thus, refer to specific developmental timing and duration of structural and functional changes or developmental processes important for optimal talent development, even critical as a make-or-break issue.

First, the developmental timing of the onset of talent development (and thus exposure) matters. For ECT, a critical task is to define the developmental timing of the onset of CA and MA, and the transition from CA to MA. Simonton's (1999) emergenic-epigenetic model of talent views the right person (with particular genetic potentials) in the right place (right exposure) at the right time as determining whether one can make the cut. My own research (Dai & Li, 2019) shows that early college entrance to a STEM program led to an accelerated rate of talent progression and career accomplishments for some top students; roughly a 3-year acceleration (ahead of peers in entry to college) in the Transitional Phase translates into a 10-year advantage in the Advanced Phase in terms of achieving milestone social recognition (e.g., National Science Foundation CAREER award)—a distinct Matthew effect, largely due to early transition to MA (the new level of dedicated effort and the institutional rigor, resources, and support; see Merton, 1996). ECT postulates several domain-related factors determining the timing issue (performance vs. productivity, technicality, the threshold requirement of social maturity, etc.).

In addition to the timing of onset, the duration of proximal processes in all phases of talent development matters with respect to the timing of peak performance or productivity, largely because talent development is a survival game. As most untenured faculty members know, maintaining a talent trajectory is of paramount importance up to the date when the tenure decision is to be made. By the same token, whether an athlete maintains a competitive edge at the state level may determine whether they have a chance to make it to Olympic games. In the expertise literature, there is a well-documented "10-year rule" (Chase & Simon, 1973; Ericsson, 2006); that is, it takes roughly 10 years or 10,000 hours of serious work and intensive training or deliberate practice (i.e., MA) to become an expert in a professional field. Although the 10-year rule is recently disputed (Hambrick et al., 2018), talent development in the advanced phase entails more staying power and persistence.

The issue of meeting institutional expectations may be less critical for young learners, but MA can still viable to those school-age individuals when their level of knowledge and skills is sophisticated enough for engaging in advanced, cutting-edge work, such as conducting an innovative research project while still in high school, inventing valuable products and procedures, or reaching a high level of performance in music by adult professional standards while still a teenager.

Summary

In sum, structural, process, and temporal regularities (the issues of what, how, and when) postulated by ECT help explicate talent development in an integrated way. ECT postulates when specific talent will likely emerge with exposure and experience, how likely it will endure (temporal regularities), and how likely related structural and functional changes (structural regularities) under the manifestation of talent will occur given the timing and duration of specific transactional experiences or proximal processes (process regularities). Together, these regularities constitute the essence of evolving complexity involved in talent development. From a developmental science point of view, ECT is a unified theory of talent development grounded in many lines of research (e.g., on talent, motivation, expertise, and creativity). Because of the developmental synthesis, talent development in a variety of domains, from highly regimented to loosely structured settings, can be mapped out.

What Distinguishes ECT From Other Talent Development Models

In a nutshell, ECT postulates talent development as contextually engendered rather than innate, dynamically shaped through person-environmental transactional experiences, and temporally evolving and going through phase transitions through increasing differentiation and hierarchical integration (hence, evolving complexity). Two main patterns of adaptive behaviors, CA and MA, regulate this developmental process, responsible for development of high-caliber performance and creative productivity. In ECT, the way that biology and culture, nature and nurture, and the endogenous and exogenous work together to advance talent and creative productivity is explicated as an evolving process of adaptation with increasing organized complexity.

The traditional models of talent development can be roughly divided into two kinds: component models typically based on psychometric, long-range prediction studies (Feist, 1998, 2006; Gagné, 2005; Lubinski & Benbow, 2006; Simonton, 2005), and process models, typically based on more up-close investigation of the person in context and developmental processes (Bloom, 1985; Csikszentmihalyi et al., 1993; Feldman, 1986; Gruber, 1986; Plucker & Barab, 2005; Subotnik et al., 2011). Renzulli's (1986) Three-Ring Conception of Giftedness is in essence a process theory (e.g., how task commitment and creativity are contextually and developmentally shaped) but is presented as a trait model based on prediction studies (see Renzulli, 1978). What distinguishes ECT from the existing models of talent development is that it is a process theory (specifying what, and how, and when of talent development) that simultaneously accounts for talent distributions and trajectories, which is of primary focus for the component models.

ECT is guided by relational developmental systems theory (Overton, 2014), according to which both micro-level and macro-level development can be captured when a multilevel integration is made across different lines of research (Cairns et al., 1996). Such integration allows ECT to integrate a model of differential development (structural regularities) and process accounts of these developmental changes (process regularities) with timing of onset and timescale in mind (temporal regularities). As a result, the theory is capable of covering a broader range of empirical observations than either a component account or a process account can, thus avoiding the problems of having two disciplines or realms of psychology (Cronbach, 1957; McCall, 1981).

Moreover, existing talent development models, whether of the component or process variety, tend to remain implicit regarding increasing differentiation and hierarchical integration involved as well as the underlying forces driving developmental processes and transitions to a new level of evolving complexity. When this happens, development (i.e., what develops, and how and when) remains a default, implicit assumption, not subject to empirical observation (see Sternberg & Davidson, 1986, for a distinction between implicit and explicit theoretical models). ECT specifies emergence of new properties and organization principles at multiple levels at different developmental junctures, showing how push-sustain mechanisms every step of the way through cognitive, affective-conative, and social forces propel further developmental changes. The articulation of these structural and process regularities (i.e., explicitness) by ECT can potentially enhance higher sensitivity of developmental assessment and more specificity in formulating research hypotheses as well as designing targeted interventions.

Finally ECT is a distinct effort to integrate talent development research and theory into a more broadly defined science of human development in that it uses talent development as a window through which to discover the nature and nurture of human potential, and treat the development of high-caliber performance and creative productivity as epitomizing the highest form of human development. It shows the adaptive nature of human development and the primacy of human activity in development; it highlights the nature of human adaptivity as involving the biological tendency to seek the best person-environment fit with characteristic adaptation (CA), as well as the cultural tendency toward maximal adaptation (MA) for its own collective agenda with its tools and resources.

ECT as a Guiding Tool for Practice

As I argue elsewhere, gifted education in the United States has inherited the legacy of what I call the *Gifted Child Paradigm* (Dai, 2011; Dai & Chen, 2013), which is predicated on the assumption of bifurcation between the gifted and nongifted, as if they are two different categories of people (see Borland, 2003, for a critique). Historically, the notion of giftedness was closely associated with high IQ (Dai, 2018). Granted that IQ can be one indicator of developmental potential, there are many other factors, such as various talents, motivation, personality characteristics, and symbol systems and cultural tools, that underlie what one can become. Therefore, if the purpose of gifted education is to cultivate human potential to the highest level humanly possible, an exclusive focus on IQ is vastly inadequate, given an understanding of the pluralistic and developmental nature of human potential. ECT (Dai, 2018) is intended to be truly a systems theory of talent development that can help facilitate a paradigm shift in gifted and talent education, to make it scientifically more compelling, socially more equitable, and educationally more productive (Dai, 2016).

A distinct advantage of ECT (particularly over component models) is that by explicating the dynamic interplay of endogenous and exogenous forces interacting in shaping talent trajectories and pathways every step of the way, it can be easily applied in educational and training settings, with interventions designed according to its theory-based principles and guidelines (see Table 1.1).

Policy Implications of ECT

The overarching principle derived from ECT is to make the education system more open and adaptive to developmental diversity, encouraging maximal participation in a diverse range of talent development opportunities promoting excellence as one of the core values for students. Cultivation of developmental potential, rather than "serving the gifted," should become the main impetus of educational provisions. This way, gifted and talented education and regular education are just a division of labor, not two separate education systems. When excellence in culturally valued domains (including but not limited to academics) becomes a priority for a school, gifted and talented education will be prominently featured, regardless of how it is labeled. The following strategies will help improve education practice.

Aligning Education With Developmental Trajectories

A main assumption of ECT is that individual characteristic adaptations (CA) can be harnessed to maximize its developmental outcomes (i.e., optimal development). In this regard, structural regularities (emergent CA, personal interests and strivings, etc.) help educators identify important developmental changes and divergent developmental patterns among students that are conducive to particular lines of talent development. Understanding of developmental continuity and discontinuity (i.e., the onset of puberty) can facilitate a developmentally responsive education (Dai, 2010). As ECT considers education an integral part of human development (with its pedagogical tools and social-cultural support), educators can be more proactive in creating talent development agendas, rather than merely react to signs of talent. For that matter, how to facilitate basic human effectivities in formative years and identify aptitudes and dispositions along the way, how to facilitate and identify CA, and how to facilitate transition to MA through affective development become main education challenges. For example, early enrichment activities in targeted domains of talent can be extremely helpful for exposure, threshold experiences, and development of early interests. In this regard, informal learning across home, community, and school can be highly valuable for the emergence of CA and identity (Barron, 2006). Although it is difficult for educators to have total control over the timing and duration of relevant proximal processes necessary to advance particular lines of talent development, educators should be more alert to the role of timely opportunities and sustainability of lines of talent work. For that matter, temporal regularities stipulated by ECT as optimal for various domains can help optimize individual talent development through timely provision of structured experience, formal learning, and training. A relevant example is the accelerated pace of academic progression and early onset of advanced learning in STEM fields. Feldhusen (2003) argued that gifted education provisions be better conceptualized as *programming* for individual development rather than providing *programs*, which tend to take a short-term, piecemeal approach without concerns for long-term development. As a developmental process theory, ECT can guide such programming.

Identification as Developmental Prognosis, Not a Status Determination

It has been long argued that identification and intervention should be tightly coupled (i.e., directly tied to educational needs; Callahan, 1996; Tomlinson, 2014). However, most models of talent development do not explicate developmental processes and transitions in a way that can guide identification. In this regard, ECT permits a phase- and stage-sensitive identification; that is, identification is no longer made of a fixed formula, administered in a once-and-for-all fashion, but is a prognosis of the person's possible future advances based on demonstrated strengths and interests and personality characteristics. In other words, developmental trajectories can be cast in a developmental corridor and mapped out for intervention purposes. Even some milestone events can be predicted in a developmental pathway to excellence. The role of teachers in shepherding the process becomes crucial. For example, a talent portfolio will help teachers and counselors keep track of a student's progress along a particular talent trajectory or pathway.

Facilitating Transition From MA to CA as the Main Task of Gifted Education

Because ECT is a developmental theory, it affords a clearer idea of when to do what. For example, it postulates that the impetus for the transition to MA is that CA can hit its plateau or bottleneck (when left to one's own devices) unless a more rigorous regiment of learning and training is put in place. This issue is more likely to occur during adolescence. Conceptualized this way, the challenge of gifted and talented education (e.g., required research projects for high school students, as practiced in specialized STEM schools) is a timely provision to help adolescents stretch their limits through maximal adaptation to challenges at hand (e.g., a robot competition, a project of solving a local pollution problem).

Counseling for Optimal Development

Talented children and adolescents have additional counseling needs precisely because they have increasingly tough challenges to face and more hurdles to overcome in individual development if they were to survive and thrive on particular lines of talent development. Evolving complexity for them implies that by living on the edge, so to speak, developmental instability is more common for them (Dai & Renzulli, 2008). Throughout the four developmental phases, self-development is always crucial (even for athletes as young as 10 years old). ECT provides direction as to what counseling and guidance should focus on for each phase of talent development. For example, ECT postulates that adolescence is the best window for encouraging exploration and expansion of personal action space (PAS). Counseling can help talented teenagers to clarify their interests and aspirations, encourage them to explore areas that they may otherwise hesitate to. For another, according to ECT, a main endogenous barrier for transition to MA is affective in nature: identity (personal vision) and commitment to a particular line of work.

Counseling and guidance have a lot to do in recognizing talented students' strengths and accomplishments, helping them cope with stress and self-related issues, and helping them envision their life trajectories and possibilities.

DISCUSSION QUESTIONS

1. What are major advantages of interaction-dominant models over component-dominant models of giftedness and talent?
2. In what way does ECT help educators rethink the nature and development of human potential?
3. Why is an emphasis on contextual and temporal emergence of structural and functional changes a fundamental rejection of reductionism in talent development theory and research? In what way does it help avoid falling into the trap of the nature-nurture dichotomy?

DISCUSSION QUESTIONS, continued

4. In what ways does ECT change the way educators think about the practice of gifted and talent education, especially the means and ends of identification and intervention?

Acknowledgments

This work was partly supported by a grant from Army Research Institute, Behavioral and Social Sciences, Grant No. W911NF-17-1-0236. Opinions expressed by the author here do not necessarily represent those of the funding agency.

References

Ackerman, P. L. (2013). Personality and cognition. In S. Kreitler (Ed.), *Cognition and motivation: Forging an interdisciplinary perspective* (pp. 62–75). Cambridge University Press.

Baltes, P. B. (1998). Testing the limits of the ontogenetic sources of talent and excellence. *Behavioral and Brain Sciences, 21*(3), 407–408. https://doi.org/10.1017/S0140525X98221236

Barron, B. (2006). Interest and self-sustained learning as catalysts of development: A learning ecology perspective. *Human Development, 49*(4), 193–224. https://doi.org/10.1159/000094368

Bloom, B. S. (Ed.). (1985). *Developing talent in young people*. Ballantine Books.

Borland, J. H. (2003). The death of giftedness. In J. H. Borland (Ed.), *Rethinking gifted education* (pp. 105–124). Teachers College Press.

Borland, J. H. (2014). Mariam L. Goldberg, a scholar of first rank. In A. Robinson & J. L. Jolly (Eds.), *A century of contributions to gifted education: Illuminating lives* (pp. 203–219). Routledge.

Bronfenbrenner, U., & Ceci, S. J. (1994). Nature-nurture reconceptualized in developmental perspective: A bio-ecological model. *Psychological Review, 101*(4), 568–586. https://doi.org/10.1037/0033-295x.101.4.568

Buss, A. H. (1989). Personality as traits. *American Psychologist, 44*(11), 1378–1388.

Cairns, R. B., Elder, G. H., & Costello, E. J. (Eds.). (1996). *Developmental science*. Cambridge University Press.

Callahan, C. M. (1996). A critical self-study of gifted education: Healthy practice, necessary evil, or sedition? *Journal for the Education of the Gifted, 19*(2), 148–163. https://doi.org/10.1177/016235329601900203

Chase, W. C., & Simon, H. A. (1973). The mind's eye in chess. In W. C. Chase (Ed.), *Visual information processing* (pp. 215–281). Academic Press.

Cronbach, L. J. (1957). The two discipline of scientific psychology. *American Psychologist, 12*(11), 671–684. https://doi.org/10.1037/h0043943

Csermely, P. (2015, October). *Cutting-edge research on talent development in Europe* [Paper presentation]. Nuremberg Conference on Talent Development, Nuremberg, Germany.

Csikszentmihalyi, M. (1996). *Creativity: Flow and the psychology of discovery and invention*. HarperCollins.

Csikszentmihalyi, M., Rathunde, K., & Whalen, S. (1993). *Talented teenagers: The roots of success and failure*. Cambridge University Press.

Csikszentmihalyi, M., & Robinson, R. E. (1986). Culture, time, and the development of talent. In R. J. Sternberg & J. E. Davidson (Eds.), *Conceptions of giftedness* (pp. 264–284). Cambridge University Press.

Dai, D. Y. (2005). Reductionism versus emergentism: A framework for understanding conceptions of giftedness. *Roeper Review 27*(3), 144–151. https://doi.org/10.1080/02783190509554308

Dai, D. Y. (2010). *The nature and nurture of giftedness: A new framework for understanding gifted education*. Teachers College Press.

Dai, D. Y. (2011). Hopeless anarchy or saving pluralism? Reflections on our field in response to Ambrose, VanTassel-Baska, Coleman, and Cross. *Journal for the Education of the Gifted, 34*(5), 705–730. https://doi.org/10.1177/0162353211416437

Dai, D. Y. (2016). Envisioning a new century of gifted education: The case for a paradigm shift. In D. Ambrose & R. J. Sternberg (Eds.), *Giftedness and talent in the 21st century: Adapting to the turbulence of globalization* (pp. 45–63). Sense.

Dai, D. Y. (2017). Envisioning a new foundation for gifted education: Evolving Complexity Theory (ECT) of talent development. *Gifted Child Quarterly, 61*(3), 172–182. https://doi.org/10.1177/0016986217701837

Dai, D. Y. (2018). A century of quest for identity: A history of giftedness. In S. Pfeiffer (Ed.), *The APA handbook on giftedness and talent* (pp. 3–23). American Psychological Association.

Dai, D. Y., & Chen, F. (2013). Three paradigms of gifted education: In search of conceptual clarity in research and practice. *Gifted Child Quarterly, 57*(3), 151–168. https://doi.org/10.1177/0016986213490020

Dai, D. Y. & Li, X. (2019). *Behind an accelerated STEM research career: Dynamic interplay of endogenous and exogenous forces in talent development* [Manuscript in preparation].

Dai, D. Y., & Renzulli, J. S. (2008). Snowflakes, living systems, and the mystery of giftedness. *Gifted Child Quarterly, 52*(2), 114–130. https://doi.org/10.1177/0016986208315732

Dai, D. Y., Steenbergen-Hu, S., & Zhou, Y. (2015). Cope and grow: A grounded theory approach to early college entrants' lived experiences and changes in a STEM program. *Gifted Child Quarterly, 59*(2), 75–90. https://doi.org/10.1177/0016986214568719

Dai, D. Y., & Sternberg, R. J. (2004). Beyond cognitivism: Toward an integrated understanding of intellectual functioning and development. In D. Y. Dai & R. J. Sternberg (Eds.), *Motivation, emotion, and cognition: Integrative perspectives on intellectual functioning and development* (pp. 3–38). Erlbaum.

Edelman, G. M. (1995). Memory and the individual soul: Against silly reductionism. In J. Cornwell (Ed.), *Nature's imagination: The frontiers of scientific vision* (pp. 200–206). Oxford University Press.

Ericsson, K. A., Krampe, R. T., & Tesch-Romer, C. (1993). The role of deliberate practice in the acquisition of expert performance. *Psychological Review, 100*(3), 363–406. https://doi.org/10.1037/0033-295X.100.3.363

Ericsson, K. A., Nandagopal, K., & Roring, R. W. (2005). Giftedness viewed from the expert-performance perspective. *Journal for the Education of the Gifted, 28*(3–4), 287–311. https://doi.org/10.4219/jeg-2005-335

Feist, G. J. (1998). A meta-analysis of personality in scientific and artistic creativity. *Personality and Social Psychology Review, 2*(4), 290–309. https://doi.org/10.1207/s15327957pspr0204_5

Feist, G. J. (2006). How development and personality influence scientific thought, interest, and achievement. *Review of General Psychology, 10*(2), 163–182. https://doi.org/10.1037/1089-2680.10.2.163

Feldman, D. H. (1986). *Nature's gambit: Child prodigies and the development of human potential*. Basic Books.

Feldman, D. H. (2003). A developmental, evolutionary perspective on giftedness. In J. H. Borland (Ed.), *Rethinking gifted education* (pp. 9–33). Teachers College Press.

Feltovich, P. J, Prietula, M. J., & Ericcson, K. A. (2006). Studies of expertise from psychological perspectives. In K. A. Ericsson, N. Charness, P. J. Feltovich, & R. R. Hoffman (Eds.), *The Cambridge handbook of expertise and expert performance* (pp. 41–67). Cambridge University Press.

Gagné, F. (1985). Gifted and talent: Reexamining a reexamination of the definitions. *Gifted Child Quarterly, 29*(3), 103–112. https://doi.org/10.1177/001698628502900302

Gagné, F. (2005). From gifts to talents: The DMGT as a developmental model. In R. J. Sternberg & J. E. Davidson (Eds.), *Conceptions of giftedness* (2nd ed., pp. 98–119). Cambridge University Press.

Gagné, F. (2009). Debating giftedness: Pronat vs. antinat. In L. Shavinina (Ed.), *International handbook on giftedness* (pp. 155–198). Springer.

Geary, D. C. (1995). Reflections of evolution and culture in children's cognition: Implications for mathematical development and instruction. *American Psychologist, 50*(1), 24–37. https://doi.org/10.1037//0003-066x.50.1.24

Gottlieb, G. (1998). Normally occurring environmental and behavioral influences on gene activity: From central dogma to probabilistic epigenesis. *Psychological Review, 105*(4), 792–802. https://doi.org/10.1037/0033-295x.105.4.792-802

Gruber, H. E. (1986). The self-construction of the extraordinary. In R. J. Sternberg & J. E. Davidson (Eds.), *Conceptions of giftedness* (pp. 247–263). Cambridge University Press.

Hambrick, D. Z., Burgoyne, A. P., Macnamara, B. M., & Ullén, F. (2018). Toward a multifactorial model of expertise: Beyond born versus made. *Annals of the New York Academy of Sciences, 1423*(1), 284–295. https://doi.org/10.1111/nyas.13586

Hilpert, J. C., & Marchand, G. C. (2018). Complex systems research in educational psychology: Aligning theory and method. *Educational Psychologist, 53*(3), 185–202. https://doi.org/10.1080/00461520.2018.1469411

Horowitz, F. D. (2000). Child development and the PITS: Simple questions, complex answers, and developmental theory. *Child Development, 71*(1), 1–10. https://doi.org/10.1111/1467-8624.00112

Lewis, M. D. (2000). The promise of dynamic systems approaches for an integrated account of human development. *Child Development, 71*(1), 36–43. https://doi.org/10.1111/1467-8624.00116

Lohman, D. F. (2005). An aptitude perspective on talent identification: Implications for identification of academically gifted minority students. *Journal for the Education of the Gifted, 28*(3–4), 333–360. https://doi.org/10.4219/jeg-2005-341

Lubinski, D. (2010, May). *Acceleration, individual differences, and the elephant in the classroom* [Paper presentation]. The Wallace Symposium on Talent Development, University of Iowa, Iowa City, IA, United States.

Lubinski, D., & Benbow, C. P. (2006). Study of mathematically precious youth after 35 years. *Perspectives on Psychological Science, 1*(4), 316–345. https://doi.org/10.1111/j.1745-6916.2006.00019.x

McAdams, D. P., & Pals, J. L. (2006). A new big five: Fundamental principles for an integrative science of personality. *American Psychologist, 61*(3), 204–217. https://doi.org/10.1037/0003-066X.61.3.204

McCall, R. B. (1981). Nature-nurture and the two realms of development: A proposed integration with respect to mental development. *Child Development, 52*(1), 1–12.

Merton, R. K. (1996). *On social structure and science.* University of Chicago Press.

Molenaar, P. C. M., Lerner, R. M., & Newell, K. M. (2014). Developmental systems theory and methodology: A view of the issues. In P. C. M. Molenaar, R. M. Lerner, & K. M. Newell (Eds.), *Handbook of developmental systems theory and methodology* (pp. 3–15). Guilford Press.

Murray, H. A. (1938). *Explorations in personality.* Oxford University Press.

Overton, W. F. (2014). Relational developmental systems and developmental science: A focus on methodology. In P. C. M. Molenaar, R. M. Lerner, & K. M. Newell (Eds.), *Handbook of developmental systems theory and methodology* (pp. 19–65). Guilford Press.

Plucker, J. A., & Barab, S. A. (2005). The importance of contexts in theories of giftedness: Learning to embrace the messy joys of subjectivity. In R. J. Sternberg & J. A. Davidson (Eds.), *Conceptions of giftedness* (2nd ed., pp. 201–216). Cambridge University Press.

Renzulli, J. S. (1978). What makes giftedness? Reexamining a definition. *Phi Delta Kappan, 60*(3), 180–184, 261.

Renzulli, J. S. (1986). The Three-Ring Conception of Giftedness: A developmental model for creative productivity. In R. J. Sternberg & J. E. Davidson (Eds.), *Conceptions of giftedness* (pp. 332–357). Cambridge University Press.

Schlaug, G. (2001). The brain of musicians: A model for functional and structural adaptation. In R. J. Zatorre & I. Peretz (Eds.), *The biological foundations of music* (pp. 281–299). New York Academy of Sciences.

Simonton, D. K. (1999). Talent and its development: An emergenic and epigenetic model. *Psychological Review, 106*(3), 435–457. https://doi.org/10.1037/0033-295X.106.3.435

Simonton, D. K. (2005). Giftedness and genetics: The emergenic-epigenetic model and its implications. *Journal for the Education of the Gifted, 28*(3–4), 270–286. https://doi.org/10.4219/jeg-2005-338

Sternberg, R. J. (1985). *Beyond IQ: A triarchic theory of human intelligence.* Cambridge University Press.

Sternberg, R. J., & Davidson, J. E. (1986). Conceptions of giftedness: A map of the terrain. In R. J. Sternberg & J. E. Davidson (Eds.), *Conceptions of giftedness* (pp. 3–18). Cambridge University Press.

Subotnik, R. F., & Jarvin, L. (2005). Beyond expertise: Conceptions of giftedness as great performance. In R. J. Sternberg & J. E. Davidson (Eds.), *Conceptions of giftedness* (2nd ed., pp. 343–357). Cambridge University Press.

Subotnik, R. F., Olszewski-Kubilius, P., & Worrell, F. C. (2011). Rethinking giftedness and gifted education: A proposed direction forward based on psychological science. *Psychological Science in the Public Interest, 12*(1), 3–54. https://doi.org/10.1177/1529100611418056

Tannenbaum, A. J. (1983). *Gifted children: Psychological and educational perspectives.* Macmillan.

Valsiner, J. (1989). *Human development and culture: The social nature of personality and its study.* Lexington Books.

Wachs, T. D. (2000). *Necessary but not sufficient: The respective roles of single and multiple influences on individual development.* American Psychological Association.

Wai, J., Lubinski, D., & Benbow, C. P. (2009). Spatial ability for STEM domains: Aligning over 50 years of cumulative psychological knowledge solidifies its importance. *Journal of Educational Psychology, 101*(4), 817–835. https://doi.org/10.1037/a0016127

Werner, H. (1957). The concept of development from a comparative and organismic point of view. In D. B. Harris (Ed.), *The concept of development* (pp. 125–148). University of Minnesota Press.

Witty, P. A. (1958). Who are the gifted? In N. B. Henry (Ed.), *Education of the gifted. 57th Yearbook of the National Society for the Study of Education, Part 2* (pp. 41–63). University of Chicago Press.

Ziegler, A., & Phillipson, S. N. (2012). Toward a systemic theory of gifted education. *High Ability Studies, 23*(1), 3–30. https://doi.org/10.1080/13598139.2012.679085

CHAPTER 2

The Talent Development Megamodel

RENA F. SUBOTNIK, PAULA OLSZEWSKI-KUBILIUS, AND FRANK C. WORRELL

Given the number of conceptions of gifted education in the literature, is there a need for another? The Talent Development Megamodel (Subotnik et al., 2011, 2012, 2018) addresses several gaps in the literature and provides an evidence-based integration of several extant models. For example, test-based models for identifying gifted and talented students dominate, particularly under two circumstances. The first is in highly competitive arenas (e.g., entrance to a selective high school). When many people apply for a limited number of spots, it is reasonable to employ test scores to identify the applicants with requisite skill to benefit from the program, provided the scores have been shown to have appropriate predictive validity for this purpose (see the following paragraph). In circumstances such as these, tests are viewed as being more objective than information such as recommendations, particularly for children and youth who may be less likely to elicit teacher endorsements. Second, tests can be used successfully to identify those who might need more advanced content and higher levels of challenge. In this case as well, broad-based testing can balance recommendation-based approaches to gifted identification.

The strengths of testing, however, are counterbalanced by two factors. One is the validity of predictive inferences drawn from test scores relative to actual performance in an area. For example, mathematical creativity or poetry writing is not likely to be tested or evaluated using standardized tests. Portfolios, auditions, or even some kinds of dynamic assessments will be more useful in these circumstances. Additionally, psychometrically sound tests with appropriate norms are not widely available in many subjects and domains (e.g., social studies). Children with strengths in domains without tests are not as likely to be identified.

An alternative practical and effective approach to addressing student needs is embodied in the framework of Advanced Academics (see Chapter 10), whereby students, whether formally identified and labeled as gifted or not, receive instruction at a level consistent with their demonstrated achievement in school subjects. Unfortunately, however, unlike in the case of standard mathematics or foreign language instruction, not all subjects are easily sequenced into basic, intermediate, and advanced stages. And if progress is assessed with tests, the problems of construct validity noted previously are again important. Additionally, the Advanced Academics framework (Peters et al., 2014) does not incorporate developing talent beyond school walls or in nonacademic domains and does not address the development of noncognitive skills that support achievement.

Older conceptions of giftedness, including Tannenbaum's (1986) star model and Sternberg's (1997) successful intelligence theory, feature additional important components missing in the models described previously. These include psychosocial skills, creativity, and chance. Well-developed psychosocial skills are essential for persistence in the face of challenge or failure. Creative productivity is the aspirational outcome of an excellent and comprehensive talent development program. Further, tacit or practical knowledge featured in Sternberg's model and the willingness to take advantage of chance opportunities are often ignored or forgotten. The missing ingredient in these older models is a developmental approach. The Talent Development Megamodel (Subotnik et al., 2011) builds on all of these important contributions to gifted and talented education by focusing on domains both inside and outside of school, on content-valid methods of identification, and on offering opportunities for advanced instruction; it also addresses the need for teaching psychosocial skills and insider knowledge explicitly. Finally, the Megamodel is organized around transitions within domains from abilities to competencies and competencies to expertise and beyond.

Main Components of the Megamodel

Several components make up the Megamodel. These are explicated briefly in the following sections.

Focus on Talent in Domains Rather Than the Gifted Person

Little direct evidence can be found for IQ as the *sole* predictor of exceptional adult achievement (Nisbett et al., 2012; Subotnik et al., 1989; Terman & Oden, 1959). Indeed, general intelligence, or *g*, accounts, on average, for about 25% of variation in work-sample performance (Brody, 1997). Although Terman's study participants were high-IQ children, other factors such as personality, gender, and environmental opportunities played a role in the fulfillment of their talent (National Association for Gifted Children & Council of State Directors of Programs for the Gifted, 2015). Yet, IQ remains predominant in school admissions to gifted and other selective programs for several reasons. For one, it is a reasonable predictor of school achievement (Neisser et al., 1996). Second, IQ scores have strong psychometric properties, allowing policymakers to make selection decisions based on a specific number rather than what are often viewed as more subjective decisions. Third, there are few globally accepted alternatives that do not also measure *g* to some extent (Wai et al., 2018). Less productively, the assumption of IQ as an unchanging measure of innate intelligence has led to conflating *g* with the person rather than viewing IQ as a measure of potential to be developed.

In contrast to privileging *g*, strong support exists for the acquisition of domain-specific abilities in predicting adult achievement and high performance. For example, physical attributes such as lung capacity, flexibility, and pitch perception are connected to sport, dance, and music expertise (Subotnik et al., 2011; Watts et al., 2003). Visual-spatial reasoning skills are associated with successful career choices in the arts (e.g., drawing) and sciences (e.g., chemistry, physics; Hegarty, 2004; Hegarty et al., 2009; Hsi et al., 1997; Sorby et al., 2013; Stieff, 2013; Winner & Casey, 1992). Additionally, the Study of Mathematically Precocious Youth demonstrated a direct connection between early math or verbal reasoning abilities and creative productivity in specific, related domains (Lubinski, 2016; Park et al., 2007).

Focus on Experiences and Skills Within Domains Needed to Move to the Next Level

The Megamodel highlights differences in performance trajectories among and within domains, in terms of beginnings, peaks, and endings across the life span. When abilities and skills in a domain coalesce determines whether a trajectory begins in early childhood or in adolescence, and when identification of talent by appropriate means can begin. For example, some talent areas, such as music performance with wind instruments, and most team sports, require physical maturation. Others, such as mathematical reasoning ability and chess, can emerge early, as can be seen in the case of prodigies (Feldman, 1993). Also, the expression of abilities is clearly recognizable in some domains and not others, thereby affecting identification. But in all domains, talent development begins with potential for future achievement, and when opportunity, motivation, study, and serious engagement come together, potential can develop into competency, expertise, and, for some individuals, eminence in the form of creative products that significantly impact the domain (Worrell et al., 2018).

As shown in Figure 2.1, boy sopranos can perform in the early elementary grades, but adult singing voices do not develop for training until after puberty. Although ability in chess and other domains identified with prodigies (see Feldman, 1986) can be recognized in the childhood years, outstanding performance in psychology does not typically occur until the completion of an advanced degree (Simonton, 2019). Outstanding performance in some sports (e.g., gymnastics) begins in childhood, whereas in other sports, more mature size, speed, flexibility, and judgment are needed (Portenga, 2019).

Some performance trajectories are short. For example, puberty will truncate further development for boy sopranos, and careers in physically demanding sports and performing arts are limited by endurance, strength, and flexibility, which diminish with age. For most academic fields, the visual arts, and some musical fields, these developmental arcs are not clearly

FIGURE 2.1
Varying Domain Trajectories

	Childhood	Adolescence			Adulthood		
		Early	Middle	Late	Early	Middle	Late
Music							
Early specialization (e.g., boy soprano)	Start/Peak	End					
Early specialization (e.g., violin)	Start			Peak		End	
Later specialization (e.g., flute)			Start		Peak	End	
Latest specialization (e.g., vocal arts)				Start		Peak	End
Athletics							
Early specialization (e.g., gymnastics)	Start			Peak/End			
Later specialization (e.g., track and field)		Start			Peak/End		
Academic							
Early specialization (e.g., mathematics)	Start			Peak		End	
Later specialization (e.g., psychology)				Start		Peak	End

Note. From "Rethinking Giftedness and Gifted Education: A Proposed Direction Forward Based on Psychological Science," by R. F. Subotnik, P. Olszewski-Kubilius, and F. C. Worrell, 2011, *Psychological Science in the Public Interest*, *12*(1), p. 32 (https://doi.org/10.1177/1529100611418056). Copyright 2011 by SAGE.

demarcated. Individuals can remain involved and active well into late adulthood, with almost no limits on productivity. Intervals between starts and peaks also vary greatly, with some fields, most particularly academic fields, requiring long periods of preparation (see extensive discussion of academic trajectories by Simonton, 1977, 1984, 1991, 1992a, 1992b, 1997, 1998, 2007, 2019).

Whether a domain begins early or late may also be arbitrarily affected by school policies. The serious study of some academic subjects, such as the social sciences, which may be intellectually accessible in middle school, is not introduced until high school or college. Domains also vary as to how much education or training is needed to achieve a domain peak. For example, medical researchers have a long and arduous journey (McWilliams et al., 2019), requiring a great deal of formal education to achieve mastery, with a significant amount of training occurring while on the job. In contrast, software engineers do not necessarily need a formal degree and can acquire many programming skills on their own or on the job. As a result, software engineers can make a unique contribution during early adulthood, or even in the teenage years (McWilliams et al., 2019). Some domains, such as psychology, religion, and writing, require the accumulation of maturity and experience to generate important contributions and creative productivity and, therefore, peak later.

Incorporate Both Inside- and Outside-of-School Contributions

In accordance with the developmental approach, the focus of the Talent Development Megamodel is on what information, skills, and insights need to be shared and promoted with gifted and talented students to move them along the continuum (see Figure 2.2), especially those children whose parents have fewer resources (Collins & Buller, 2003).

Opportunity provides a context for talent to be nurtured, sometimes even before it is recognized (Gottfried et al., 1994; Syed, 2010). That is, many specific abilities are viewed as malleable and susceptible to the important benefits of education, training, and deliberate practice (Barnett & Durden, 1993; Drake & Winner, 2018; Ericsson, 1996; Macnamara et al., 2018; Tannenbaum, 1986). Universal enrichment, particularly in early specialization domains, can expose children to interesting challenges that may provoke behaviors that display abilities. These opportunities are particu-

FIGURE 2.2
The Talent Development Megamodel

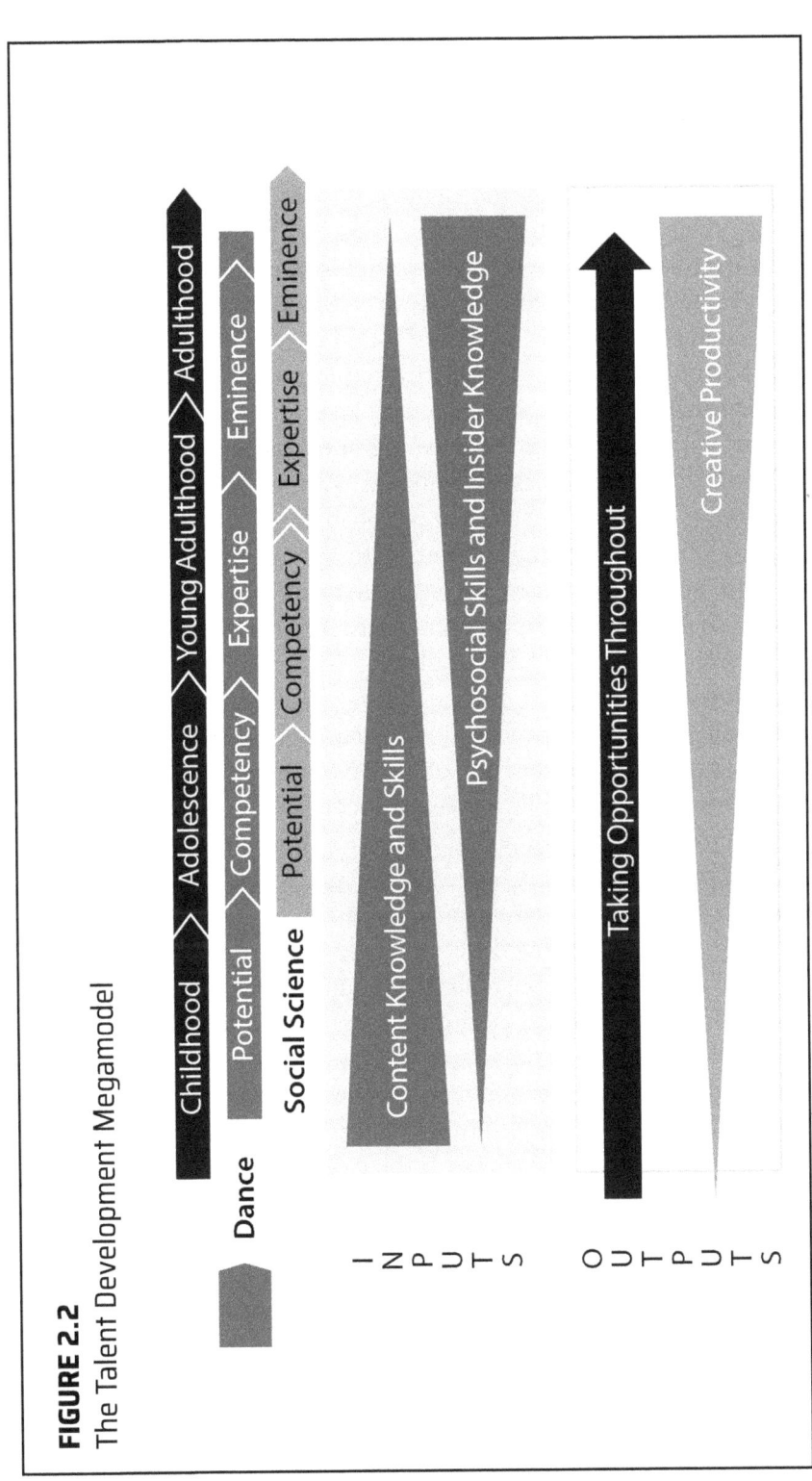

larly important for youth from underrepresented groups that are not well represented in a domain and who are more likely to feel that they do not belong (Worrell, 2010).

Opportunities are not simply those that come in the form of skills and content. One often-forgotten element includes insider knowledge, or knowledge gained from gatekeepers or those with a highly experienced viewpoint from which to provide advice. Zuckerman (1977) traced the ways in which her study participants, American Nobel laureates in science, were labeled early in their careers as "comers"—that is, they were able to capitalize on opportunities for outstanding education and mentorship. She discovered that their choice of postsecondary institution and mentor proved to be more advantageous than their demographic backgrounds (also noted by Simonton [2019] as typical of eminent psychologists). In fact, more than half of the laureates had studied or collaborated with previous laureates. These mentors inculcated students with the culture and values of the domain, and, most importantly, helped them to develop a feel for promising research questions and elegant solutions. The mentors also generated productive connections for their protégées with regard to publications, funding, fellowships, and jobs. Although it is not always clear whether the nurturing will pay off, it is abundantly clear that, without opportunities, the gift will never mature into what it could be (Worrell et al., 2018).

Even if educators and policymakers are compelled to offer opportunities for talent development, opportunities must be taken. According to Wai et al. (2010), participation in precollege educational activities such as competitions, academic clubs, and advanced and accelerated classes provides students with a higher "STEM dose" (p. 860), which is related to a higher rate of notable STEM accomplishments as adults. Individuals must possess the desire, motivation, and self-confidence to engage in talent development opportunities that challenge them and promote growth.

Students may refuse or avoid opportunities for many reasons, such as family pressure to pursue more culturally valued professional tracks or peer pressure to follow what is considered "cool." Sometimes, talented individuals are extraordinarily able in an area but are not interested enough to take time away from other pastimes. Other reasons for not opting for opportunities include performance anxieties, fear of failure, or antipathy toward competition. We argue that these fears might be addressed by psychosocial skills training.

What Helps Individuals Stand Out at Advanced Levels of Talent Development Is the Strength of Their Psychosocial Skills

Performing well at each level of the talent development trajectory requires mastery of various mental and social skills at different points along the trajectory (Simonton, 2000; Subotnik & Jarvin, 2005). Jarvin and Subotnik (2010) suggested that the type and relative importance of psychosocial skills required for transformation of musical abilities into competencies, competencies into expertise, and expertise into eminence vary at each transition point, and that one of the functions of a good teacher is to offer appropriate psychological strength training in addition to knowledge and skills specific to the talent domains. For example, being open to instruction and critique from coaches, teachers, or mentors—being "teachable"—is important for individuals to acquire the foundational skills and knowledge of a domain. At higher stages, particularly when transitioning from competence to expertise, pushing back against the mentor (Subotnik & Jarvin, 2005) by developing a personal style or niche is critical (Olszewski-Kubilius et al., 2015).

Martindale et al. (2007) studied the contributions of elite coaches in 13 sports. These coaches viewed their job as guiding their athletes through various major transitions to higher levels of competition and performance, including explicit instruction for psychosocial skills related to performance. Additional studies have highlighted a number of these skills and techniques, including goal setting, imagery, relaxation, concentration, and self-talk, as particularly helpful for coaches, their teams, and individual protégées (Burton & Raedeke, 2008; Hanton et al., 2009; Kornspan, 2009; Lehman et al., 2007; Macnamara & Collins, 2009; Macnamara et al., 2008; Weinberg & Comar, 1994; Williams & Krane, 2005).

Academically gifted students also require psychological strength to deal with the high-stakes examinations, competitions, demonstrations, and other demands for manifestations of creative productivity (Preuss & Dubow, 2004; Shaunessy & Suldo, 2010; Suldo et al., 2008). Yet before the doctoral level, few young scholars experience the kind of intensive coaching acquired by equally talented athletes. Even at the doctoral level, exposure is uneven, given that school and college teachers receive no systematic training in this dimension of talent development.

Implications for Education From the Megamodel

Subotnik et al. (2011) provided this grounding definition from which to derive implications for education:

> Giftedness is a developmental process that is domain specific and malleable. Although the path may begin with demonstrated potential, giftedness must be developed and sustained by way of training and interventions in domain specific skills and programs and deliberate development of the psychological and social skills needed to pursue difficult new paths. The goal of this developmental process is to transform potential talent during youth into outstanding performance and innovation in adulthood. (p. 7)

The objectives of talent development are important both to the individual and to society. The Megamodel assumes that fulfillment of talent is a rewarding pursuit that reinforces persistence through good times and bad. Abilities that are underidentified, underdeveloped, or discouraged diminish the possibility of individuals' contributions to communities and societies at large. This approach is in contrast to viewing gifted education as mastery of the K–12 school curriculum, or giftedness as a personal attribute that remains constant whether accompanied by actual achievement/productivity or not.

What does it mean to fulfill potential? Finding what a person genuinely likes to do and is good at is a good way to start. In an experiment conducted by Project Spectrum at Harvard University, Krechevsky and Gardner (1990) observed young children interacting with classroom learning centers featuring toys and objects reflecting the intelligences from Gardner's (1983/2011) model. The observers noted which children gravitated to specific centers and how long and intensely they engaged in the activities. Exposing children to an array of enrichment opportunities in this way facilitates the idea that interests can lead to exploration as well as enable recognition of emergent talent. Providing opportunities for children to experience different domains is particularly important in the early years and for children who have limited opportunities for such exposure within their homes and communities. Identification efforts at initial stages should focus on ferreting out interest and potential, with teachers acting as talent scouts, always on the lookout for indications of ability. The basis for providing activities at later stages of talent development should increasingly focus on demonstrated achievement in the domain, reflecting the interaction of interest with opportunity. Achievement can be demonstrated in a number of ways including through traditional tests and grades as well as creative production or serious participation in competitions or clubs.

Proclivities and interests need to be enhanced through opportunity. Educators are responsible for knowing the best evidence-based activities and instructional strategies to excite further interest and persistence through some of the more tedious aspects of learning. For example, children might be enthralled by music, drawing, writing, or public speaking, but less excited about investing time in practice to get good enough to display high levels of creativity. Artful use of role models and extrinsic motivation can help children and youth who are reluctant to get through stages of skill acquisition that require intense, deliberate practice. Additionally, familiarity with what experiences or opportunities were particularly motivating and important to promoting passion and cementing interest for eminent people in particular domains (e.g., early research experience in STEM field) is important for educators at all levels of schooling, so as to better guide students in terms of setting both short- and long-term goals.

According to the Megamodel, the types of opportunities and programs most helpful to developing talent vary depending on the stage of talent development. Initially, exposure and the chance to fall in love with a domain or identify interests are important. Building domain-relevant skills and knowledge through courses, school, and outside-of-school engagement at an appropriate pace and level enables children to progress and helps to nurture motivation, self-efficacy, and persistence. A preview of authentic work in a domain and exposure to domain professionals and experts can cement commitment and build a domain-related scholar identity for adolescents, as well as impart tacit knowledge about career and educational paths. A mismatch of opportunities and stage of talent development (e.g., a focus on developing specific knowledge and skills prior to falling in love with a domain) may negatively affect interest and motivation, and inadvertently truncate talent development.

Providing an original or transformative solution to a social, scientific, or aesthetic problem in the community or even beyond (Jackson & Messick 1965) is the ultimate goal of talent development. Is that not the hope and dream of those who are working for years in an area they love on a topic they are good at? Fulfilling talent provides a sense of purpose and meaning to life. That is not to say that those without exceptional talent have no purpose. Nor do we deny that some people with enormous gifts are content to explore their gifts without solving problems for anyone but themselves. However, the focus of educators and talent development programs should be on providing individuals with the support, opportunities, and tacit knowledge they need to pursue their talents to the highest level possible, if they so choose. Achieving this goal requires knowing both the appropriate learning experiences needed at a current stage of talent development as well as what is involved in the next stage, with an eye toward preparing students for the transition to the higher level.

The Talent Development Megamodel promotes deliberate and systemic focus on cultivating psychosocial skills that support talent development and high achievement. These skills include intellectual risk-taking, maintaining confidence, self-efficacy, performance under pressure, resiliency, dealing with competition, and managing one's reputation. Although educators know intuitively that these are critical skills for the fulfillment of talent, they are rarely addressed deliberately outside of performance realms such as sport and art. These skills can, however, be actively facilitated through the messages that children get from teachers about their abilities and performances, particularly ones that promote a growth mindset and reframe setbacks and perceived failures as opportunities for growth and improvement, and by providing appropriate experiences that require students to deal with increased challenge or competition.

One of the most neglected components of talent development is providing access to insider knowledge. This information includes whom to meet, what courses to take, what clubs to join, and how to dress for certain occasions. Information on how to find or attract the right mentor, develop optimal research questions, or select creative problems to pursue are inequitably distributed among families. Contrast, for example, the potential advantage in the domain of science one student has if their parent is a researcher at National Institutes of Health compared to an equally able classmate whose parent is a banker, police officer, waiter, or elementary school teacher. Educators can help to fill the gap by facilitating students' access to professionals in a domain of interest.

Advantages of the Talent Development Approach

If the field of education were to identify specific abilities associated with domains and distribute information about those abilities widely, more children could be exposed to enrichment and accelerative opportunities. For example, the criteria for auditioning for the Juilliard School are available to anyone on the web. Music teachers all over the world can use these criteria to help shape their curriculum if they so choose and prepare students to audition for Juilliard. Additionally, a focus on domain-specific abilities makes programming choices more feasible for education institutions inside and outside of school, because classes in that subject can be organized with less variability in the students' interests and preparation.

Focus Identification on Outstanding Potential in Domains So More Children Can Be Served, With Services Targeted to Their Strengths

With a long-term, domain-specific approach, fewer children will fall through the cracks. Working with out-of-school program providers, educators may be able to identify children with interests that they are too shy to share in school, or interests that may not respond to or be addressed by the school curriculum. For example, a recreational mathematics curriculum may focus more on geometric rather than algebraic aspects of the subject, and children with visual-spatial and aesthetic interests may then be drawn to mathematics via an alternative route to the one provided in school.

Most school-based gifted programs require high scores in math and verbal domains in order to gain admission, yet educators who have worked in these environments have seen enormously talented children denied services if they are at the very top of the scoring range in only one of these two domains. Educators do not expect children who are talented in drawing to also be talented in acting, so why assume that children will be exceptionally strong across all academic domains?

Providing Psychological Strength Training and Support Will Open Doors to Additional Opportunities and Relationships to Expand Students' Intellectual and Creative Horizons

When children with great potential or talent do not succeed, it often results from a lack of opportunity or lack of needed psychosocial skills. Fear of failure is a powerful force that can limit willingness to engage in challenge in all aspects of life. Successful adults have developed strategies for shutting out disruptive thoughts and facing their fears through trial and error. Professional coaches and performance psychologists have developed evidence-based techniques that go beyond homegrown strategies, and these should be shared with young people who enter increasingly selective environments where self-concept is constantly being challenged, reassessed, and rebuilt. Finally, the public responds more easily to celebrating talent in something, be it music or science. It is more difficult to enjoin enthusiasm for children who are labeled by virtue of an abstract concept like g. This is particularly true when intelligence is presented as immutable and there are no expectations of productivity in response to education or training.

Communities have less resistance to giftedness in performance, whether for winners of science fairs or spelling bees. With community support comes more resources and recognition—something sorely needed in gifted education—and less likelihood of programs being targeted when budgets are tight. Additionally, selection for domain-specific talent programs tend to be more content valid—by asking for demonstrations of aptitudes for writing, dancing, drawing, or mathematical problem solving.

Implications for Policy

- **Focus on domain-specific abilities over general abilities in programming.** Talent development, by definition, is focused on talent *in something*. Many "somethings" are closely tied to general ability, yet other domains are more aligned with a subdomain of g, such as visual-spatial reasoning. And a different set of abilities may be important in performance domains, such as physical flexibility in dance or sport. Finally, creativity, as applied to the domain, is essential to the fulfillment of talent development.

- **For some students, particularly those from disadvantaged circumstances, enrichment will be necessary before exceptional specific abilities can be obvious.** Once observed, talent requires continuous development. Too often gifted education emphasizes identification over the time and resource-intensive development of the talent. Talent development, as implied by the terminology, implies that abilities need to go through transformations over time to meet different levels of accomplishment: competency, expertise, and beyond expertise to creative productivity or eminence (see Figure 2.3). Transformations result from instruction, appropriate role models, experiences with creative problem solving in the domain, and appropriate engagement of psychosocial skills. Individuals may take longer to make those transformations depending upon the opportunities and support available, but it is the job of educators to provide appropriate opportunities for all children so that talent can be enhanced and developed. In the Talent Development Megamodel, talent development is a process of honing ability and developing skills, knowledge, and creativity.

- **Talent development should be offered at different ages depending on the domain trajectory.** Traditional conceptions of identification have concentrated on mid-elementary school as the ideal time when IQ scores stabilize, most children have mastered some degree of reading and mathematics, and schools have a record of children's achievement. However, a talent development approach would require additional opportunities for domain-specific identification at different ages based on trajectories found in the literature. Elementary programs could focus on early identification in mathematics, drawing, and chess. Concurrently, one can be labeled gifted for the first time in high school or university level if the domain is late-starting, such as social science. Identification should be tied to what is known about the optimal time when skills, interests, and abilities coalesce within particular domains.

- **Ensure the availability of coaching and psychosocial strength training for academically talented students.** Children and youth may be offered opportunities to develop their talent, but not all will take advantage of the opportunities presented. Getting involved in a highly creative arena in any domain requires a high level of self-confidence, which is not always evident during adolescence. To

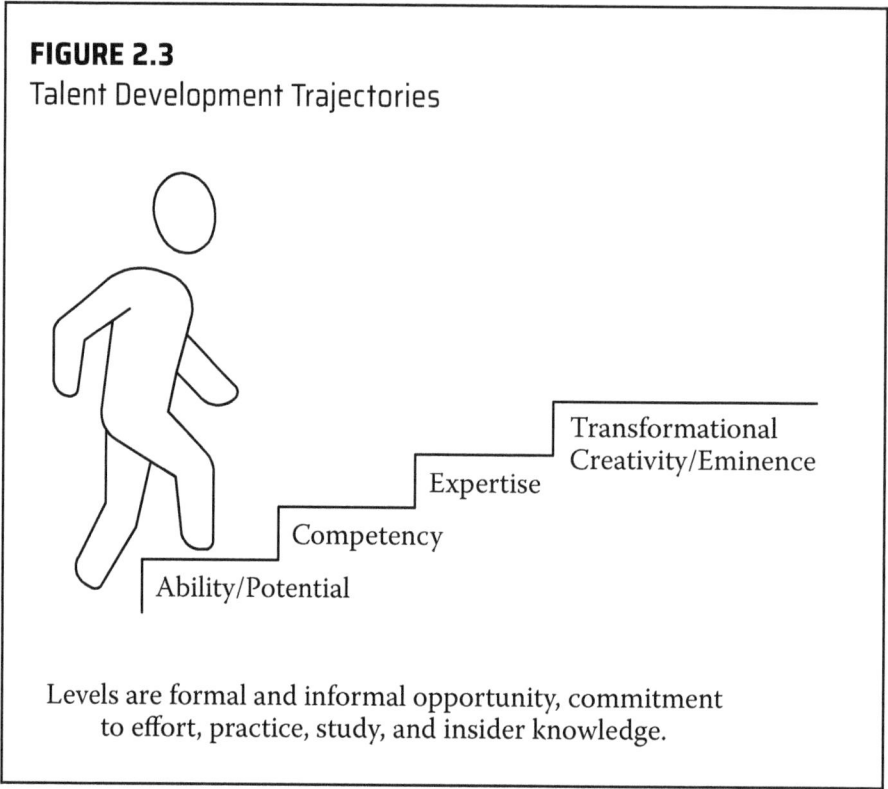

FIGURE 2.3
Talent Development Trajectories

Transformational Creativity/Eminence
Expertise
Competency
Ability/Potential

Levels are formal and informal opportunity, commitment to effort, practice, study, and insider knowledge.

develop talent, educators and coaches must be focused not only on offering opportunities, but also on helping students to understand the importance of taking advantage of them and providing supports and encouragement so that students choose them. Psychosocial strength is essential to pursuing risky endeavors, and talent development classifies as such. It requires stretching beyond current capacities, dealing with setbacks and self-doubt, and overcoming those feelings, and it also may involve absorbing the criticisms of those who are respected when a student breaks with the status quo. Educators and coaches can cultivate psychosocial strengths by providing the appropriate level of challenge in training or programs and also by emphasizing the role of effort and use of strategies to control anxiety.

- **Personnel with deep knowledge and experience with community resources and talent trajectories in each domain should be part of the gifted education team.** Talent development needs to be conceptualized as long-term, ongoing, and conducted both inside and outside of school. In fact, in some domains, almost the entire transformation of abilities into competencies and beyond takes place outside of school. We argue that school-based and informal education professionals need to be familiar with paths or trajectories in domains including secondary, undergraduate, and graduate training, and outside-of-school programs that are most likely to enhance the talents of their students. Talent development, therefore, requires that adults involved in the process be familiar with the key groups, programs, and opportunities that are influential in domains, whether clubs, competitions, mentorships, summer programs, or higher education.

A Proposal to Consolidate Different Approaches to Giftedness and Talent Development

Often, as we have done earlier in the chapter, different models for giftedness and talent development are presented in contrast to each other (McBee et al., 2012). We argue, however, that the field is helped by integration rather than segregation of varied perspectives (Worrell et al., 2019). The name we gave to the Megamodel reflects its appreciation for its constituent components and contributing factors.

- Our focus on specific abilities and psychosocial skills as critical to the identification and development of talent is consistent with the views of Tannenbaum (1986), Renzulli (1978, 2016), and Gagné (2005, 2018), although we put greater emphasis on the domain-specific and developmental nature of these in the Megamodel.
- We feature the importance of insider knowledge, made explicit by the theory of Successful Intelligence (Sternberg, 1997).
- We integrate the Advanced Academics model (Peters et al., 2014), with its greater focus on the nature of interventions at the school and classroom level, as a curricular component of academic talent.
- We see a role for IQ-based views of identification, particularly for young children who have not had significant exposure to domains or for talent areas with later starting trajectories. Global enrichment programs can fill in gaps for children who have had fewer early opportunities to learn and can provide a context to seek out interest and exceptional potential, even if demonstrated potential is not exceptional.

- The Megamodel is consistent with other models in recognizing the importance of beginning as early as possible in light of domain trajectories, including the use of gifted education best practices such as acceleration options, grouping strategies, advanced content, and differentiation in instructional pacing. We add psychosocial skills training, out-of-school programming, and mentoring.
- We acknowledge the importance of deliberate practice, a main concept of expertise models (Ericsson, 1996), at some point in all talent domains.
- We also acknowledge that models such as the Actiotope (Ziegler & Stoeger, 2017) or Dai's (2010) contextual, emergent, and dynamic model go deeper into the situational and contextual aspects of talent development and recognize the interactive nature of talent development.
- Finally, Bloom's (1985) model of talent development domains and Sternberg's (1998) stages of expertise development inspired our developmental perspectives. We agree that a stage of talent development is reaching expertise in a domain, although we support the scholarly productivity/artistry model (Subotnik & Jarvin, 2005) in recognizing that a stage beyond expertise exists as creative productivity in the form of scholarly work or artistry. Additionally, in the Megamodel, we argue that an ultimate goal of gifted education should be eminent performance or creative productivity, thus demanding a longer-term view of talent development (beyond K–12) than has been traditional for the field.

DISCUSSION QUESTIONS

1. Which domains of giftedness are supported in your community?
2. How soon should students be able to specialize? How does this decision vary with domains? How soon after specializing should students be exposed to related disciplines that might inform their creative development (e.g., exploring cultural history associated with a piece of art)?
3. What are the most important psychosocial skills needed for each domain at each level of talent development?

DISCUSSION QUESTIONS, continued

4. What are the most effective ways of teaching these mental and social skills? Who is best suited to provide this instruction?
5. How much influence should a teacher's or a coach's connections to the talent domain (familiarity with clubs, summer programs, mentors, internships, university programs, and professors) have toward their hiring or promotion?
6. Is it okay to use one's gifts for one's own satisfaction and not share the outcome with others?
7. What political and practical challenges need to be addressed in order to transform more of gifted education into talent development?

References

Barnett, L. B., & Durden, W. G. (1993). Education patterns of academically talented youth. *Gifted Child Quarterly, 37*(4), 161–168. https://doi.org/10.1177/001698629303700405

Bloom, B. S. (Ed.). (1985). *Developing talent in young people.* Ballantine Books.

Brody, N. (1997). Intelligence, schooling, and society. *American Psychologist, 52*(10), 1046–1050. https://doi.org/10.1037/0003-066X.52.10.1046

Burton, D., & Raedeke, T. D. (2008). *Sports psychology for coaches.* Human Kinetics.

Collins, M. F., & Buller J. R. (2003). Social exclusion from high-performance sport: Are all talented young sports people being given an equal opportunity of reaching the Olympic podium? *Journal of Sport & Social Issues, 27*(4), 420–442. https://doi.org/10.1177/0193732503255483

Dai, D. Y. (2010). *The nature and nurture of giftedness: A new framework for understanding gifted education.* Teachers College Press.

Dai, D. Y. (2018). A history of giftedness: A century of quest for identity. In S. I. Pfeiffer, E. Shaunessy-Dedrick, & M. Foley-Nicpon (Eds.), *APA handbook of giftedness and talent* (pp. 3–23). American Psychological Association. https://doi.org/10.1037/0000038-001

Drake, J. E., & Winner, E. (2018). Why deliberate practice is not enough: Evidence of talent in drawing. In D. Z. Hambrick, G. Campitelli, & B. N. Macnamara (Eds.), *The science of expertise: Behavioral, neural, and genetic approaches to complex skill* (pp. 101–128). Routledge.

Ericsson, K. A. (Ed.). (1996). *The road to excellence: The acquisition of expert performance in the arts and sciences, sports, and games*. Erlbaum.

Feldman, D. H. (1986). *Nature's gambit: Child prodigies and the development of human potential*. Basic Books.

Feldman, D. H. (1993). Child prodigies: A distinctive form of giftedness. *Gifted Child Quarterly, 37*(4), 188–193. https://doi.org/10.1177/001698629303700408

Gagné, F. (2005). From gifts to talents: The DMGT as a developmental model. In R. J. Sternberg & J. E. Davidson (Eds.), *Conceptions of giftedness* (2nd ed., pp. 98–119). Cambridge University Press.

Gagné, F. (2018). Academic talent development: Theory and best practices. In S. I. Pfeiffer, E. Shaunessy-Dedrick, & M. Foley-Nicpon (Eds.), *APA handbook of giftedness and talent* (pp. 163–183). American Psychological Association. https://doi.org/10.1037/0000038-011

Gardner, H. (2011). *Frames of mind: The theory of multiple intelligences*. Basic Books. (Original work published 1983)

Gottfried, A. W., Gottfried, A. E., Bathurst, K., & Guerin, D. W. (1994). *Gifted IQ: Early developmental aspects: The Fullerton longitudinal study*. Plenum.

Hanton, S., Thomas, O., & Mellalieu, S. D. (2009). Management of competitive stress in elite sport. In B. Brewer (Ed.), *International Olympic Committee sport psychology handbook* (pp. 30–42). Wiley-Blackwell.

Hegarty, M. (2004). Mechanical reasoning by mental simulation. *Trends in cognitive sciences, 8*(6), 280–285. https://doi.org/10.1016/j.tics.2004.04.001

Hegarty, M., Keener, M., Kooshabeh, P., & Montello, D. R. (2009). How spatial abilities enhance and are enhanced by dental education. *Learning and Individual Differences, 19*(1), 61–70. https://doi.org/10.1016/j.lindif.2008.04.006

Hsi, S., Linn, M. C., & Bell, J. E. (1997). The role of spatial reasoning in engineering and the design of spatial instruction. *Journal of Engineering Education, 86*(2), 151–158. https://doi.org/10.1002/j.2168-9830.1997.tb00278.x

Jackson, P. W., & Messick, S. (1965). The person, the product, and the response: Conceptual problems in the assessment of creativity. *Journal of*

Personality, 33(3), 309–329. https://doi.org/10.1111/j.1467-6494.1965.tb01389.x

Jarvin, L., & Subotnik, R. F. (2010). Wisdom from conservatory faculty: Insights on success in classical music performance. *Roeper Review, 32*(2), 78–87. https://doi.org/10.1080/02783191003587868

Kornspan, A. S. (2009). *Fundamentals of sport and exercise psychology.* Human Kinetics.

Krechevsky, M., & Gardner, H. (1990). The emergence and nurturance of multiple intelligences: The Project Spectrum approach. In M. J. A. Howe (Ed.), *Encouraging the development of exceptional skills and talents.* The British Psychological Society.

Lehman, A. C., Sloboda, J. A., & Woody, R. H. (2007). *Psychology for musicians: Understanding and acquiring the skills.* Oxford University Press

Lubinski, D. (2016). From Terman to today: A century of findings on intellectual precocity. *Review of Educational Research, 86*(4), 900–944. https://doi.org/10.3102/0034654316675476

Macnamara, Á., & Collins, D. (2009). More than the "X" factor! A longitudinal investigation of the psychological characteristics of developing excellence in musical development. *Music Education Research, 11*(3), 377–392. https://doi.org/10.1080/14613800903144270

Macnamara, Á., Holmes, P., & Collins, D. (2008). Negotiating transitions in musical development: The role of psychological characteristics of developing excellence. *Psychology of Music, 36*(3), 335–352. https://doi.org/10.1177/0305735607086041

Macnamara, B. N., Hambrick, D. Z., Frank, D. J., King, M. J. Burgoyne, A. P., & Meinz, E. J. (2018). The deliberate practice view: An evaluation of definitions, claims, and empirical evidence. In D. Z. Hambrick, G. Campitelli, & B. N. Macnamara (Eds.), *The science of expertise: Behavioral, neural, and genetic approaches to complex skill* (pp. 151–168). Routledge.

Martindale, R. J. J., Collins, D., & Abraham, A. (2007). Effective talent development: The elite coach perspective in UK sport. *Journal of Applied Sport Psychology, 19*(2), 187–206. https://doi.org/10.1080/10413200701188944

McBee, M. T., McCoach, D. B., Peters, S. J., & Matthews, M. S. (2012). The case for a schism: A commentary on Subotnik, Olszewski-Kubilius, and Worrell (2011). *Gifted Child Quarterly, 56*(4), 210–214. https://doi.org/10.1177/0016986212456075

McWilliams, M. A., Holding, E. Z., & Knotek, S. E. (2019). Talent development in medicine and software engineering. In R. F. Subotnik, P.

Olszewski-Kubilius, & F. C. Worrell (Eds.), *The psychology of high performance: Developing human potential into domain-specific talent* (pp. 109–134). American Psychological Association. https://doi.org/10.1037/0000120-006

National Association for Gifted Children & Council of State Directors of Programs for the Gifted. (2015). *2014–2015 state of the states in gifted education: Policy and practice data.* https://www.nagc.org/sites/default/files/key%20reports/2014-2015%20State%20of%20the%20States%20%28final%29.pdf

Neisser, U., Boodoo, G., Bouchard, T. J., Jr., Boykin, A. W., Brody, N., Ceci, S. J., Halpern, D. F., Loehlin, J. C., Perloff, R., Sternberg, R. J., & Urbina, S. (1996). Intelligence: Knowns and unknowns. *American Psychologist, 51*(2), 77–101. https://doi.org/10.1037/0003-066X.51.2.77

Nisbett, R. E., Aronson, J., Blair, C., Dickens, W., Flynn, J., Halpern, D. F., & Turkheimer, E. (2012). Intelligence: New findings and theoretical developments. *American Psychologist, 67*(2), 130–159. https://doi.org/10.1037/a0026699

Olszewski-Kubilius, P., Subotnik, R. F., & Worrell, F. C. (2015). Conceptualizations of giftedness and the development of talent: Implications for counselors. *Journal of Counseling and Development, 93*(2), 143–152. https://doi.org/10.1002/j.1556-6676.2015.00190.x

Park, G., Lubinski, D., & Benbow, C. P. (2007). Contrasting intellectual patterns predict creativity in the arts and sciences: Tracking intellectually precocious youth over 25 years. *Psychological Science, 18*(11), 948–952. https://doi.org/10.1111/j.1467-9280.2007.02007.x

Peters, S. J., Matthews, M. S., McBee, M. T., & McCoach, D. B. (2014). *Beyond gifted education: Designing and implementing advanced academic programs.* Prufrock Press.

Portenga, S. T. (2019). High performance talent development in golf. In R. F. Subotnik, P. Olszewski-Kubilius, & F. C. Worrell (Eds.), *The psychology of high performance: Developing human potential into domain-specific talent* (pp. 23–51). American Psychological Association. https://doi.org/10.1037/0000120-003

Preuss, L. J., & Dubow, E. F. (2004). A comparison between intellectually gifted and typical children in their coping responses to a school and a peer stressor. *Roeper Review, 26*(2), 105–111. https://doi.org/10.1080/02783190409554250

Renzulli, J. S. (1978). What makes giftedness? Reexamining a definition. *Phi Delta Kappan, 60*(3), 180–184, 261.

Renzulli, J. S. (2016). The three-ring conception of giftedness: A developmental model for promoting creative productivity. In S. M. Reis (Ed.), *Reflections on gifted education: Critical works by Joseph S. Renzulli and colleagues* (pp. 55–90). Prufrock Press.

Shaunessy, E., & Suldo, S. M. (2010). Strategies used by intellectually gifted students to cope with stress during their participation in a high school International Baccalaureate program. *Gifted Child Quarterly, 54*(2), 127–137. https://doi.org/10.1177/0016986209355977

Simonton, D. K. (1977). Creative productivity, age, and stress: A biographical time-series analysis of 10 classical composers. *Journal of Personality and Social Psychology, 61*(5), 829–840. https://doi.org/10.1037/0022-3514.61.5.829

Simonton, D. K. (1984). Artistic creativity and interpersonal relationships across and within generations. *Journal of Personality and Social Psychology, 46*(6), 1273–1286. https://doi.org/10.1037/0022-3514.46.6.1273

Simonton, D. K. (1991). Emergence and realization of genius: The lives and works of 120 classical composers. *Journal of Personality and Social Psychology, 61*(5), 829–840. https://doi.org/10.1037/0022-3514.61.5.829

Simonton, D. K. (1992a). Leaders of American psychology, 1879–1967: Career development, creative output, and professional achievement. *Journal of Personality and Social Psychology, 62*(1), 5–17. https://doi.org/10.1037/0022-3514.62.1.5

Simonton, D. K. (1992b). The social context of career success and course for 2,026 scientists and inventors. *Personality and Social Psychology Bulletin, 18*(4), 452–463. https://doi.org/10.1177/0146167292184009

Simonton, D. K. (1997). Creative productivity: A predictive and explanatory model of career trajectories and landmarks. *Psychological Review, 104*(1), 66–89. https://doi.org/10.1037/0033-295X.104.1.66

Simonton, D. K. (1998). Achieved eminence in minority and majority cultures: Convergence versus divergence in the assessments of 294 African Americans. *Journal of Personality and Social Psychology, 74*(3), 805–817. https://doi.org/10.1037/0022-3514.74.3.804

Simonton, D. K. (2000). Creative development as acquired expertise: Theoretical issues and an empirical test. *Developmental Review, 20*(2), 283–318. https://doi.org/10.1006/drev.1999.0504

Simonton, D. K. (2007). Creative life cycles in literature: Poets versus novelists or conceptualists versus experimentalists? *Psychology of Aesthetics, Creativity and the Arts, 1*(3), 133–139. https://doi.org/10.1037/1931-3896.1.3.133

Simonton, D. K. (2019). Talent development in the domain of academic psychology. In R. F. Subotnik, P. Olszewski-Kubilius, & F. C. Worrell (Eds.), *The psychology of high performance: Developing human potential into domain-specific talent* (pp. 201–218). American Psychological Association. https://doi.org/10.1037/0000120-010

Sorby, S., Casey, B. M., Veurink, N., & Dulaney, A. (2013). The role of spatial training in improving spatial and calculus performance in engineering students. *Learning and Individual Differences, 26*, 20–29. https://doi.org/10.1016/j.lindif.2013.03.010

Sternberg, R. J. (1997). *Successful intelligence: How practical and creative intelligence determine success in life.* Plume.

Sternberg, R. J. (1998). Abilities are forms of developing expertise. *Educational Researcher, 27*(3), 11–20. https://doi.org/10.3102/0013189X027003011

Stieff, M. (2013). Sex differences in the mental rotation of chemistry representations. *Journal of Chemical Education 90*(2), 165–170. https://doi.org/10.1021/ed300499t

Subotnik, R. F., & Jarvin, L. (2005). Beyond expertise: Conceptions of giftedness as great performance. In R. J. Sternberg & J. E. Davidson (Eds.), *Conceptions of giftedness* (2nd ed., pp. 343–357). Cambridge University Press.

Subotnik, R. F., Karp, D. E., & Morgan, E. R. (1989). High IQ children at mid-life: An investigation into the generalizability of Terman's "Genetic Studies of Genius." *Roeper Review, 11*(3), 139–144. https://doi.org/10.1080/02783198909553190

Subotnik, R. F., Olszewski-Kubilius, P., & Worrell, F. C. (2011). Rethinking giftedness and gifted education: A proposed direction forward based on psychological science. *Psychological Science in the Public Interest, 12*(1), 3–54. https://doi.org/10.1177/1529100611418056

Subotnik, R. F., Olszewski-Kubilius, P., & Worrell, F. C. (2012). A proposed direction forward for gifted education based on psychological science. *Gifted Child Quarterly, 56*(4), 176–188. https://doi.org/10.1177/0016986212456079

Subotnik, R. F., Olszewski-Kubilius, P., & Worrell, F. C. (2018). Talent development as the most promising focus of giftedness and gifted education. In S. I. Pfeiffer, E. Shaunessy-Dedrick, & M. Foley-Nicpon (Eds.), *APA handbook of giftedness and talent* (pp. 231–245). American Psychological Association. https://doi.org/10.1037/0000038-015

Suldo, S. M., Shaunessy, E., Michalowski, J., & Shaffer, E. J. (2008). Coping strategies of high school students in an International Baccalaureate program. *Psychology in the Schools, 45*(10), 960–975. https://doi.org/10.1002/pits.20345

Syed, M. (2010). *Bounce: Mozart, Federer, Picasso, Beckham, and the science of success.* HarperCollins.

Tannenbaum, A. J. (1986). Giftedness: A psychosocial approach. In R. J. Sternberg & J. E. Davidson (Eds.), *Conceptions of giftedness* (pp. 21–52). Cambridge University Press.

Terman, L. M., & Oden, M. H. (1959). *Genetic studies of genius: Vol. 5. The gifted group at mid-life: 35 years' follow up of the superior child.* Stanford University Press.

Wai, J., Lubinski, D., Benbow, C. P., & Steiger, J. H. (2010). Accomplishment in science, technology, engineering and mathematics (STEM) and its relation to STEM educational dose: A 25-year longitudinal study. *Journal of Educational Psychology, 102*(4), 860–871. https://doi.org/10.1037/a0019454

Wai, J., Worrell, F. C., & Chabris, C. (2018). The consistent influence of general cognitive ability in college, career, and lifetime achievement. In K. Larsen-McClarty, K. Mattern, & M. Gaertner (Eds.), *Preparing students for college and careers: Theory, measurement, and educational practice* (pp. 46–56). Routledge.

Watts, C., Barnes-Burroughs, K., Andrianopoulos, M., & Carr, M. (2003). Potential factors related to untrained singing talent: A survey of singing pedagogues. *Journal of Voice, 17*(3), 298–307. https://doi.org/10.1067/S0892-1997(03)00068-7

Weinberg, R. S., & Comar, W. (1994). The effectiveness of psychological interventions in competitive sport. *Sports Medicine, 18*(6), 406–418. https://doi.org/10.2165/00007256-199418060-00005

Williams, J. M., & Krane, V. (2005). Psychological characteristics of peak performance. In J. Williams (Ed.), *Applied sport psychology: Personal growth to peak performance* (5th ed., pp. 162–178). McGraw-Hill.

Winner, E., & Casey, M. B. (1992). Cognitive profiles of artists. In G. D. Cupchik, G. C. Cupchik, & J. Laszlo (Eds.), *Emerging visions of the aesthetic process in psychology and semiology* (pp. 154–170). Cambridge University Press.

Worrell, F. C. (2010). Psychosocial stressors in the development of gifted learners with atypical profiles. In J. L. VanTassel-Baska (Ed.), *Patterns and profiles of promising learners from poverty* (pp. 33–58). Prufrock Press.

Worrell, F. C., Subotnik, R. F., & Olszewski-Kubilius, P. (2018). Talent development: A path toward eminence. In S. I. Pfeiffer, E. Shaunessy-Dedrick,

& M. Foley-Nicpon (Eds.), *APA handbook of giftedness and talent* (pp. 247–258). American Psychological Association. https://doi.org/10.1037/0000038-016

Worrell, F. C., Subotnik, R. F., Olszewski-Kubilius, P., & Dixson, D. D. (2019). Gifted students. *Annual Review of Psychology, 70*, 551–576. https://doi.org/10.1146/annurev-psych-010418-102846

Ziegler, A., & Stoeger, H. (2017). Systematic gifted education: A theoretical introduction. *Gifted Child Quarterly, 61*(3), 183–193. https://doi.org/10.1177/0016986217705713

Zuckerman, H. (1977). *Scientific elite: Nobel laureates in the United States.* Free Press.

CHAPTER 3

Toward a Science of Expertise

Obstacles, Implications, and Applications

DAVID Z. HAMBRICK AND BROOKE N. MACNAMARA

Some people are more highly skilled at complex tasks than other people. But why? This question is of enduring interest to scientists, and a central focus of contemporary research on expertise. In this chapter, we briefly review evidence concerning the origins of individual differences in expertise, focusing on a multifactorial perspective. We then discuss obstacles to progress in the field. We focus on *scientific authoritarianism*—advocacy of a theoretical view using antiscientific tactics, at the expense of scientific progress—and discuss ways of combating this pernicious problem. We then reflect on implications of expertise research for social justice and end with a discussion of practical applications of expertise research.

Toward a Science of Expertise

Most everyone has dreamed of becoming highly skilled at something, whether a hobby or an occupation. Yet, the harsh reality is that few people achieve this goal, or even come close to doing so. Consider the odds of playing professional basketball, a dream for millions of children around the world. According to a National Collegiate Athletic Association (NCAA, 2019) report, 3.6% of people who play basketball in high school play in college, but only 0.03% of this select group are drafted to play professionally. The odds of becoming a professional in other talent domains are at least as slim. As but one example, only a handful of the millions of people who play chess make a living doing so (Knapp, 2017).

What differentiates people who make it to the top of their field? This is a question that parents, coaches, and talent scouts all seek to answer, and a question of central concern of the science of expertise. *Expertise* refers to a person's level of skill in a domain. In some domains, it is possible to determine level of skill by purely objective means. As examples, in the marathon, a person's expertise can be quantified in terms of running time, and in chess, a person's skill level can be determined by tournament rating. In other domains, expertise must be determined using criteria that have at least an element of subjectivity. For example, there are technical aspects of music skill, but also expressive and creative aspects, the evaluation of which is ultimately subjective.

Across domains, expertise varies on a continuum from unidimensional to highly multidimensional. In unidimensional domains, a single type of task can be used to measure expertise. For example, in darts, the essence of expertise is accurate dart throwing, and it is obvious how to measure expertise: Have people throw darts at a dartboard and measure their accuracy. By contrast, in multidimensional domains, multiple tasks are required to measure expertise in its totality, or research must focus on one aspect of expertise. For example, there are numerous facets of music skill, including sight-reading, composing, playing memorized pieces, and improvisation. A musician may be strong in some of these aspects of skill but weaker in others; no single task will suffice to measure all of these aspects of expertise.

However expertise is defined, it may be useful for descriptive or applied purposes to assign labels to different skill ranges, such as *beginner, novice, intermediate, expert,* and *elite.* For example, in chess, an "elite" player might be defined as a player with an Elo rating of 2,400 or higher, while an elite marathoner might be defined as a runner who consistently finishes in under 2 hours and 10 minutes. However, these labels are ultimately arbitrary, based as they are on cuts on a continuously (although not necessarily normally) distributed variable. In other words, these labels do not describe discrete, naturally occurring categories, like eye color or genotype. The goal of scientific research on expertise is to explain the full range of performance variation in a domain, not differences between arbitrary groups of performers.

Theoretical Issues in Expertise Research

Although the term *expertise* has only been in widespread use in the English language since the 1950s (Hambrick & Campitelli, 2018), scientific interest in the origins of human skill dates to the earliest days of psychology. In fact, the question of what accounts for individual differences in what is now called expertise was the subject of one of the first major debates in the field. In his 1869 book *Hereditary Genius,* Francis Galton argued that eminence arises from "natural ability," based on his observation that highly accomplished people in art, music, science, and other fields tended to be biologically related to each other. The Swiss botanist Alphonse de Candolle (1873) countered that the real source of individual differences was "causes favorable"—environmental advantages ranging from a good upbringing to a temperate climate (see Fancher, 1983). The debate over the origin question—whether expertise is "born" or "made"—has raged on ever since. Recent research has focused on the contributions of training and ability to individual differences in expertise. We briefly review evidence from this research next.

The Role of Training

There is no doubt that training, in its various forms, is necessary for any individual to develop a high level of skill in a domain. No person becomes a professional athlete, a concert pianist, or a world-class lawyer without a great deal of training. This is simply to say that no one is *literally* born an expert, innately endowed with the type of specialized knowledge that is necessary for these types of activities. This type of knowledge can *only* be acquired through some type of learning experience. In more technical terms, training is what drives a person's improvement in a domain, as reflected in *within-person variability* (also called *intra-individual variability*).

The controversial question is the extent to which training history explains *between-person variability* in performance (also called *inter-individual variability*). Our own research has focused on empirically testing the influential *deliberate practice view*. As proposed by Ericsson and colleagues (Ericsson et al., 1993), this view proposes that "individual differences in ultimate performance can largely be accounted for by differential amounts of past and current levels of practice" (p. 392). This claim is not supported by the available evidence. Our research indicates that, under various operationalizations, deliberate practice explains a sizeable amount of the between-person variance in performance but leaves an even larger amount of the variance unexplained and potentially explainable by other factors (see Macnamara et al., 2014; Macnamara et al., 2016). Research by other scientists arrived at the same conclusion. For example, in a meta-analysis, Platz et al. (2014) found that deliberate practice explained 37% of the between-person variance in music achievement, after correcting for measurement error (see Figure 3.1). This finding implies that people may require massively different levels of deliberate practice to reach a given level of skill.

It should be added that the case for deliberate practice is based almost entirely on correlational evidence. That is, nearly all research on deliberate practice has used cross-sectional research designs in which performers of different levels of skill are compared at a single point in time (e.g., novices vs. experts). The fundamental limitation of this design is that aptitude (talent) and training are confounded: A person with a high level of aptitude for a domain may be more inclined to engage in deliberate practice than a person with a lower level of aptitude (see Sternberg, 1996; Winner & Drake, 2013). Ericsson seemed to reject this argument on the grounds that "deliberate practice does not involve a mere execution or repetition of already attained skills but repeated attempts to reach beyond one's current level which is associated with frequent failures" (Ericsson et al., 2007, p. 18). Ericsson's argument appears to be that because deliberate practice is not "more of the same," success in previously practiced activities should not predict whether a person will engage in future deliberate practice. But this conclusion is not logically required—and it seems doubtful that it is true. Imagine two high school basketball players. One is among the best players in the state, is a top prospect for a college basketball scholarship, and has a long history of

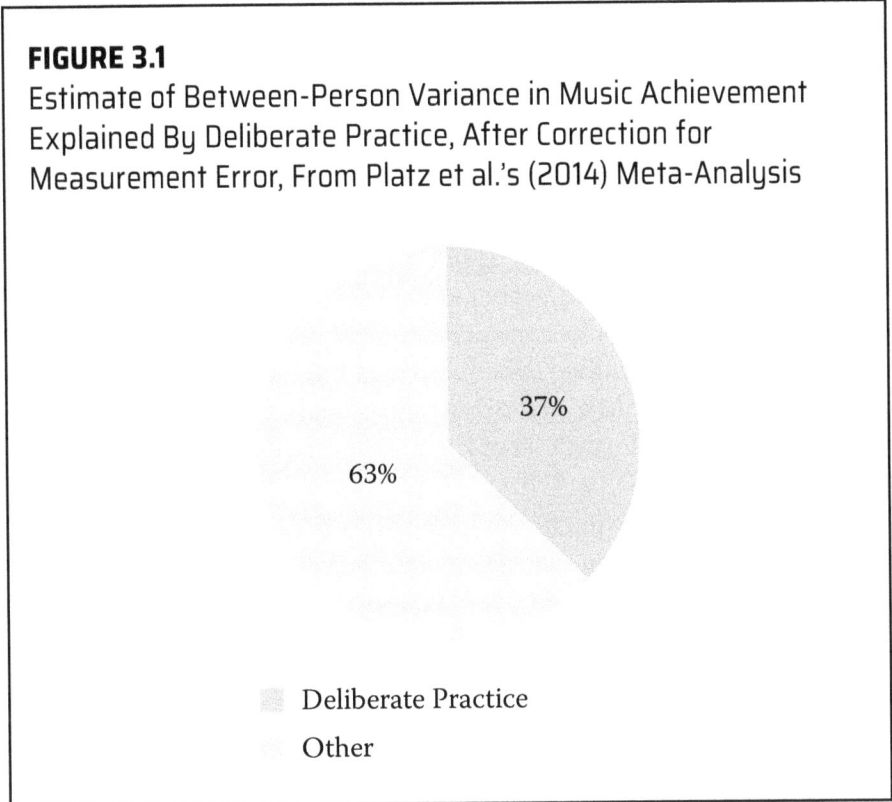

FIGURE 3.1
Estimate of Between-Person Variance in Music Achievement Explained By Deliberate Practice, After Correction for Measurement Error, From Platz et al.'s (2014) Meta-Analysis

being positively reinforced for practicing basketball; the other is the worst player on the team. Who seems more likely to engage in a gruelling regimen of deliberate practice in the future—the star or the benchwarmer? This is an empirical question, but it seems likely that it would be the star.

In general, Ericsson has defended his view by claiming that other researchers do not understand what deliberate practice is (Ericsson, 2014d, 2016). Most recently, he and colleagues stated that "it has been common for scientists to be confused about the definition of DP [deliberate practice]" (Dearani et al., 2017). This is surely true, because as illustrated in Table 3.1, Ericsson's definition of and criteria for deliberate practice have repeatedly shifted. For example, although Ericsson sometimes stipulated that deliberate practice activities must be designed by a teacher or coach (e.g., Ericsson & Pool, 2016; Krampe & Ericsson, 1996), other times he explicitly stated that the activities can be designed by such individuals or the "performers themselves" (e.g., Ericsson, 1998, p. 84; Keith & Ericsson, 2007, p. 136). As another example, although Ericsson recently emphasized that deliberate practice must be individualized (Ericsson & Pool, 2016), in a previous study

TABLE 3.1

Illustrations of Shifts in Ericsson's Definition of and Criteria for Deliberate Practice (in Chronological Order)

Is a Teacher Required to Design DP?	Quotation From Ericsson's Writings
Yes	"Given the cost of individualized instruction, the teacher designs practice activities that the individual can engage in between meetings with the teacher. We call these practice activities deliberate practice and distinguish them from other activities."—Ericsson et al. (1993), p. 368
Yes	"In distinction from leisurely or normal job-related experience, Ericsson et al. defined deliberate practice as a very specific activity designed for an individual by a skilled teacher explicitly to improve performance."—Krampe & Ericsson (1996), p. 333
No	"Ericsson et al. (1993) proposed the term deliberate practice to refer to those training activities that were designed solely for the purpose of improving individuals' performance by a teacher or the performers themselves."—Ericsson (1998), p. 84
Yes	"Ericsson et al. (1993) identified activities that met the necessary requirements for effective training and were designed by a teacher to improve a specific individual's performance. They termed these activities 'deliberate practice.'"—Ericsson (2000), p. 368
No	"Ericsson et al. (1993) introduced the term deliberate practice to describe focused and effortful practice activities that are pursued with the explicit goal of performance improvement....These activities can be designed by external agents, such as teachers or trainers, or by the performers themselves."—Keith & Ericsson (2007), p. 136
Yes	"Deliberate practice requires a teacher who is capable of individualizing instruction and practice and knowledgeable of practice methods with verified performance outcomes."—Ericsson (2020), p. 163

he and his colleagues collected measures of both "solitary deliberate practice" and "deliberate practice with a partner" (Duffy et al., 2004, p. 232). Given these inconsistencies in the definition of and criteria for deliberate practice, it is not surprising that scientists are commonly confused about the definition of deliberate practice.

There are other serious problems with Ericsson's conclusions and arguments, which we will mention briefly here (see Hambrick et al., 2016, for further discussion). One is that Ericsson has sometimes used a double standard for evidence. For example, in a commentary, Ericsson (2014b) rejected studies that Macnamara et al. (2014) included in their meta-analyses for not meeting his criteria for deliberate practice, even though he had previously used some of the same studies to argue for the importance of deliberate practice. Most bizarrely, among the studies Ericsson (2014b) rejected are some of his own studies in which he explicitly claimed to be studying deliberate practice (see Table 3.2), which would seem to undermine the case he has for decades been attempting to make for his view.

More recently, Ericsson and Harwell (2019) conducted a reanalysis of Macnamara et al.'s (2014) meta-analytic data, and used a more lenient teacher/coach involvement criterion for deliberate practice than Ericsson (2014b) had when he commented on the same set of studies. This led Ericsson and Harwell to code seven studies as deliberate practice that Ericsson (2014b) had previously rejected for not meeting the criteria for deliberate practice. (For additional details, see Hambrick et al., in press; see also the presentation "Is the Deliberate Practice View Defensible?" on the Open Science Framework at https://osf.io/buqsk.) Ericsson and Harwell did not acknowledge and explain this criterion shift. Consequently, it remains unclear what the definition of deliberate practice is, or even whether there is a fixed definition of deliberate practice.

Another problematic issue is what can be called *theoretical term swapping*. Without explicitly acknowledging doing so, Ericsson and colleagues have swapped out one term for another in describing past research. In particular, they have recently relabeled activities they once referred to as "deliberate practice" as a distinct and less effective form of practice that Ericsson and Pool (2016) termed "purposeful practice"—training that has a goal and structure but is self-directed rather than teacher-directed. For example, referring to two studies of chess by Charness et al. (2005), Ericsson (2005) wrote that "this paper reports the most compelling and detailed evidence for how designed training (deliberate practice) is the crucial factor in developing expert chess performance" (p. 237). Later, he added that "the amount of solitary chess study was the best predictor of performance at

TABLE 3.2
Illustrations of Double Standard for Evidence in Ericsson's Writings

Study Rejected by Ericsson (2014b) for Violating His Criteria for Deliberate Practice	Previous Use of the Same Study by Ericsson and Colleagues to Argue for the Importance of Deliberate Practice
Hodges & Starkes (1996)[1]	"Several studies and reviews have since found a consistent relation between performance and amount and quality of *deliberate practice* . . . in sports (. . . Hodges & Starkes, 1996 . . .)."—Ericsson (1998), p. 87
Helsen, Starkes, & Hodges (1998)[1]	"Research conducted in several domains such as . . . sports (Helsen, Starkes, & Hodges, 1998 . . .) suggests that the amount of accumulated *deliberate practice* is closely related to an individual's attained level of performance."—Keith & Ericsson (2007), p. 136
Duffy, Baluch, & Ericsson (2004)[2]	"The engagement of the dart-related activities differed between groups for three types, namely playing in league darts, solitary practice and total *deliberate practice*. The latter two findings were in line with prior expectations namely; the more an individual engages in *deliberate practice* (particularly solitary practice) the more proficient their performance is likely to be. This finding supports one of the main tenets of Ericsson et al.'s (1993) theory whereby expertise is acquired through a vast number of hours spent engaging in activities purely designed to improve performance, i.e., *deliberate practice*."—Duffy et al. (2004), pp. 242–243

TABLE 3.2, continued

Study Rejected by Ericsson (2014b) for Violating His Criteria for Deliberate Practice	Previous Use of the Same Study by Ericsson and Colleagues to Argue for the Importance of Deliberate Practice
Charness, Tuffiash, Krampe, Reingold, & Vasyukova (2005)[2]	"The paper by Charness, Tuffiash, Krampe, Reingold, and Vasyukova (this issue) extends an earlier classic chapter by Charness, Krampe, and Mayr (1996) and examines retrospective estimates by a large sample of chess players about their training during the development of their skill and expertise. This paper reports the most compelling and detailed evidence for how designed training (*deliberate practice*) is the crucial factor in developing expert chess performance."—Ericsson (2005), p. 237

"In chess, Charness and his colleagues (Charness, Krampe, & Mayr, 1996; Charness, Tuffiash, Krampe, Reingold, & Vasyukova, 2005) have found that the amount of solitary chess study was the best predictor of performance at chess tournaments, and when this type of deliberate practice was statistically controlled, there was no reliable benefit from playing chess games."—Ericsson (2014a), p. 190 |
| Tuffiash, Roring, & Ericsson (2007)[2] | "Several researchers have reported a consistent association between the amount and quality of solitary activities meeting the criteria of *deliberate practice* and performance in different domains of expertise, such as . . . Scrabble (Tuffiash et al., 2007)."—Ericsson et al. (2009), p. 9 |

TABLE 3.2, continued

Study Rejected by Ericsson (2014b) for Violating His Criteria for Deliberate Practice	Previous Use of the Same Study by Ericsson and Colleagues to Argue for the Importance of Deliberate Practice
Duckworth, Kirby, Tsukayama, Berstein, & Ericsson (2011)[2]	"Our major findings in this investigation are as follows: *Deliberate practice*—operationally defined in the current investigation as the solitary study of word spellings and origins—was a better predictor of National Spelling Bee performance than either being quizzed by others or engaging in leisure reading. With each year of additional preparation, spellers devoted an increasing proportion of their preparation time to *deliberate practice*. . . . Grittier spellers engaged in *deliberate practice* more so than their less gritty counterparts, and hours of *deliberate practice* fully mediated the prospective association between grit and spelling performance." —Duckworth et al. (2011), p. 178 "In that study [Duckworth et al., 2011] we (as I was also one of the co-authors) collected data on '*deliberate practice*.'" —Ericsson (2012), p. 4

Note. In each quotation, the emphasis on "deliberate practice" is added. [1]Rejected because article "do[es] not record assigned individualized practice tasks with immediate feedback and goals for practice" (see Ericsson, 2014c, Table 3). [2]Rejected because article "do[es] not record a teacher or coach supervising and guiding all or most of the practice" (see Ericsson, 2014c, Table 2). For additional examples of studies rejected/previously used by Ericsson, see Macnamara et al.'s (2018) Table 9.1.

chess tournaments, and when this type of deliberate practice was statistically controlled, there was no reliable benefit from playing chess games" (Ericsson, 2014a, p. 190). However, Ericsson and colleagues recently stated that "Charness et al. (2005) found evidence for an independent effect of engagement in purposeful practice for chess skill, even after controlling for other types of practice activities" (Moxley et al., 2019, p. 17). Likewise, Ericsson and Harwell (2019) pointed to an initial report of data from the Charness et al. (1996) studies to illustrate purposeful practice—although it should also be noted that in the very same article they coded the studies as deliberate practice for their meta-analysis. (For a timeline of Ericsson's varying characterizations of the Charness et al. studies, see the Appendix of Hambrick et al.'s [in press] article.)

It is, of course, appropriate to revise a theory as evidence accumulates. This is part of what the philosopher Imre Lakatos (1976) called a "progressive" program of research. Obviously, however, the revisions must be explicitly acknowledged and justified. Otherwise, to use Lakatos's terminology, a theory can be endlessly adjusted through "auxiliary hypotheses" that form a "protective belt" around its "hard core"—the central theses of the theory that are essentially irrefutable. The research program becomes "degenerative" rather than progressive. The theory is then difficult, if not impossible, to empirically test and enters the realm of pseudoscience. The theorist fends off challenge by, for example, claiming that other researchers did not use the "correct" definition, and past claims and evidence that are problematic for the theory are effectively erased through obfuscation.

The Role of Ability

There is no reason to doubt that elite performers in a given domain vary in basic abilities and capacities—elements of "talent." For example, if all of the chess grandmasters in the world were given an IQ test, the average would likely be above that for the general population (Grabner et al., 2007), but there would still be a range of scores, and it is entirely possible that some grandmasters would score near, or even below, the population average. Similarly, if the 100 best marathoners in the world were give a test of aerobic capacity (VO_2max), the average would be much higher than the average for the general population, but there would still be a range of values.

In research on individual differences, the relevant question is not whether any one person with a low level of some ability can reach a certain level of performance in a domain; it is whether the probability of doing so differs for people of differing levels of the ability. Do measures of abilities predict acquisition of skill in complex domains? The answer is yes. Meta-analyses with extremely large samples have established that measures of general cognitive ability (g) predict real-world outcomes such as job training success better than any single variable, including personality, motivation, prior job experience, and interview ratings (Schmidt & Hunter, 2004). Measures of other types of abilities predict future performance, as well. For example, in a longitudinal study of elite tennis players, Schneider and colleagues (1993) found that measures of physical and psychological characteristics had a significant positive effect on subsequent tennis rank. Furthermore, basic motor abilities had an indirect impact on ranking through tennis-specific skills (see Hambrick et al., 2016, for further discussion of this rare longitudinal study of elite performers).

According to one popular view, which we have termed the *circumvention-of-limits hypothesis* (Hambrick & Meinz, 2011), basic abilities predict performance differences initially during skill acquisition, but their influence diminishes as specialized knowledge is acquired and is eventually eliminated. Ericsson and Pool (2016) explained the idea as follows: "While people with certain innate characteristics . . . may have an advantage when first learning a skill, that advantage gets smaller over time, and eventually the amount and quality of practice take on a much larger role in determining how skilled a person becomes" (p. 233). In line with this claim, based on his own review of the evidence, Ericsson (2018a) wrote that "traditional tests of intelligence and IQ are not predictive of individual differences in attained performance among skilled performers" (p. 97).

One might think that there is extensive evidence to support these conclusions, but in reality, there is not. In some cases, Ericsson has made inferences that are not licensed by well-established conventions of statistical inference in psychological research, arguing for his view based on a finding that an ability-performance correlation was statistically significant in a lower skill group but not in a higher skill group, even though the correlations are not significantly different from each other. For example, in making the argument that ability-performance correlations drop with increasing skill, Ericsson has in multiple reviews (Ericsson, 2014b, 2018a, 2018b) pointed to Ruthsatz et al.'s (2008) finding that a measure of intelligence (Raven's score) correlated with musical performance in high school band members ($r = .25$, $p < .01$, $N = 178$) but not in more skilled groups of university music majors ($r = .24$, $p > .05$, $N = 19$) or in music institute students ($r = .12$, $p > .05$, $N = 64$). However, these correlations are not significantly different from each other (all test of differences in r's are nonsignificant, z's < 1). Thus,

Ruthsatz et al.'s results actually *fail* to support Ericsson's claim of a diminishing ability-performance correlation with increasing skill.

In other cases, Ericsson's arguments do not make sense. For example, in one review, he (Ericsson, 2014d) cited a report in the German magazine *Der Spiegel* that former chess world champion Garry Kasparov's IQ was estimated at 120 based on his score on Raven's Progressive Matrices, and noted that this score is "very close to the average of all chess players . . . thus not very predictive of world-class chess performance" (p. 87). However, even if this estimate of Kasparov's IQ is valid, the strength of a predictive relationship between two variables (i.e., a correlation) cannot be inferred from a single case. That is, if other world-class chess players (e.g., Bobby Fischer, Anatoly Karpov, Magnus Carlsen, Viswanathan Anand) had much higher IQs, then IQ could still correlate *highly* with world-class chess performance.

In still other cases, Ericsson has been selective in his reporting of evidence. For example, citing Schmidt and Hunter's (2004) review of the job performance literature, Ericsson (2014d) explained, "The expert-performance approach proposes that performance on tests of general cognitive ability [and performance] will be correlated for beginners" (p. 84). However, he failed to mention that, in this same review, Schmidt and Hunter noted that this is true for nonbeginners, as well. Indeed, they specifically stated: "One might hypothesize that the validity of GMA [general mental ability] declines over time as workers obtain more job experience. However, research does not support this hypothesis" (p. 167). Failing to mention evidence contrary to a hypothesis leads to a biased portrayal of the strength of the evidence for that hypothesis.

Finally, Ericsson has made numerous material errors in his reviews. For example, Ericsson (2013) claimed that "Kopiez and Lee (2006) found that for musicians with lower sight-reading skill there was a correlation with their working memory. For musicians with a higher level of sight-reading skill there was no significant relation between their performance and their working memory" (p. 236). However, Kopiez and Lee (2006) reported no such finding. In fact, they did not report any analyses comparing the correlation between working memory and sight-reading performance in groups representing lower versus higher levels of sight-reading skill. As another example, referring to a subsequent report of data from this study of sight-reading, Ericsson (2018b) noted that "Kopiez and Lee (2008) found that speed of alternating finger movements [music-specific speed trilling] and amount of accumulated sight-reading experience were the only significant predictors of sight-reading performance" (p. 707). This is incorrect: Sight-reading performance was also significantly predicted by a nonmusic measure of processing speed (i.e., number combination, $r = -0.44$, $p = 0.001$; see Kopiez & Lee, 2008, Tables 2 and 4), indicating faster processing for more skilled sight-readers. These material errors create confusion in the literature and need to be corrected (for further examples, see Hambrick et al., 2014, 2016; Macnamara et al., 2016).

We carried out our own review of evidence relevant to the circumvention-of-limits hypothesis (Hambrick, Burgoyne, & Oswald, 2018), conducting systematic searches for relevant articles in the literature on expertise in five domains (games, music, science, sports, surgery/medicine, and aviation), as well as the literature on job performance. Altogether, we searched approximately 1,300 documents. We found that, on balance, evidence from the expertise literature does not support the circumvention-of-limits hypothesis: Only three of 15 studies provide support for this hypothesis, either in the form of significantly different ability-performance correlations across skill groups or significant ability × skill interactions on performance. What might be regarded as the strongest evidence comes from one of our own meta-analyses (Burgoyne et al., 2016). In that meta-analysis, we found that the correlation between Gf (as measured by tests of reasoning ability) and chess expertise was significantly higher for less-skilled chess players than for more-skilled players. However, as we urged, this finding must be interpreted cautiously, because the measure of chess skill was highly confounded with age (i.e., the more-skilled players were adults, the less-skilled players were children).

A more consistent picture emerged in the review of evidence from the job performance literature. Ability-performance correlations may decrease in relatively simple lab tasks, and especially those with consistent demands (Ackerman, 1988). However, even after an extensive amount of job experience, general cognitive ability remains a statistically and practically significant predictor of actual job performance (see also Reeve & Bonaccio, 2011). Some of the most compelling evidence for this conclusion comes from a reanalysis of data from the Joint-Service Job Performance Measurement/Enlistment (JPM) Standards Project. Initiated in 1980 by the U.S. Department of Defense, the purpose of this study was to develop measures of military job performance (see Hambrick, Burgoyne, & Oswald, 2018, for further description). The JPM data set includes 31 jobs and a total sample size of 10,088 military personnel; the measure of general cognitive ability was the Armed Forces Qualifying Test (AFQT) score, and job performance was measured with hands-on job performance (HOJP) tests for the different jobs. Using this data set, Figure 3.2 shows the correlation between AFQT and HOJP for four levels of job experience (top panel) and for eight

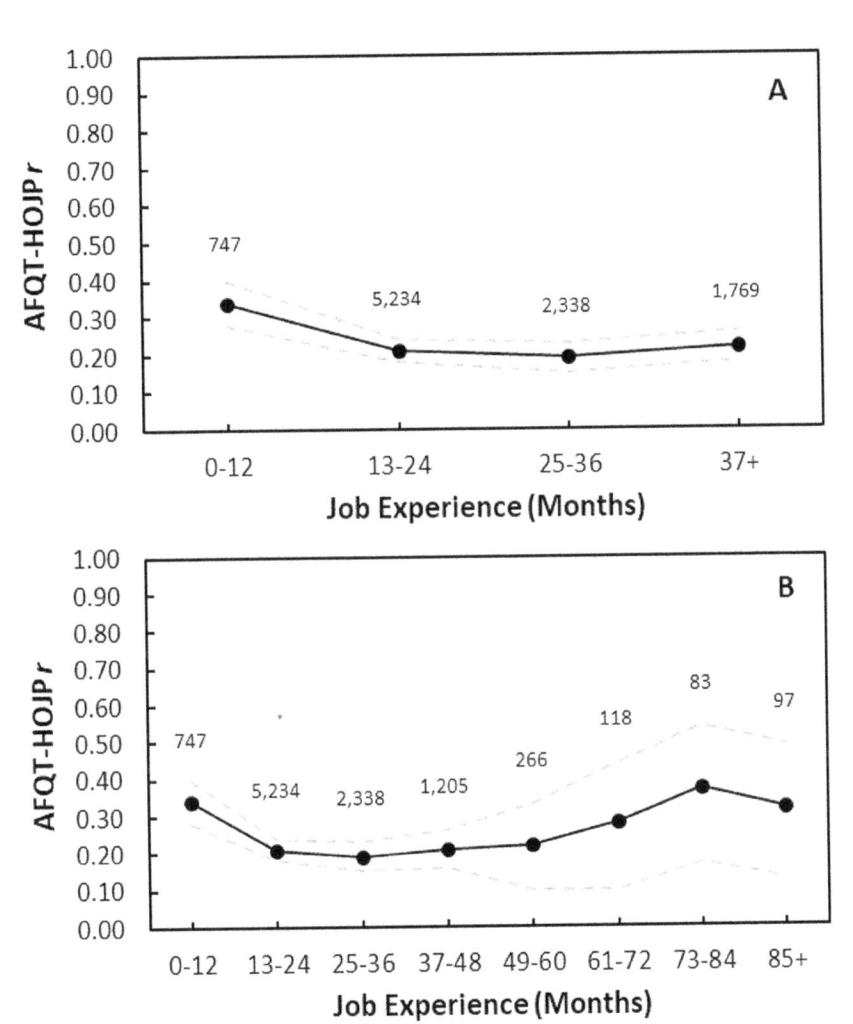

FIGURE 3.2
Correlation Between Cognitive Ability (AFQT Score) and Hands-On Job Performance (HOJP) at Different Levels of Job Experience

Note. Data from JPM project. Each dot represents a correlation; dashes represent 95% confidence intervals. Values above dots are sample sizes. From "Domain-General Models of Expertise: The Role of Cognitive Ability," by D. Z. Hambrick, A. P. Burgoyne, and F. L. Oswald, in P. Ward, J. M. Schraagen, J. Gore, and E. Roth (Eds.), *The Oxford Handbook of Expertise* (p. 70), 2018, Oxford University Press. Copyright 2018 by Oxford University Press. Reprinted with permission.

levels of job experience (bottom panel). As can be seen in both panels, the AFQT-HOJP correlation decreases from the first year to the second, but does not decrease further after that. The overall picture to emerge from this and other large-scale studies (e.g., Farrell & McDaniel, 2001; Schmidt & Hunter, 2004) is that general cognitive ability remains a significant predictor of job performance, even after extensive job experience, and even if validity drops initially. It is possible that ability effects would be attenuated with even more training, but this has not yet been established.

The Multifactorial Perspective on Expertise

To sum up, evidence converges on two complementary conclusions. The first is that training history is important, but does not account for all, nearly all, or even most of the between-person variance in expertise across a wide range of domains. This discovery indicates that people may differ greatly in the amount of training that it takes them to reach a given level of skill. The second conclusion is that basic abilities—elements of "talent"—explain a practically and statistically significant amount of the remaining variance. Moreover, at this point, there is not consistent and compelling evidence that the predictive validity of ability factors is eliminated at high levels of skill.

Based on this evidence, we have argued that models of expertise should take into account all potentially relevant factors. Figure 3.3 illustrates one such model: the *multifactorial gene-environment interaction* model (MGIM; Ullén et al., 2016). There are two core assumptions of this model. The first is that expertise reflects the influence of multiple factors, which may have both direct and indirect influences on performance. This includes not only domain-specific factors (i.e., training and specialized knowledge), but also domain-general factors (i.e., ability and nonability traits). The second assumption is that individual differences in expertise arise from the interplay between genetic and environmental factors.

According to the *first law of behavioral genetics* (Turkheimer, 2000), any behavioral trait or characteristic that varies across people has a genetic component. Accordingly, between-person variation in every behavioral variable in the MGIM is assumed to be influenced by both genetic and environmental factors. This includes factors that have traditionally been regarded as purely "environmental" variables—namely, training variables. As a case in point, in a study of more than 2,500 twin pairs, Mosing and colleagues (2014) found an average heritability estimate of around 50% for accumu-

FIGURE 3.3
The Ullén-Hambrick-Mosing Multifactorial Gene-Environment Interaction Model of Expertise

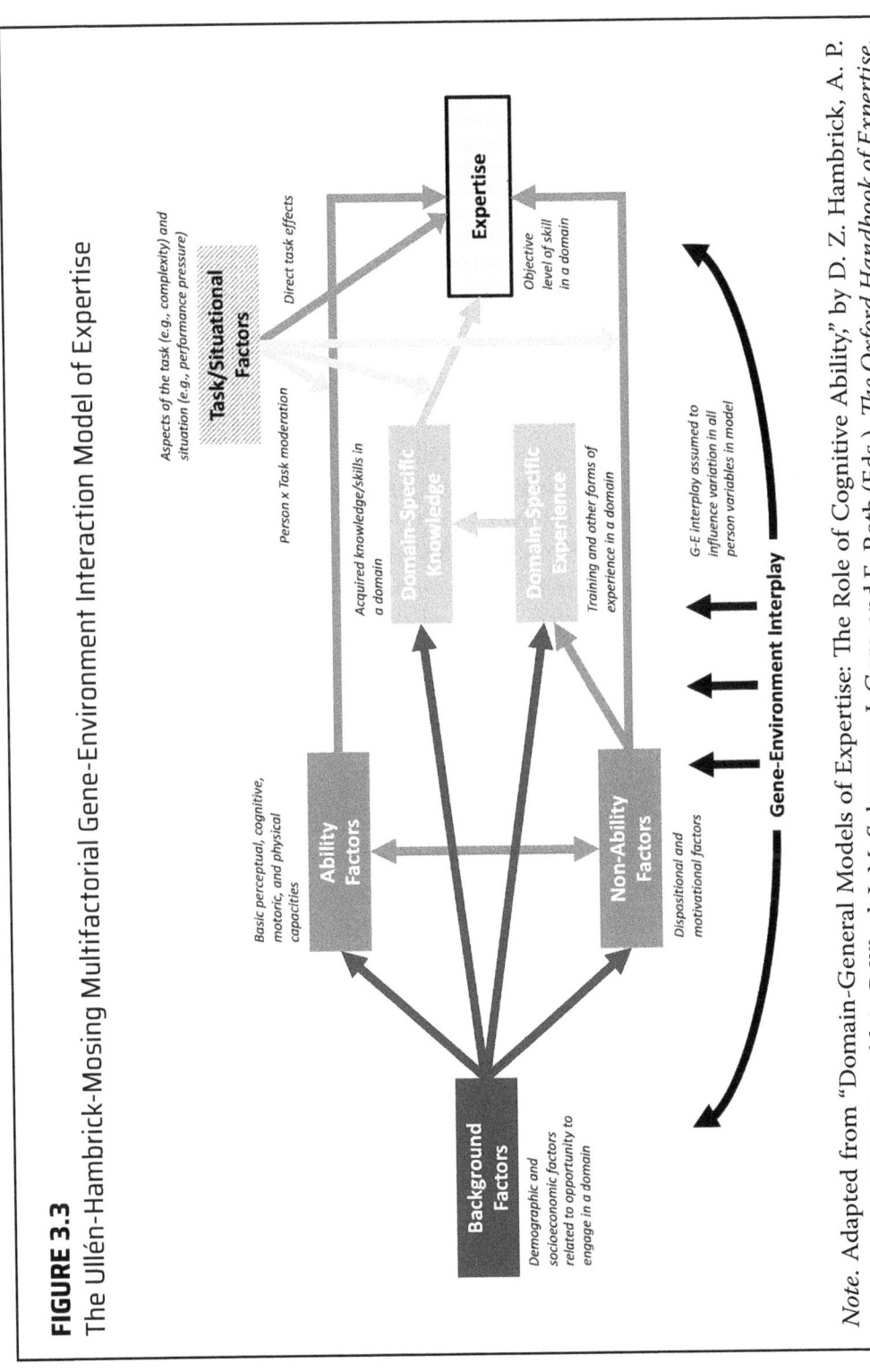

Note. Adapted from "Domain-General Models of Expertise: The Role of Cognitive Ability," by D. Z. Hambrick, A. P. Burgoyne, and F. L. Oswald, in P. Ward, J. M. Schraagen, J. Gore, and E. Roth (Eds.), *The Oxford Handbook of Expertise*, 2018, Oxford University Press. Copyright 2018 by Oxford University Press.

lated amount of music practice (see also Hambrick & Tucker-Drob, 2015). This finding is readily explainable as an instance of gene-environment correlation (*r*GE), which occurs when a person's genetically influenced ability and preferences influence the experience they seek out for themselves (see Tucker-Drob, 2018).

Obstacles in Expertise Research

We believe that research aimed at testing multifactorial models of expertise will advance scientific understanding of the nature and origin of expertise. There are, however, three major obstacles to the advancement of the field. The first is that expertise is difficult to study. As already noted, given that expertise develops over a long period of time, researchers have often used cross-sectional research designs. However, there is no way around it: Group differences in expertise may be confounded with motivation, aptitude, and other traits. An alternative is the longitudinal design, in which performers are followed over time. This approach takes years—even decades—to complete in research on expertise. Furthermore, researchers cannot know who will persist in a domain and who will drop out. However, one way to think about a longitudinal study is that it is never complete—it is always ongoing. Indeed, in other areas of research, longitudinal studies have been running for decades. For example, the Seattle Longitudinal Study began in 1956 (Schaie, 2005). Large-scale longitudinal studies will be critical to achieve greater understanding of expertise but will require major commitment of resources and coordinated efforts among many scientists.

Another approach to research on expertise is to experimentally manipulate expertise in laboratory tasks designed to capture elements of more complex tasks. We have made use of this *knowledge activation* approach in our own research. In a recent study, Hambrick, Altmann, and Burgoyne (2018; see also Hambrick & Oswald, 2005) had participants complete tests of cognitive ability, as well as a procedural task in which the goal was to perform a sequence of steps in a particular order. Task-relevant knowledge was experimentally manipulated between subjects. In one condition, participants were given a piece of task-relevant knowledge, in the form of a mnemonic, to keep their place in the sequence, whereas in the other condition, participants were not given the mnemonic. The question was whether the provision of task-relevant knowledge would mitigate the effect of cognitive ability on performance in the procedural task—and it did not. The effect of cognitive ability on performance in the procedural task was as great in the mnemonic condition as in the no-mnemonic condition. This finding provides converging evidence for the conclusion that domain-specific knowledge may not always mitigate effects of cognitive ability on performance.

The second obstacle in expertise research is reliance on bad research practices. Among the methodological issues plaguing research on expertise are use of small samples, use of measures with unknown or poor psychometric properties, and use of extreme groups designs (e.g., novice vs. expert). Use of small samples leads not only to low statistical power, but also to low precision, meaning there is a low likelihood the findings will replicate. Use of measures with unknown or poor psychometric properties makes it difficult to interpret relationships among these measures. For example, if a near zero correlation between some measure of ability and a measure of expertise is reported without reliability estimates, it is unclear whether there is no relationship between the measures or whether the measures have poor reliability, limiting the degree to which they can correlate with each other. Finally, use of extreme-groups designs (e.g., novice vs. expert) in expertise research leads to inflated effect size estimates, among other problems (see Preacher et al., 2005). A lack of transparency, including a refusal to share data so that other researchers may address limitations of a study through reanalyses, compounds these problems. The advent of data repositories such as Open Science Framework makes it especially easy to share data.

The final—and perhaps greatest—obstacle in expertise research is expertise researchers themselves. Professed commitment to objectivity notwithstanding, scientists often enter an area of research with preconceived notions about what they study. This is surely the case in expertise research. Nearly everyone has beliefs about why some people are so much better at complex endeavors than other people. Ericsson (2007), for example, commented: "My own thoughts on exceptional ability were influenced by my family and education in Sweden, where views that genetic endowment limited the acquisition of superior performance among otherwise healthy individuals were discouraged" (p. 5). As a teenager, one of us (Hambrick) suspected that his failed effort to achieve golfing greatness reflected a lack of talent, plus limited opportunity for good golf instruction (see Konnikova, 2016). The problem is not that scientists have preconceptions about what they study; the problem is that these preconceptions may influence the research they conduct, with or without the researchers' awareness.

One way that preconceptions may corrupt research is by influencing study design. For example, a researcher who believes that individual differences in expertise largely, or entirely, reflect training history may only measure training history and fail to measure basic abilities that could account for additional variance, or may effectively "engineer" the results by including measures of abilities that have little relevance to the criterion task (e.g., a visuospatial perceptual speed task for a verbal problem-solving game). Preconceptions may also influence the interpretation, reporting, and review of research results—and, again, this may occur even without the researcher's awareness. For example, a researcher may fail to conduct and report relevant statistical tests to make an argument for a favored viewpoint and omit problematic findings in literature reviews. In extreme cases, a scientist's preconceptions can have more destructive consequences, as we now discuss.

Scientific Authoritarianism

The sociologist Robert Merton (1973) proposed four principles of science that promote open, nonauthoritarian, scientific discourse and review. The first is *communism*: All scientists should have access and ownership of scientific goods, such as theories; that is, one researcher should not claim ownership and authority over a theory and attempt to keep aspects of research (e.g., data) secret. The second is *universalism*: Scientific validity is independent of the status of the people conducting the research; that is, the merit of ideas should be evaluated based on evidence rather than the status or prominence of the person proposing the ideas. The third is *disinterestedness*: Scientists should conduct work to progress science rather than for self-interest and personal gain. The fourth is *organized skepticism*: Scientific claims should be scrutinized prior to acceptance.

When researchers in a scientific field stray from Merton's principles, the conditions are ripe for *scientific authoritarianism*: the emergence of an individual (or group of individuals) who advocate for a theoretical view using antiscientific tactics, at the expense of progress toward the truth. Scientific authoritarianism may arise from ideology—a religious-like devotion to some view—or from a desire for profit, fame, and/or power. Any (or all) of these motives can operate within an individual to produce scientific authoritarianism, and sometimes without the individual's awareness or malevolent intent. If they *are* aware of their conduct, the scientific authoritarian may justify it (if only to themselves) with an end-justifies-means argument: The favored view is beneficial to society and "must" be right, and thus it is justifiable to maintain and promote it through any means necessary, including antiscientific tactics. Scientific authoritarians may also attract adherents who use such tactics.

Scientific authoritarians use the same types of tactics as political authoritarians (e.g., U.S. President Donald Trump). Political authoritarians and scientific authoritarians may even combine forces, as infamously illustrated by the case of the Soviet agronomist Trofim Lysenko. With the support of Joseph Stalin, Lysenko rejected Mendelian genetics and promoted bogus ideas about inheritance, including that heredity could be changed by "educating" plants (Borinskaya et al., 2019). In 1940, Lysenko was named the Director of the Institute for Genetics; scientists who rejected his ideas were fired from their posts, arrested, or even executed (Ings, 2017). Of course, political authoritarians may also exert pressure on scientists for political ends. As one especially disturbing example, there were reports in Spring 2020 that the Trump administration was pressuring the Centers for Disease Control and Prevention to change how it calculated deaths due to COVID-19 to lower the count (Van Dongen, 2020).

Table 3.3 presents a working list of the scientific authoritarian's tactics, along with some other tipoffs. The cardinal trait underlying scientific authoritarianism is narcissism: a consuming desire by an individual to promote themselves and/or their view, without regard for the impact of their actions on others and science. This often takes on the form of self-aggrandizing. The scientific authoritarian may emphasize their (or their theory's) "greatness" (seniority, accolades, pedigree, etc.) and use their position of power to promote their view by pressuring editors to publish their work and (equally important) reject critics' work. The scientific authoritarian may further attempt to suppress dissent through petty sleights such as failing to cite critics' relevant research, misspelling their names, and emphasizing their junior status in the field; panning critics' manuscripts with tangential and disingenuous criticisms in peer review; and so on. Like the political authoritarian, the scientific authoritarian may even act as if delusional, overstating the importance of their theory and claiming that it has more explanatory power than it does, and going beyond the data (e.g., making bold causal claims based on correlational evidence). In the philosopher Isaiah Berlin's (1953) terminology, the scientific authoritarian is typically a "hedgehog"—a theoretical dogmatist who knows "one great thing"—rather than a data-driven "fox" who knows "many things."

The scientific authoritarian's ultimate goal is to insulate their theory from falsification—to keep it "alive"—and they employ a range of tactics to achieve this goal. One of the most common and insidious is *shifting*: in response to challenge, changing and "tweaking" theoretical definitions and

TABLE 3.3
Scientific Authoritarianism Tactics and Tipoffs (in Alphabetical Order)

Attacking critics	Questioning the credibility/competence of those who challenge a favored view, while ignoring the substance of their criticisms.
Blathering	Addressing challenge to a favored view using arguments that are superficially plausible but turn out to be nonsensical.
Bullying	Trying to intimidate critics when they challenge a favored view and accusing critics of misconduct.
Covering the bases	Articulating multiple, conflicting positions on key theoretical issues, so as to never be wrong.
Emotionality	Becoming hostile ("testy") when a favored view is challenged; taking criticism personally; being thin-skinned in the face of challenge.
Externalizing	Blaming critics for confusion created by problems with scholarship; refusal to accept responsibility.
Going beyond the data	Drawing conclusions that aren't warranted by findings (e.g., making strong causal claims from correlational data).
Grandstanding	Overstating the importance of a favored view and the evidence for it.
Hypocrisy	Holding a double standard; using one set of standards to argue for a favored view, but demanding that others adhere to a more stringent standard when testing the view.
Invoking tradition	Using "back in the old days" arguments to justify unsound research practices; invoking tradition for such practices ("this is the way it's always been done").
Mis-characterizing	Mischaracterizing evidence so that it supports a favored view; making frequent material errors in direction of the view.
Projecting	When confronted with misbehavior, claiming it is the *critics* who are misbehaving.
Rewriting history	Continually "clarifying" theoretical claims to fend off challenge; altering previous claims; playing word games to deflect criticism.

TABLE 3.3, continued

Secretiveness	Being unwilling to share data (concocting "the dog ate my data" excuses) and other resources.
Selective reviewing	Ignoring evidence that contradicts a favored view; excessively citing one's own work to support a view.
Self-aggrandizing	Emphasizing one's own greatness (e.g., accolades, seniority); describing one's own work in flattering terms.
Shifting arguments	Changing theoretical definitions and criteria in the face of challenge, without acknowledgment and explanation.
Subverting peer review	Making unauthorized substantive changes in articles after they are accepted for publication (i.e., at the galley proof stage).
Suppressing critics	Dismissing work of challengers by failing to cite their work, even when it supports a favored view; seeking to damage critics' careers (e.g., by writing negative tenure letters).
Thwarting norms	Deviating from professional standards (e.g., drawing conclusions without conducting appropriate statistical tests).
Vague theorizing	Proposing theories that are nonfalsifiable and defending them with infinitely regressing arguments; making abstruse claims so that they can be later "clarified" in the face of disconfirming evidence.

criteria so that the favored theory cannot be falsified. A similar tactic is *covering the bases*: articulating multiple, conflicting positions on key theoretical issues, so that the theory can never be wrong. The scientific authoritarian is also prone to *hypocrisy*—relying on one set of standards to argue for their theory but demanding that others adhere to more stringent standards when testing the theory. They may also attempt to *rewrite history* by revising past claims and interpretations of evidence that become problematic when the theory comes under scrutiny. Yet another tactic is *thwarting norms*: drawing conclusions without performing the appropriate statistical analyses or "nudging" data toward a favorable result through arbitrary and undisclosed data exclusions and *p*-hacking (see John et al., 2012). The scientific authoritarian's writings will also frequently be riddled with material errors, because with or without awareness, they have mischaracterized evidence so that it favors their theory. They also tend to be secretive—unwilling to share their data and other resources—and fail to disclose financial conflicts of interest in their research.

What is the best way to confront someone who is behaving in a way that indicates they might be a scientific authoritarian? We offer some advice. First, *don't accuse, but dispassionately document.* Line up inconsistent and contradictory claims, definitions, and criteria; point out double standards for evidence; and identify material errors in scholarship. Second, *don't presume.* Be careful not to put words in the mouth of the possible scientific authoritarian; rely on direct quotations to characterize their views. Third, *expect to be attacked.* Keep your cool when you are attacked; the person's conduct will not have gone unnoticed in the field. You will not be alone in your fight. Finally, *check yourself.* In confronting the possible scientific authoritarian, be careful not to become one yourself, and remain open to the possibility that there are innocent explanations for the problems with the person's scholarship you have identified.

In government, authoritarianism threatens democracy and people's rights; in science, it threatens progress toward the truth about some scientific issue or question. Clearly, political authoritarianism has a much more direct, and devastating, impact on people's lives than scientific authoritarianism does. However, if left unchecked, scientific authoritarianism will have a corrosive effect on a field of research, and society. This is to say that science is not just an abstract endeavor, carried out in the laboratory; it affects people's lives in myriad ways. Science drives technological innovation in everything from medicine to transportation to computing. What's more, and particularly relevant to this discussion, the layperson looks to science (and scientists) for guidance in making decisions, from how to eat a healthy diet to what precautions to take during a pandemic. There is an implicit trust that scientists have the public's best interest at heart. Scientific authoritarianism betrays this trust and limits the good that science can do.

Implications of Expertise Research for Social Justice

Science also has implications for social justice. *Social justice* refers to fairness in terms of the distribution of resources and privilege in a society. Different views about the origins of expertise have different implications for how resources should be distributed to cultivate expertise. The view that people are created equal strikes a deep chord in people, especially in democratic societies. In the United States, this idea is enshrined in the Declaration of Independence as a self-evident truth. At the same time, as is known in psychological science, behavioral phenotypes such as intelligence and personality are substantially heritable (Knopik et al., 2016), meaning that genotypic variation is correlated with phenotypic variation. Through molecular genetic research, scientists are even beginning to identify specific genes associated with variation in these traits (e.g., Savage et al., 2018). There is no longer serious scientific debate about whether genetic factors contribute to individual differences in psychological traits.

However, in the context of expertise, one might argue that it is better to act *as if* people are created equal, because the consequences of acting otherwise are harmful to individuals and society. In particular, even if there is compelling evidence for an impact of ability on accomplishment, one might argue that people will give up on their dreams of developing expertise (e.g., becoming a world-class musician or athlete) if they believe that talent is a limiting factor in their potential. In *Peak: Secrets From the New Science of Expertise,* Ericsson and Pool (2016) described this as the "dark side of believing in innate talent" (p. 241).

We argue that this view is wrong-headed in two ways. First, it is antiscientific. If conclusions in research are to be based on anything other than what evidence from sound research indicates, then there is no point in conducting research in the first place. Science becomes a charade—a political project. Second, this view may lead to ill-advised decisions about how to distribute resources for cultivating expertise and squandered opportunities for doing good. For example, if an aptitude (a "talent" variable) turns out to be a predictor of achieving a high level of performance in some domain, then resources (e.g., educational funding) can be channeled to people with lower levels of that ability to help them achieve a higher level of performance than they could otherwise, or used in efforts to remove structural barriers that prevent some people from succeeding despite high aptitude.

We further observe that although discussions about social justice frequently focus on the distribution of monetary resources, as in the preceding example, *knowledge* is also a resource that can be distributed more or less fairly in society. As a case in point, when scientists downplay, falsely portray, or suppress evidence concerning the impact of ability on the development of expertise, they deny laypeople with knowledge that they may use to make decisions that are best for them (and their children). For example, there is compelling evidence that cognitive ability predicts real-world accomplishments, including earning a Ph.D. in a science, technology, engineering, and mathematics field (e.g., Makel et al., 2016; Robertson et al., 2010). If a person with a below-average IQ sets out to earn a Ph.D. in, say, math or physics, they are unlikely to achieve this goal, relatively speaking. Failure, in turn, can have a host of negative consequences for the person, included a diminished sense of confidence, not to mention loss of time and money. Provided with accurate information about the role of cognitive ability in academic and occupational success, the same person might make a different decision about what type of career to pursue. We argue that the public has a right to an accurate accounting of the results of scientific research. After all, through taxpayer dollars, it is very often the public that is paying for the research.

What people believe about the nature of expertise is not life or death like, for example, what they believe about the efficacy of vaccines for their children. But it is not unimportant, either. People devote tremendous amounts of time, money, and effort pursuing expertise in hobbies and vocations, and their success in this pursuit affects their quality of life. People's beliefs about the nature of expertise may also affect parenting decisions, such as how hard to push a child in sports or music training. In short, findings from research on expertise should be accurately disseminated to the public, so that people can use the knowledge in their lives.

Applications of Expertise Research

How can findings from scientific research on expertise inform principles, practices, and procedures that will help more people develop expertise, and in doing so, make their lives and the lives of others better? One area of application is skill training. Training is necessary for anyone to become highly skilled in some domains, but some approaches to training may be more effective for some people than for others. This idea is already being embraced in sports science. For example, it is well-established that people differ in their response to aerobic training and that genetics plays a role in this between-person variation (Bouchard, 2012). In turn, genotype may have implications for what training—in terms of considerations such as the intensity and frequency of training and amount of rest—a person needs (see Mann et al., 2014). Training can be tailored in other domains, as well. For example, if a cognitive ability such as working memory capacity is identified as a limiting factor in acquiring some aspect of musical skill (e.g., sight-reading; see Meinz & Hambrick, 2010), then it may be possible to structure the training to mitigate demands on working memory capacity, bringing the skill within the reach of a greater number of people.

Findings from research on expertise can also be used to improve personnel selection and classification in the workplace. As industrial-organizational psychologists have known for nearly a century (Taylor & Russell, 1939), measures of psychological traits can substantially improve prediction of real-world performance, even when correlations between the predictors and the outcomes (i.e., validity coefficients) seem low (see Hambrick et al., 2019, for further discussion). Take the case of an ability measure that correlates .20 with a measure of success in skill training. A correlation of this magnitude will sometimes be dismissed as unimportant, on the grounds that it indicates that the predictor variable accounts for "only" 4% of the variance in the outcome. However, using this measure for selection can substantially improve prediction of an outcome. This can be demonstrated using Rosenthal and Rubin's (1982) binomial effect size display (BESD). Table 3.4 presents a BESD for a hypothetical scenario in which 100 individuals must be selected for a training program. In one case, a selection test with validity of .20 is used; that is, individuals are selected for the program using a cut score on the hypothetical ability test. In the other case, the selection test is not used. As shown, when the selection test is used, the chances that a trainee will pass the training program increase by 20% (i.e., 20 more people out of 100 pass). Depending on the outcome, ability tests may have considerably higher validity than the .20 value used for this illustration. For example, correlations between general cognitive ability and job performance are typically around .50 (Schmidt & Hunter, 2004). Thus, using ability tests for personnel selection can yield *massive* improvements in the prediction of training outcomes.

Findings from the science of expertise can also serve as the basis for recommendations designed to help people (including parents) make decisions about how they want to devote their time, money, and effort pursu-

TABLE 3.4
Example of Binomial Effect Size Display

	Training Outcome	
Ability test used to select?	Fail	Pass
No	60	40
Yes	40	60

Note. Correlation between score on predictor test and training outcome assumed to be $r = .20$.

ing the development of expertise. The question of when children should begin focused training in some domain provides an excellent example of this application. According to the *early specialization view*, a child should begin training in a particular domain as early as possible. The logic of this view is that the child who begins training early will have a virtually insurmountable advantage over the child who begins later. However, the best available evidence on this question indicates that *later specialization* leads to higher levels of ultimate performance, while reducing the likelihood of burnout and injury (e.g., Baker, 2003; Moesch et al., 2011).

Conclusions

Over the past decade, there has been an explosion of scientific and popular interest in expertise. Expertise research has traditionally focused on well-defined domains such as chess, but there is growing interest in studying "messy" domains in which performance criteria are not always clear (see Hoffman et al., 2014). Although expertise research has focused primarily on environmental factors, there is a growing recognition that genetically influenced abilities and capacities are important pieces of the expertise puzzle. The nature-versus-nurture debate has been over in many fields for decades, and slowly but surely, it appears to be ending in the field of expertise. Finally, expertise research is becoming more methodologically sophisticated, making use of advanced statistical techniques and research designs, and embracing tenets of the open science movement.

Nevertheless, there are significant obstacles to progress in the science of expertise. The greatest of all, we argue, is expertise researchers themselves. When a field of scientific study becomes a battleground for competing ideologies and rife with scientific authoritarianism, progress is no longer possible. The field stagnates, because sound research is no longer the point. The way forward is to embrace Merton's (1973) principles of science: communism, universalism, disinterestedness, and organized skepticism. These principles put the focus in expertise research where it should be: conducting research that will increase understanding of the origins and nature of complex skill, laying the foundation for practical applications that will bring expertise into reach of more people than is currently the case.

DISCUSSION QUESTIONS

1. What is expertise, and how is it measured in scientific research? What does it mean to say that expertise varies on a continuum from unidimensional to multidimensional?

2. What is gene-environment correlation, and how is it relevant to understanding how expertise develops in people?

3. Describe a major controversy in research on expertise, focusing on the difference between within-person variability and between-person variability.

4. What is deliberate practice, and what are some problems with the way it has been defined? How does deliberate practice differ from other forms of experience?

5. What is scientific authoritarianism, and what are some tipoffs to it in scientific writing? How does scientific authoritarianism impede progress in research?

References

Ackerman, P. L. (1988). Determinants of individual differences during skill acquisition: Cognitive abilities and information processing. *Journal of*

Experimental Psychology: General, 117(3), 288–318. https://doi.org/10.1037/0096-3445.117.3.288

Baker, J. (2003). Early specialization in youth sport: A requirement for adult expertise? *High Ability Studies, 14*(1), 85–94. https://doi.org/10.1080/13598130304091

Berlin, I. (1953). *The hedgehog and the fox: An essay on Tolstoy's view of history.* Princeton University Press.

Borinskaya, S. A., Ermolaev, A. I., & Kolchinsky, E. I. (2019). Lysenkoism against genetics: The meeting of the Lenin All-Union Academy of Agricultural Sciences of August 1948, its background, causes, and aftermath. *Genetics, 212*(1), 1–12. https://doi.org/10.1534/genetics.118.301413

Bouchard, C. (2012). Genomic predictors of trainability. *Experimental Physiology, 97*(3), 347–352. https://doi.org/10.1113/expphysiol.2011.058735

Burgoyne, A. P., Sala, G., Gobet, F., Macnamara, B. N., Campitelli, G., & Hambrick, D. Z. (2016, November–December). The relationship between cognitive ability and chess skill: A comprehensive meta-analysis. *Intelligence, 59*, 72–83. https://doi.org/10.1016/j.intell.2016.08.002

Charness, N., Krampe, R., & Mayr, U. (1996). The role of practice and coaching in entrepreneurial skill domains: an international comparison of life-span chess skill acquisition. In K. A. Ericsson (Ed.), *The road to excellence: The acquisition of expert performance in the arts and sciences, sports and games* (pp. 51–80). Erlbaum.

Charness, N., Tuffiash, M., Krampe, R., Reingold, E., & Vasyukova, E. (2005). The role of deliberate practice in chess expertise. *Applied Cognitive Psychology, 19*(2), 151–165. https://doi.org/10.1002/acp.1106

de Candolle, A. (1873). *Histoire des sciences et des savants depuis deux siècles: Suivie d'autres études sur des sujets scientifiques* [History of science and scientists for two centuries: Followed by other studies on scientific subjects]. Fayard.

Dearani, J. A., Gold, M., Leibovich, B. C., Ericsson, K. A., Khabbaz, K. R., Foley, T. A., Julsrud, P. R., Matsumoto, J. M., & Daly, R. C. (2017). The role of imaging, deliberate practice, structure, and improvisation in approaching surgical perfection. *The Journal of Thoracic and Cardiovascular Surgery, 154*(4), 1329–1336. https://doi.org/10.1016/j.jtcvs.2017.04.045

Duckworth, A. L., Kirby, T. A., Tsukayama, E., Berstein, H., & Ericsson, K. A. (2011). Deliberate practice spells success: Why grittier competitors triumph at the National Spelling Bee. *Social Psychological and Personality Science, 2*(2), 174–181. https://doi.org/10.1177/1948550610385872

Duffy, L. J., Baluch, B., & Ericsson, K. A. (2004). Dart performance as a function of facets of practice amongst professional and amateur men and women players. *International Journal of Sport Psychology, 35*(3), 232–245.

Ericsson, K. A. (1998). The scientific study of expert levels of performance: General implications for optimal learning and creativity. *High Ability Studies, 9*(1), 75–100. https://doi.org/10.1080/1359813980090106

Ericsson, K. A. (2000). How experts attain and maintain superior performance: Implications for the enhancement of skilled performance in older individuals. *Journal of Aging and Physical Activity, 8*(4), 366–372. https://doi.org/10.1123/japa.8.4.366

Ericsson, K. A. (2005). Recent advances in expertise research: A commentary on the contributions to the special issue. *Applied Cognitive Psychology, 19*(2), 233–241. https://doi.org/10.1002/acp.1111

Ericsson, K. A. (2007). Deliberate practice and the modifiability of body and mind: Toward a science of the structure and acquisition of expert and elite performance. *International Journal of Sport Psychology, 38*(1), 4–34.

Ericsson, K. A. (2012). *The danger of delegating education to journalists: Why the APS Observer needs peer review when summarizing new scientific developments* [Unpublished manuscript]. Department of Psychology, Florida State University.

Ericsson, K. A. (2013). My exploration of Gagné's "evidence" for innate talent: It is Gagné who is omitting troublesome information so as to present more convincing accusations. In S. B. Kaufman (Ed.), *The complexity of greatness: Beyond talent or practice* (pp. 223–254). Oxford University Press.

Ericsson, K. A. (2014a). Adaptive expertise and cognitive readiness: A perspective from the expert-performance approach. In H. F. O'Neil, R. S. Perez, & E. Baker (Eds.), *Teaching and measuring cognitive readiness* (pp. 179–197). Springer.

Ericsson, K. A. (2014b). *Challenges for the estimation of an upper-bound on relations between accumulated deliberate practice and the associated performance of novices and experts: Comments on Macnamara, Hambrick, and Oswald's (2014) published meta analysis* [Unpublished manuscript]. Department of Psychology, Florida State University.

Ericsson, K. A. (2014c). *Supplemental online materials for "A challenge to estimates of an upper-bound on relations between accumulated delib-*

erate practice and the associated performance in domains of expertise: Comments on Macnemara (sic), Hambrick, and Oswald's (2014) published meta-analysis" [Unpublished manuscript]. Department of Psychology, Florida State University.

Ericsson, K. A. (2014d, July–August). Why expert performance is special and cannot be extrapolated from studies of performance in the general population: A response to criticisms. *Intelligence, 45*, 81–103. https://doi.org/10.1016/j.intell.2013.12.001

Ericsson, K. A. (2016). Summing up hours of any type of practice versus identifying optimal practice activities: Commentary on Macnamara, Moreau, & Hambrick (2016). *Perspectives on Psychological Science, 11*(3), 351–354. https://doi.org/10.1177/1745691616635600

Ericsson, K. A. (2018a). Intelligence as domain-specific superior reproducible performance: The role of acquired domain-specific mechanisms in expert performance. In R. J. Sternberg (Ed.), *The nature of human intelligence* (pp. 85–100). Cambridge University Press. https://doi.org/10.1017/9781316817049.007

Ericsson, K. A. (2018b). The differential influence of experience, practice, and deliberate practice on the development of superior individual performance of experts. In K. A. Ericsson, R. R. Hoffmann, A. Kozbelt, & A. M. Williams (Eds.), *The Cambridge handbook of expertise and expert performance* (2nd ed., pp. 745–769). Cambridge University Press.

Ericsson, K. A. (2020). Towards a science of the acquisition of expert performance in sports: Clarifying the difference between deliberate practice and other types of practice. *Journal of Sports Sciences, 38*(2), 159–176. https://doi.org/10.1080/02640414.2019.1688618

Ericsson, K. A., & Harwell, K. W. (2019). Deliberate practice and proposed limits on the effects of practice on the acquisition of expert performance: Why the original definition matters and recommendations for future research. *Frontiers in Psychology,* Article 10:2396. https://doi.org/10.3389/fpsyg.2019.02396

Ericsson, K. A., Krampe, R. T., & Tesch-Romer, C. (1993). The role of deliberate practice in the acquisition of expert performance. *Psychological Review, 100*(3), 363–406. https://doi.org/10.1037/0033-295X.100.3.363

Ericsson, K. A., Perez, R. S., Eccles, D. W., Lang, L., Baker, E. L., Bransford, J. D., VanLehn, K., & Ward, P. (2009). The measurement and development of professional performance: An introduction to the topic and a background to the design and origin of this book. In K. A. Ericsson (Ed.), *Development of professional expertise: Toward measurement of expert performance and design of optimal learning environments* (pp.

1–24). Cambridge University Press. https://doi.org/10.1017/CBO9780 511609817.001

Ericsson, K. A., & Pool, R. (2016). *Peak: Secrets from the new science of expertise.* Houghton Mifflin Harcourt.

Ericsson, K. A., Roring, R. W., & Nandagopal, K. (2007). Giftedness and evidence for reproducibly superior performance: An account based on the expert performance framework. *High Ability Studies, 18*(1), 3–56. https://doi.org/10.1080/13598130701350593

Fancher, R. E. (1983). Alphone de Candolle, Francis Galton, and the early history of the nature-nurture controversy. *Journal of the History of the Behavioral Sciences, 19*(4), 341–352. https://doi.org/10.1002/1520-669 6(198310)19:4<341::aid-jhbs2300190403>3.0.co;2-7

Farrell, J. N., & McDaniel, M. A. (2001). The stability of validity coefficients over time: Ackerman's (1988) model and the General Aptitude Test Battery. *Journal of Applied Psychology, 86*(1), 60–79. https://doi.org/10.1037/0021-9010.86.1.60

Galton, F. (1869). *Hereditary genius: An inquiry into its laws and consequences.* Macmillan. https://doi.org/10.1037/13474-000

Grabner, R. H., Stern, E., & Neubauer, A. C. (2007). Individual differences in chess expertise: A psychometric investigation. *Acta Psychologica, 124*(3), 398–420. https://doi.org/10.1016/j.actpsy.2006.07.008

Hambrick, D. Z., Altmann, E., & Burgoyne, A. P. (2018). A knowledge-activation approach to testing the circumvention-of-limits hypothesis. *American Journal of Psychology, 131*(3), 307–321. https://doi.org/10.54 06/amerjpsyc.131.3.0307

Hambrick, D. Z., Altmann, E. M., Oswald, F. L., Meinz, E. J., Gobet, F., & Campitelli, G. (2014). Accounting for expert performance: The devil is in the details. *Intelligence, 45,* 112–114. https://doi.org/10.1016/j.intell.2014.01.007

Hambrick, D. Z., Burgoyne, A. P., & Oswald, F. L. (2018). Domain-general models of expertise: The role of cognitive ability. In P. Ward, J. M. Schraagen, J. Gore, & E. Roth (Eds.), *The Oxford handbook of expertise.* Oxford University Press.

Hambrick, D. Z., Burgoyne, A. P., & Oswald, F. L. (2019). The role of interests in the development of expertise: A multifactorial perspective. In C. D. Nye & J. Rounds (Eds.), *Vocational interests in the workplace: Rethinking behavior at work* (pp. 280–299). Routledge.

Hambrick, D. Z., & Campitelli, G. (2018). Editorial: Introducing the Journal of Expertise. *Journal of Expertise, 1*(1), 1–5.

Hambrick, D. Z., Macnamara, B. N., & Oswald, F. L. (2019). *Is the deliberate practice view defensible? A summary of the empirical evidence and reply to K. Anders Ericsson.* Open Science Framework. https://osf.io/buqsk

Hambrick, D. Z., Macnamara, B. N., & Oswald, F. L. (in press). Is the deliberate practice view defensible? A review of evidence and discussion of issues. *Frontiers in Psychology.*

Hambrick, D. Z., Macnamara, B. N., Campitelli, G., Ullén, F., & Mosing, M. A. (2016). Beyond born versus made: A new look at expertise. *Psychology of Learning and Motivation, 64,* 1–55. https://doi.org/10.1016/bs.plm.2015.09.001

Hambrick, D. Z., & Meinz, E. J. (2011). Limits of the predictive power of domain-specific experience. *Current Directions in Psychological Science, 20*(5), 275–279. https://doi.org/10.1177/0963721411422061

Hambrick, D. Z., & Oswald, F. L. (2005). Does domain knowledge moderate involvement of working memory capacity in higher-level cognition? A test of three models. *Journal of memory and language, 52*(3), 377–397. https://doi.org/10.1016/j.jml.2005.01.004

Hambrick, D. Z., & Tucker-Drob, E. M. (2015). The genetics of music accomplishment: Evidence for gene–environment correlation and interaction. *Psychonomic Bulletin & Review, 22*(1), 112–120. https://doi.org/10.3758/s13423-014-0671-9

Helsen, W. F., Starkes, J. L., & Hodges, N. J. (1998). Team sports and the theory of deliberate practice. *Journal of Sport & Exercise Psychology, 20*(1), 12–34. https://doi.org/10.1123/jsep.20.1.12

Hodges, N. J., & Starkes, J. L. (1996). Wrestling with the nature expertise: A sport specific test of Ericsson, Krampe and Tesch-Römer's (1993) theory of "deliberate practice." *International Journal of Sport Psychology, 27*(4), 400–424.

Hoffman, R. R., Ward, P., Feltovich, P. J., DiBello, L., Fiore, S. M., & Andrews, D. H. (2014). *Accelerated expertise: Training for high proficiency in a complex world.* Psychology Press.

Ings, S. (2017). *Stalin and the scientists: A history of triumph and tragedy, 1905–1953.* Atlantic Monthly Press.

John, L. K., Loewenstein, G., & Prelec, D. (2012). Measuring the prevalence of questionable research practices with incentives for truth telling. *Psychological Science, 23*(5), 524–532. https://doi.org/10.1177/0956797611430953

Keith, N., & Ericsson, K. A. (2007). A deliberate practice account of typing proficiency in everyday typists. *Journal of Experimental Psychology: Applied, 13*(3), 135–145. https://doi.org/10.1037/1076-898X.13.3.135

Knapp, A. (2017, May 5). *Making a living in chess is tough—But the internet is making it easier.* Forbes. https://www.forbes.com/sites/alexknapp/2017/05/05/making-a-living-in-chess-is-tough-but-the-internet-is-making-it-easier

Knopik, V. S., Neiderhiser, J. M., DeFries, J. C., & Plomin, R. (2016). *Behavioral genetics.* Macmillan Higher Education.

Konnikova, M. (2016). *Practice doesn't make perfect.* The New Yorker. https://www.newyorker.com/science/maria-konnikova/practice-doesnt-make-perfect

Kopiez, R., & Lee, J. I. (2006). Towards a dynamic model of skills involved in sight reading music. *Music Education Research, 8*(1), 97–120. https://doi.org/10.1080/14613800600570785

Kopiez, R., & Lee, J. I. (2008). Towards a general model of skills involved in sight reading music. *Music Education Research, 10*(1), 41–62. https://doi.org/10.1080/14613800701871363

Krampe, R. T., & Ericsson, K. A. (1996). Maintaining excellence: Deliberate practice and elite performance in young and older pianists. *Journal of Experimental Psychology: General, 125*(4), 331–359. https://doi.org/10.1037//0096-3445.125.4.331

Lakatos, I. (1976). Falsification and the methodology of scientific research programmes. In S. G. Harding (Ed.), *Can theories be refuted?* (pp. 205–259). Springer.

Macnamara, B. N., Hambrick, D. Z., & Moreau, D. (2016). How important is deliberate practice? Reply to Ericsson. *Perspectives on Psychological Science, 11*(3), 355–358. https://doi.org/10.1177/1745691616635614

Macnamara, B. N., Hambrick, D. Z., & Oswald, F. L. (2014). Deliberate practice and performance in music, games, sports, education, and professions: A meta-analysis. *Psychological Science, 25*(8), 1608–1618. https://doi.org/10.1177/0956797614535810

Makel, M. C., Kell, H. J., Lubinski, D., Putallaz, M., & Benbow, C. P. (2016). When lightning strikes twice: Profoundly gifted, profoundly accomplished. *Psychological Science, 27*(7), 1004–1018. https://doi.org/10.1177/0956797616644735

Mann, T. N., Lamberts, R. P., & Lambert, M. I. (2014). High responders and low responders: Factors associated with individual variation in response to standardized training. *Sports Medicine, 44*(8), 113–1124. https://doi.org/10.1007/s40279-014-0197-3

Meinz, E. J., & Hambrick, D. Z. (2010). Deliberate practice is necessary but not sufficient to explain individual differences in piano sight-reading skill: The role of WMC. *Psychological Science, 21*(7), 914–919. https://doi.org/10.1177/0956797610373933

Merton, R. (1973). *The sociology of science: Theoretical and empirical investigations.* University of Chicago Press.

Moesch, K., Elbe, A. M., Hauge, M. L., & Wikman, J. M. (2011). Late specialization: The key to success in centimeters, grams, or seconds (cgs) sports. *Scandinavian Journal of Medicine & Science in Sports, 21*(6), e282–e290. https://doi.org/10.1111/j.1600-0838.2010.01280.x

Mosing, M. A., Madison, G., Pedersen, N. L., Kuja-Halkola, R., & Ullén, F. (2014). Practice does not make perfect: No causal effect of music practice on music ability. *Psychological Science, 25*(9), 1795–1803. https://doi.org/10.1177/0956797614541990

Moxley, J. H., Ericsson, K. A., & Tuffiash, M. (2019). Gender differences in SCRABBLE performance and associated engagement in purposeful practice activities. *Psychological Research, 83*, 1147–1167. https://doi.org/10.1007/s00426-017-0905-3

National Collegiate Athletic Association. (2019). *Estimated probability of competing in professional athletics.* https://www.ncaa.org/about/resources/research/estimated-probability-competing-professional-athletics

Platz, F., Kopiez, R., Lehmann, A. C., & Wolf, A. (2014). The influence of deliberate practice on musical achievement: A meta-analysis. *Frontiers in Psychology, 5,* Article 646. https://doi.org/10.3389/fpsyg.2014.00646

Preacher, K. J., Rucker, D. D., MacCallum, R. C., & Nicewander, W. A. (2005). Use of the extreme groups approach: A critical reexamination and new recommendations. *Psychological Methods, 10*(2), 178–192. https://doi.org/10.1037/1082-989X.10.2.178

Reeve, C. L., & Bonaccio, S. (2011). On the myth and the reality of the temporal validity degradation of general mental ability test scores. *Intelligence, 39*(5), 255–272. https://doi.org/10.1016/j.intell.2011.06.009

Robertson, K., Smeets, S., Lubinski, D., & Benbow, C. P. (2010). Beyond the threshold hypothesis: Even among the gifted and top math/science graduate students, cognitive abilities, vocational interests, and lifestyle preferences matter for career choice, performance, and persistence. *Current Directions in Psychological Science, 19*(6), 346–351. https://doi.org/10.1177/0963721410391442

Rosenthal, R., & Rubin, D. B. (1982). A simple, general purpose display of magnitude of experimental effect. *Journal of Educational Psychology, 74*(2), 166–169. https://doi.org/10.1037/0022-0663.74.2.166

Ruthsatz, J., Detterman, D., Griscom, W. S., & Cirullo, B. A. (2008). Becoming an expert in the musical domain: It takes more than just practice. *Intelligence, 36*(4), 330–338. https://doi.org/10.1016/j.intell.2007.08.003

Savage, J. E., Jansen, P. R., Stringer, S., Watanabe, K., Bryois, J., De Leeuw, C. A., Nagle, M., Awasthi, S., Barr, P. B., Coleman, J. R. I., Grasby, K. L., Hammerschlag, A. R., Kaminski, J. A., Karlsson, R., Krapohl, E., Lam, M., Nygaard, M., Reynolds, C. A., Trampush, J. W., . . . Grasby, K. L. (2018). Genome-wide association meta-analysis in 269,867 individuals identifies new genetic and functional links to intelligence. *Nature Genetics, 50*(7), 912–919. https://doi.org/10.1038/s41588-018-0152-6

Schaie, K. W. (2005). *Developmental influences on adult intelligence: The Seattle longitudinal study*. Oxford University Press.

Schmidt, F. L., & Hunter, J. (2004). General mental ability in the world of work: occupational attainment and job performance. *Journal of Personality and Social Psychology, 86*(1), 162–173. https://doi.org/10.1037/0022-3514.86.1.162

Schneider, K., Bös, K., & Rieder, H. (1993). Performance prediction in young top athletes. In J. Beckmann, H. Strang, & E. Hahn (Eds.), *Aufmerksamkeit und Energetisierung. Facetten con Konzentration und Leistung* (pp. 277–299). Hogrefe.

Sternberg, R. J. (1996). Costs of expertise. In K. A. Ericsson (Ed.), *The road to excellence: The acquisition of expert performance in the arts and sciences, sports, and games* (pp. 347–354). Erlbaum.

Taylor, H. C., & Russell, J. T. (1939). The relationship of validity coefficients to the practical effectiveness of tests in selection: Discussion and tables. *Journal of Applied Psychology, 23*(5), 565–578. https://doi.org/10.1037/h0057079

Tucker-Drob, E. (2018). Primer—Theoretical concepts in the genetics of expertise. In D. Z. Hambrick, G. Campitelli, & B. N. Macnamara (Eds.), *The science of expertise: Behavioral, neural, and genetic approaches to complex skill* (pp. 241–252). Routledge.

Tuffiash, M., Roring, R. W., & Ericsson, K. A. (2007). Expert performance in SCRABBLE: Implications for the study of the structure and acquisition of complex skills. *Journal of Experimental Psychology: Applied, 13*(3), 124–134. https://doi.org/10.1037/1076-898X.13.3.124

Turkheimer, E. (2000). Three laws of behavior genetics and what they mean. *Current Directions in Psychological Science, 9*(5), 160–164. https://doi.org/10.1111/1467-8721.00084

Ullén, F., Hambrick, D. Z., & Mosing, M. A. (2016). Rethinking expertise: A multifactorial gene–environment interaction model of expert performance. *Psychological Bulletin, 142*(4), 427–446. https://doi.org/10.1037/bul0000033

Van Dongen, R. (2020). *The daily 202: Coronavirus death toll is possible casualty of growing rift between President Trump and CDC*. The Washington Post. https://www.washingtonpost.com/news/powerpost/paloma/daily-202/2020/05/18/daily-202-coronavirus-death-toll-is-possible-casualty-of-growing-rift-between-president-trump-and-cdc/5ec1918788e0fa17cde01dac

Winner, E., & Drake, J. E. (2013). The rage to master: The decisive role of talent in the visual arts. In S. B. Kaufman (Ed.), *The complexity of greatness: Beyond talent or practice* (pp. 333–366. Oxford University Press.

CHAPTER 4

Tannenbaum's Psychosocial Conception of Giftedness

LANNIE KANEVSKY

Abraham J. Tannenbaum (1983) was one of the first to propose a developmental conception of giftedness that distinguished early childhood promise from its fulfillment in extraordinary adult accomplishments:

> Keeping in mind that developed talent exists only in adults, a proposed definition of giftedness in children is that it denotes their potential for becoming critically acclaimed performers or exemplary producers of ideas in spheres of activity that enhance the moral, physical, emotional, social, intellectual or aesthetic life of humanity. (p. 86)

Rather than considering children gifted, Tannenbaum (2009) felt that they could *become* gifted if the right combination of internal and external factors were able to interact: "Adults are proven gifted if they excel in any of these major domains of productivity and performance; children are potentially gifted if there is reason to hope that they can be groomed for these high-level pursuits in future years" (p. 506).

Tannenbaum identified five sets of psychosocial factors essential to developing giftedness: general intelligence, domain-specific abilities, nonintellective attributes, environmental influences, and chance. The first four were frequently included in others' accounts of talent development, but Tannenbaum was the first to formally include the role of unpredictable events and opportunities. Giftedness emerges from the accumulating contributions of the factors at the center of a five-pointed star (see Figure 4.1). As in other multifactor models of talent development, inseparable interactions among the factors over time "transform potential talent during youth into outstanding performance and innovation in adulthood" (Subotnik et al., 2011, p. 6). However, Tannenbaum did not specify the processes involved as others have (e.g., Jarvin & Subotnik, 2015; Subotnik et al., 2009, 2011).

Tannenbaum was also one of the first to situate giftedness and its development in its sociocultural context. He did this in two ways. First, he acknowledged that realms of excellence are culturally determined, and second, he included external influences (the environmental and chance factors). Like others (Csikszentmihalyi, 1988; Simonton, 1994; Sternberg, 2005a; Subotnik et al., 2011), he felt that giftedness in any domain might be valued (or not) in different cultures, to differing degrees, at different times. These aspects of his work have impacted many subsequent conceptions of extraordinary abilities (e.g., Gagné, 2005; Subotnik et al., 2011).

When Tannenbaum's definition and model first appeared in 1983, it reflected a research base that relied heavily on studies that operationally defined giftedness as an IQ above a certain cut-off as modeled by Terman (1925) and Hollingworth (1936, 1942). As conceptual and operational definitions have proliferated, so have methods for defining and investigating each set of factors. In the upcoming pages, findings of recent and seminal studies will be synthesized to demonstrate the continuing validity and value of Tannenbaum's work. After a brief introduction to Tannenbaum's terminology, each set of factors in his star (1983, 1986a, 1986b, 1991, 1997) or "Sea Star" (2003, 2009) will be described and explored.

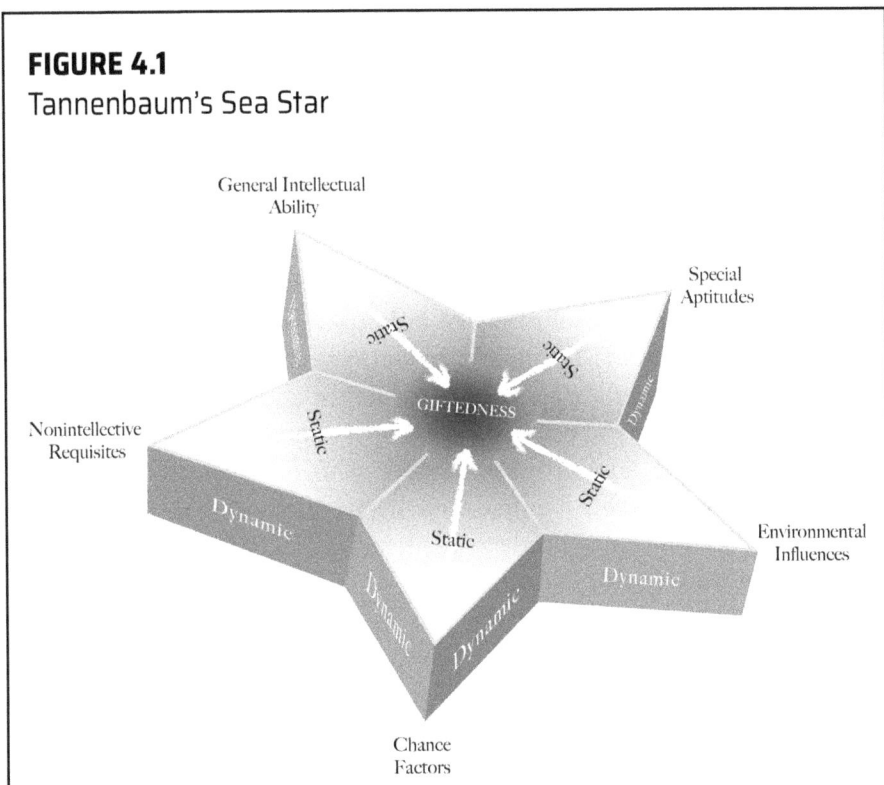

FIGURE 4.1
Tannenbaum's Sea Star

Note. Adapted from "Defining, Determining, Discovering, and Developing Excellence" by A. J. Tannenbaum, in J. S. Renzulli, E. J. Gubbins, K. S. McMillen, R. D. Eckert, and C. A. Little (Eds.), *Systems and Models for Developing Programs for the Gifted and Talented* (2nd ed., p. 509), 2009, Taylor & Francis. Copyright 2009 by Taylor & Francis. Adapted with permission.

Tangled Terms

Before launching into his model, it is valuable to understand how Tannenbaum uses vocabulary associated with giftedness. The adjective *gifted* is used interchangeably with *brilliant, excellent, high ability, extraordinary, exceptionally bright,* and *talented*. A *prodigy* was gifted in childhood on the basis of adult standards, not just in comparison to same-age peers. Finally, "genius" was the most advanced extension of giftedness in its various forms. Akin to "eminence" (Worrell et al., 2018), "genius" denotes

Olympian-level accomplishments, usually by the rarest of adults, especially those who make lasting changes in the disciplines in which they excel.

Creativity and proficiency represent two dimensions of giftedness. Creativity pertains to the generation of new knowledge and innovation that deserves critical acclaim. Proficiency refers to exceptional insight when facing mentally challenging tasks. Tannenbaum (1997) did not believe that

> only the creative are gifted and that mastery is merely a sign of high-level consumption, of little use to anybody except the consumer. . . . There is room for outstanding proficiency in sophisticated domains of production and performance that deserve to be recognized as signs of excellence. Think, for example, of the microsurgeon who operates "by the book" as only few can in order to save life and limb. That kind of proficiency needs to be included in any definition of giftedness. (p. 40)

Tannenbaum (1997, 2003, 2009) posed and answered three questions to be considered when seeking different types of excellence (see Table 4.1). His answers to these three questions identified eight possible groups of potentially gifted individuals, including both those who produce thoughts or tangible products creatively or proficiently and those who perform staged artistry or human services creatively or proficiently:

1. **A creatively gifted producer of thoughts:** A Nobel Laureate in Literature.
2. **A proficiently gifted producer of thoughts:** A copyeditor who can turn chaotic text into admirable publications.
3. **A creatively gifted producer of tangible products:** A doctor who invents a life-saving medical device.
4. **A proficiently gifted producer of tangible products:** An elite, meticulous diamond-cutter.
5. **A creatively gifted performer of staged artistry:** A professional dancer in an elite troupe who creates a novel interpretation of traditional work.
6. **A proficiently gifted performer of staged artistry:** A professional dancer who executes a choreographer's plan exactly (without interpretation).
7. **A creatively gifted performer of human services:** An innovative educator who creates new pedagogy.
8. **A proficiently gifted performer of human services:** An educator who precisely implements instructional guidelines.

TABLE 4.1
Tannenbaum's Essential Questions for Determining Giftedness

Questions	Answers
1. Who should be included in the pool of gifted children who might become gifted adults?	Potential producers and performers
2. a) What do producers produce? b) What do performers perform?	a) Thoughts or tangible products b) Staged artistry and human services
3. How do pool members demonstrate their giftedness?	Creatively or proficiently

The Sea Star Model of Giftedness

Tannenbaum (1983, 1986a, 1986b, 1991, 1997, 2003, 2009) inductively arrived at five factors linking "promise and fulfillment" (Tannenbaum, 1983, p. 95) after an extensive review of the literature related to the development of giftedness: (a) superior general intellectual ability; (b) outstanding special aptitudes; (c) nonintellective, facilitative personal habits and attitudes; (d) challenging and supportive environmental conditions; and (e) chance events or opportunities. Every factor is involved in every form of giftedness; however, the strength of its contribution and threshold levels required for excellence vary across domains. No combination of strengths in four of the factors can compensate for weakness in the fifth.

Initially, Tannenbaum represented their relationships to each other as a two-dimensional star (1983, 1986b) with giftedness resulting from their interacting contributions at the center, where the factors overlapped. Later, as shown in Figure 4.1, the model gained a third dimension when he distinguished the static and dynamic aspects of each set of factors (1997, 2003, 2009). The arrows flowing through each arm toward giftedness indicate that static and dynamic aspects of all factors must operate in unison, over time, for potential giftedness to develop.

The surface of the star represents the static aspects of each factor and the depth represents the dynamic. Static subfactors denote an individual's status when compared to others of the same age at the same moment, "usually relating to group norms, group identity, or other external criteria . . . single impressions frozen in time and place" (Tannenbaum, 2009, p. 508). A child's standing on a normed test would be an example. The test provides a descriptive "aerial view" of a child: what they know and can do in relation to items on the test. However, their test score does not offer insight into the processes involved in how they came to know the information. Those processes are examples of the dynamic aspects of each factor, or the "processes of human functioning and of the situational contexts in which individual behavior is shaped" (Tannenbaum, 2009, p. 509). They are evident in "how and how well" individuals learn and engage in activities that extend their abilities (Tannenbaum, 1997, p. 40).

In the next five sections, static and dynamic aspects of each set of factors will be described as well as a small, illustrative sample of the studies scrutinizing their importance and roles in giftedness.

Superior General Intellectual Ability

General intellectual ability is a multidimensional, hierarchical, psychometric construct (Lohman, 2006; Schneider & McGrew, 2018). More than a century ago, Charles Spearman (1904, 1927) developed factor analysis (a statistical technique) to distinguish g, the general mental power involved in all complex tasks, from more specific abilities involved to varying degrees across different types of tasks. Although still controversial, the g construct not only has endured but also has been supported by an extensive body of research. Gottfredson (1997), with 51 scholars and researchers involved in work focusing on the meaning and assessment of intelligence, defined g as:

> a very general mental capability that, among other things, involves the ability to reason, plan, solve problems, think abstractly, comprehend complex ideas, learn quickly and learn from experience. It is not merely book learning, a narrow academic skill, or test-taking smarts. Rather, it reflects a broader and deeper capability for comprehending our surroundings—"catching on," "making sense" of things, or "figuring out" what to do. (p. 13)

Static Aspects of General Intellectual Ability

G can be measured with IQ tests that assess "high-level mental skills such as the ability to draw inferences, see similarities and differences, and process complex information of virtually any kind" (Gottfredson, 2004, p. 35). These tests measure static aspects of *g* and are often used to compare individuals. They became the "coin of the realm" in gifted education after Terman used an IQ of 135 or higher as the cutoff for participation in his seminal, longitudinal study (Terman, 1925; Terman & Oden, 1947, 1959). For many years, IQ was used as the sole criterion for giftedness and access to special programs.

Originally, *g* was believed to be entirely innate. In 1931, when asked for a brief description, Spearman stated, "G is in the normal course of events determined innately; a person can no more be trained to have it in higher degree than he can be trained to be taller" (as cited in Deary et al., 2008). It is true that *g* is more difficult to train than specific cognitive abilities, such as working memory or executive functioning, but some believe *g*, as well as the non-*g* components of IQ, can be enhanced with training (e.g., Melby-Lervåg et al., 2016; Protzko, 2017).

In studies of giftedness and efforts to identify students for special programs, a contentious question is always "How high is high enough?" As mentioned earlier, Tannenbaum (1983) argued that "thresholds" should be expected to vary across disciplines:

> The "g" factor, or tested general intelligence, figures on a sliding scale in all high-level talent areas. This means that different threshold IQs are required for various kinds of accomplishment, higher in academic subjects than, for example in the performing arts. There is no basis for making extreme assertions about the IQ, such as discounting its relevance to giftedness entirely or claiming that all those destined to become great producers or performers in any area of human activity need to score at the ninety-ninth percentile or better. Instead, positions along this continuum should be adjusted according to the talent area, which means taking a stance closer to one extreme for some kinds of giftedness and nearer the opposite extreme for others. (p. 87)

Tannenbaum's notion of a "sliding scale" continues to receive support from scholars investigating talent development in different domains (e.g., Simonton & Song, 2009; Sternberg & Davidson, 2005; Subotnik et al., 2011).

IQ scores are earned on normed tests designed to assess the types of knowledge and skills believed to distinguish more and less intelligent individuals. Thus, no matter how theorists conceptually define intelligence, in practice it has been operationally defined by the items on the test. As Edwin Boring (1923) said a century ago, "Intelligence is what the tests test" (p. 35).

Hundreds of tests have been developed to assess general intellectual ability. Those that can be administered to groups include the Otis-Lennon School Ability Test (Otis & Lennon, 1997), the Cognitive Abilities Test (Lohman, 2012), and Raven's Progressive Matrices (Raven, 1998). Individual intelligence tests sample a greater range of cognitive abilities than group tests. Four that are frequently used when assessing potentially gifted students are the Stanford-Binet Intelligence Scales, Fifth Edition (Roid, 2003), Wechsler Intelligence Scales for Children, Fifth Edition (Wechsler, 2014), Wechsler Preschool and Primary Scale of Intelligence, Fourth Edition (Wechsler, 2012), and the Woodcock-Johnson IV Tests of Cognitive Abilities (Schrank et al., 2014).

The content of many intelligence tests has been biased in favor of individuals most like those who created them (i.e., White, middle-class males of European descent) and against others. Evidence from exploratory factor analyses conducted on non-Western samples (less than 50% White or European) indicated that g is universal (e.g., Canivez & Watkins, 2010; Warne & Burningham, 2019); however, the scores of individuals whose cultural, socioeconomic, and linguistic backgrounds differ from those in the norm group reflect the extent to which they have had opportunities to develop the specific knowledge and abilities involved in items on any test used to assess their abilities.

The concept and assessment of intelligence continue to be two of the most controversial topics in psychology, particularly educational psychology and gifted education. Debates continue over what intelligence is, if and how it should be assessed, the interpretation of results, and how results should be used (e.g., Carroll, 1993; Gottfredson & Saklofske, 2009; Tannenbaum, 1996; Thorndike, 1985).

Dynamic Aspects of General Intellectual Ability

The dynamic aspects of general intellectual ability involve the skills, strategies, and cognitive processes involved in learning, thinking, and problem solving. Differences in their acquisition, nature and execution distinguish high-ability individuals from their peers and contribute to their potential for giftedness. Dynamic aspects underlie superior scores on static IQ tests as well as the precocious and sustained development of talents. A brief sketch of the research on ability-related differences in general cognitive processes is followed by another focusing on differences in learning.

Cognitive Processes. A vast and ever-expanding body of research on the speed, complexity, and extent of high-ability learners' cognitive, executive, and self-regulatory processes has demonstrated many of the advantages associated with a high IQ. A few highlights are provided here; however, more extensive summaries are available (e.g., Alexander et al., 1995; Johnsen, 1997; Shore & Kanevsky, 1993; Tannenbaum, 1983). Cognitive abilities that distinguish individuals with high IQs from their peers include the following:

- They are more aware of what they know and how to use it (Shore & Kanevsky, 1993).
- They are better able to identify relevant declarative and procedural knowledge, and reorganize it when problem solving (Davidson & Sternberg, 1984; Keating & Bobbitt, 1978; Siegler & Kotovsky, 1986).
- They weave new knowledge into prior knowledge immediately with rich interconnections (Larkin et al., 1980).
- They understand and respond to tasks more quickly and efficiently (Deary, 1995; Jackson & Myers, 1982; Scruggs & Mastropieri, 1985).
- They are better able to distinguish relevant and irrelevant information (Davidson & Sternberg, 1984).
- They are better at finding problems, solving them, and monitoring their problem solving process (Rogers, 1986).
- They spend more time on higher order planning when problem solving (Davidson & Sternberg, 1984).
- They have more metacognitive knowledge (Shore & Dover, 1987), and many are more aware of and better able to describe their thinking (Sheppard & Kanevsky, 1999).
- Their knowledge, thinking, and learning are more flexible (Johnsen, 1997; Shore & Dover, 1987).
- They organize knowledge so it is easy to generalize (Geary & Brown, 1991; Shavinina & Kholodnaja, 1996).

- They are able "to see alternate representations or adopt alternate strategies" (Shore & Kanevsky, 1993, p. 138), which is essential to outstanding performance in mathematics (Krutetskii, 1968/1976) as well as great accomplishments in many disciplines.
- They seek, prefer, and create challenge and complexity in activities (Bowen et al., 1992; Kanevsky, 1990, 1992; Kanevsky & Keighley, 2003; Shore & Kanevsky, 1993).

Learning. The ease, speed (e.g., Klausmeier & Check, 1962), flexibility (Scruggs & Mastropieri, 1988), independence, and sophistication (Klausmeier & Loughlin, 1961) of a young child's learning in their areas of strength often provide startling evidence of their general intelligence and potential giftedness. They can apply knowledge and strategies learned on one task to novel tasks, even when the tasks differ in significant ways (Alexander et al., 1995; Borkowski & Peck, 1986; Davidson & Sternberg, 1984; Kanevsky, 1990; Kanevsky & Rapagna, 1990; Shore et al., 1992). For example, Subotnik et al. (2019) found that the ability to learn and quickly adapt to change was essential to the elite performances of eminent adults in diverse domains, from dance and sports to medicine and culinary arts.

Many of the earliest intelligence theorists and researchers considered learning potential to be synonymous with g (Binet, 1905; Dearborn, 1921; Henmon, 1921). However, Dearborn (1921) reported with dismay, "For practical reasons most tests now in common use are not tests of the capacity to learn, but are tests of what has been learned" (pp. 210–211). Vygotsky (1978) shared their frustration and proposed the "zone of proximal development," a construct that includes both the past products of learning, those that are developing, as well as the interactions contributing to learning. Further, he designed learning experiments as dynamic assessment procedures to provide opportunities for children to demonstrate how they benefit from instruction.

Studies employing contemporary dynamic assessment protocols have provided rich insights on ability-related differences in learning processes (e.g., Kanevsky, 1990; Kanevsky & Geake, 2004; Sternberg & Grigorenko, 2002; Swanson & Lussier, 2001). For example, Kanevsky (1990, 1992, 1994) was not surprised to find that the 4- and 5-year-olds with high IQs mastered problem-solving strategies more quickly and independently than their agemates with average IQs, but she also found that their learning and far transfer were superior to 7- and 8-year-olds who had been matched to the 4- and 5-year-olds' mental age. The younger children with high IQs spontaneously pointed out similarities in the tasks and solutions, had a better understanding of their mistakes, and learned more from them (Kanevsky, 1992). In addition, they set their own criteria for success (speed, accuracy) and volunteered suggestions to make the puzzle problems more elaborate and challenging.

Special Aptitudes

> A general factor may predominate, but children also possess special aptitudes, some of which are much more fully developed than others, especially in gifted individuals. Furthermore, there are signs of extraordinary aptitudes even among children who are too young to undergo formal, standardized testing in *any* domain of specialization. Consider, for example the case of child prodigies, some of them not yet of school age. (Tannenbaum, 2003, p. 52)

The importance of special abilities is clear when hearing "gatekeepers," coaches, and mentors of elite performers in many domains describe what they look for in a top prospect (Subotnik et al., 2019). Gradually, researchers and educators of potentially gifted individuals are accepting "the need for selection based on specific abilities" (Lubinski, 2016, p. 901) rather than relying solely on assessments of *g*.

Differences in domain-specific abilities appear in children's behavior before they can be assessed reliably (Robinson, 2000; Tannenbaum, 2003). These abilities vary within domains as well as between them. Retrospective studies of the lives of eminent individuals have documented differences in the developmental trajectories of talents in different domains (Bloom, 1985; Subotnik et al., 2019). Each has "different start, peak, and end times for outstanding performance" (Subotnik et al., 2011, p. 33). For example, musical giftedness can appear as a child's ability to sing a song they have just heard for the first time with extreme accuracy in their first or second year of life (Winner & Drake, 2018), "whereas insight in to social and political structures develops much later in childhood" (Tannenbaum, 1983, p. 88).

Proponents of multipotentiality suggests an individual who excels in one domain will excel in others as well. Tannenbaum (1983) and others disagreed, including Vygotsky (1926/1997). As early as 1926, Vygotsky made examples of his colleagues to demonstrate the need to replace the concept of *general* and *abstract* giftedness with that of *special* and *concrete* giftedness.... Every form of giftedness is unfailingly a special form of giftedness toward some one thing. Tolstoy, for example, would be first in any list if it was giftedness in writing which was under study, though he would occupy a very modest position, perhaps one of the last spots, if it was musical abilities, suitability for engineering activity, or mathematical talent which was being investigated. Chekhov was a very average physician and a great writer.... All these examples only go to show that there does not exist any kind of "giftedness in general," rather that there exist special predispositions to certain types of activity. (pp. 324–325)

Static Aspects of Special Aptitudes

In addition to *g*, the number, nature, and roles of more specific abilities involved in achievements has been disputed continuously since Spearman (1904, 1927) first reported them. Carroll (1993) provided solid psychometric evidence of eight "broad" abilities organized hierarchically beneath *g*: fluid intelligence, crystallized intelligence, general memory and learning, broad visual perception, broad auditory perception, broad retrieval ability, broad cognitive speediness, and processing speed. A third level comprised of more concrete, task-specific abilities (e.g., induction, numerical facility, and visualization) extends beneath each of the broad abilities. The importance of these broad and specific abilities differs across disciplines. Among studies focusing on the development of specific talents within disciplines, mathematicians have been most extensively and rigorously investigated. As a result, examples of static and dynamic aspects of special aptitudes will be drawn from the literature exploring mathematical ability.

Longitudinal studies of mathematically talented individuals have provided rich insights on their aptitudes and accomplishments. Julian Stanley's (1996) innovative use of the Scholastic Aptitude Test (SAT) in the early 1970s launched the Study of Mathematically Precocious Youth (SMPY) and its continuous, ongoing, comprehensive data collection. Stanley introduced the practice of "off-level" or "above-level" testing by using the SAT for mathematics (SAT-M), a test designed for 16- to 18-year-olds, to find students able to earn a score of at least 500 (out of a possible 800) before age 13, putting them in the top 1% of students of their age. He believed that "gifted children need to be assessed with tests commensurate with their abilities, developmental rates, and pre-existing knowledge and skills, not their chronological age or grade" (Thomson & Olszewski-Kubilius, 2013, p. 33). Since 1972, SMPY researchers have been following approximately 4,000 individuals who scored in the top 1% on either the SAT-M or SAT-V (Verbal), using a range of additional assessments to monitor their interests, values, education, careers, creative accomplishments, and other aspects of their lives.

SMPY researchers have taken up fundamental questions related to the measurement and development of academically advanced students with these data. For example, Achter et al. (1996) constructed profiles from the SAT scores, values, and interests of students in the SMPY cohorts and examined them for evidence of multipotentiality. A profile with one peak indicated a single area of strength, while a high "flat" profile across subjects and interests indicated multiple strengths. Their findings concur with Vygotsky's and Tannenbaum's position. They found that less than 5% of the of students had high "flat" profiles and concluded that the popular belief in multipotentiality was a persistent myth. In other words, a multitalented individual, like Leonardo da Vinci, is the rare exception.

Park et al. (2007) found that "distinct ability patterns uncovered by age 13 portend contrasting forms of creative expression by middle age" (p. 948). Twenty-five years after earning SAT scores in the top 1% as 13-year-olds, the distribution of SMPY participants' professional accomplishments reflected levels and patterns in their verbal and mathematical ability that were detectable in adolescence. Those whose SAT-M exceeded their SAT-V were most likely to engage in careers in science, technology, engineering, and mathematics (STEM), while those with higher verbal than math scores gravitated to the humanities.

The understanding of the importance of spatial abilities has also grown (Lubinski & Kell, 2018). This ability to manipulate visual patterns (Lohman, 1994) plays a powerful role in the likelihood and nature of academic and creative achievements in STEM. In their analysis of the 11-year follow-up of 400,000 adolescents in Project TALENT, Wai et al. (2009) found that the likelihood of earning an advanced degree in STEM increased with spatial ability and more of the individuals earning Ph.D.s than master's degrees had earned top spatial ability scores. Further, Kell et al. (2013) demonstrated that spatial ability added incrementally to the prediction of creative outcomes (patents and publications) of 563 SMPY participants who had scored in the top 0.5% on the SAT 30 years earlier. They found, as one might expect, that different abilities were associated with accomplishments in different fields.

For example, the spatial abilities of patent-holders and those who publish in STEM outlets were similar, but the mathematical and verbal reasoning of those who publish was superior. In contrast, SMPY participants who published in art, humanities, law, and social sciences were the lowest in spatial ability (Lubinski, 2016, p. 924). Tannenbaum (1997) warned that although the findings of these studies indicate that spatial ability plays a significant role in school and later life accomplishments, the findings are not causal (i.e., they should not be used to guide adolescents' career choices).

Dynamic Aspects of Special Aptitudes

Interest in the dynamic aspects of abilities have a rich history, particularly in mathematics. It has benefitted from the renewed interest in innovative and creative thinking in STEM education. Poincaré (1908/1952), Krutetskii (1968/1976), and many others described an aesthetic sensitivity associated with their experience of mathematics. They used words like *elegance* and *beauty* to refer to, for example, a clear, "simple" solution to a complex problem. Krutetskii witnessed this in his intensive 12-year investigation of the nature and development of the problem-solving abilities of approximately 200 mathematically gifted children in primary and secondary school. He provided a rich account of the components and structure of the distinctive abilities of mathematically gifted students and their "mathematical cast of mind" (p. 361). This cast of mind was a "synthesis" of their ability to understand the formal structure of problems; think logically about quantitative, symbolic, and spatial relationships; reason elegantly, planfully, and flexibly; and retain and generalize their rich mathematical knowledge. Krutetskii recounted, "their whole demeanor testified to the aesthetic feeling they were experiencing: their eyes sparkled, they rubbed their hands in satisfaction and smiled, they invited one another to admire a keen train of thought or a particularly 'elegant' solution" (p. 347).

This aesthetic sensitivity is not limited to mathematicians. Kay (1991) observed a similar distinctive character, a "personal aesthetic bias," (p. 248) in the ways professional artists engaged with two- and three-dimensional figural problems when compared to nonartists. Instead of solving the problem as it was presented to them, the professionals redefined it and solved it as they saw it, according to their preferences and personal principles. They infused it with their love of beauty "and a vivid individuality, which are the dynamic underpinnings of creativity" (Tannenbaum, 2009, p. 518).

Returning to Krutetskii's (1968/1976) study, his team observed other noticeable differences in the ways mathematically gifted students solved challenging problems as compared to their less capable peers: "The trials of the capable pupils were always purposeful, systematized attempts, directed toward verifying assumptions they had made" (p. 138). Krutetskii repeatedly noted their "ability to see alternative representations or adopt alternative strategies," emphasizing that this flexibility was one of the most important qualities of their outstanding performance in mathematics. It may be related to the "dual processing" Gross (2009) noticed in the participants in her longitudinal study of children with IQs of more than 160: "the seeming ability to process two sets of information simultaneously and in parallel" (p. 339). These findings have been replicated in math and other domains (Leikin et al., 2014).

Neuroscience also suggests that there are cognitive and neural correlates of giftedness. For example, there is evidence indicating the primary structures and functions that distinguish the brains of mathematically gifted individuals are their highly developed right hemisphere coupled with highly coordinated, efficient interhemispheric interactions at the frontal and parietal regions. These results are promising but must be considered tentative, as they are based on studies with small sample sizes and "backward inferencing" (i.e., attributing specific cognitive functions to regions of the brain based on neuroimaging data, such as fMRIs and EEGs; Myers et al., 2017).

A growing body of evidence has provided a better understanding of differences in the progression of talent development, from its early beginnings of raw ability, to competence, expertise, and perhaps scholarly productivity, artistry, or eminence (Subotnik & Jarvin, 2005; Subotnik et al., 2011) across diverse domains, including the arts (acting, dance, music, visual arts, culinary arts), sports (swimming, tennis, golf, gymnastics, game sports), mathematics, and sciences (e.g., Bloom, 1985; Chua, 2014; Jarvin & Subotnik, 2015; Subotnik & Jarvin, 2005; Subotnik et al., 2019). Winner and Drake (2018) observed,

> adults who achieve eminence and are considered to be major creators were often prodigies as children. However, the reverse is not the case: Most prodigies do not become domain-altering creators. Many drop out and turn to other pursuits; of those who do not drop out, most do not become known as creative geniuses. (p. 7)

Thus, precocity and extreme aptitude are not sufficient for talent to develop; other factors are essential. In Tannenbaum's (2003) words,

> special aptitudes can help a child excel in a specific discipline, *if* she or he also shows evidence of superior general ability. But to bring giftedness fully to life, these cognitive faculties have to be energized by an encouraging disposition, an enriching environment, and timely elements of chance. (p. 53)

Nonintellective Requisites

Nonintellective requisites include the social, emotional, and behavioral characteristics, as well as aspects of personality, temperament and motivation that can release the full use of a person's abilities:

> It is not known which of the nonintellective attributes are *responsible* for creative achievement, which are merely *associated* with it, and which are *by-products* of it. Among the facilitative traits, there are two types that function in different ways. Some are of direct help to individual performance, and these include the familiar advantages of ambition, dedication and intellectual "perspiration." Others are unrelated to the product or performance at hand, but they help make it possible for gifted individuals to maximize their impact on audiences, patients or clients by calling attention to themselves and their work through personal charm or through a keen sense of promotional acumen. (Tannenbaum, 1986b, p. 396)

To a greater degree than their peers, individuals who are or have the potential to be gifted are *more* driven, persistent, curious, sensitive, intuitive, imaginative, independent, courageous, and risk-taking. They are those who learn to find venues and colleagues who appreciate, promote, and extend their work. Greta Thunberg, the young Swedish environmental activist, is one example. She began her campaign to raise concern for climate change by inspiring young people to leave school on "Fridays for Future." Her pleas and challenges to world leaders inspired millions to support her efforts to change the world in 2019.

Static Aspects of Nonintellective Requisites

Investigators who examined relationships between ability and measurable traits, like motivation and personality, have documented differences in their nature and extent that are associated with high potential.

Motivation. Motivation is "the process whereby goal-directed activity is instigated and sustained" (Schunk et al., 2008, p. 4), and potential will not be fulfilled without motivation and engagement (Csikszentmihalyi et al., 1993). The intense engagement of highly talented individuals can appear early. Gottfried et al. (2006) found that, by age 7, children with IQs higher than 130 were more academically intrinsically motivated than their agemates, and this was maintained through their school years (i.e., they enjoyed learning more). Although the intrinsic motivation of highly successful students and adults is often prioritized in descriptions of their personality, it may be the balance or tension between intrinsic (valuing the joy of learning) and extrinsic (valuing external recognition for their learning from parents, teachers, awards, etc.) motivation that keeps them moving forward. Al-Dhamit and Kreishan (2013) found a strong positive correlation ($r = .61$) between the intrinsic and extrinsic motivation of academically gifted secondary students, suggesting they were both intrinsically and extrinsically motivated. This is consistent with Covington and Dray's (2002) observation that these students may be "driven simultaneously by high hopes of success and by an excessive fear of failure" (p. 37).

This tension also appeared in interviews exploring high-ability 8- to 12-year-old students' motivation to learn in school (Garn & Jolly, 2014). Two themes emerged from their descriptions: Learning was "fun" when it was relevant to their interests and goals (intrinsically motivated), and learning was driven by the rewards and pressures associated with parents' expectation that students earn good grades (extrinsically motivated). The more dynamic aspects of motivation will be discussed in the next section.

Personality. One of Lewis Terman's (1925) motives for undertaking his study of children with high IQs was to investigate, and hopefully dispel, the belief that they were emotionally fragile, more likely than their peers to experience social and emotional difficulties, and perhaps destined for insanity. He and others found little evidence that his high-IQ cohort struggled any more than others their age. Leta Hollingworth (1942) was not convinced that the relationship between IQ and mental health was as simple as Terman had reported. She compared 12 "profoundly gifted" students with IQs of at least 180 to age-mates with "superior" IQs of 130 and found that those above 180 were more likely to struggle socially and emotionally. The results of a later analysis of individuals with IQs of 170 and higher in Terman's study reinforced Hollingworth's findings (Terman & Oden, 1947). According to Tannenbaum (2009), "relating personality traits to giftedness is basically a chicken-and-egg problem. Nobody knows for sure whether and to what extent, these attributes are *causes, concomitants,* or *consequences* of successful achievement" (p. 519).

With Tannenbaum's (2009) caveat in mind, studies investigating the Big Five factors in the Five Factor Model (FFM; McRae et al., 2002) of personality have shown that some traits correlate with intelligence and creative productivity more than others. The five factors are Agreeableness, Conscientiousness, Neuroticism, Extraversion, and Openness to Experience. Openness to Experience has the strongest, most consistent association with intellectual abilities and creative productivity (Ackerman & Heggestad, 1997; Hong et al., 2014; Limont et al., 2014; McCrae et al., 2002; Vuyk et al., 2016; Wirthwein et al., 2019; Zeidner & Shani-Zinovich, 2011). It represents "aesthetic sensitivity, intellectual curiosity, vivid imagination, and evolving value systems" (Vuyk et al., 2016, p. 192). Gifted adolescents also scored lower on Neuroticism than their nongifted peers, which indicates greater emotional stability (Limont et al., 2014; Zeidner & Shani-Zinovich, 2011). Contrary to public perception, as a group, this suggested these gifted adolescents were a bit less vulnerable than other adolescents rather than fragile (Baudson, 2016). Inconsistent relationships between intellectual ability and agreeableness, conscientiousness, and extraversion show that individuals with high IQs are as diverse as their peers in terms of these factors. Although individuals should be expected to differ from each other, these recent findings create a more favorable picture of them as a group than might be expected.

Perfectionism and suicide are two concerns frequently associated with giftedness, but there is little evidence to support them. The prevalence of maladaptive perfectionism among gifted individuals is similar to nongifted, so educators should expect as many gifted students as nongifted to experience it (Mofield & Parker Peters, 2018). Further, the data and research addressing prevalence rates are limited and insufficient to support or challenge the popular belief that gifted individuals are more likely to consider, attempt, or complete an attempt to take their own life (Cross & Cross, 2018).

Differences in the methods in studies investigating static aspects of nonintellective dimensions of giftedness contribute to differences in their findings. For example, some studies operationally defined giftedness using an IQ cutoff, while others relied on school districts' designations. Further, a variety of instruments have been used to assess personality and socioemotional status (e.g., Martin et al., 2010). After systematically reviewing the 11 studies that used IQ as a selection criterion, Francis et al. (2016) concluded, "intellectual giftedness was associated with decreased levels of psychopathology among children and adolescents" (pp. 292–293); however, they warned that the "gifted population is not a homogeneous group" (p. 294) and that many internal and external influences contribute to their strengths and difficulties. It seems, as a group, individuals with extreme intellectual strengths may also be associated with social and emotional strengths for some, but not all.

Dynamic Aspects of Nonintellective Requisites

The dynamic aspects of nonintellective factors influencing fulfillment of potential "can only be discerned through diagnosis at levels below the surface" (Tannenbaum, 2003, p. 48). This section returns to the topics of motivation and personality, looking beneath the quantitative findings.

Motivation. Since the late 1800s, the intensity and nature of intrinsic motivation associated with the strength of gifted children's and adults' domain-specific, persistent passion for learning have been a constant in accounts of developing talent (e.g., Cohen, 2011; Galton, 1869; Krutetskii, 1968/1976; Tannenbaum, 1983; Winner & Drake, 2018). It is evident in the spontaneous "undivided interest" (Rathunde & Csikszentmihalyi, 1993) and chronic "rage to master" that Winner (1996) argued is an inescapable force in talent development that can appear early in the lives of young artists and musicians (Cohen, 2011; Coleman & Guo, 2013; DeLoache et al., 2007). Krutetskii (1968/1976) also witnessed this "insatiable striving to acquire information" in mathematically gifted students as well (p. 346).

The theory of "flow" accounts for the optimal intrinsic motivation experienced by those who pursue creative goals (Csikszentmihalyi et al., 2018). It is an absorbing, pleasurable state of consciousness associated with activities that match one's level of challenge with one's skill so "they are more likely to practice, persist, and succeed in their creative endeavors" (p. 224). To maintain it, "individuals must take on tougher challenges as their skills increase, and must develop new skills through deliberate practice to meet increasing challenges in order to remain in flow" (p. 216). Individuals are driven to seek and create challenges, and if they cannot, they disengage (Kanevsky & Keighley, 2003).

This hunger for challenge also distinguished the problem solving of high-IQ 4- to 8-year-olds from that of same-age peers with average IQs in Kanevsky's (1992) dynamic assessments of their problem solving and learning. In their self-talk, only children with high IQs maintained their motivation by challenging themselves to solve the problems more efficiently.

For creative and gifted individuals, truly challenging tasks feel like "play with a purpose" (Rea, 2000). In the words of one of the elite mathematical researchers in Bloom's study of talent development, "It's half hard work and it's half play, but mostly it's just engrossing" (Gustin, 1985, p. 327). Dewey (1933) also recognized the value of opportunities for serious play: "To be playful and serious at the same time is possible, and it defines the ideal mental condition" (p. 286). It seems the need for serious play begins early and endures into adulthood.

In school, unfortunately, flow and serious play experiences are rare for many bright learners. In their "beeper study," Csikszentmihalyi et al. (1993) provided vivid insights into the lives of talented adolescents. Participants wore electronic pagers (i.e., beepers), and each time they went off, students recorded their location, companions, activities, thoughts, and feelings:

> Three fourths of the time when the talented teens reported from the classroom they did not want to do what they were doing. When they did want to do what they were doing, they tended to be doing and thinking about something other than academic work. The pager found them talking with classmates, falling asleep, daydreaming, or planning the next free period. (p. 180)

Adolescents identified as gifted in elementary school who were "underachieving" in high school shared descriptions of their boredom that resonate with those shared previously (Kanevsky & Keighley, 2003). They were "bored," but unlike the boredom of others their age, their boredom had an ethical dimension. They described a sense of injustice, a double standard; attending school was mandatory, but they were offered little, if anything, to learn. This resentment grew throughout their years in school, and by the time they reached high school, most had disengaged academically. Eventually, a few left school. They clearly distinguished schooling from learning and identified learning as the antidote to boredom. The learning they sought resonated with Csikszentmihalyi et al.'s (2018) flow experiences. In it, the students had challenge, complexity, control, choice, and caring teachers: "the five C's."

Persistence. Ability, the raw material of talent, will remain just potential without commitment and hard work. Elite dancers have grit; they work through pain, recover from injuries and setbacks, overcome adversity, and make personal sacrifices to pursue their art (Chua, 2014). Their enduring belief that their abilities can be developed reflects a growth mindset. In mathematics, talent development also requires the same perseverance and commitment (Krutetskii, 1968/1976).

Developing expertise also requires deliberate practice, and it appears that one's willingness to practice may have a genetic component. Mosing et al. (2014) investigated the relationship between music ability (voice or playing an instrument) and the deliberate practice habits of 10,500 Swedish twins to see if ability and the willingness to practice was inherited. Twin studies enable educators to distinguish the relative contributions of genetics and environment to behaviors essential to talent development, like one's inclination to practice. The studies found that genetics played a significant role in both music ability and inclination to practice and that the amount of music practice was surprisingly heritable (40%–70%), so it seems some individuals are born with a greater propensity to practice as well as having more music ability.

Personality. In his Theory of Positive Disintegration (TPD), Dabrowski (1964), a Polish psychiatrist, took a very different perspective on the personality development of extraordinary individuals such as Mahatma Gandhi. He viewed personality as the outcome of an individual's efforts to develop "the most essential positive human qualities" by "working internally on his own improvement and education" (Dabrowski, 1967, p. 5). These qualities include "personal and social responsibility and sense of justice, courage, honesty, and discipline" (Mendaglio, 2008, p. 22). According to Dabrowski (1964), one's developmental potential is determined by the nature and extent of their "overexcitabilities" (OEs). OEs are heightened sensitivities to five types of experiences: intellectual, imaginational, emotional, psychomotor, and sensual. The first three are considered prerequisites for the development of higher levels of personality through cycles of positive disintegration and integration. In most of the studies investigating ability-related differences, intellectual, imaginational, and emotional OEs have distinguished high-ability children and adults from others (Silverman, 2008). Dabrowski emphasized the role these sensitivities and intensities play in higher levels of moral, emotional, and spiritual development (Piechowski, 2003, 2008).

Although the OEs have helped many make sense of the lived experiences of highly creative individuals, researchers have often struggled to establish their validity. Vuyk et al. (2016) demonstrated the conceptual equivalence of the OEs and one of the factors in the FFM, Openness to Experience; they argued that the superior strength and depth of the psychological science supporting the FFM makes it a clearer lens for viewing personality development. The FFM and TPD both converge on an understanding that the highly talented minority experience their inner and outer worlds differently from the less talented majority, and the differences in those experiences play an essential role in the fulfillment of their potential.

Environmental Influences

The societal, cultural, community, and school contexts in which a potentially gifted individual lives and learns can test and inspire their development:

> Human potential cannot flourish in an arid cultural climate; it needs nurturance, urgings, encouragement, and even pressures from a world that cares. The child lives in several worlds, the closest of which are the family, peer group, school, and community, while the remotest are the various economic, social, legal, and political institutions. These environments all help to determine the *kinds* of talent that society is willing to honor as well as the *amount* of investment that it is willing to make in cultivating them. Societal conditions are therefore critical in stimulating the gifted child's pursuit of excellence. (Tannenbaum, 1983, p. 184)

A lack of political will to recognize and nurture talents often reflects a society's ambivalence toward individuals with extraordinary intellectual abilities (Gottfredson, 2001, 2003; Tannenbaum, 1996). For example, those opposing ability grouping and acceleration resist years of research evidence demonstrating their benefits for many academically advanced students even when shown that they pose no harm. At the same time, they buy season tickets to attend professional sports populated with elite athletes who have had access to superior instructors, coaches, and facilities at ages younger than others. Clearly, some talents are celebrated while others are suppressed. The reasons are complex and, at least in North America, may be connected to a concern that practices like ability grouping, acceleration, and gifted education in general will "help the rich get richer" (Gottfredson, 2003, p. 24).

Societal, cultural, community, school, and home contexts external to an individual interact in idiosyncratic ways with their internal resources (e.g., g, special aptitudes, nonintellective resources) throughout the lifespan to fulfill or frustrate the development of potential:

> Many children show signs of giftedness only in response to pressure or even oppressiveness in their environments. For most of them, however, stimulating home, school, and community settings are indispensable not only for maximizing potentialities but also for helping to determine the directions they take. Parents will serve as role models through their own achievement orientation while creating an enriched educational environment outside of school and urging their offspring to advance their studies to the fullest extent. The quality of classroom instruction also makes a difference, as do the attitudes of peers in and out of the classroom toward the life of the mind. As for the resources in the neighborhood, there are formal cultural institutions such as local museums, concert halls, and libraries as well as human resources that can inspire and instruct. Without proper stimulation in the human ecological structure, there is always the possibility, and often the likelihood, that children with outstanding mental endowment will "hide their lights under a bushel." (Tannenbaum, 1983, p. 88)

Static Aspects of Environmental Influences

Depending on alignment with a child's needs, experiences in school may or may not contribute to the fulfilment of promise. Sosniak (1985) highlighted the timing, source (e.g., parents, teachers, mentors), and types of learning experienced by the highly accomplished musicians, artists, athletes, mathematicians, and scientists in Bloom's (1985) retrospective study in the early, middle, and later years of developing their talent. These phases began and ended at different ages in different domains and involved opportunities that were qualitatively different from those most of these individuals experienced in school (Bloom & Sosniak, 1981). In the early years, they had been encouraged by parents to informally play with and explore their area of talent, first with family members and then with teachers. Even as children, they began to see themselves as members of their disciplines (e.g., pianists, mathematicians). In the middle years, their talent became their priority. Although parents continued to be supportive, their reliance on parents to organize activities diminished as their passion and aspirations motivated them to advance and deliberately practice and refine their knowledge and techniques with the support of an expert teacher (usually outside of school). They received increasing public recognition for their accomplishments and sought further feedback from experts. The later years were fully committed to their talent, finding and working with a top-tier, master teacher and like-minded peers. All were focused on "perfecting" their talent, developing their "style," and "on the larger purpose and meaning of the talent" (Bloom, 1985, p. 527).

Many models have been proposed to guide the design of curriculum, instruction, and programs for advanced learners. Most evidence-based programs and practices involve a combination of forms of acceleration, ability grouping, and curriculum involving greater depth, abstraction, complexity, challenge, and creativity in learning (VanTassel-Baska & Stambaugh, 2006). The education of potentially gifted individuals needs to be structured but flexible, with opportunities for them to inquire deeply (e.g., Eysinck et al., 2015) and apply their sophisticated understandings in creative ways to real problems in order to appreciate the beauty within a domain (Mann, 2006).

Many forms of acceleration can be employed to accommodate the rapid pace of gifted children's learning. In addition to grade-skipping, Rogers (2015) and Southern and Jones (2015) have identified as many as 20 forms of acceleration that can be used to accommodate the rapid pace of a gifted learner's learning. Some are subject-based (e.g., independent study, honors classes, mentorships), allowing students "to flexibly progress through the general K–12 curriculum" while others are grade-based (e.g., skipping one or more grades, telescoping 3 years of middle school into one). The latter enable students "to progress more quickly through the general K–12 curriculum, leaving the system anywhere from one to four years earlier than the normal age/grade lockstep system provides" (Rogers, 2015, p. 23).

Numerous studies have compared accelerants with nonaccelerants of the same age and ability (e.g., Gross, 2006; Kulik, 2003; Kulik & Kulik, 1984; Rogers, 2015). Academic effects have been consistently significant and positive. Contrary to popular belief, effects on social and emotional variables have either been positive or neutral. For example, Gross (2009) found that "radical accelerants" with IQs of 160 or higher who entered university when they were between 11 and 15 years old "reported warm and fulfilling friendships with the older students," while peers of the same age and ability who stayed with their agemates or skipped only one grade "experienced significant and ongoing difficulties with peer relationships" (p. 342). All studies concluded that decisions regarding who should be accelerated and how must be made based on an individual learner's strengths, preferences, and interests, and the resources available, not based on aggregated research findings.

Based on her longitudinal study of children with high IQs, Hollingworth (1936) explained that difficulties with peer relationships were not due to social skill deficits; rather, they were

> largely a result of the infrequency of persons who are like-minded. The more intelligent a person is, regardless of age, the less often can he find a truly congenial companion. The average child finds playmates in plenty who can think and act on a level congenial to him, because there are so many average children. (p. 79)

Children who differ in their level of giftedness (as defined by IQ) also differ in their social acceptance. For example, 8-year-olds with very high IQs (163+) were more likely to experience social difficulties than peers with IQs between 125 and 140 (Janos et al., 1985). Children with IQs above a 150 or 165 tended to have more problems connecting with peers than age-mates just below those cutoffs (DeHaan & Havighurst, 1961; Gallagher, 1958; Janos, 1983). Hollingworth (1942) characterized IQs between 125–155 as "most favorable to the development of successful and well-rounded personality in the world" (p. 264).

In their search for friends, young intellectually gifted children often seek out older children who are a closer match to their mental age (Gross, 2009). From adolescence onward, most gifted students appear to be able to find friends. Their friendships are based on socioemotional concerns (providing guidance, trust, respect, etc.) rather than intellectual match (Shore et al., 2019).

Dynamic Aspects of Environmental Influences

Receptive, supportive families create the "prime context" children need to pursue their passions (Coleman & Guo, 2013). Parents who value education and are committed to locating resources and opportunities for their talented children contribute significantly to the development of their child's abilities (Bloom, 1985). They also need teachers, coaches, or mentors with domain-specific expertise who shared their passions and are able to adjust the depth, pace, and direction of their instruction, support, and feedback to maintain their interest and need for challenge (Bloom, 1985; Gross, 1993, 2004; Subotnik et al., 2019). These needs increase in intensity as children and their talent mature, from play to a commitment, from commitment to formal instruction and deliberate practice, and later to self-determined immersion and commitment to their discipline. Wai et al. (2010) found that the strength of the "educational dose" (the "density of advanced precollegiate educational opportunities," p. 860) was related to adult accomplishments of SMPY. Studies in many diverse fields recounting the young lives of extraordinary artists, athletes, and academics also validate the need for a strong, sustained educational dose (Bloom, 1985; Muratori et al., 2006; Subotnik et al., 2019). In order to achieve a sufficient dose, advanced and enriched opportunities offered in school are especially important for students from families with limited financial resources, as they will be unable to afford costs associated with those offered outside of school.

Through mentorships, youngsters can develop their abilities and introduce them to peers as well as the culture of a discipline. Zuckerman (1977) found that more than half of the 92 Nobel Laureates she interviewed had been mentored by previous laureates. Mentorships can take place in school or community settings. They offer opportunities for intellectual *and* psychosocial growth as talented youngsters learn to identify and solve significant, elegant problems while developing the social skills needed to interact appropriately with members of the discipline, sponsors, the media, and others.

A lack of supportive peers may interfere with the fulfillment of promise (Subotnik et al., 2019). Relationships with peers may motivate talented adolescents to maintain their commitment to their talent, or they may interfere with it. Patrick et al. (1999) found that a major factor in a student's decision to continue or quit an activity was whether or not they felt it involved opportunities to "make new friends and maintain a social support system" (p. 759).

The potential for being stigmatized is a major concern when attempting to understand the psychosocial effects of school on children. Children whose abilities and interests develop at an accelerated pace often sense and are made aware of these differences most sharply in school where they are placed in classrooms according to their chronological age (Coleman et al., 2015; Gross, 2009; Robinson, 2008). For example, Dauber and Benbow (1990) found that teenagers with exceptional verbal talent rated themselves lower for social standing than those with extreme mathematical ability. They suggested this may have been because their "linguistic precocity" was more difficult to hide. By adolescence, in settings where their atypical behavior is not understood or accepted, many talented students experience their "gifts" as a social handicap (Coleman & Cross, 2014) often until they reach university (Gross, 2009; Robinson, 2008).

Out-of-school programs can play an important role in talent development by bringing high-potential youth into contact with people, resources, and experiences they would be unlikely to encounter in school. They include summer, afterschool, weekend, or online courses; academic clubs; or competitions. Participation in demanding encounters that engage students' "rage to master" (Winner, 1996, p. 371) during adolescence was found to predict their careers and attainments as adults (Milgram, 2003; Milgram & Hong, 1999). Talented teens can be introduced to ideas, skills, and "the process of acculturation and socialization into the field" (Olszewski-Kubilius, 2015, p. 266), as well as find peers who share their passion and commitment. Participating in competitions in their talent domain can enable them to determine their standing among peers and experts. Out-of-school programs are even more crucial for recognizing early indicators of high potential among gifted students from culturally and linguistically diverse backgrounds.

Opportunities in and beyond school, family members, teachers, mentors, and like-minded peers are some of the environmental factors that can nurture potential. That said, brilliance can develop despite a lack of financial resources and in the presence of adversity and trauma:

> there is no simple connection between extraordinary accomplishment and a favorable environment. Many people have to overcome all kinds of adversity to distinguish themselves in the crowd. They seem to succeed *because* of the pressures, not just *despite* them. Hardships that discourage most people from achieving somehow challenge a few to "beat the odds" and "make it big." Their drive toward

excellence may be basically an act of defiance against what they consider hostile, inhibiting forces in the world. But they constitute a minority among people with high potential, most of whom need a supportive environment and would wither on the vine if they did not have it. (Tannenbaum, 1983, p. 184)

Chance

As mentioned early in this chapter, Tannenbaum (1983) was first to propose a conception of giftedness that included the role of luck, good or bad, in the development and expression of talent:

> Generally overlooked in the studies of the fulfillment of talent are the entirely unpredictable events in a person's life that are critical both to the realization of promise and to the demonstration of developed talents. It is not only a matter of being in the right place at the right time, although that is important, too. (Tannenbaum, 1983, pp. 88–89)

Unexpected chance events and opportunities change lives. They can unleash, facilitate, redirect, or obstruct the development of one's abilities. Whether they involve good fortune or misfortune, they consistently arise as career-defining moments in biographies and retrospective accounts of the lives of eminent and extraordinary individuals in many fields (e.g., literature, science, dance, and more). Some are wonderful, and others excruciatingly painful. For example, Frida Kahlo began painting while recovering from critical injuries she sustained in a collision between a streetcar and a bus she was riding. While she was in a body cast for months, her parents brought her painting supplies and had a special easel designed so she could begin to paint while confined to her bed. It will never be known if her artistry would have emerged if she not been involved in that random accident.

Tannenbaum (1983) felt that social scientists avoided the role of chance or luck in the development of giftedness because they were more concerned with "influences that are more easily observable, measurable, and perhaps eventually controllable" (p. 205). It's true that methodologies for investigating random events are problematic; however, as will be described, mathematical models and other accounts have been able to simulate their effects on the likelihood that talented individuals will succeed (Pluchino et al., 2018).

Static Aspects of Chance

Not only psychologists but also statisticians, economists, and risk analysts have concluded that "chance events play a much larger role in life than many people once imagined" (Pluchino et al., 2018, p. 3). Atkinson (1978) felt that the role of chance in one's accomplishments was clearest in "two crucial rolls of the dice over which no individual exerts any personal control. These are the accidents of birth and background. One roll of the dice determines an individual's heredity; the other his formative environment" (p. 221). Many have interpreted the latter as family environment, but Subotnik et al. (2011) suggested that geographic location matters as well. It determines one's proximity to potential mentors and resources, making it easier to be in the right place at the right time.

Two physicists and an economist who also felt that the relationship between random events and career achievements was underappreciated recently combined their skills in an attempt to quantify the roles of luck and talent in success for the first time (Pluchino et al., 2018). In earlier retrospective studies, when describing the path to their success, they, like others, found that many of the most successful individuals in competitive Western cultures often attributed their accomplishments to traits like intelligence, skill, hard work, or risk-taking, or they made their accomplishments sound inevitable rather than crediting providence. Pluchino and his colleagues suggested "hindsight bias" and "narrative fallacy" were at work in results of studies that minimized or ignored the influence of chance. Hindsight bias is the tendency to overestimate one's ability to have predicted an outcome that could not possibly have been predicted, and narrative fallacy is the tendency to weave observed facts into a story and then to believe it explains more than what was observed. Pluchino et al. created an "agent-based" mathematical model that simulated the contributions of luck and talent to the likelihood of success from ages 20 to 60. Kaufman's (2018) cheeky summary of their findings highlights the importance of unforeseen events:

> talent was definitely not sufficient because *the most talented individuals were rarely the most successful.* In general, mediocre-but-lucky people were much more successful than

> more-talented-but-unlucky individuals. The most successful agents tended to be those who were only slightly above average in talent but with a lot of luck in their lives. (para. 10)

If the correlation between talent and success (as measured by performance-based indicators of success like money) were perfect, individuals with the greatest amount of talent would be the most successful; however, this is seldom true. Pluchino et al. (2018) attributed the success of individuals with moderate talent to "naïve meritocracy," a system that equates success with talent. In it, those who have succeeded in the past continue to be rewarded with the resources needed to succeed without acknowledging the role luck or random events may have played in their achievements. Pluchino et al. suggested that if organizations funding research really wanted to increase the likelihood of finding innovative solutions and insights, "the best funding strategy of them all was one where an equal number of funding was distributed to everyone . . . to counterbalance the unpredictable role of luck and give more opportunities and resources to the most talented ones" (p. 27). Although dispersing research funds without considering past productivity may have merit when seeking projects that might result in radical innovations, it is unlikely that resources will be distributed in this way while fiscal accountability is valued more than innovation (Perkins, 1994; Simonton, 2004; Yaqub, 2018).

Dynamic Aspects of Chance

The complex, nuanced ways in which individuals influence and are influenced by chance represent its dynamic aspects. What underlies or surrounds a potentially gifted individual's responsiveness to chance events? With this in mind, Tannenbaum (2009) invited educators to consider these questions:

> Is chance simply a stroke of luck, a random event in the life of an individual and totally unrelated to the lawful functioning of the psyche or the environment? Is it a static condition, improbable and fateful, or can the person reach out and develop any kind of dynamic relationship with it? (p. 527)

J. H. Austin (1978/2003), a neurologist, suggested that all chance events were not created equal. He proposed four different types of relationships one might have with random events. Although the types can be distinguished from each other, he felt that most breakthroughs involved more than one. He defined Chance I as blind luck, a completely random event that occurs in the presence of the passive but lucky individual. In Chance II events, good luck results from an active, curious individual's persistent, broad exploration of ideas and possibilities. Although their activity "is mostly wasteful, it increases the chances they will stumble upon a good idea" (Tannenbaum, 1983, p. 206). Austin (1978/2003) referred to Chance III as *The Pasteur Principle*, as it depicts the "sagacity" (p. 68) implied in Pasteur's words, "chance favors only the prepared mind." Rather than general exploration, Chance III events are the result of an individual's "special receptivity born from past experience" (p. 76). *Altamirage*, or Chance IV events, arise due to an individual's specific, perhaps unique, behaviors, such as a distinctive hobby or lifestyle "in domains seemingly far removed from the area of the discovery" (p. 76). In the lives of eminent historical and contemporary figures, Piechowski (1998) found Chance IV in the "synergistic effect of opportunity (chance) and a person's readiness to seize it" (p. 193).

Bloom (1985) noted that the impact of chance events was greatest at the time that the child chose a specific field within a talent domain. These included:

> securing positive initial learning experiences in a talent field, the support of a patron or sponsor when essential, and especially the extent to which an individual's physical, intellectual, and personal characteristics were matched with qualities that were of special value in a given talent field. (p. 528)

Once these pieces were in place, "chance events played only a minor role" (p. 529).

In the arts, dancers in elite professional troupes differed in their estimates of the role of luck in their accomplishments (Chua, 2014, 2019). Some attributed their success to "effort and perseverance" alone, while others considered themselves "lucky to have met influential people at the right place at the right time" (Chua, 2014, p. 260). Gatekeepers (e.g., artistic directors for dance companies and heads of dance conservatories) reported a blend of both: "If you are at the right place for a longer time, you may be successful" (Chua, 2019, p. 278). The difference in the dancers' and gatekeepers' perspectives is a good example of the difference between Chance I and Chance III in Austin's (1978/2003) model. The gatekeepers acknowledged the efforts dancers had made to be in that place at that time, but the dancers did not. On the other hand, Atkinson's (1978) reference to home and heredity resonated with the dancers' beliefs. Some credited having had a family that supported their passion for dance and having been born with the physical attributes to be a dancer.

To explore the role of random events involved in different fields, Weber and Perkins (1992) brought together a small, diverse group of eminent innovators (cognitive psychologists, historians of technology, and world-class inventors) to examine the thinking involved in their major discoveries. They found that "the inventor's search process involves a mix of chance and craft, with even the chance a craft of sorts. The balance between the two depends on the circumstances" (Perkins, 1994, p. 132). Perkins noticed that these innovators employed six different "styles of search" in which the role and nature of chance fluctuated:

- *Sheer chance.* An invention not particularly sought gets discovered by an active searcher exploring widely and incidentally.
- *Cultivated chance.* The searcher deliberately opens himself or herself to a variety of semirandom input, harvesting the occasional useful connections.
- *Systematized chance.* The searcher systematically surveys a sizable number of options that fall within a defined set, seeking ones with the target characteristics.
- *Fair bet.* The searcher conceives and develops one or a few prototypes, relying on science and craft, with reasonable expectations that one or another will serve.
- *Good bet.* The searcher conceives and develops a prototype from principle and experience that probably will work.
- *Safe bet.* The searcher deduces with formal methods something that almost certainly will do the job. (Perkins, 1994, p. 131)

Systemized chance, fair bet, and good bet activities were most prevalent in these inventors' discovery processes. Safe bets were common when at the stage of testing prototypes. Sheer chance and cultivated chance helped but were not mainstays.

Evidence of the nature and role of chance in talent development is pervasive in retrospective studies of the lives of eminent individuals and their creative processes (e.g., Bloom, 1985; Piechowski, 1998; Simonton, 2004; Subotnik et al., 2019; Weber & Perkins, 1992). Tannenbaum (2009) insisted that chance events "should never be trivialized or neglected in any study of giftedness, especially since so many eminent people place emphasis on their experiencing unpredictable events that help them reach the top" (p. 527). And yet, luck of any kind is not sufficient. The individual will need to work hard for their good luck and must be ready to act when lucky opportunities arise.

Implications and Connections

Although unpredictable events play a role in the development of expertise, brilliant individuals cannot rely on chance alone. In Tannenbaum's Sea Star, no combination of strengths in four of the factors can compensate for weakness in the fifth. This means that efforts to nurture a young person's potential will need to enlist them all. Outstanding performances and products will not appear as some inevitable outcome of a predetermined internal, biological process or as the result of one "lucky break." Talented children will need significant, ongoing opportunities to invest and extend their internal resources (general ability, special aptitudes, and nonintellective requisites) in inspiring programs and experiences in and out of school with educators, coaches, mentors, peers, and supportive family members.

Tannenbaum (2009) insisted that comprehensive K–12 *programs* were imperative rather than "ad hoc *provisions* [emphasis added], . . . fragmentary learning experiences lacking in complex form, long-range purpose, or clear directionality" (p. 534). Children need to be introduced to the content and culture of the disciplines in which their talents are valued and can thrive. In these experiences, they need to develop the psychosocial skills involved in locating personal and financial resources, sustaining growth, and overcoming obstacles. Further, they will need emotional skills and insight to maintain their momentum and relationships through times of struggle. Highly able youths from underserved populations, in particular, must work with role models and peers who share their lived experiences and cultural backgrounds as well as their passion and commitment (Worrell & Dixson, 2018, p. 219).

The availability of these opportunities is likely to vary greatly depending on location, size of community, cost, and the procedures used to select recipients. Access may be limited to students in suburban and urban centers or communities with moderate to high incomes because only they can afford the fees and the technology needed to participate in such programs online. Children from all economic, cultural, and linguistic backgrounds should have equal access to the conditions, opportunities, and resources needed to have their abilities recognized and their potential fulfilled if they are to have a fair chance to become creatively or proficiently gifted performers and producers. Whenever possible, offering these experiences as a part of school programs, at no cost, can give students from all socioeconomic levels opportunities they might experience if they took place in afterschool programs requiring registration fees.

During the school years and beyond, efforts to understand and enhance a child's trajectory toward giftedness benefit from the ongoing collection of information regarding the nature and extent of a youngster's accomplishments. This information can inform educational planning and communication. For example, Kay (1996, 2019) developed a system, a *Talent Record*, to track the emergence of students' talents throughout their K–12 education by documenting their experiences, behavior, and achievements in six areas: intellectual ability, academics, creativity, leadership, visual/performing arts, and psychomotor/kinesthetic. The Talent Record process enlists educators, mentors, coaches, and family members as talent scouts who all contribute to this cumulative record of static and dynamic aspects of students' general and domain-specific abilities, nonintellective characteristics (i.e., cast of mind, curiosity, intensity, social and emotional well-being, interests, etc.), activities, chance events, and achievements. In addition to acknowledging excellence, the *Talent Record* can be used to develop short- and long-term goals, inform curriculum planning, monitor progress, and promote effective communication between the students, their families, the community, and school.

Efforts to locate potentially gifted children should begin early and continue through adolescence in order to accommodate diverse developmental trajectories across disciplines. In addition to, or perhaps instead of, superficial, static assessment protocols, these efforts should include rich, challenging opportunities to stimulate the dynamic processes involved in each set of factors; this will feed students' curiosity and cast of mind, letting them discover and extend their passions and strengths while they engage in the communities of practitioners associated with their talent domains.

Connections to Other Models

When Tannenbaum initially proposed his conception of giftedness, he had no idea it would provide a foundation for the growth of developmental models. Each model specifies domain-specific trajectories accounting for the transformation of childhood potential to outstanding adult giftedness: what to expect, who should be involved, what is needed, and how abilities should be nurtured along the way (e.g., Subotnik & Jarvin, 2005; Subotnik et al., 2011). He considered giftedness to be an outcome of that process, while some, such as Gagné (2017), referred to "gifts" as undeveloped potential (Sternberg & Kaufman, 2018). Tannenbaum was most interested in explaining what Renzulli (2005) called "creative/productive giftedness" (i.e., discovering and developing innovative, valued new ideas and products in any domain), unlike his peers who were more interested in "schoolhouse giftedness" (i.e., the top 3%–5% in IQ, cognitive ability, or achievement tests; Sternberg et al., 2011).

Like other multifactor models, such as the Talent Development Megamodel (Subotnik et al., 2011), the WICS Model of Giftedness (Sternberg, 2005b), the Integrative Model of Talent Development, and the Munich Model of Giftedness (Heller et al., 2005), interactions between all five sets of factors are essential to the emergence of giftedness. All of these models consider general intellectual abilities and specific aptitudes to be necessary but not sufficient for talent to develop. Tannenbaum's factors include external influences as well as internal resources (e.g., general intellectual ability, specific aptitudes, and nonintellective requisites), which distinguish his model from models that include only internal factors, like Renzulli's (2005). Further, Renzulli's model limits its recognition of nonintellective factors to task commitment, while Tannenbaum's considers many other personality and psychosocial variables.

Tannenbaum was the first to include uncontrollable, chance factors as an essential force in talent development; however, this inclusion is a common feature of many contemporary multifactor models (Gagné, 2017; Heller et al., 2005; Sternberg, 2005b). For example, Gagné (2005) acknowledged borrowing the notion of chance factors and their role in the transformation of ability to talent from Tannenbaum's work. Its prominence in Gagné's model has increased since first appearing in his model in 1993. Gagné (2017) now considers chance to be an *éminence grise*—in essence, a powerful, inconspicuous determinant of giftedness (p. 158).

Conclusion

Tannenbaum's conception of giftedness launched a paradigm shift away from static orientations driven by IQ to broader, more inclusive, dynamic, developmental, multifactor perspectives in which childhood promise is distinguished from adult excellence. He also situated the notion of giftedness in its cultural context by acknowledging that the types of products and performances that might be valued at any point in time would be determined by sociocultural forces beyond the individual. The complex and unpredictable relationships among the factors within and beyond the individual help educators understand the intriguing differences found among individuals who are or have the potential to become gifted. He warned, "a rude awakening awaits those who ignore the map of personal idiosyncrasy and rely only on cognitive perspectives and their measures to forecast later success" (Tannenbaum, 2003, p. 54). Ultimately, Tannenbaum sought to help educators value, understand, and nurture those who have the greatest potential to "enhance the moral, physical, emotional, social, intellectual or aesthetic life of humanity" (Tannenbaum, 1983, p. 86).

DISCUSSION QUESTIONS

1. Does including "chance" in Tannenbaum's conception of giftedness strengthen it . . . weaken it? Discuss the value and implications of including random events in a developmental model of giftedness.

2. Whose responsibility is it to coordinate and offer the environmental conditions (programs, materials, technology, teachers, etc.) needed to nurture potential to its fruition, and why? Or should these experiences be left to chance?

3. Brainstorm examples of each set of static and dynamic factors in Tannenbaum's Sea Star. Working with others, classify each example as static or dynamic in nature.

DISCUSSION QUESTIONS, continued

4. Generate a collection of celebrated or uncelebrated individuals, living or dead, who would be examples of each of Tannenbaum's eight types of giftedness. Each should come from a different talent domain (e.g., arts, sports, medicine, science, literature, technology, culinary arts, architecture, etc.). Share your justification for considering each to be gifted. In what way does each "enhance the moral, physical, emotional, social, intellectual or aesthetic life of humanity" (Tannenbaum, 1983, p. 86)?

5. In what ways is Tannenbaum's conception of giftedness sociocultural? What types of giftedness do you think are valued in the mainstream culture in your community? Which are not? How is "value" determined?

6. What types of environmental resources and opportunities are available in your local community? Are they accessible to families with little or no income ... recent immigrants ... individuals who are often underrepresented in programs for children with high potential? What are some barriers to their participation? How might these barriers be removed or reduced?

7. What research is needed to validate Tannenbaum's conception of giftedness? Imagine studies that would do this.

8. What are the implications or consequences of relying primarily on IQ to operationally define giftedness in studies cited in support of a particular way of conceptualizing giftedness? Who might be missed?

9. What is the relationship between giftedness and creativity?

References

Achter, J. A., Lubinski, D., & Benbow, C. P. (1996). Multipotentiality among the intellectually gifted: "It was never there and already it's vanishing." *Journal of Counseling Psychology, 43*(1), 65–76. https://doi.org/10.1037/0022-0167.43.1.65

Ackerman, P. L., & Heggestad, E. D. (1997). Intelligence, personality, and interests: Evidence for overlapping traits. *Psychological Bulletin, 121*(2), 219–245. https://doi.org/10.1037/0033-2909.121.2.219

Al-Dhamit, Y., & Kreishan, L. (2013). Gifted students' intrinsic and extrinsic motivations and parental influence on their motivation: From the self-determination theory perspective. *Journal of Research in Special Education Needs, 16*(1), 13–23. https://doi.org/10.1111/1471-3802.12048

Alexander, J. M., Carr, M., & Schwanenflugel, P. J. (1995). Development of metacognition in gifted children: Directions for future research. *Developmental Review, 15*(1), 1–37. https://doi.org/10.1006/drev.1995.1001

Atkinson, J. W. (1978). Motivational determinants of intellective performance and cumulative achievement. In J. W. Atkinson & J. O. Raynor (Eds.), *Personality, motivation, and achievement* (pp. 221–242). Wiley.

Austin, J. H. (2003). *Chase, chance, and creativity: The lucky art of novelty.* MIT Press. (Original work published 1978)

Baudson, T. G. (2016). The mad genius stereotype: Still alive and well. *Frontiers in Psychology, 7,* 368. https://doi.org/10.3389/fpsyg.2016.00368

Binet, A. (1905). New methods for the diagnosis of the intellectual level of subnormals. *L'Année Psychologique, 12,* 191–244.

Bloom, B. S. (Ed.). (1985). *Developing talent in young people.* Ballantine Books.

Bloom, B. S., & Sosniak, L. A. (1981). Talent development vs. schooling. *Educational Leadership, 39*(2), 86–94.

Boring, E. G. (1923). Intelligence as the tests test it. *New Republic, 36,* 35–37.

Borkowski, J. G., & Peck, V. A. (1986). Causes and consequences of metamemory in gifted children. In R. J. Sternberg & J. E. Davidson (Eds.), *Conceptions of giftedness* (pp. 182–200). Cambridge University Press.

Bowen, S., Shore, B. M., & Cartwright, G. F. (1992). Do gifted children use computers differently? A view from The Factory. *Gifted Education International, 8*(3), 151–154. https://doi.org/10.1177/026142949200800306

Canivez, G. L., & Watkins, M. W. (2010). Investigation of the factor structure of the Wechsler Adult Intelligence Scale—4th ed. (WAIS-IV): Exploratory and higher order factor analyses. *Psychological Assessment, 22*(4), 827–836. https://doi.org/10.1037/a0020429

Carroll, J. B. (1993). *Human cognitive abilities: A survey of factor-analytic studies.* Cambridge University Press.

Chua, J. (2014). Dance talent development: Case studies of successful dancers in Finland and Singapore. *Roeper Review, 36*(4), 249–263. https://doi.org/10.1080/02783193.2014.945220

Chua, J. (2019). Talent development in dance: Perspectives from gatekeepers in Hong Kong and Finland. In R. F. Subotnik, P. Olszewski-Kubilius, & F. C. Worrell (Eds.), *The psychology of high performance: Developing human potential into domain-specific talent* (pp. 261–290). American Psychological Association.

Cohen, L. M. (2011). Natural acceleration: Supporting creative trajectories. *Roeper Review, 33*(4), 218–227. https://doi.org/10.1080/02783193.2011.603109

Coleman, L. J., & Cross, T. L. (2014). Is being gifted a social handicap? *Journal for the Education of the Gifted, 37*(1), 5–17. https://doi.org/10.1177/016235328801100406

Coleman, L. J., & Guo, A. (2013). Exploring children's passion for learning in six domains. *Journal for the Education of the Gifted, 36*(2), 155–175. https://doi.org/10.1177/0162353213480432

Coleman, L. J., Micko, K. J., & Cross, T. L. (2015). Twenty-five years of research on the lived experience of being gifted in school: Capturing the students' voices. *Journal for the Education of the Gifted, 38*(4), 358–376. https://doi.org/10.1177/0162353215607322

Covington, M. V., & Dray, E. (2002). The developmental course of achievement motivation: A need-based approach. In A. Wigfield & J. S. Eccles (Eds.), *Development of achievement motivation* (pp. 33–56). Academic Press.

Cross, T. L., & Cross, J. R. (2018). Suicide among students with gifts and talents. In S. I. Pfeiffer, E. Shaunessy-Dedrick, & M. Foley-Nicpon (Eds.), *APA handbook of giftedness and talent* (pp. 601–614). American Psychological Association.

Csikszentmihalyi, M. (1988). Society, culture, and person: A systems view of creativity. In R. J. Sternberg (Ed.), *The nature of creativity* (pp. 325–339). Cambridge University Press.

Csikszentmihalyi, M., Montijo, M. N., & Mouton, A. R. (2018). Flow theory: Optimizing elite performance in the creative realm. In S. I. Pfeiffer, E. Shaunessy-Dedrick, & M. Foley-Nicpon (Eds.), *APA handbook of giftedness and talent*. American Psychological Association.

Csikszentmihalyi, M., Rathunde, K., & Whalen, S. (1993). *Talented teenagers: The roots of success and failure.* Cambridge University Press.

Dabrowski, K. (1964). *Positive disintegration.* Little, Brown.

Dabrowski, K. (1967). *Personality-shaping through positive disintegration*. Little, Brown.

Dauber, S. L., & Benbow, C. P. (1990). Aspects of personality and peer relations of extremely talented adolescents. *Gifted Child Quarterly, 34*(1), 10–14. https://doi.org/10.1177/001698629003400103

Davidson, J. E., & Sternberg, R. J. (1984). The role of insight in intellectual giftedness. *Gifted Child Quarterly, 28*(2), 58–64. https://doi.org/10.1177/001698628402800203

Dearborn, W. F. (1921). Intelligence and its measurement: A symposium. *Journal of Educational Psychology, 12*(3), 210–212. https://doi.org/10.1037/h0076078

Deary, I. J. (1995). Auditory inspection time and intelligence: What is the causal direction? *Developmental Psychology, 31*(2), 237–250. https://doi.org/10.1037/0012-1649.31.2.237

Deary, I. J., Lawn, M., & Bartholomew, D. J. (2008). A conversation between Charles Spearman, Godfrey Thomson, and Edward L. Thorndike: The International Examinations Inquiry Meetings 1931–1938. *History of Psychology, 11*(2), 122–142. https://doi.org/10.1037/1093-4510.11.2.122

DeHaan, R. F., & Havighurst, R. J. (1961). *Educating gifted children* (Rev. ed.). University of Chicago Press.

DeLoache, J. S., Simcock, G., & Macari, S. (2007). Planes, trains, automobiles--and tea sets: Extremely intense interests in very young children. *Developmental Psychology, 43*(6), 1579–1586. https://doi.org/10.1037/0012-1649.43.6.1579

Dewey, J. (1933). *How we think*. Heath & Company.

Eysinck, T. H. S., Gersen, L., & Gijlers, H. (2015). Inquiry learning for gifted children. *High Ability Studies, 26*(1), 63–74. https://doi.org/10.1080/13598139.2015.1038379

Francis, R., Hawes, D. J., & Abbott, M. (2016). Intellectual giftedness and psychopathology in children and adolescents: A systematic literature review. *Exceptional Children, 82*(3), 279–302. https://doi.org/10.1177/0014402915598779

Gagné, F. (2005). From gifts to talents: The DMGT as a developmental model. In R. J. Sternberg & J. E. Davidson (Eds.), *Conceptions of giftedness* (2nd ed., pp. 98–119). Cambridge University Press.

Gagné, F. (2017). The Integrative Model of Talent Development (IMTD): From theory to educational applications. In J. A. Plucker, A. N. Rinn, & M. C. Makel (Eds.), *From giftedness to gifted education: Reflecting theory in practice* (pp. 149–182). Prufrock Press.

Gallagher, J. J. (1958). Peer acceptance of highly gifted children in the elementary school. *The Elementary School Journal, 58*, 465–470.

Galton, F. (1869). *Hereditary genius: An inquiry into its laws and consequences.* Macmillan. https://doi.org/10.1037/13474-000

Garn, A. C., & Jolly, J. L. (2014). High ability students' voice on learning motivation. *Journal of Advanced Academics, 25*(1), 7–24. https://doi.org/10.1177/1932202X13513262

Geary, D. C., & Brown, S. C. (1991). Cognitive addition: Strategy choice and speed-of-processing differences in gifted, normal, and mathematically disabled children. *Developmental Psychology, 27*(3), 398–406. https://doi.org/10.1037/0012-1649.27.3.398

Gottfredson, L. S. (1997). Mainstream science on intelligence: An editorial with 52 signatories, history and bibliography [Editorial]. *Intelligence, 24*(1), 13–23. https://doi.org/10.1016/S0160-2896(97)90011-8

Gottfredson, L. S. (2001). Intelligence and the American ambivalence toward talent. In N. Colangelo & S G. Assouline (Eds.), *Talent development IV: Proceedings from the 1998 Henry B. and Jocelyn Wallace National Research Symposium on Talent Development* (pp. 41–58). Great Potential Press.

Gottfredson, L. S. (2003). The science and politics of intelligence in gifted education. In N. Colangelo & G. A. Davis (Eds.), *Handbook of gifted education* (3rd ed., pp. 24–40). Allyn & Bacon.

Gottfredson, L. S. (2004). Schools and the g factor. *Wilson Quarterly, 28*(3), 35–45.

Gottfredson, L. S., & Saklofske, D. H. (2009). Intelligence: Foundations and issues in assessment. *Canadian Psychology, 50*(3), 183–195. https://doi.org/10.1037/a0016641

Gottfried, A. W., Gottfried, A. E., & Guerin, D. W. (2006). The Fullerton Longitudinal Study: A long-term investigation of intellectual and motivational giftedness. *Journal for the Education of the Gifted, 29*(4), 430–450. https://doi.org/10.4219/jeg-2006-244

Gross, M. U. M. (1993). *Exceptionally gifted children.* Routledge.

Gross, M. U. M. (2004). *Exceptionally gifted children* (2nd ed.). Routledge.

Gross, M. U. M. (2006). Exceptionally gifted children: Long-term outcomes of academic acceleration and non-acceleration. *Journal for the Education of the Gifted, 29*(4), 404–429. https://doi.org/10.4219/jeg-2006-247

Gross, M. U. M. (2009). Highly gifted young people: Development from childhood to adulthood. In L. V. Shavinina (Ed.), *International handbook on giftedness* (pp. 337–351). Springer.

Gustin, W. C. (1985). The development of exceptional research mathematicians. In B. S. Bloom (Ed.), *Developing talent in young people* (pp. 270–331). Ballantine Books.

Heller, K. A., Perleth, C., & Lim, T. K. (2005). The Munich Model of Giftedness designed to identify and promote gifted students. In R. J. Sternberg & J. E. Davidson (Eds.), *Conceptions of giftedness* (2nd ed., pp. 147–170). Cambridge University Press.

Henmon, V. A. C. (1921). Intelligence and its measurement: A symposium. *Journal of Educational Psychology, 12*(4), 195–198. https://doi.org/10.1037/h0076078

Hollingworth, L. S. (1936). The development of personality in highly intelligent children. *National Elementary Principal, 15*, 272–281.

Hollingworth, L. S. (1942). *Children above 180 IQ Stanford-Binet: Origin and development.* World Book.

Hong, E., Peng, Y., & O'Neil, H. G. (2014). Activities and accomplishments in various domains: Relationships with creative personality and creative motivation in adolescence. *Roeper Review, 36*(2), 92–103. https://doi.org/10.1080/02783193.2014.884199

Jackson, N., & Myers, M. (1982). Letter naming time, digit span, and precocious reading achievement. *Intelligence, 6*(3), 311–329. https://doi.org/10.1016/0160-2896(82)90007-1

Janos, P. M. (1983). *The psychological vulnerabilities of children of very superior intellectual ability* [Unpublished doctoral dissertation]. New York University.

Janos, P. M., Marwood, K. A., & Robinson, N. M. (1985). Friendship patterns in highly intelligent children. *Roeper Review, 8*(1), 46–49. https://doi.org/10.1080/02783198509552929

Jarvin, L., & Subotnik, R. F. (2015). Understanding elite talent in academic domains: A developmental trajectory from basic abilities to scholarly productivity/artistry. In F. A. Dixon & S. M. Moon (Eds.), *The handbook of secondary gifted education* (2nd ed., pp. 217–235). Prufrock Press.

Johnsen, S. K. (1997). Assessment beyond definitions. *Peabody Journal of Education, 72*(3–4), 136–152. https://doi.org/10.1080/0161956X.1997.9681870

Kanevsky, L. (1990). Pursuing qualitative differences in the flexible use of a problem-solving strategy by young children. *Journal for the Education of the Gifted, 13*(2), 115–140. https://doi.org/10.1177/016235329001300202

Kanevsky, L. (1992). The learning game. In P. S. Klein & A. J. Tannenbaum (Eds.), *To be young and gifted* (pp. 204–241). Ablex.

Kanevsky, L. (1994). A comparative study of children's learning in the zone of proximal development. *European Journal for High Ability, 5*(2), 163–175. https://doi.org/10.1080/0937445940050206

Kanevsky, L., & Geake, J. (2004). Inside the zone of proximal development: Validating a multifactor model of learning potential with gifted students and their peers. *Journal for the Education of the Gifted, 28*(2), 182–217. https://doi.org/10.1177/016235320402800204

Kanevsky, L., & Keighley, T. (2003). To produce or not to produce? Understanding boredom and the honor in underachievement. *Roeper Review, 26*(1), 20–28. https://doi.org/10.1080/02783190309554235

Kanevsky, L., & Rapagna, S. O. (1990). Dynamic analysis of problem-solving by average and high ability children. *Canadian Journal of Special Education, 6*(1), 15–30.

Kaufman, S. B. (2018). *The role of luck in life success is far greater than we realized*. Scientific American. https://blogs.scientificamerican.com/beautiful-minds/the-role-of-luck-in-life-success-is-far-greater-than-we-realized

Kay, S. I. (1991). The figural problem solving and problem finding of professional and semi-professional artists and nonartists. *Creativity Research Journal, 4*(3), 233–252. https://doi.org/10.1080/10400419109534396

Kay, S. I. (1996). The Talent Profile—Translating theory into practice. *Gems of AGATE, 20*, 4.

Kay, S. I. (2019). *On human potential: Nurturing talents and cultivating expertise*. Rowman & Littlefield.

Keating, D. P., & Bobbitt, B. L. (1978). Individual and developmental differences in cognitive processing components of mental ability. *Child Development, 49*(1), 155–167. https://doi.org/10.2307/1128604

Kell, H. J., Lubinski, D., Benbow, C. P., & Steiger, J. H. (2013). Creativity and technical innovation: Spatial ability's unique role. *Psychological Science, 24*(9), 1831–1836. https://doi.org/10.1177/0956797613478615

Klausmeier, H. J., & Check, J. (1962). Retention and transfer in children of low, average, and high intelligence. *Journal of Educational Research, 55*(7), 319–322.

Klausmeier, H. J., & Loughlin, L. J. (1961). Behaviors during problem solving among children of low, average, and high intelligence. *Journal of Educational Psychology, 52*(3), 148–152. https://doi.org/10.1037/h0042140

Krutetskii, V. A. (1976). *The psychology of mathematical abilities in school children* (J. Teller, Trans.). University of Chicago Press. (Original work published 1968)

Kulik, J. A. (2003). Grouping and tracking. In N. Colangelo & G. A. Davis (Eds.), *Handbook of gifted education* (3rd ed., pp. 268–281). Allyn & Bacon.

Kulik, J. A., & Kulik, C. C. (1984). Effects of accelerated instruction on students. *Review of Educational Research, 54*(3), 409–425. https://doi.org/10.3102/00346543054003409

Larkin, J. H., McDermott, J., Simon, D. P., & Simon, H. A. (1980). Expert and novice performance in solving physics problems. *Science, 208*(4450), 1335–1342. https://doi.org/10.1126/science.208.4450.1335

Leikin, R., Paz-Baruch, N., & Leikin, M. (2014). Cognitive characteristics of students with superior performance in mathematics. *Journal of Individual Differences, 35*(3), 119–129. https://doi.org/10.1027/1614-0001/a000140

Limont, W., Dreszer-Drogoród, J., Bedyńska, S., Śliwińska, K., & Jastrzębska, D. (2014). 'Old wine in new bottles'? Relationships between overexcitabilities, the Big Five personality traits and giftedness in adolescents. *Personality and Individual Differences, 69*, 199–204. https://doi.org/10.1016/j.paid.2014.06.003

Lohman, D. F. (1994). Spatial ability. In R. J. Sternberg (Ed.), *Encyclopedia of intelligence* (Vol. 2, pp. 1000–1007). Macmillan.

Lohman, D. F. (2006). Beliefs about differences between ability and accomplishment: From folk theories to cognitive science. *Roeper Review, 29*(1), 32–40. https://doi.org/10.1080/02783190609554382

Lohman, D. F. (2012). *Cognitive Abilities Test: Directions for administration (Form 7: Levels 10–17/18)*. Riverside.

Lubinski, D. (2016). From Terman to today: A century of findings on intellectual precocity. *Review of Educational Research, 86*(4), 900–944. https://doi.org/10.3102/0034654316675476

Lubinski, D., & Kell, H. J. (2018). Three crucial dimensions for students with intellectual gifts: It's time to stop talking and start thinking. In S. I. Pfeiffer, E. Shaunessy-Dedrick, & M. Foley-Nicpon (Eds.), *APA handbook of giftedness and talent* (pp. 479–496). American Psychological Association.

Mann, E. L. (2006). Creativity: The essence of mathematics. *Journal for the Education of the Gifted, 30*(2), 236–260. https://doi.org/10.4219/jeg-2006-264

Martin, L. T., Burns, R. M., & Schonlau, M. (2010). Mental disorders among gifted and nongifted youth: A selected review of the epidemiologic literature. *Gifted Child Quarterly, 54*(1), 31–41. https://doi.org/10.1177/0016986209352684

McCrae, R. R., Costa, P. T., Parker, W. D., & Mills, C. J. (2002). Personality trait development from age 12 to age 18: Longitudinal, cross-sectional, and cross-cultural analyses. *Journal of Personality and Social Psychology, 83*(6), 1456–1468. https://doi.org/10.1037/0022-3514.83.6.1456

Melby-Lervåg, M., Redick, T. S., & Hulme, C. (2016). Working memory training does not improve performance on measures of intelligence or other measures of "far transfer": Evidence from a meta-analytic review. *Perspectives on Psychological Science, 11*(4), 512–534. https://doi.org/10.1177/1745691616635612

Mendaglio, S. (2008). Dabrowski's Theory of Positive Disintegration: A personality theory for the 21st century. In S. Mendaglio (Ed.), *Dabrowski's theory of positive disintegration* (pp. 13–40). Great Potential Press.

Milgram, R. M. (2003). Challenging out-of-school activities as a predictor of creative accomplishments in art, drama, dance, and social leadership. *Scandinavian Journal of Educational Research, 47*(3), 305–315. https://doi.org/10.1080/00313830308599

Milgram, R. M., & Hong, E. (1999). Creative out-of-school activities in intellectually gifted adolescents as predictors of their life accomplishments in young adults: A longitudinal study. *Creativity Research Journal, 12*(2), 77–87. https://doi.org/10.1207/s15326934crj1202_1

Mofield, E. L., & Parker Peters, M. (2018). Shifting the perfectionistic mindset: Moving to mindful excellence. *Gifted Child Today, 41*(4), 177–185. https://doi.org/10.1177/1076217518786989

Mosing, M. A., Madison, G., Pedersen, N. L., Kuja-Halkola, R., & Ullén, F. (2014). Practice does not make perfect: No causal effect of music practice on music ability. *Psychological Science, 25*(9), 1795–1803. https://doi.org/10.1177/0956797614541990

Muratori, M. C., Stanley, J. C., Ng, L., Ng, J., Gross, M. U. M., Tao, T., & Tao, B. (2006). Insights from SMPY's greatest former child prodigies: Drs. Terence ("Terry") Tao and Lenhard ("Lenny") Ng reflect on their talent development. *Gifted Child Quarterly, 50*(4), 307–324. https://doi.org/10.1177/001698620605000404

Myers, T., Carey, E., & Szűcs, D. (2017). Cognitive and neural correlates of mathematical giftedness in adults and children: A review. *Frontiers in Psychology, 8,* 1646. https://doi.org/10.3389/fpsyg.2017.01646

Olszewski-Kubilius, P. (2015). The role of out-of-school program in talent development for secondary students. In F. A. Dixon & S. M. Moon (Eds.), *The handbook of secondary gifted education* (2nd ed., pp. 261–281). Prufrock Press.

Otis, A. S., & Lennon, R. T. (1997). *Otis-Lennon School Ability Test* (7th ed.). Harcourt Brace.

Park, G., Lubinski, D., & Benbow, C. P. (2007). Contrasting intellectual patterns predict creativity in the Arts and Sciences: Tracking intellectually precocious youth over 25 years. *Psychological Science, 18*(11), 948–952. https://doi.org/10.1111/j.1467-9280.2007.02007.x

Patrick, H., Ryan, A. M., Alfeld-Liro, C., Fredricks, J. A., Hruda, L. Z., & Eccles, J. C. (1999). Adolescents' commitment to developing talent: The role of peers in continuing motivation for sports and the arts. *Journal of Youth and Adolescence, 28*(6), 741–763. https://doi.org/10.1023/A:1021643718575

Perkins, D. N. (1994). Creativity: Beyond the Darwinian paradigm. In M. A. Boden (Ed.), *Dimensions of creativity* (pp. 119–142). MIT Press.

Piechowski, M. M. (1998). The self victorious: Personal strengths, chance, and co-incidence. *Roeper Review, 20*(3), 191–199. https://doi.org/10.1080/02783199809553890

Piechowski, M. M. (2003). Emotional and spiritual giftedness. In N. Colangelo & G. A. Davis (Eds.), *Handbook of gifted education* (3rd ed., pp. 403–416). Allyn & Bacon.

Piechowski, M. M. (2008). Discovering Dabrowski's theory. In S. Mendaglio (Ed.), *Dabrowski's theory of positive disintegration* (pp. 41–77). Great Potential Press.

Pluchino, A., Biondo, A. E., & Rapisarda, A. (2018). Talent versus luck: The role of randomness in success and failure. *Advances in Complex Systems, 21*(3–4), 1850014. https://doi.org/10.1142/S0219525918500145

Poincaré, H. (1952). *Science and method* (F. Maitland, Trans.). Dover. (Original work published 1908)

Protzko, J. (2017). Effects of cognitive training on the structure of intelligence. *Psychonomic Bulletin & Review, 24*, 1022–1031. https://doi.org/10.3758/s13423-016-1196-1

Rathunde, K., & Csikszentmihalyi, M. (1993). Undivided interest and the growth of talent: A longitudinal study of adolescents. *Journal of Youth and Adolescence, 22*(4), 385–405. https://doi.org/10.1007/BF01537720

Raven, J. C. (1998). *Raven's Progressive Matrices*. Pearson.

Rea, D. (2000). Optimal motivation for talent development. *Journal for the Education of the Gifted, 23*(2), 187–216. https://doi.org/10.4219/jeg-2000-574

Renzulli, J. S. (2005). The three-ring conception of giftedness: A developmental model for promoting creative productivity. In R. J. Sternberg &

J. E. Davidson (Eds.), *Conceptions of giftedness* (2nd ed., pp. 246–279). Cambridge University Press.

Robinson, N. M. (2000). Giftedness in very young children: How seriously should it be taken? In R. C. Friedman & B. M. Shore (Eds.), *Talents unfolding: Cognition and development* (pp. 7–26). American Psychological Association.

Robinson, N. M. (2008). The social world of gifted children and youth. In S. Pfeiffer (Ed.), *Handbook of giftedness in children: Psychoeducational theory, research, and best practices* (pp. 33–51). Springer.

Rogers, K. B. (1986). Do the gifted think and learn differently? A review of recent research and its implications for instruction. *Journal for the Education of the Gifted, 10*(1), 17–39. https://doi.org/10.1177/016235328601000103

Rogers, K. B. (2015). The academic, socialization, and psychological effects of acceleration: Research synthesis. In S. G. Assouline, N. Colangelo, J. VanTassel-Baska, & A. Lupkowski-Shoplik (Eds.), *A nation empowered: Evidence trumps the excuses holding back America's brightest students* (Vol. 2, pp. 19–29). The University of Iowa, The Connie Belin & Jacqueline N. Blank International Center for Gifted Education and Talent Development.

Roid, G. H. (2003). *Stanford-Binet Intelligence Scales* (5th ed.). Riverside.

Schneider, W. J., & McGrew, K. S. (2018). The Cattell-Horn-Carroll theory of cognitive abilities. In D. P. Flanagan & E. M. McDonough (Eds.), *Contemporary intellectual assessment: Theories, tests, and issues* (4th ed., pp. 73–163). Guilford Press.

Schrank, F. A., McGrew, K. S., Mather, N., Wendling, B. J., LaForte, E. M., & Riverside Publishing Company. (2014). *Woodcock-Johnson IV tests of achievement*. Riverside.

Schunk, D. H., Pintrich, P. R., & Meece, J. L. (2008). *Motivation in education: Theory, research, and applications* (3rd ed.). Pearson.

Scruggs, T. E., & Mastropieri, M. A. (1985). Spontaneous verbal elaborations in gifted and nongifted youths. *Journal for the Education of the Gifted, 9*(1), 1–10. https://doi.org/10.1177/016235328500900102

Scruggs, T. E., & Mastropieri, M. A. (1988). Acquisition and transfer of learning strategies by gifted and nongifted students. *Journal of Special Education, 22*(2), 153–166. https://doi.org/10.1177/002246698802200203

Shavinina, L. V., & Kholodnaja, M. A. (1996). The cognitive experience as a psychological basis of intellectual giftedness. *Journal for the Education of the Gifted, 20*(1), 3–35. https://doi.org/10.1177/016235329602000102

Sheppard, S., & Kanevsky, L. S. (1999). Nurturing gifted students' metacognitive awareness: Effects of training in homogeneous and heterogeneous classes. *Roeper Review, 21*(4), 266–272. https://doi.org/10.1080/02783199909553974

Shore, B. M., Chichekian, T., Gyles, P. D. T., & Walker, C. L. (2019). Friendships of gifted children and youth: Updated insights and understanding. In B. Wallace, D. A. Sisk, & J. Senior (Eds.), *The SAGE handbook of gifted and talented education* (pp. 184–195). SAGE.

Shore, B. M., Coleman, E. B., & Moss, E. (1992). Cognitive psychology and the use of protocols in the understanding of giftedness and high level thinking. In F. Monks & W. Peters (Eds.), *Talent for the future: Social and personality development of gifted children* (pp. 259–263). Van Gorcum.

Shore, B. M., & Dover, A. C. (1987). Metacognition, intelligence and giftedness. *Gifted Child Quarterly, 31*(1), 37–39. https://doi.org/10.1177/001698628703100108

Shore, B. M., & Kanevsky, L. (1993). Thinking processes: Being and becoming gifted. In K. A. Heller, F. J. Monks, & A. H. Passow (Eds.), *International handbook for research and development on giftedness and talent* (pp. 133–148). Pergamon.

Siegler, R. S., & Kotovsky, K. (1986). Two levels of giftedness: Shall ever the twain meet? In R. J. Sternberg & J. E. Davidson (Eds.), *Conceptions of giftedness* (pp. 417–435). Cambridge University Press.

Silverman, L. K. (2008). The theory of positive disintegration in the field of gifted education. In S. Mendaglio (Ed.), *Dabrowski's theory of positive disintegration* (pp. 157–173). Great Potential Press.

Simonton, D. K. (1994). *Greatness: Who makes history and why*. Guilford Press.

Simonton, D. K. (2004). *Creativity in science: Chance, logic, genius and zeitgeist*. Cambridge University Press.

Simonton, D. K., & Song, A. V. (2009). Eminence, IQ, physical and mental health, and achievement domain: Cox's 282 geniuses revisited. *Psychological Science, 20*(4), 429–434. https://doi.org/10.1111/j.1467-9280.2009.02313.x

Skuy, M., Kaniel, S., & Tzuriel, D. (1988). Dynamic assessment of intellectually superior Israeli children in a low socio-economic status community. *Gifted Education International, 5*(2), 90–96. https://doi.org/10.1177/026142948800500207

Sosniak, L. (1985). Phases of learning. In B. S. Bloom (Ed.), *Developing talent in young people* (pp. 409–438). Ballantine Books.

Southern, W. T., & Jones, E. D. (2015). Types of acceleration: Dimensions and issues. In S. G. Assouline, N. Colangelo, J. VanTassel-Baska, & A. Lupkowski-Shoplik (Eds.), *A nation empowered: Evidence trumps the excuses holding back America's brightest students* (Vol. 2, pp. 9–18). The University of Iowa, The Connie Belin & Jacqueline N. Blank International Center for Gifted Education and Talent Development.

Spearman, C. (1904). "General intelligence," objectively determined and measured. *The American Journal of Psychology, 15*(2), 201–292. https://doi.org/10.2307/1412107

Spearman, C. (1927). *The abilities of man: Their nature and measurement.* Macmillan.

Stanley, J. C. (1996). In the beginning: The Study of Mathematically Precocious Youth. In C. P. Benbow & D. Lubinski (Eds.), *Intellectual talent: Psychometric and social issues* (pp. 225–235). Johns Hopkins University Press.

Sternberg, R. J. (2005a). WICS: A model of giftedness in leadership, *Roeper Review, 28*(1), 37–44. https://doi.org/10.1080/02783190509554335

Sternberg, R. J. (2005b). The WICS Model of Giftedness. In R. J. Sternberg & J. E. Davidson (Eds.), *Conceptions of giftedness* (2nd ed., pp. 327–342). Cambridge University Press.

Sternberg, R. J., & Davidson, J. E. (Eds.). (2005). *Conceptions of giftedness* (2nd ed.). Cambridge University Press.

Sternberg, R. J., & Grigorenko, E. L. (2002). *Dynamic testing: The nature and measurement of learning potential.* Cambridge University Press.

Sternberg, R. J., & Kaufman, S. B. (2018). Theories and conceptions of giftedness. In S. I. Pfeiffer (Ed.), *Handbook of giftedness in children: Psychoeducational theory, research, and best practices* (pp. 29–47). Springer.

Sternberg, R. J., Jarvin, L., & Grigorenko, E. L. (2011). *Explorations in giftedness.* Cambridge University Press.

Subotnik, R. F., & Jarvin, L. (2005). Beyond expertise: Conceptions of giftedness as great performance. In R. J. Sternberg & J. E. Davidson (Eds.), *Conceptions of giftedness* (2nd ed., pp. 343–357). Cambridge University Press.

Subotnik, R. F., Olszewski-Kubilius, P., & Worrell, F. C. (2011). Rethinking giftedness and gifted education: A proposed direction forward based on psychological science. *Psychological Science in the Public Interest, 12*(1), 3–54. https://doi.org/10.1177/1529100611418056

Subotnik, R. F., Olszewski-Kubilius, P., & Worrell, F. C. (Eds.). (2019). *The psychology of high performance: Developing human potential into domain-specific talent.* American Psychological Association.

Subotnik, R. F., Pillmeier, E., & Jarvin, L. (2009). The psychosocial dimensions of creativity in mathematics. In R. Leikin, A. Berman, & B. Koichu (Eds.), *Creativity in mathematics and the education of gifted students* (pp. 165–179). Sense.

Swanson, H. L., & Lussier, C. M. (2001). A selective synthesis of the experimental literature on dynamic assessment. *Review of Educational Research, 71*(2), 321–363. https://doi.org/10.3102/00346543071002321

Tannenbaum, A. J. (1983). *Gifted children: Psychological and educational perspectives.* Macmillan.

Tannenbaum, A. J. (1986a). Giftedness: a psychosocial approach. In R. J. Sternberg & J. E. Davidson (Eds.), *Conceptions of giftedness* (pp. 21–52). Cambridge University Press.

Tannenbaum, A. J. (1986b). The enrichment matrix model. In J. S. Renzulli (Ed.), *Systems and models for developing programs for the gifted and talented* (pp. 391–428). Creative Learning Press.

Tannenbaum, A. J. (1996). The IQ controversy and the gifted. In C. P. Benbow & D. Lubinski (Eds.), *Intellectual talent: Psychometric and social issues* (pp. 44–77). Johns Hopkins University Press.

Tannenbaum, A. J. (1997). The meaning and making of giftedness. In N. Colangelo & G. A. Davis (Eds.), *Handbook of gifted education* (2nd ed., pp. 27–42). Allyn & Bacon.

Tannenbaum, A. J. (2003). Nature and nurture of giftedness. In N. Colangelo & G. A. Davis (Eds.), *Handbook of gifted education* (3rd ed., 45–59). Allyn & Bacon.

Tannenbaum, A. J. (2009). Defining, determining, discovering, and developing excellence. In J. S. Renzulli, E. J. Gubbins, K. S. McMillen, R. D. Eckert, & C. A. Little (Eds.), *Systems and models for developing programs for the gifted and talented* (2nd ed., pp. 503–569). Prufrock Press.

Terman, L. M. (1925). *Genetic studies of genius: Vol. 1. Mental and physical traits of a thousand gifted children.* Stanford University Press.

Terman, L. M., & Oden, M. H. (1947). *Genetic studies of genius: Vol. 4. The gifted group grows up: Twenty-five years' follow-up of a superior group.* Stanford University Press.

Terman, L. M., & Oden, M. H. (1959). *Genetic studies of genius: Vol. 5. The gifted group at mid-life: Thirty-five years' follow up of the superior child.* Stanford University Press.

Thomson, D., & Olszewski-Kubilius, P. (2013). The increasingly important role of off-level testing in the context of the talent development perspective. *Gifted Child Today, 37*(1), 33–40. https://doi.org/10.1177/1076217513509619

Thorndike, R. (1985). The central role of general ability in prediction. *Multivariate Behavioral Research, 20*(3), 241–254. https://doi.org/10.1207/s15327906mbr2003_1

VanTassel-Baska, J., & Stambaugh, T. (2006). *Comprehensive curriculum for gifted learners* (3rd ed.). Pearson Education.

Vuyk, M. A., Krieshok, T. S., & Kerr, B. A. (2016). Openness to experience rather than overexcitabilities: Call it like it is. *Gifted Child Quarterly, 60*(3), 192–211. https://doi.org/10.1177/0016986216645407

Vygotsky, L. S. (1978). *Mind in society: The development of higher psychological processes*. Harvard University Press.

Vygotsky, L. S. (1997). *Educational psychology* (R. Silverman, Trans.). St. Lucie Press. (Original work published 1926)

Wai, J., Lubinski, D., & Benbow, C. P. (2009). Spatial ability for STEM domains: Aligning over 50 years of cumulative psychological knowledge solidifies its importance. *Journal of Educational Psychology, 101*(4), 817–835. https://doi.org/10.1037/a0016127

Wai, J., Lubinski, D., Benbow, C. P., & Steiger, J. H. (2010). Accomplishment in science, technology, engineering, and mathematics (STEM) and its relation to STEM educational dose: A 25-year longitudinal study. *Journal of Educational Psychology, 102*(4), 860–871. https://doi.org/10.1037/a0019454

Warne, R. T., & Burningham, C. (2019). Spearman's g found in 31 non-Western nations: Strong evidence that g is a universal phenomenon. *Psychological Bulletin, 145*(3), 237–272. https://doi.org/10.1037/bul0000184

Weber, R. J., & Perkins, D. N. (1992). *Inventive minds: Creativity in technology*. Oxford University Press.

Wechsler, D. (2012). *Wechsler preschool and primary scale of intelligence* (4th ed.). Pearson.

Wechsler, D. (2014). *Wechsler intelligence scale for children* (5th ed.). Pearson.

Winner, E. (1996). The rage to master: The decisive case for talent in the visual arts. In K. A. Ericsson (Ed.), *The road to excellence: The acquisition of expert performance in the arts and sciences, sports and games* (pp. 271–301). Erlbaum.

Winner, E., & Drake, J. E. (2018). Giftedness and expertise: The case for genetic potential. *Journal of Expertise, 1*(2), 1–7.

Wirthwein, L., Bergold, S., Preckel, F., & Steinmayr, R. (2019). Personality and school functioning of intellectually gifted and nongifted adolescents: Self-perceptions and parents' assessments. *Learning and Individual Differences, 73*, 16–29. https://doi.org/10.1016/j.lindif.2019.04.003

Worrell, F. C., & Dixson, D. D. (2018). Recruiting and retaining underrepresented gifted students. In S. Pfeiffer (Ed.), *Handbook of giftedness in children: Psychoeducational theory, research, and best practices* (2nd ed., pp. 209–226). Springer.

Worrell, F. C., Subotnik, R. F., & Olszewski-Kubilius, P. (2018). Talent development: A path toward eminence. In S. I. Pfeiffer, E. Shaunessy-Dedrick, & M. Foley-Nicpon (Eds.), *APA handbook of giftedness and talent* (pp. 247–258). American Psychological Association.

Yaqub, O. (2018). Serendipity: Towards a taxonomy and a theory. *Research Policy, 47*(1), 169–179. https://doi.org/10.1016/j.respol.2017.10.007

Zeidner, M., & Shani-Zinovich, I. (2011). Do academically gifted and nongifted students differ on the Big-Five and adaptive status? Some recent data and conclusions. *Personality and Individual Differences, 51*(5), 566–570. https://doi.org/10.1016/j.paid.2011.05.007

Zuckerman, H. (1977). *Scientific elite: Nobel laureates in the United States*. Free Press.

CHAPTER 5

The Three-Ring Conception of Giftedness and the Schoolwide Enrichment Model

A Talent Development Approach for All Students

JOSEPH S. RENZULLI AND SALLY M. REIS

> You never change things by fighting the existing reality. To change something, build a new model that makes that existing model obsolete.
>
> —R. Buckminster Fuller

When Ian signed up for an enrichment cluster called "Young Inventors," he never dreamed that he would eventually compete in the finals of the National Invention Convention. Enrichment clusters are one of the talent development components in the Schoolwide Enrichment Model (SEM) that are open to all students (Renzulli et al., 2013). Ian, who is an average-achieving student, is interested in electronics and mechanics, and he is also very creative. This enrichment cluster allowed him to express his creativity through his interests. Ian came up with an idea for an electronic attachment that would turn on a light when his dog's water bowl needed to be refilled. Ian's classroom teacher and the facilitator of the enrichment cluster on inventions provided the opportunities, resources, and encouragement that helped Ian turn his idea into an award-winning reality that led to an appearance on local television and a trip to the Henry Ford Museum in Detroit for the National Invention Convention.

Any plan to define, identify, and develop gifted behaviors and talents in young people, like the one described in this chapter, should integrate a series of guidelines or considerations based on research and many years of collective experience gained from involvement in gifted education programming and lessons learned from students like Ian (Callahan et al., 2012). We believe that the enjoyable, creative productive, and talent development experiences that children and young adults have in school can and will increase the likelihood that they will seek to find and create these opportunities in their subsequent work and personal lives. And when they do, the world will benefit from an increasing number of creative and personally meaningful contributions.

General Issues Related to Theories of Gifted Education and Talent Development

Taken collectively, our introductory considerations can be summarized in two general principles that will be addressed in this chapter. First and foremost, a direct relationship should exist between the identification system and the types of services offered in the talent development program developed for schools. If, for example, the program is designed to provide advanced level curriculum in math, then it is logical and appropriate to examine math scores and achievement levels in this discipline to make identification and selection decisions. If, on the other hand, a program is developed to respond to individual student interests, to promote investigative skills and mindsets, and to encourage creative productivity in students' strength areas, then a logical identification system that assesses these areas should be considered. The information-gathering and identification process for this type of program should include performance-based assessment as well as other instruments and procedures. In other words, the identification system should follow rather than precede the development of program practices.

A second principle is that the educational services provided to students should be theory-based and research-driven. The identification practices, therefore, should also maintain some integrity to the theory and respect for the research generated by the theory. A theory is simply an organized and integrated set of ideas formed by speculation based on previous knowledge, experience, reflection, observation, and past practice. Theories are not inherently "good" or "bad," but they do reflect ideas, purposes, and values deemed important to persons who have developed or adopted a given theory. The most important roles of a theory are, first, to guide an action-oriented service delivery plan or model that effects practical activities taking place in schools, classrooms, and other places where learning occurs; and second, to guide research about the effectiveness of those practices.

Theories themselves are not really the objects of research and evaluation. Rather, the purposes and practical applications guided by the theories should be the objects of research and evaluation. A caution should be offered, however, about interpreting this research. Some outcome behaviors are more easily and precisely measured than others. In the two examples mentioned previously (math achievement and creative productivity), it is far easier to measure gains in math achievement than it is to evaluate the quality, innovation, and impact of a creative product, be it a story, science experiment, or community action project. These nuances are important to consider when evaluating the research that supports a theory.

To summarize, theories provide the big ideas, foundational values, purposes, and consistency designed to guide practice. The components of a service delivery model based on a theory should leverage one another so that recommended practices are consistent with the purposes set forth in the theory, rather than being merely a random collection of activities and "flavor-of-the-month" events. Theories provide guidance for research and program evaluation, but practice is what counts when examining the quality of models designed to develop talents in young people.

The Big Picture About Talent Development

The first thing to consider when examining the big picture is that talent development initiatives are influenced by the larger changes taking place in the world. Recent shifts in the goals of general education, the unprecedented changes happening in technology, and rapidly changing world conditions all affect the field of talent development. Who would have thought 3 or 4 decades ago that gifted education leaders would have advocated developing creativity and thinking skills for all students, or that a student at a rural school in the middle of the country could take an Advanced Placement or online accelerated course remotely from an Ivy League university, or that most of the world's knowledge could be downloaded into a young person's computer at any hour of the day or night? Who would have imagined that the majority of today's jobs would depend upon computers or be replaced by robots and applications of artificial intelligence and virtual reality? These changes have been compared to the transformations that took place during the Industrial Revolution. The resulting necessity is that education must adapt to a digitally based rather than an industrial economy.

Changes in technology and the demands of present and future job market realities have also set the stage for a new interest in the ongoing theme of our Schoolwide Enrichment Model (Renzulli & Reis, 1985, 1997, 2014). Simply stated, we believe now, as we have over the last 4 decades in which the SEM has been implemented, that *schools should be places for talent development*. A talent development approach must move beyond various iterations of standards-based learning and the current knowledge-based curriculum, no matter how fast and advanced those standards and that curriculum may be. Our SEM talent development model resists the temptation to standardize students. Our focus in the SEM is on the flexible development of a broad range of thinking skills, an attitudinal focus on and mindset of creative productivity, and the effective *application* of both stored knowledge and just-in-time knowledge.

Today's students must acquire a broad range of thinking skills and executive functions that will be able to be applied to careers and conditions that don't currently exist, and they must become lifelong learners who are experts in learning how to learn, because they will need to continually adapt to a future that cannot be predicted. Countries interested in improving their economy and in promoting the social and cultural contributions that improve people's lives need to have teachers who can prepare their students in the topics of creativity, thinking skills, problem solving, and executive functions so critical for today's changing job market. Employers in all businesses and industries desperately need young people with these skills. One need only look at the growth in places such as Silicon Valley and the design centers in Italy to see how changing demands in the workplace should provide a new direction for the education system.

What does this unprecedented change mean for the ways educators assess student potential, manage classrooms, and attempt to promote talent development in young people? This question and an examination of the skills of creative and productive people guided us in the development of the SEM. Regardless of how, when, or where learning takes place, one thing that has remained stable in our work is the knowledge is that all learning exists on a continuum ranging from deductive, didactic, and prescriptive on one hand, to inductive, investigative, and inquiry-oriented on the other. Our SEM talent development approach favors the inductive-investigative side of the continuum because we believe that the major purpose of talent development programs should be to increase the world's reservoir of creative and productive young people.

The Theories Underlying the SEM

The second part of the big picture is the set of theories underlying the Schoolwide Enrichment Model, which is the major focus of this chapter. Fundamental to the four theories related to talent development that are depicted in Figure 5.1 is a general theory of knowledge that focuses on the interaction between and among Received Knowledge, Analyzed Knowledge, and Applied Knowledge (Renzulli & De Wet, 2010; Renzulli, 2016). This theory calls attention to the important differences between To-Be-Presented Knowledge (textbooks, standards, unit plans, and test prep) and Just-In-Time Knowledge (knowledge a person only accesses when it is needed to address a problem they are working on). The four theories in Figure 5.1 are described in detail elsewhere (Renzulli, 2012); therefore, we briefly review them before moving on to the more practical aspects of our approach to talent development using the Three-Ring Conception of Giftedness and the Schoolwide Enrichment Model.

The Three-Ring Conception of Giftedness (Renzulli, 1978) calls attention to the fact that educators must examine a variety of potentials in addition to measures of cognitive ability; this interaction between and among

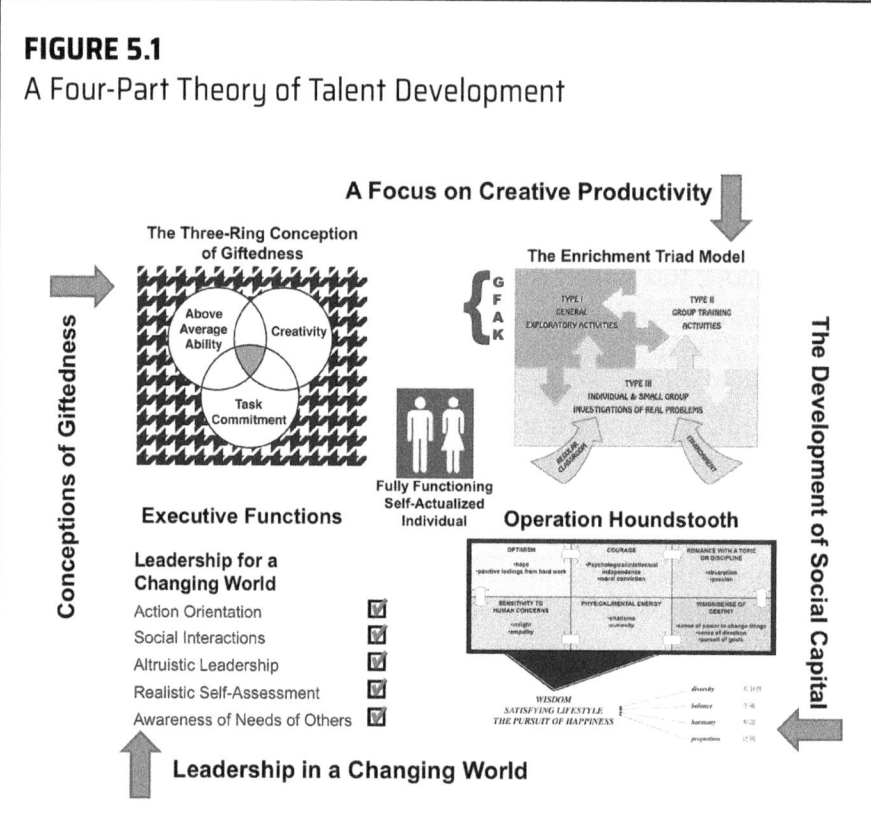

FIGURE 5.1
A Four-Part Theory of Talent Development

Note. From *The Schoolwide Enrichment Model: A How-to Guide for Talent Development* (3rd ed., p. 14), by J. S. Renzulli and S. M. Reis, 2014, Taylor & Francis. Copyright 2014 by Taylor & Francis. Reprinted with permission.

Above-Average Ability, Creativity, and Task Commitment produces "gifted behaviors." It should be noted that "ability" takes into consideration both traditional academic performance and areas such as music, the arts, leadership, physical performance, and other non- or co-cognitive skills. It should also be pointed out that creativity and task commitment feed upon one another. A creative idea may ignite the task commitment for an active talent development project, and likewise, a commitment to bring about a needed change may promote the generation of creative ideas.

The Enrichment Triad Model is the pedagogical core of the SEM, and it identifies two categories of general enrichment (Types I and II), which we recommend for all students, and a third category (Type III), which is appropriate for some students. These three types of enrichment are explained in depth later in this chapter but are introduced briefly here for context. Type I Enrichment consists of general exploratory experiences that expose young people to new interests and potential areas of follow-up. Type II Enrichment consists of training activities in the following six categories: Cognitive Thinking Skills; Character Development Skills; Learning How-To-Learn Skills; Using Advanced Research and Reference Skills; Written, Oral, and Communication Skills; and Metacognitive Technology Skills. Type III Enrichment includes individual and small-group investigations of real problems; it is this type of enrichment that we have seen the most innovative and creative examples of talent development (c.f., Ian's dog bowl light).

The theory entitled Operation Houndstooth (Renzulli et al., 2006; Renzulli & D'Souza, 2012) calls attention to the development of social and emotional factors that that can help young people use their gifts and talents to do good work and to make the world a better place. The theory entitled Leadership for a Changing World focuses on executive function skills, such as organizing, planning, having an action orientation, realistic self-assessment, and communication and collaboration.

Note that the four theories interact with one another. Our focus in this chapter is on the practical applications of the Three-Ring Conception of Giftedness and the Schoolwide Enrichment Model.

The Three-Ring Conception of Giftedness

The Three-Ring Conception of Giftedness (Renzulli, 1978, 1986, 2005; see Figure 5.2) is the definition of giftedness that accompanies the SEM programming model, and it is designed to develop both academic/high-achieving and creative productive types of giftedness (Renzulli & Reis, 1985, 1997, 2014). Both types of giftedness are important; they often interact, and both should be developed in high-potential youth who participate in special gifted and talented and enrichment programs.

The SEM programming model discussed in this chapter is supported by decades of research (Reis & Renzulli, 2003; Renzulli & Reis, 1997), as are the clusters of ability that describe highly intelligent, creative productive individuals. This research about these models has consistently demonstrated

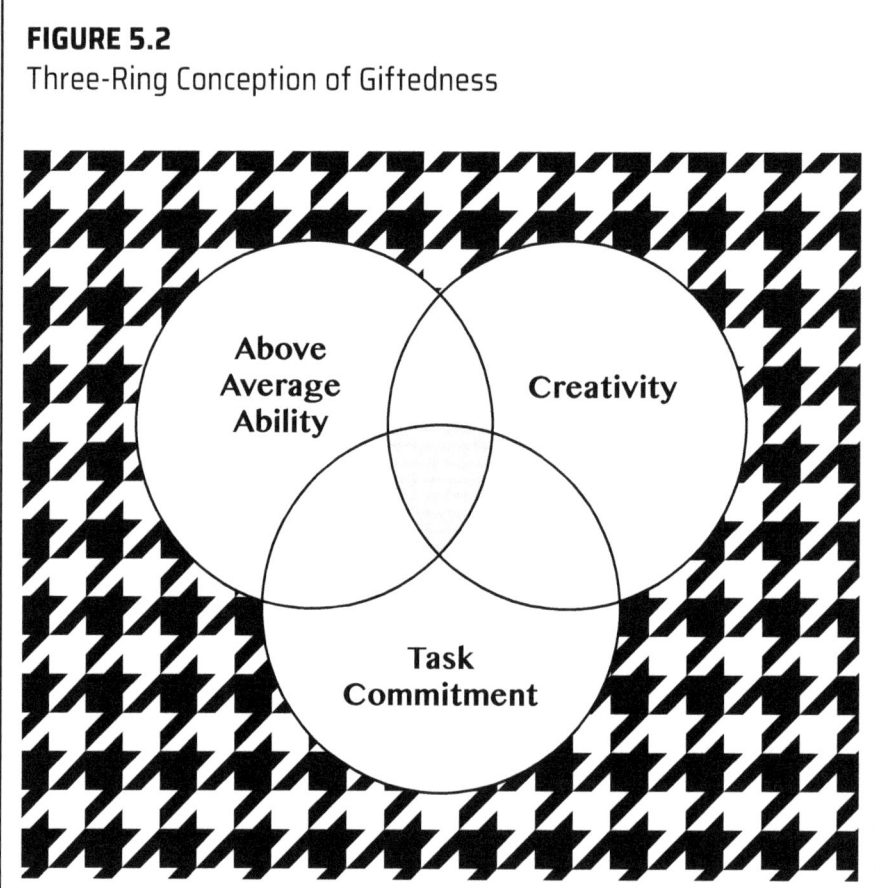

FIGURE 5.2
Three-Ring Conception of Giftedness

Note. From *The Schoolwide Enrichment Model: A How-to Guide for Talent Development* (3rd ed., p. 22), by J. S. Renzulli and S. M. Reis, 2014, Taylor & Francis. Copyright 2014 by Taylor & Francis. Reprinted with permission.

that although no single criterion can be used to determine giftedness, persons who have achieved recognition because of their unique accomplishments and creative contributions possess a relatively well-defined set of three interlocking clusters of traits (Renzulli, 1978, 1986, 1988, 1999, 2002, 2005). These clusters include above-average (not necessarily superior) ability, task commitment, and creativity. No single cluster "makes giftedness"; rather, the interaction, represented by the shaded portion in Figure 5.2, has been shown to be the necessary ingredient for creative productive accomplishment (Renzulli, 1978, 1986, 2005). Each cluster plays an important role in contributing to the display of gifted behaviors. Comprehensive reviews of the literature on these clusters have, over time, provided updated pertinent research supporting this definition (Renzulli, 1978, 1986, 1988, 1999, 2002, 2005). Each cluster is described in detail in the sections that follow.

Above Average Ability

Above Average Ability includes both general and specific ability. We define *general ability* as the capacity to process information, integrate experiences that result in appropriate and adaptive responses in new situations, and engage in abstract thinking in areas such as verbal and numerical reasoning, spatial relations, memory, and word fluency. General abilities are most often measured by tests of general aptitude or intelligence and are broadly applicable to a variety of traditional learning situations. General ability can be applied across all domains (e.g., general intelligence) or broad domains (e.g., general verbal ability applied to several dimensions of the language arts). Examples of general ability are verbal and numerical reasoning, spatial relations, memory, and word fluency, which can usually be measured by tests of general aptitude or intelligence and are broadly applicable to a variety of traditional learning situations. Research support for the concept of the Above Average Ability cluster has been discussed in previous research syntheses (Renzulli, 1978, 1986, 1988, 1992, 1999, 2005) but is also found in Sternberg's (1985, 1988, 1996) voluminous work.

Sternberg's (1988) Triarchic Theory of Intelligence includes analytical intelligence, defined as evaluation, comparison, and contrast of information, which is precisely the type of intelligence typically considered in traditional academic settings. Practical intelligence, the second component of the triarchic theory, involves the application of an individual's abilities to the types of problems one encounters in daily life by adapting to, shaping, and selecting the environment. Sternberg (1996) asserted that practical intelligence is a better predictor of successful academic and occupational outcome in life than standard IQ tests and other cognitive tests. Sternberg's third dimension of his triarchic theory, creative intelligence, also provides research support for that cluster in the Three-Ring Conception.

Specific ability is the capacity to acquire knowledge and skill or the ability to perform in one or more activities of a specialized kind and within a restricted range, defined as the ways human beings express themselves in real-life, authentic situations. Examples of specific abilities include areas such as biology, ballet, mathematics, musical composition, sculpture, and photography. Each specific ability can further subdivide into more specific areas (e.g., portrait photography, astrophotography, photojournalism, etc.). Certain specific abilities, in areas such as mathematics and chemistry, have a strong relationship with general ability, and, therefore, some indication of potential in these areas can be determined from tests of general aptitude and intelligence. Some specific abilities can be measured by achievement tests and tests of specific aptitude, but other specific abilities are not easily measured by standardized tests. Examples include leadership, fine arts abilities, "street smarts," and planning and decision-making abilities that must be evaluated in different ways. Assessment of this type of specific abilities usually can only occur by highly skilled observers using specific performance assessments.

In the Three-Ring Conception of Giftedness, the Above Average Ability cluster includes both general and specific abilities. Above-average ability is an upper range of potential within any given area, and although it is difficult to assign numerical values to specific areas of ability, we define above-average ability individuals as those who are capable of high-level performance or the potential for performance. This potential is usually representative of the top quintile of any given area of human endeavor, or in other words, individuals who are generally capable of graduating from competitive 4-year colleges, universities, or conservatories.

Task Commitment

The second cluster of traits consistently exhibited by creative productive persons is a refined or focused form of motivation, which Renzulli (1978) termed "task commitment" more than 3 decades ago and which has more recently gained attention in Duckworth's theory of grit (Duckworth et al., 2007). Whereas motivation is usually defined in terms of a general energizing process that triggers responses, task commitment represents focused motivation that is brought to bear upon a particular problem (task) or specific performance area. The terms that are most frequently used to describe task commitment are *perseverance, endurance, hard work, dedicated practice, self-confidence,* and *a belief in one's ability to carry out important work.* In addition to perceptiveness and a better capacity to identify significant problems, research on persons of high levels of accomplishment has consistently shown that a special fascination for and involvement with content that is of high interest is of critical importance in the talent development process (Renzulli, 1978, 1986, 2005). The young people studied by Bloom and

Sosniak (1981) in one of the most well-regarded studies of sustained talent development, for example, displayed early evidence of task commitment.

Research support for including task commitment in a definition of giftedness has increased in recent years. From popular maxims and autobiographical accounts to research about the role of effort and sustained interest (Duckworth et al., 2007; Dweck, 2006/2016; Tough, 2012), task commitment, as well as focus and effort, have emerged as necessary traits employed by successful individuals who can immerse themselves totally in a specific problem or area for an extended period of time. Indeed, grit is defined as the tendency to sustain interest in and effort toward very long-term goals (Duckworth et al., 2007).

Renzulli's earlier research (1978, 1986, 2005) on persons with high levels of creative productive behavior consistently reinforced that high levels of task commitment were part of a cluster of characteristic traits. Although this second cluster of traits is not as easily and objectively identifiable as general cognitive abilities, task commitment is a major contributor to the development of gifted behaviors.

Creativity

The third cluster of traits necessary for the development of skills leading to creative productivity includes factors usually characterized under the general heading of "creativity." Kaufman and Beghetto (2009) estimated that there have been more than 10,000 papers written about creativity in the last decade or so, across diverse areas of psychology, so summarizing research on this increasingly complex area is challenging. Several researchers, including Kaufman and Beghetto (2009), suggested that current creativity research follows one of two trends. The first focuses on eminence and creative genius, usually labeled as *Big-C* creativity. The second trend focuses on everyday creativity (Richards, 1990) and includes the creative work or activities of students or children, often called *little-c* creativity. Our work on the Three-Ring Conception of Giftedness has led us to understand that the little-c opportunities that are a core part of the SEM can inspire students to pursue the Big-C creativity that may emerge in the years that follow. Longitudinal research suggests that this is the case. Hébert (1993) found that the creative projects of school-age students had an impact on their postsecondary decisions and plans. He also found that the high creative opportunities in elementary and middle SEM programs encouraged students to seek creative outlets in high school. Students who experienced high levels of creative productivity, especially those who completed sustained creative projects based on their interests, maintained these interests and aspirations during college. One student we recently interviewed, for example, who had graduated from college as an aspiring writer explained that the high levels of creative enjoyment and engagement that she experienced in the enrichment program led her to seek similar opportunities in her college and future work. Delcourt (1993), in another longitudinal study of participants in SEM programs, learned that high school student creative productivity, as manifested in performances and product development, was predicted by earlier high levels of creative productive behaviors in elementary and middle school. In another recent longitudinal study, students who participated in SEM programs maintained strong interests over time and were still involved in creative productive work both during and after graduation from college (Westberg, 2010).

Traits associated with creativity in the Three-Ring Conception of Giftedness include novelty, curiosity, originality, ingenuity, flow (Beghetto & Kaufman, 2007; Csikszentmihalyi, 1996), and a willingness to challenge convention and tradition. The SEM provides opportunities for students to experience various types of creativity in three types of enrichment experiences. The belief that creativity is developmental is inherent in the Three-Ring Conception of Giftedness and is shared by other creativity researchers, including Runco (2004) and Sternberg and Lubart (1995). Another theory that is compatible with the creativity cluster in the Three-Ring Conception is Amabile's (1996) componential model of creativity. She argued that three variables were needed for creativity to occur: domain-relevant skills, creativity-relevant skills, and task motivation, similar to the interaction of the three clusters in the Three-Ring Conception.

Creativity is an essential component of the highest levels of creative-productive giftedness. Gifted scientists have emerged throughout history, but the scientists whose work is revered, whose names have remained recognizable in scholarly communities and among the general public, are those scientists who used their creativity to envision, analyze, and help to resolve scientific questions in new, original ways. We believe that teachers, parents, and mentors can stimulate and develop young people's creativity in school, and in this way prevent and alleviate the boredom and underachievement that too often afflict high-potential students (Reis & McCoach, 2000). And because the occurrence of Big-C is rare, we remain fascinated by whether educators can increase the likelihood that it can occur more often in students who participate in consistently planned enrichment opportunities.

It is difficult to measure creativity, as challenges exist in establishing relationships between creativity assessments and later creative lifetime accomplishments. Some research exists about school-based experiences that have increased creativity and had an impact on later creative productivity (Delcourt, 1993; Hébert, 1993; Westberg, 2010). Although case studies do not represent the type of hard data that are the contemporary vogue in research and evaluation, when examining a different "brand" of learning, educators must be open to equally different brands of evaluation. Accordingly, we advocate increasing longitudinal case study research in the assessment of students' potential for future creativity with an analysis of the types of project-based work completed in school and the effects of this work on future creative productivity.

Defining Gifted Behaviors

Although no single statement can effectively integrate the many ramifications of the research studies that underlie the Three-Ring Conception of Giftedness, our definition of gifted behavior attempts to summarize the major conclusions and generalizations resulting from extensive reviews of research (Renzulli, 1978, 1986, 2005): *Gifted behavior consists of behaviors that reflect an interaction among three basic clusters of human traits—above-average ability, high levels of task commitment, and high levels of creativity. Individuals capable of developing gifted behavior are those possessing or capable of developing this composite set of traits and applying them to any potentially valuable area of human performance. Persons who manifest or are capable of developing an interaction among the three clusters require a wide variety of educational opportunities and services that are not ordinarily provided through regular instructional programs.*

The three-ring representation of this definition (see Figure 5.2) portrays a summary of the major concepts and conclusions emanating from decades of our work. As is always the case with traits suggesting gifted behavior, an overlap exists among the general categories and specific traits. All of the traits need not be present in any given individual to lead to the development of gifted behaviors. It is for this reason that the Three-Ring Conception of Giftedness emphasizes the interaction among the clusters rather than any single cluster. It is also for this reason that we believe gifted behaviors take place in certain people (not all people), at certain times (not all of the time), under certain circumstances (not all circumstances), and within certain contexts or areas of study.

The Schoolwide Enrichment Model: Focusing on Student Strengths and Interests

The SEM (Renzulli & Reis, 1985, 1997, 2014), a product of almost 4 decades of research and field-testing, emerged from earlier work on the previously developed Enrichment Triad and Revolving Door Identification Models. The SEM has been implemented in school districts worldwide, and extensive evaluations and research studies indicate the effectiveness of the model, which VanTassel-Baska and Brown (2007) called one of the megamodels in the field (Reis & Renzulli, 2003; Renzulli & Reis, 1994; VanTassel-Baska & Brown, 2007). Prior and current research suggests that the model is effective at serving high-ability students in a variety of educational settings and works well in different types of schools across the globe (Reis & Renzulli, 2003; Renzulli & Reis, 1994). The SEM has been implemented in schools across the world in addition to the United States. Schools in China, Mexico, Chile, Argentina, Brazil, Canada, the Virgin Islands, Spain, Germany, Portugal, Turkey, Hungary, Holland, Lebanon, Switzerland, Croatia, South Korea, England, Japan, Peru, India, Dubai, Austria, Switzerland, and Brazil make use of SEM. At the time of this writing, efforts to implement the SEM in some of these countries (e.g., China) are just beginning.

In the SEM, a talent pool of approximately 10%–20% of above-average ability/high-potential students is identified through a variety of measures, including achievement tests, teacher nominations, assessment of potential for creativity and task commitment, as well as alternative pathways of entrance (self-nomination, parent nomination, etc.). Students in SEM programs receive several kinds of services. First, interest, learning style, and product style assessments should be completed with talent pool students, but these can be done with all students. The online tool Renzulli Learning (https://renzullilearning.com) can be used to efficiently collect and organize these data. A creativity test is also available through this tool. On Renzulli Learning, each student creates a profile that identifies their unique strengths and talents, and that helps teachers to identify patterns in students' interests, products, and learning styles. The tool also connects students to resources matched to their profile in order to encourage students to develop and pursue these interests in various ways.

Most of our work on the SEM has been devoted to research and development on identification practices and teaching strategies for promoting talent development (Reis & Renzulli, 2003; Renzulli & Reis, 1997). Over the decades, we learned that many students, in addition to those formally identified as gifted, can and do benefit from enriching school experiences that are engaging and challenging, and that help to develop their interests and talents. We also realized that in order to make changes in *entire* schools, we needed to implement an organizational plan or model for the delivery of these strategies and the professional development that is guided by our theories and research. The SEM is designed to infuse various types of enrichment and planned talent development practices into all aspects of the school curriculum and to ensure that certain types of enrichment activities are available to the larger school population. We believe that a total talent development model must take into account the mission, culture, and commitment of entire schools in addition to what happens in special programs.

Our approach to applying the pedagogy of gifted education to the talent development of more students is a departure from most traditional approaches that focus on identified gifted students. Although persons representing more conservative positions in our field may disagree, national interests in both promoting 21st-century skills for all students and recognizing talent potentials in students from underrepresented groups have resulted in a growing number of adoptions of our SEM. The explanatory information about SEM that follows is organized around the three major service delivery components listed on the face of the cube in Figure 5.3. The three major service delivery components should be viewed as brought to bear on the three school organizational structures listed on the top of the cube.

Comprehensive Strength Assessment in the SEM

The first service in the SEM, Comprehensive Strength Assessment, is achieved by compiling a strength-based profile for students that includes information about their academic achievement; student interests; learning preferences, such as projects or simulations; and preferred modes of expression. Each of these areas include research-based questionnaires: teacher ratings of students' potential for creativity and task commitment (e.g., Renzulli et al., 2010) and self-ratings that students complete about their interests, learning styles (Renzulli & Sullivan, 2009), and preferred modes of expression (Kettle et al., 1998). Interest questionnaires cover the full range

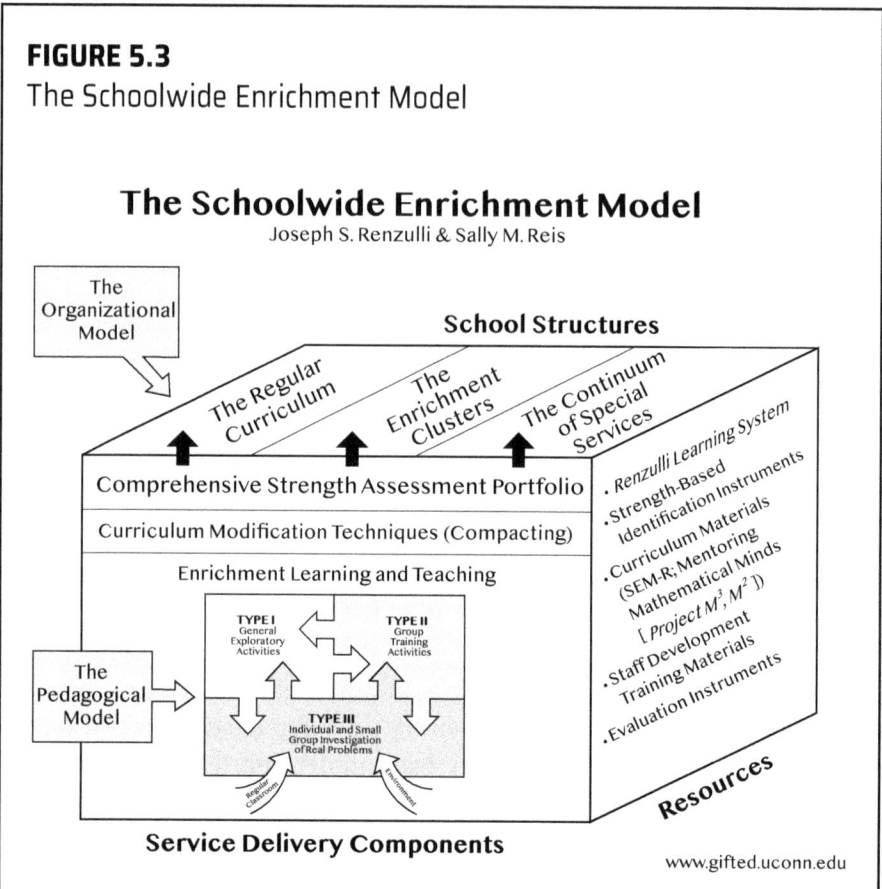

FIGURE 5.3
The Schoolwide Enrichment Model

Note. Adapted from *The Schoolwide Enrichment Model: A How-to Guide for Talent Development* (3rd ed., p. 47), by J. S. Renzulli and S. M. Reis, 2014, Taylor & Francis. Copyright 2014 by Taylor & Francis. Adapted with permission.

of academic areas as well as questions about topics in which students may have interests that are outside traditional academic areas. Learning style preferences include projects, independent study, teaching games, simulations, peer teaching, computer-assisted instruction, lecture, drill and recitation, and discussion. Expression style preferences include written, oral, artistic, graphic, dramatic, and service-oriented ways in which students like to express themselves. This information can be gathered through the use of paper-and-pencil assessments or a computer-generated profile completed by each student on Renzulli Learning (Field, 2009; Renzulli & Reis, 2007).

We strongly recommend that this talent development profile process focus on student *strengths*.

Curriculum Compacting, Enrichment, and Acceleration

Our approach to addressing students' advanced learning needs in the regular curriculum is the second service provided in the SEM. We recommend a process called curriculum compacting to provide content acceleration for students who can cover regular curriculum material faster. In this way, the SEM is compatible with acceleration practices and models (Colangelo et al., 2004). Curriculum compacting is one of the most well-researched and practiced methods of differentiation (Reis et al., 2016). It is traditionally offered and provided to all eligible above-average students. Compacting enables classroom teachers to modify the regular curriculum by eliminating portions of previously mastered content when students demonstrate content strengths in a particular area(s). Research on compacting has demonstrated that academically talented students can have up to 50%–75% of their regular curriculum eliminated or streamlined to avoid repetition of previously mastered work while guaranteeing mastery and simultaneously substituting more appropriately challenging activities (Reis & Purcell, 1993; Reis, Westberg, et al., 1998). Compacting enables teachers to document the content areas that have been compacted and substitute them with alternative work that is more interesting, challenging, and engaging. In a certain sense, compacting allows students to "buy time" that can then be devoted to talent development activities.

Enrichment Learning and Teaching: The Enrichment Triad Model

The curriculum/instructional focus in the SEM for all learning activities is the Enrichment Triad Model (Renzulli, 1977). This was initially implemented in school districts as a gifted and talented program and is often now integrated into whole-school programming. Research on the use of the Enrichment Triad Model and its integration into the SEM has consistently shown positive outcomes for students, finding that the enriched and accelerated content can reverse underachievement and increase achievement

(Baum, 1988; Baum et al., 1999; Baum et al., 2014; Delcourt, 1993; Hébert, 1993; Reis et al., 2008; Reis et al., 2011). The Enrichment Triad Model is designed to provide talent development opportunities for students and to encourage their creative productivity by exposing them to various topics, areas of interest, and fields of study. Further it is designed to train them to *apply* advanced content, process skills, and methodology training to self-selected areas of interest. Accordingly, three types of enrichment are included in the Enrichment Triad Model. In order for enrichment learning and teaching to be applied systematically to the education of all students, it must be organized in a way that makes sense to teachers and students, and the Enrichment Triad Model can be used for this purpose.

The Enrichment Triad Model is based on the ways in which people learn in a natural environment rather than the artificially structured environment that characterizes most curricular-focused classrooms. External stimulation, internal curiosity, necessity, or combinations of these three starting points cause people to develop an interest in a topic, problem, or area of study. Children are curious beings and they enjoy solving problems, but in order for them to act upon a problem or interest with some degree of commitment and enthusiasm, the interest must be sincere, and they must feel a personal reason for taking action. In the Enrichment Triad Model, the *interaction* between and among the following three types of enrichment is as important as any single type of enrichment or the sum of all three types.

The Enrichment Triad Model is the curriculum core of the SEM, and it includes three types of enrichment. Type I Enrichment includes general exploratory experiences to expose students to new topics and areas in which they may develop an interest. Type I experiences include guest speakers, field trips, demonstrations, interest centers, and the use of audiovisual materials and technology (such as webinars) that introduce students to exciting topics, ideas, and fields of knowledge not ordinarily covered in the regular curriculum. Type II Enrichment includes instructional methods and materials purposefully designed to promote the development of thinking, feeling, research, communication, and methodological processes. Type II training, usually carried out both in classrooms and in enrichment programs, includes the development of creative thinking, problem solving, critical thinking, and affective processes; a variety of specific learning-how-to-learn skills; skills in the appropriate use of advanced-level reference materials; written, oral, and visual communication skills; and metacognitive technology skills (i.e., the ability to identify trustworthy and useful information, selectively self-assess reliable information, use relevant information for independent and small-group research projects, and communicate what has been learned effectively). We typically integrate these skills into teaching by collecting and categorizing skill-based activities in various subject matter areas and infusing these activities into required or standards-driven curriculum.

Type III Enrichment is the most advanced level of the Enrichment Triad Model, and it is completed by students whose above-average abilities, task commitment, and creativity are brought to bear upon an area of interest or the development of a creative product. This is the most intense and exciting stage in the SEM talent development process. Although Types I and II Enrichment, interest assessment, and curriculum compacting should be provided on a regular basis to talent pool students, the ability to revolve into Type III Enrichment depends on an individual's interests, motivation, and desire to pursue advanced-level study. Type III Enrichment is defined as investigative activities and artistic productions in which the learner assumes the role of a firsthand inquirer, thinking, feeling, and acting like a practicing professional within a specific domain or area of interest. Type III Enrichment is pursued at as advanced or professional a level as possible given the student's level of development and age. The most important feature of the Enrichment Triad Model is the "flow" or connection among the experiences. Each type of enrichment is viewed as a component part of a holistic process that blends present or newly developed interests (Type I) and advanced-level thinking and research skills (Type II) with application situations based on the modus operandi of the firsthand inquirer (Type III).

Enrichment Clusters

Enrichment clusters, another component of the Schoolwide Enrichment Model, are nongraded, often multiage groups of students who share common interests and who are grouped together during specially designated time blocks to work with an adult who shares their interests and who has some degree of advanced knowledge and expertise in the area (Renzulli et al., 2013). A series of clusters is usually planned and implemented for all students in an SEM school both in the fall and the spring semester. Students complete an interest inventory to assess their interests, and an enrichment coordinator tallies all of the major families of interests (or uses technology to do so automatically). Teachers and parents who want to facilitate clusters also complete an interest questionnaire to help them decide which interest areas to offer as clusters. SEM schools try to offer enrichment clusters in the areas of high student interest as well as talent development opportunities, such as the arts, drama, history, creative writing, drawing, music, science, inventions, archeology, and other areas. Training is provided to the facilitators who agree to offer the clusters, and a brochure is developed and sent to all parents and students with descriptions of enrichment clusters. Students select their top three choices for the clusters and scheduling is completed to place all children into their first or, in some cases, second choice. Like extracurricular activities and programs such as 4-H and Junior Achievement, the main rationale for participation in one or more clusters is that *students and teachers want to be there.* All teachers (including music, art, physical education, etc.) are involved in facilitating the clusters, and their involvement in any particular cluster is based on the same type of interest assessment that is used for students in selecting clusters of choice. The desired outcome of all enrichment clusters is a student-developed product, performance, or service based on students' interests and using authentic learning. Authentic learning includes investigative activities and the development of creative products in which students assume roles as firsthand investigators, writers, artists, or other types of practicing professionals. Although students pursue these kinds of involvement at a more junior level than adult professionals, the overriding purpose is to create situations in which young people are thinking, feeling, and doing what practicing professionals do in the delivery of products and services within domains or areas of interest. These experiences should be viewed as vehicles through which students can apply their interests, knowledge, thinking skills, creative ideas, and task commitment to self-selected problems or areas of study, completing a product, performance, or service in every cluster.

How Do Students Develop Their Gifts and Talents in the SEM?

Young people identified as gifted and talented are as diverse and eclectic as the paths they take to develop their gifts and talents. They exhibit a wide range of characteristics in ability, achievement, temperament, and effort invested in reaching goals. Our years of research on the SEM have enabled us to identify some patterns or paths to talent development, as well given us insights about the development of qualities that are the key components of creative productive giftedness. In the SEM, students' abilities, task commitment, and creativity are applied to areas of interest or passion over time. The development of their above-average abilities is accomplished when they begin the process of developing their academic abilities and interests both in and out of school. The development of their task commitment and creativity occurs when they find an area in which an interest is activated; they develop these skills in order to pursue that interest. When children experience and enjoy creative and productive experiences, based on their interests, and pursue independent or small-group investigative projects, they will be more likely to seek additional creative experiences later in life. These projects are the Enrichment Triad Model's (Renzulli, 1977) Type III experiences described previously and are an essential service in the SEM.

More traditional models of education that focus on compliance, memorization, and test preparation are now giving way to approaches that emphasize thinking skills and the application of knowledge that reflect what professionals do in their daily work. The theory of knowledge (Renzulli, 2016) underlying our SEM approach is designed to guide teachers to help students use received and analyzed knowledge in applied ways to produce Type III outcomes that approximate the work of persons who use an investigative and creative mindset to become producers rather than consumers of knowledge. The theory also makes distinctions between presented knowledge that typifies the traditional curriculum and the just-in-time knowledge needed by professionals to address a problem or project of current interest.

Recently, we interviewed a university student who had participated in an SEM program in elementary, middle, and high school. She described the intensity of her interests when working on creative projects, such as theater and puppetry. She shared the memories of her excitement when she wrote, starred in, and produced her own play in elementary school and the passion she felt when doing something that made others laugh. She is currently a theater major who is passionate about continuing to seek these types of opportunities in her later life and career. She explained that the experience of completing her creative productive work in elementary and secondary school talent development programs enabled her to identify a college major and pursue it with intensity, and she explained that she craved the opportunity to participate in theater in college and in her subsequent career. Like for this student, we have found that early creative productive experiences in elementary or secondary school enable some academically talented students to learn to relish creative experiences and to become more likely to pursue these options in their adult lives. This leads to a more creative and productive personal life, regardless of the work and career they select.

Research on the SEM

Hundreds of separate studies have been conducted on the SEM, and a complete summary of that work is beyond the scope of this chapter (Gubbins, 1995; Reis & Renzulli, 2003; Renzulli & Reis, 1997), but its effectiveness has been demonstrated in schools with widely differing socioeconomic levels and program organization patterns. The SEM has been adopted in thousands of schools across the country and internationally, and its effectiveness has been studied in more than 40 years of research and field-testing. That research relates to student creative productivity (Brigandi et al., 2018); students' personal and social development (Baum et al., 2014); the use of SEM with culturally diverse students or populations with special needs (Reis & Morales-Taylor, 2011); the use of SEM as a curricular framework, such as with the SEM-R (Reis et al., 2011); research about curriculum compacting and differentiation (Field, 2009); and longitudinal research on the SEM (Westberg, 2010).

This research on the SEM suggests that it is effective at serving high-ability students in a variety of educational settings and in schools serving diverse ethnic and socioeconomic populations. These studies also suggest that the pedagogy of the SEM can be applied to various content areas resulting in higher achievement when implemented in a wide variety of settings. The SEM has also been found to be effective with all populations of students studied, including high-ability students with learning disabilities and those who underachieve. Due to space, only a few more recent studies are briefly summarized in this chapter.

A recent study (Brigandi et al., 2018) examined participation in SEM enrichment and environmental perceptions of gifted secondary school students. Participants included 10 gifted secondary school students, their parents, and their classroom teacher, who were interviewed in semistructured interviews, responded to short-answer surveys, and submitted student work for analysis. Findings indicated a relationship between participation in enrichment and positive environmental perceptions. Environmental perceptions were positively influenced by students' positive perceptions of their gifted classes, teachers, enrichment program opportunities, and opportunities for challenge and engagement. Student participants benefited from working with a teacher trained in gifted education who nurtured both affective and cognitive development, homogeneous grouping with like-minded peers, involved parents, and relationships with project mentors.

Baum et al. (2014) investigated the experiences of a cohort of students who entered a strength-based independent school for twice-exceptional students that used components of SEM, such as enrichment clusters and Type III projects. These students enrolled during middle school and successfully completed graduation requirements. Using a case study design, the researchers identified four benefits from the talent development opportunities offered to students. Participating in talent development activities enabled students to become part of a social group; overcome some social, emotional, and cognitive challenges in context; develop ongoing mentor and professional relationships with people in talent areas; and develop expertise in an area of talent. This research supports the incorporation of a strengths-based, SEM-talent-focused approach for twice-exceptional learners.

Westberg (2010) conducted a retrospective study examining the lives of students 25 years after they participated in an elementary gifted program based on the SEM that used a more expanded identification system. The purpose of the multiple case-study research was to investigate the relationship between students' early interests and their subsequent vocations and avocations as young adults. A correlation was found between students' early and subsequent interests; for example, interests in creative writing as a child were still present decades later. The results from the study provide support for an SEM approach that develops the interests and talents of young people.

In a 25-year follow-up study of students who participated in a school based on the SEM model (Booji et al., 2016), three Dutch economists reported that participating students obtained higher grades, followed a more science-intensive curriculum (most notably for girls), and reported stronger beliefs about their academic abilities. They also found that the positive SEM program effects persisted in university, where students chose more challenging fields of study with, on average, higher returns. The students also entered career tracks at higher levels of challenge and financial rewards. Together, these results are consistent with a human capital interpretation of the effect of an SEM education program that promotes both academic excellence and creative productivity.

Talent development education programs based on the SEM have been found to longitudinally benefit gifted and talented students by helping them to identify interests, determine postsecondary and career plans (Booji et al., 2016; Delcourt, 1993; Hébert, 1993), and develop creativity and motivation that are applied to later work (Delcourt, 1993; Hébert, 1993). More recent research has found that gifted programs based on the SEM help focus students' interest development and productivity in their areas of interest, had a positive effect on students' subsequent interests, and positively affected postsecondary plans (Brigandi et al., 2018; Westberg, 2010). Hébert (1993) reported that nonintellectual characteristics, such as creativity, interests, and task commitment, remain consistent in gifted and talented students over time (e.g., from elementary and middle school to college graduation). Westberg (2010), who investigated longitudinal patterns in students who participated in SEM-type programs, also found that students maintained interests and were still involved in both those interests and creative productive work after they finished college and graduate school.

In summary, both qualitative and quantitative longitudinal studies of SEM gifted programs demonstrate positive outcomes in the cognitive, affective, and social development of participating students. Participants in SEM programs had higher college and work aspirations, and they maintained interests and creative productive work that begin in gifted programs after they finished college and graduate school. It is our hope that more schools and districts will continue to implement talent development programs based on the SEM in the years to come, whether as part of gifted or enrichment programs, magnet or theme schools, or a general education program. During the last decade, several "Renzulli Academies" have been developed that focus on implementing the pedagogy described in this chapter with high-potential students. These schools have been successful at ensuring academic achievement as well as providing many opportunities for creative productivity (Reis & Morales-Taylor, 2011). Renzulli Academies incorporate all components of SEM and are designed for students who have a passion for learning and are capable of advanced and creative performance in school. Students who attend academies are academically talented, task-committed, and curious. Especially important to recruit for Renzulli Academies are original thinkers, students who are open to discovering their talents in a creative educational environment, and those who are interested in innovation and creativity. Approximately 45 Renzulli Academies have been developed and implemented across the world at the current time.

Additional resources have been published or are in preparation that focus on implementing the SEM philosophy in science (Heilbronner & Renzulli, 2015), technology (Housand et al., 2017), social studies, and mathematics (Gavin & Renzulli, 2018). As previously described, Renzulli Learning (https://renzullilearning.com) can also help to scale up SEM. Using its integrated digital tools can greatly increase the speed and ease with which a teacher or enrichment team can identify interests and resources to use with students, or students can use it independently to explore and create.

The success of enrichment clusters in the SEM has caused us to recommend this component as the starting point of new programs. There are three reasons for this recommendation. First and foremost, enrichment clusters provide occasions for *all students and teachers* to become involved in an organized enrichment teaching and learning opportunity. Second, our research has shown that many classroom teachers have learned from and then subsequently applied their enrichment cluster teaching experiences to their regular curriculum teaching responsibilities (Reis, Gentry, & Maxfield, 1998). In a certain sense, they have become their own professional development "consultants." This development is also consistent with our current emphasis on infusing more enrichment into the regular curriculum (Reis, 2016). Finally, with more thinking skills and general enrichment taking place in the clusters and the regular curriculum, the gifted education or enrichment specialists can spend the majority of their time working with students on advanced Type III Enrichment projects.

Common Goals and Unique Means

Three general goals exist for schools implementing the SEM, and educators have a wide degree of flexibility for achieving these goals (see Figure 5.4). The first goal is *enjoyment*. Anything a person enjoys doing they generally do better, and they tend to grow and try to improve in the process.

Enjoyment leads to *engagement*, a commitment to become intrinsically involved in and energetic about what one is learning or doing. Research has shown that higher engagement results in higher achievement (Dotterer & Lowe, 2011; Reyes et al., 2012; Wang & Holcombe, 2010). This research also demonstrates that engagement leads to *enthusiasm* for learning. We recommend that high-end learning objectives are used to plan all enrichment activities, including the ability to formulate meaningful questions, apply knowledge and problem-solving strategies to real-world problems, work effectively with others, derive enjoyment from active engagement in the act of learning, and creatively solve problems and produce new ideas.

These learner-centered skills grow young minds, promote genuine student engagement, and increase achievement. Although focusing on these outcomes may be counterintuitive to the "more practice is better" pedagogy, educators need to be courageous enough to explore bold, innovative alternatives that will provide all students with a more highly enriched diet—the kind of diet that characterizes learning in the nation's best public and private schools. This is not to say that educators should abandon a strong,

FIGURE 5.4
The Three Es of the Schoolwide Enrichment Model

Note. From *The Schoolwide Enrichment Model: A How-to Guide for Talent Development* (3rd ed., p. 3), by J. S. Renzulli and S. M. Reis, 2014, Taylor & Francis. Copyright 2014 by Taylor & Francis. Reprinted with permission.

standards-based curriculum that ensures basic competencies, nor that they should forget to demand data to evaluate returns on investment when implementing alternatives.

But educators also need to infuse into the curriculum a series of motivationally rich experiences that promote student engagement, enjoyment, and a genuine enthusiasm for learning. Common sense and experience support the idea that people always do a better job when they are working on something in which they are personally engaged—something they are really "into" and truly enjoy doing. Take, for example, the demonstrated benefits in performance that result from extracurricular activities that are based on a pedagogy that is the opposite of the pedagogy of drill and practice. How many *dis*engaged students participate in the Math League, school newspaper staff, basketball team, chess club, debate team, or concert choir? Their engagement occurs because these students have some choice in the area in which they will participate, and they interact in a goal-oriented environment with other likeminded students interested in developing expertise in their chosen area. They use authentic problem-solving, interpersonal, and creative strategies in order to produce a product, service, or performance, and their work is brought to bear on one or more intended audiences other than (or, at least, in addition to) the teacher. The engagement that results from these kinds of experiences exemplifies the best way to approach learning, one that differs completely from the behaviorist theory that guides so much of prescriptive and remedial education.

As mentioned earlier, all learning, from diapers to doctorate, exists on a continuum ranging from deductive, didactic, and prescriptive on one hand, to inductive, investigative, and inquiry-oriented on the other. Students who have not achieved a certain, predetermined score are subjected to repetitive practice material in the didactic model. Then, if their scores do not improve, some educators believe that the obvious solution is to simply redouble their efforts with what has been popularly called a "drill and kill" approach to learning. Proponents of popular but extremely prescriptive reading programs may boast of slightly higher test scores; however, the endless drill and practice only prepares students for more test taking. This approach has turned many schools into joyless places that promote boredom, lack of genuine student and teacher engagement, absenteeism, increased dropout rates, and the other byproducts of overdependence on mechanized learning. The goal should be that students not only learn, but also *learn to love learning and creating,* allowing them to make learning and creating important parts of their lives.

All Roads Lead to Rome

With these three common goals and objectives in mind (see Figure 5.4), we encourage school leaders to make their own decisions about how the goals will be achieved. The metaphor that we sometimes use is that "all roads lead to Rome" (in this case, the Three Es). However, there are many ways to get to Rome. We believe that the unique means for getting there are based on the selection and use of a program development model that maintains two essential requirements. A model should consist of a *shared mission* and *set of objectives.* Everyone (or at the very least, almost everyone) involved in the selection and implementation of a model should agree that the mission and objectives represent a "destination" that they would like to reach. If an agreed-upon goal is to get to Rome, then there is no ambiguity, vagueness, or misunderstanding about where everyone is going. This first requirement of a model means that a great deal of front end time should be spent exploring alternative models, discussing and debating the advantages and disadvantages of various approaches, and examining related factors, such as underlying research, implementation in other schools, and the availability of supportive resources. Reaching consensus before embarking upon a journey will help ensure that everyone involved will get to Rome rather than to Venice or Moscow!

Although we advocate that programs based on the SEM should strive to accomplish an agreed-upon mission and set of objectives, we also believe that plans for program development must allow for a great deal of flexibility in the achievement of its objectives. This flexibility is necessary because no written plan or set of procedures can take into account the variations that exist at the local school level. Differences in school populations, financial resources, the availability of persons from the community at large, and a host of other local variables must be considered in the implementation of this or any other approach to school improvement. The SEM enables flexibility, as some schools will have supplementary resource teachers for advanced-level students, and others will not. Some school districts will have an abundance of community resources readily available, and others, perhaps more geographically isolated, will have limited access to museums, planetariums, colleges, and universities. Some schools may serve larger proportions of culturally diverse students than others, and certain highly selective schools may have such a large number of high-achieving students that they have been designated as a school for the gifted.

Another reason why we believe that a model for program development must maintain a large degree of flexibility is that educators tend to quickly lose interest in "canned" programs and models that do not allow for local initiative, creativity, and teacher input. New and better ways to provide enrichment experiences to students will be discouraged if program development does not encourage local adaptation and innovation to occur. The SEM does provide a certain amount of general direction in both the development of program objectives and in the procedures for pursuing these objectives. At the same time, the specific types of activities that educators select and develop for their programs and the ways in which they make these activities available to various populations of students will actually result in the creation of their own programming model. Educators will, in effect, be writing their own resource guide based on the activities that they select and develop. Program sustainability is a function of building an SEM program in the way it works best for educators, developing ownership, and experiencing pride in individual creative input.

If the three general goals of the Schoolwide Enrichment Model are maintained, a school's program can and will achieve the integrity that we hope to develop in the SEM approach. In this regard, the program that educators develop will attempt to achieve the best of two worlds. First, their program will benefit from the theoretical and research developments and the many years of field-testing and practical application that have led to this particular approach for total talent development. Second, the ideas, resources, innovations, and adaptations that emerge from local situations will create a unique program that is tailored to local needs. We have been delighted to see how many teachers and leaders from excellent SEM schools have contributed to their profession by sharing their work at conferences, workshops, and in various publications. We view this type of sharing as a best-case example of teacher leadership and the extended professionalization of the work of teachers who have achieved the best of both worlds.

We have consistently recommended that educators should make whatever modifications and adaptations are necessary to the particular procedures recommended for accomplishing various program tasks. We believe that there are many pathways and alternatives to reaching desired program outcomes. Once everyone in a school has agreed upon a destination, the uniqueness and excitement of the journey should involve the creation of an individualized plan for getting there. If all roads lead to Rome, what an unimaginative world it would be if everyone followed the same strip of pavement to get there! Each school develops ownership of the SEM by the ways in which it selectively adopts, adapts, and creates the methods, materials, and organizational components that will make the school and program an *original* application of the Schoolwide Enrichment Model.

Similarities exist between and among the several talent development models discussed in various chapters of this book. Most authors agree that underlying theory and research should be a foundation for talent development programs and that greater attention should be given to practical procedures for finding and developing talents in low-income and underrepresented groups. Most authors also agree on a broader conception of domain-specific talent potentials and gifted behaviors and that a continuum of services that includes both acceleration and enrichment should be made available for individuals with varying interests and potentials. There is general agreement about the use of multicriteria in the identification process and that performance-based assessment is important for determining who should receive supplementary opportunities, resources, and services for advanced talent development options.

Our SEM model has been in operation for 4 decades, so it is difficult to compare its implementation with newer approaches, but we can say that the SEM can and has been used with various content and grade-level enrichment and acceleration approaches. The SEM has also been used with various curriculum development approaches that are the focus of several talent development models. We advise readers to examine all of the talent development models discussed in this book and adopt, adapt, and combine features that are compatible with the goals, demographics, and resources that characterize the uniqueness of their respective school districts.

In conclusion, SEM programs are a natural place to develop talents, innovation, and creativity, and our goal is to produce the next generations of leaders and creators who can invent, lead, and make a positive difference in the world. Ian is a perfect example of a student who benefitted from an SEM experience in his participation in an enrichment cluster that eventually led to a national competition that may have changed his life. In SEM programs, innovation and creative productivity are nurtured, taught, and systematically developed.

DISCUSSION QUESTIONS

1. Can the Enrichment Triad Model be implemented without the SEM?
2. Can the SEM be implemented with underachieving gifted and talented students?
3. Should or could the Three-Ring Conception of Giftedness be used in identification and programming models that are not the SEM?
4. Do all three clusters have to be present for creative productivity to be developed?
5. Why are the Three Es so important in the SEM?
6. What other models in gifted education can coexist with the SEM in the same school or program?
7. What would distinguish a Renzulli Academy from another school for high-potential or gifted students?

References

Amabile, T. M. (1996). *Creativity in context: Update to "The social psychology of creativity."* Westview Press.

Baum, S. M. (1988). An enrichment program for gifted learning disabled students. *Gifted Child Quarterly, 32*(1), 226–230. https://doi.org/10.1177/001698628803200108

Baum, S. M., Renzulli, J. S., & Hébert, T. P. (1999). Reversing underachievement: Creative productivity as a systematic intervention. *Gifted Child Quarterly, 39*(4), 224–235. https://doi.org/10.1177/001698629503900406

Baum, S. M., Schader, R. M., Hébert, T. P. (2014). Through a different lens: Reflecting on a strengths-based, talent-focused approach for twice-exceptional learners. *Gifted Child Quarterly, 58*(4), 311–327. https://doi.org/10.1177/0016986214547632

Beghetto, R. A., & Kaufman, J. C. (2007). Toward a broader conception of creativity: A case for "mini-c" creativity. *Psychology of Aesthetics, Creativity, and the Arts, 1*(2), 73–79. https://doi.org/10.1037/1931-3896.1.2.73

Bloom, B. S., & Sosniak, L. A. (1981). Talent development vs. schooling. *Educational Leadership, 39*(2), 86–94.

Booji, A., Haan, F., & Plug, E. (2016). *Enriching students pays off: Evidence from an individualized gifted and talented program in secondary education* (Discussion Paper No. 9757). University of Amsterdam.

Brigandi, C. B., Weiner, J. M., Siegle, D., Gubbins, E. J., & Little, C. A. (2018). Environmental perceptions of gifted secondary school students engaged in an evidence-based enrichment practice. *Gifted Child Quarterly, 62*(3), 289–305. https://doi.org/10.1177/0016986218758441

Callahan, C. M., Renzulli, J. S., Delcourt, A. B., & Hertberg, H. L. (2012). Considerations for identification of gifted and talented students: An introduction to identification. In C. M. Callahan & H. Hertberg-Davis (Eds.), *Fundamentals of gifted education: Considering multiple perspectives* (pp. 83–91). Routledge.

Colangelo, N., Assouline, S. G., & Gross, M. U. M. (2004). *A nation deceived: How schools hold back America's brightest students* (Vol. 1). The University of Iowa, The Connie Belin & Jacqueline N. Blank International Center for Gifted Education and Talent Development.

Csikszentmihalyi, M. (1996). *Creativity: Flow and the psychology of discovery and invention.* HarperCollins.

Delcourt, M. A. B. (1993). Creative productivity among secondary school students: Combining energy, interest, and imagination. *Gifted Child Quarterly, 37*(1), 23–31. https://doi.org/10.1177/001698629303700104

Dotterer, A. M., & Lowe, K. (2011). Classroom context, school engagement, and academic achievement in early adolescence. *Journal of Youth and Adolescence, 40*(12), 1649–1660. https://doi.org/ 10.1007/s10964-011-9647-5

Duckworth, A. L., Peterson, C., Matthews, M. D., & Kelly, D. R. (2007). Grit: Perseverance and passion for long-term goals. *Journal of Personality and Social Psychology, 92*(6), 1087–1101. https://doi.org/10.1037/0022-3514.92.6.1087

Dweck, C. S. (2016). *Mindset: The new psychology of success*. Ballantine Books. (Original work published 2006)

Field, G. B. (2009). The effects of using Renzulli Learning on student achievement: An investigation of internet technology on reading fluency, comprehension, and social studies. *International Journal of Emerging Technology, 4*(1), 29–39.

Gavin, M. K., & Renzulli, J. S. (2018). *Using the Schoolwide Enrichment Model in mathematics: A how-to guide for developing student mathematicians*. Prufrock Press.

Gubbins, E. J. (Ed.). (1995). *Research related to the Enrichment Triad Model* (RM95212). University of Connecticut, The National Research Center on the Gifted and Talented. https://nrcgt.uconn.edu/research-based_resources/gubbins

Hébert, T. P. (1993). Reflections at graduation: The long-term impact of elementary school experiences in creative productivity. *Roeper Review, 16*(1), 22–28. https://doi.org/10.1080/02783199309553529

Heilbronner, N., & Renzulli, J. S. (2015). *The Schoolwide Enrichment Model in science: A hands-on approach for engaging young scientists*. Prufrock Press.

Housand, A. M., Housand, B. C., & Renzulli, J. S. (2017). *Using the Schoolwide Enrichment Model with technology*. Prufrock Press.

Kaufman, J. C., & Beghetto, R. A. (2009). Beyond big and little: The four c model of creativity. *Review of General Psychology, 13*(1), 1–12. https://doi.org/10.1037/a0013688

Kettle, K. E., Renzulli, J. S., & Rizza, M. G. (1998). Products of mind: Exploring student preferences for product development using My Way . . . an expression style instrument. *Gifted Child Quarterly, 42*(1), 49–60. https://doi.org/10.1177/001698629804200106

Reis, S. M. (Ed.). (2016). *Reflections on gifted education: Critical works by Joseph S. Renzulli and colleagues*. Prufrock Press

Reis, S. M., Eckert, R. D., McCoach, D. B., Jacobs, J. K., & Coyne, M. (2008). Using enrichment reading practices to increase reading fluency, comprehension, and attitudes. *Journal of Educational Research, 101*(5), 299–314. https://doi.org/10.3200/JOER.101.5.299-315

Reis, S. M., Gentry, M., & Maxfield, L. R. (1998). The application of enrichment clusters to teachers' classroom practices. *Journal for Education of the Gifted, 21*(3), 310–324. https://doi.org/10.1177/016235329802100304

Reis, S. M., & McCoach, D. B. (2000). The underachievement of gifted students: What do we know and where do we go? *Gifted Child Quarterly, 44*(3), 152–170. https://doi.org/10.1177/001698620004400302

Reis, S. M., McCoach, D. B., Little, C. M., Muller, L. M., & Kaniskan, R. B. (2011). The effects of differentiated instruction and enrichment pedagogy on reading achievement in five elementary schools. *American Educational Research Journal, 48*(2), 462–501. https://doi.org/10.3102/0002831210382891

Reis, S. M., & Morales-Taylor, M. (2011). From high potential to gifted performance: Encouraging academically talented urban students. *Gifted Child Today, 33*(4), 28–38. https://doi.org/10.1177/107621751003300408

Reis, S. M., & Purcell, J. H. (1993). An analysis of content elimination and strategies used by elementary classroom teachers in the curriculum compacting process. *Journal for the Education of the Gifted, 16*(2), 147–170. https://doi.org/10.1177/016235329301600205

Reis, S. M., & Renzulli, J. S. (2003). Research related to the Schoolwide Enrichment Triad Model. *Gifted Education International, 18*(1), 15–40. https://doi.org/10.1177/001698629403800102

Reis, S. M., Renzulli, J. S., & Burns, D. E. (2016). *Curriculum compacting: A guide to differentiating curriculum and instruction through enrichment and acceleration* (2nd ed.). Prufrock Press.

Reis, S. M., Westberg, K. L., Kulikowich, J. M., & Purcell, J. H. (1998). Curriculum compacting and achievement test scores: What does the research say? *Gifted Child Quarterly, 42*(2), 123–129. https://doi.org/10.1177/001698629804200206

Renzulli, J. S. (1977). *The Enrichment Triad Model: A guide for developing definsible program for the gifted and talented*. Creative Learning Press.

Renzulli, J. S. (1978). What makes giftedness? Reexamining a definition. *Phi Delta Kappan, 60*(3), 180–184, 261.

Renzulli, J. S. (1986). The Three-Ring Conception of Giftedness: A developmental model for creative productivity. In R. J. Sternberg & J. E.

Davidson (Eds.), *Conceptions of giftedness* (pp. 332–357). Cambridge University Press.

Renzulli, J. S. (1988). A decade of dialogue on the three-ring conception of giftedness. *Roeper Review, 11*(1), 18–25. https://doi.org/10.1080/02783 198809553154

Renzulli, J. S. (1992). A general theory for the development of creative productivity in young people. In F. J. Mönks & W. A. M. Peters (Eds.), *Talent for the future: Social and personality development of gifted children* (pp. 51–72). Van Gorcum.

Renzulli, J. S. (1999). What is this thing called giftedness, and how do we develop it? A twenty-five year perspective. *Journal for the Education of the Gifted, 23*(1), 3–54. https://doi.org/10.1177/016235329902300102

Renzulli, J. S. (2002). Expanding the conception of giftedness to include co-cognitive traits and to promote social capital. *Phi Delta Kappan, 84*(1), 33–40, 57–58. https://doi.org/10.1177/003172170208400109

Renzulli, J. S. (2005). The Three-Ring Conception of Giftedness: A developmental model for promoting creative productivity. In R. J. Sternberg & J. Davidson (Eds.), *Conceptions of giftedness* (2nd ed., pp. 217–245). Cambridge University Press.

Renzulli, J. S. (2012). Reexamining the role of gifted education and talent development for the 21st century: A four-part theoretical approach. *Gifted Child Quarterly, 56*(3), 150–159. https://doi.org/10.1177/00169 86212444901

Renzulli, J. S. (2016). The role of blended knowledge in the development of creative productive giftedness. *International Journal for Talent Development and Creativity, 4*(1), 13–24.

Renzulli, J, S., & De Wet, C. F. (2010). Developing creative productivity in young people through the pursuit if ideal acts of learning. In R. A. Beghetto & J. C. Kaufman (Eds.), *Nurturing creativity in the classroom* (pp. 24–72). Cambridge University Press.

Renzulli, J. S., & D'Souza, S. (2012). Intelligences outside the normal curve: Co-Cognitive: factors that contribute to the creation of social capital and leadership skills in young people. In A. Ziegler, C. Fischer, H. Stoeger, & M. Reutlinger (Eds.), *Gifted education as a life-long challenge: Essays in honour of Franz Mönks* (pp. 157–177). LIT-Verlag.

Renzulli, J. S., Gentry, M., & Reis, S. M. (2013). *Enrichment clusters: A practical plan for real-world, student-driven learning* (2nd ed.). Prufrock Press.

Renzulli, J. S., Koehler, J., & Fogarty, E. (2006). Operation Houndstooth intervention theory: Social capital in today's school. *Gifted Child Today, 29*(1), 14–24. https://doi.org/10.4219/gct-2006-189

Renzulli, J. S., & Reis, S. M. (1985). *The Schoolwide Enrichment Model: A comprehensive plan for educational excellence*. Creative Learning Press.

Renzulli, J. S., & Reis, S. M. (1994). Research related to the Schoolwide Enrichment Triad Model. *Gifted Child Quarterly, 38*(1), 7–20. https://doi.org/10.1177/001698629403800102

Renzulli, J. S., & Reis, S. M. (1997). *The Schoolwide Enrichment Model: A how-to guide for educational excellence* (2nd ed.). Prufrock Press.

Renzulli, J. S., & Reis, S. M. (2007). A technology based program that matches enrichment resources with student strengths. *International Journal of Emerging Technologies in Learning, 2*(3), 1–12.

Renzulli, J. S., & Reis, S. M. (2014). *The Schoolwide Enrichment Model: A how-to guide for talent development* (3rd ed.). Prufrock Press.

Renzulli, J. S., Smith, L. H., White, A. J., Callahan, C. M., Hartman, R. K., Westberg, K. L., Gavin, M. K, Reis, S. M., Siegle, D., & Sytsma Reed, R. E. (2010). *Scales for rating the behavioral characteristics of superior students* (3rd ed.). Prufrock Press.

Renzulli, J. S., & Sullivan, E. E. (2009). Learning styles applied: Harnessing students' instructional style preferences. In L. Zhang & R. J. Sternberg (Eds.), *Perspectives on the nature of intellectual styles* (pp. 209–232). Springer.

Reyes, M. R., Brackett, M. A., Rivers, S. E., White, M., & Salovey, P. (2012). Classroom emotional climate, student engagement, and academic achievement. *Journal of Educational Psychology, 104*(3), 700–710. https://doi.org/10.1037/a0027268

Richards, R. (1990). Everyday creativity, eminent creativity, and health: "Afterview" for CRJ issues on creativity and health. *Creativity Research Journal, 3*(4), 300–326. https://doi.org/10.1080/10400419009534363

Runco, M. A. (2004). Everyone has creative potential. In R. J. Sternberg, E. L. Grigorenko, & J. L. Singer (Eds.), *Creativity: From potential to realization* (pp. 21–30). American Psychological Association.

Sternberg, R. J. (1985). *Beyond IQ: A triarchic theory of human intelligence*. Cambridge University Press.

Sternberg, R. J. (1988). *The triarchic mind: A theory of human intelligence*. Viking.

Sternberg, R. J. (1996). *Successful intelligence: How practical and creative intelligence determine success in life*. Simon & Schuster.

Sternberg, R. J., & Lubart, T. I. (1995). *Defying the crowd: Cultivating creativity in a culture of conformity*. Free Press.

Tough, P. (2012). *How children succeed: Grit, curiosity, and the hidden power of character*. Random House.

VanTassel-Baska, J., & Brown, E. F. (2007). Toward best practice: An analysis of the efficacy of curriculum models in gifted education. *Gifted Child Quarterly, 51*(4), 342–358. https://doi.org/10.1177/0016986207306323

Wang, M. T., & Holcombe, R. (2010). Adolescents' perceptions of school environment, engagement, and academic achievement in middle school. *American Educational Research Journal, 47*(3), 633–662. https://doi.org/10.3102/0002831209361209

Westberg, K. L. (2010). Young creative producers: Twenty-five years later. *Gifted Education International, 26*(2), 261–270.

CHAPTER 6

Nonuniversal Theory and the Development of Gifts and Talents[1]

DAVID HENRY FELDMAN

Most approaches to giftedness and talent development focus on assessing the amount of a talent or gift that a child possesses, and then finding ways to nurture those gifts and talents. In this tradition, gifts and talents tend to be thought of as entities that exist in the child, waiting to be assessed, and development tends to be thought of as making sure that these natural gifts and talents are recognized and nurtured. Historically, giftedness has been most often identified with this approach, with psychometric intelligence (IQ) its primary target (Borland, 2003).

Nonuniversal Theory takes a different approach; it locates giftedness and talent within domains of expertise that range from universal domains to unique ones (see Figure 6.1). A child or person's degree of expertise and

---

1 The author wishes to thank Frank C. Worrell, Ph.D., for helpful discussions and for providing materials used in the preparation of this chapter.

> **FIGURE 6.1**
> The Universal to Unique Continuum
>
> Universal | Pancultural | Cultural | Discipline | Idiosyncratic | Unique

pace of movement through a domain's developmental levels marks their degree of talent for that domain. The theory assumes that both general gifts (of the IQ sort) and specific talents (e.g., musical, artistic, mathematical) contribute to the child's movement through the levels of a specific domain. It does not assume, however, that whatever gifts and talents a child brings to the learning situation are inborn, unchanging, or set for life.

In Nonuniversal Theory, giftedness and talent are marked by performance as much as they are marked by potential, although in extreme cases such as prodigies (see Feldman, 1986), there is little doubt that great natural potential is a key part of the development of expertise (Feldman, 1986; Feldman & Katzir, 1998). There have been children whose gifts and talents were not extreme who became world-class performers (Bloom, 1985) and others whose abilities were clear and obvious who did not. The processes through which a child's potentials become expressed are complex; Nonuniversal Theory seeks to illuminate these processes and, in doing so, enhance the likelihood that children will be able to express their unique potentials by achieving expertise in valued domains (Subotnik et al., 2018).

The Universal to Unique Continuum

The heart of Nonuniversal Theory is the Universal to Unique continuum (see Figure 6.1). It is a simple line that attempts to capture in broad strokes the diversity of knowledge domains that exist at a given period of time. The line is divided loosely into regions of domains ranging from Universal at the left end of the continuum to Unique at the right end. Between Universal and Unique regions are Pancultural, Culturally Mandated, Discipline-Based, and Idiosyncratic regions, with each region containing numerous distinct domains.

The theory provides criteria for placing a domain in each region of the Universal to Unique continuum. For example, Pancultural domains are marked by being found in all human cultures, acquired with relatively little focused instruction, and supported by natural abilities shared with all other human beings. In comparison, Culturally Mandated domains are considered essential for participation in a given culture (but not necessarily in all cultures), are explicitly required of all members, and require cultural resources to ensure their achievement (e.g., schools, intervention techniques, and pedagogies). There are often laws and policies that formalize a culture's commitment to ensure that all members have access to and achieve targeted levels of mastery in mandated domains.[2]

Across the Universal to Unique Continuum there exist hundreds, possibly thousands, of knowledge domains. A small number of domains exist in all human cultures. A larger number (but not a large number) are achieved in many cultures (e.g., literacy, numeracy). A much larger number of disciplines, trades, professions, and practices are found around the world. A potentially even larger number of idiosyncratic forms of all of the disciplines, and an unlimited number of possible unique forms, are found in widely dispersed cultures. In rare cases, fundamentally new domains emerge (e.g., psychoanalysis through Freud, genetics, computer science).

The continuum is characterized by the assumption that all domains along its regions are developmental in the sense that they can be usefully characterized by a sequence of levels of expertise. Along with the assumed levels within each domain there are also assumed to exist dynamic processes of change within and across domains (Feldman, 1994). For the Universal region, for example, Piaget's equilibration processes of assimilation and accommodation are involved in all shifts from one level to another. In Pancultural domains, equilibration is also involved, along with domain-specific requirements that mark each level in the domain (e.g., grammatical forms for speech, notational forms for music, maps for space, number systems, etc.). Moving further along the continuum, additional change processes are introduced, which require the systematic efforts of others to assist in developing expertise (mandated schooling, cultural transmission practices, religious rituals, etc.).

Some empirical work has been done in some regions of the Universal to Unique continuum. There have been literally hundreds of studies of Piaget's stages (albeit most not within the framework of Nonuniversal Theory) testing their claimed invariant sequence, cross-cultural validity, and many

---

2 Knowledge domains may appear in more than one region of the Universal to Unique continuum. Some may appear in virtually every region in various forms. For example, music is quite possibly Universal, certainly Pancultural, sometimes Culturally Mandated, a Discipline for professional practice, Idiosyncratic in more advanced forms, and Unique when a novel composition or performance is achieved.

other issues (Feldman, 2004). Similarly, studies of language development and development in other areas like space, time, music, art, and dance have charted levels of expertise in Pancultural domains, while studies of curriculum sequences have been done in the Culturally Mandated region (Olson, 1970, 2003). Studies explicitly aimed at the development of expertise have tended to be carried out in regions to the right of Culturally Mandated (Disciplined, Idiosyncratic, and Unique regions), some of which were done explicitly within a Nonuniversal Theory framework (e.g., Benjamin, 1989; Campbell et al., 1992; Feldman, 1994; Snyder & Feldman, 1997; Walton, 1987), although most were not (e.g., Chase & Simon, 1973; Ericsson, 1996).

Although the research base is not extensive, results to date have tended to affirm the assumption that knowledge domains as defined in Nonuniversal Theory can be organized productively into a sequence (or, in some cases, more than one sequence) of levels of expertise. In comparison with other research on expertise (e.g., Simon & Chase, 1973), Nonuniversal Theory utilizes several levels between novices and experts, while most other expertise research focuses on contrasts between novices and experts. The number of levels depends upon the domain as well as the purposes for which the levels will be used. Most domains have yielded between six and nine levels. Levels are constructed in consultation with experts in the target domain and tested empirically on samples of individuals attempting to master the challenges of the domain.

To date, empirical studies of computer programming, visual arts, spatial reasoning (map drawing), computer programming, juggling, preschool teaching, and moral reasoning have been done (Campbell et al., 1992; Feldman, 1994). Some domains have established levels on their own; chess and some martial arts fields, for example, have carefully articulated levels that are used in ranking participants. For a chess player to be named a Grand Master, an A Player, or any other of about a dozen levels is a precise and well-recognized way of summarizing their level of mastery of the domain of chess.

Nonuniversal Theory and Giftedness

Nonuniversal Theory was not intended to be a theory of giftedness. It was created to try to extend the field of cognitive development beyond Piaget's focus on universals (Feldman, 1980). The central claim of the theory was that there are domains of cognitive development that are not universal but have some of the same qualities as universal domains: primarily that they can be organized into a sequence of developmental levels and that movement from level to level can be explained by domain-specific and domain-general processes of transition. Because universal domains are spontaneously achieved (by definition for Piaget), they are essentially guaranteed to occur in all children and to occur without much help from anyone else.

Nonuniversal domains, on the other hand, although also achieved through a sequence of developmental levels, are not spontaneously acquired and will only be mastered with sustained and focused efforts by others—others with expertise that they often desire to share (Vygotsky, 1978). The conscious efforts of most people most of the time are devoted to achieving mastery of nonuniversal domains. Because universal domains will be achieved spontaneously and universally, they are essentially guaranteed to be mastered. Nonuniversal Theory proposes that a better understanding of nonuniversal development should be a focus of the field's efforts beyond the universals of Piaget.

Nonuniversal Theory makes an additional claim that brings it closer to giftedness and talent. That claim is that human beings have a natural desire to express their gifts and talents in satisfying, productive ways. A related claim is that human beings are able to gauge how well their gifts and talents are being expressed, or how much a given experience contributes to or does not contribute to the fulfillment of their unique potentials (Feldman, 1994).

In contrast with Piaget's theory that proposes that human beings are essentially the same with respect to the development of the universal structures of cognitive development, Nonuniversal Theory proposes that in addition to whatever universal abilities humans share, they also have an array of abilities that they may share with some others or no others, and that one of the goals of human existence is to be able to express and fulfill the potential that exists in those more unique abilities.

To be sure, none of the claims made by Nonuniversal Theory about human potentials, universal or nonuniversal, speak directly to notions of giftedness and talent. It does not take much of a leap, however, to go from claims that have been made about human experience in general to see their implications for gifts and talents. Although Nonuniversal Theory claims that each person has a unique set of abilities, it follows that each person varies one from another in how strong these abilities might be, how amenable they are to enhancement, how rare they are, and how well matched they are to existing opportunities to express them. Olga Korbutt, the Romanian gymnast who achieved a perfect 10 for the first time in Olympic history, is said to have remarked: "If gymnastics didn't exist, I would have had to invent it" (Feldman, 1986, 1994).

Most other theories of giftedness and talent focus on the abilities that children have. Nonuniversal Theory focuses on the areas of activity where those abilities might find expression—the many knowledge, skill, and practice domains that may be found in a given society at a given point in time, and the extent to which individuals have mastered them.

The main goals of Nonuniversal Theory are to understand how the numerous domains of knowledge, skill, and practice have developed and to understand how individuals who try to achieve mastery in one or more domain move through their levels of expertise toward becoming experts or masters. Some domains have stayed relatively the same over centuries (e.g., chess, ceramics), while others have changed dramatically over a few decades (e.g., high jumping, gymnastics, ice skating). Domains also tend to have "signatures" that differentiate them from other domains, special techniques, technologies, or practices and vocabularies. Nonuniversal Theory provides a framework within which similarities and differences among domains can be studied on a systematic basis. For example, it has been learned, albeit informally (Feldman, 1994), that some domains (e.g., yoga) resist the idea that they can be organized into a sequence of developmental levels, while others (e.g., taekwondo, chess) have organized their practices around such levels.

In studying individual movement through the developmental levels of domains, Feldman (1994) found patterns of stability and change that often seem to hold across domains. For example, virtually all participants perform at more than one level at a given point in time in terms of their levels of mastery, and several different levels exist in their profile at a given point in time. The latter is a good predictor of how rapidly they are likely to move to the next level of expertise in their domain (Feldman, 1994).

Additionally, backward movement in expertise is an important, perhaps necessary, phase in movement from one level to the next. The data seem to confirm the old adage "Two steps forward, one step back" when it comes to the development of expertise in the domains studied thus far. The timing of backward movement also is often predicted by the general distribution of levels of performance, where high concentrations of skills around a central mode predict little movement backward, while a wide distribution of skills away from a central mode predicts relatively high amounts of backward movement.

A gap in gifted education practice that may be in part filled through the application of Nonuniversal Theory is in the *content* of gifted education programming. A frequent lament in the field is that students are identified as gifted, but there is no systematic way to guide the construction of curriculum and instruction that engages and enhances the development of students' gifts and talents. This is not so much of a problem when the main issue is the pace of instruction and the rapidity at which new material is introduced; here acceleration often works quite well (Assouline et al., 2015). However, many students' gifts and talents are more domain-specific (e.g., the arts, music, technology, the environment, politics, etc.). Most gifted education programs offer little programming targeted at these more specific domains (Borland, 2003; Killas, 2019).

As is almost always true, no single theory does everything needed to serve the needs of the field. In the next sections of this chapter, I will try to show how Nonuniversal Theory, *in combination with several other approaches*, may offer more comprehensive guidance for the field than any single approach can provide. I will discuss the theories that complement Nonuniversal Theory and can be applied in combination with it: Gardner's theory of multiple intelligences, Dai's Evolving Complexity Theory, and Gagné's Integrative Model of Talent Development theory.

I will also discuss a recent framework proposed by Subotnik, Olszewski-Kubilius, and Worrell aimed to guide the field of gifted education (the Talent Development Megamodel). Although not a theory itself, the framework draws on theory and is consistent with many of the features of those theories discussed here.

Gardner's Theory of Multiple Intelligences

When Howard Gardner published *Frames of Mind* in 1983, it almost immediately became a widely cited and applied approach to intelligence (Gardner, 1983/2011). Gardner challenged the prevailing view that intelligence was best understood as a single broad ability, usually described as g, or general ability, and indexed with an IQ score from a standardized psychometric test. Gardner proposed that a better framework for intelligence was a set of seven (more recently eight or nine; cf. Gardner,

2006) more or less independent intelligences that ranged from spatial and logical-mathematical, to inter- and intrapersonal intelligence.

Gardner also challenged the hegemony of psychometric assessment as the only way to gauge intelligence(s). He and the present author set about demonstrating that informal, classroom-based assessment of intelligences could be achieved in preschool (Gardner et al., 1998). Project Spectrum (as the project was called) showed the feasibility of detecting the strengths of about a dozen intelligences in young children based on their behavior in their classrooms and their involvement and performance on a set of specially designed "games" or activities administered by researchers in their classroom settings.

The theory of multiple intelligences (MI) proposed that all children have varying strengths in all of the intelligences, but that each child also would show distinctive areas of relative strength and weakness across the intelligences. Some children showed exceptional strength in mechanical ability, others in musical ability, others in linguistic ability, and so forth. Children's "profiles" rarely perfectly duplicated those of other children. Their strengths ranged from relative to their other abilities, to relative to those of the other children in their classroom, to relative to children in general. The abilities assessed by Project Spectrum provided a variegated profile of talents and proclivities each child brought to the classroom (Gardner et al., 1998).

The theory also assumed that the various intelligences were natural but not unchangeable, in contrast with traditional IQ-based frameworks. MI did not, however, at least in its original form, provide much guidance about how to support and develop the intelligences in school or elsewhere (although later publications [e.g., Gardner, 2006] did begin to address these issues).

A difference between MI and Nonuniversal Theory is that MI argues against G, while Nonuniversal Theory incorporates this way of describing ability (Feldman & Morelock, 2020). MI proposes to *replace* IQ with the seven, eight, or nine intelligences so far established, while Nonuniversal Theory acknowledges that G is a likely evolutionary adaptation that gives humans the flexibility to thrive in highly diverse environments and to do a wide range of symbolic and logical activities (Feldman, 1986). Unlike most other species, humans are blessed with both the general intelligence form of ability as well as a set of more specific talents that make mastering specific domains more likely.

Whereas MI provides an approach to intellectual abilities that gives all children the opportunity to show their strengths, Nonuniversal Theory shows how these various strengths, singly and in combination, can be utilized to master knowledge and skills in domains that offer opportunities for the development of expertise, which in turn offer career possibilities or provide pursuits for personal fulfillment. For almost everyone there is a domain, sometimes more than one, that may engage their distinct strengths and provide a structure and sequence through which to develop them.

Taken in combination, MI and Nonuniversal Theory offer two mostly complementary perspectives on intelligence that share the assumption that abilities are numerous and domain-specific, that each person has at least some of each one, and that abilities can be developed. Nonuniversal Theory adds that people are at least somewhat aware of what their abilities are and when they are being appropriately developed, virtually from birth, and that the ultimate goal of development of abilities is to develop them in a personally satisfying way.

Gagné's Integrative Model of Talent Development

Francoys Gagné created a comprehensive and wide-ranging framework for the field of gifted education. The Integrative Model of Talent Development (IMTD) begins with what are called natural "gifts" that, if sufficiently cultivated, become the "talents" that make accelerated achievement in various fields possible (Gagné, 2005; Gagné & McPherson, 2016).

One of Gagné's goals was to provide a clear, research-based set of analytic tools that can be used for research and practice in gifted education contexts. The field of gifted education has been burdened with conflicting views of the definitions of "giftedness" and "talent," making it difficult for practitioners to sort out and evaluate possible sources of application for selection and programming. Gagné hoped to resolve the issue by giving the label "gifts" only to natural abilities and "talent" to those abilities developed to potentially excellent levels.

Gagné's framework is admirably detailed and systematic, focusing on intellectual, physical, and personal qualities that contribute to the development of gifts into talent; on resources such as teachers, families, technologies, institutions, and competitions; and on material resources, such as scholarships and family income. However, the framework is not focused on gender, birth order, and several other aspects that have been shown to influence the talent development process (Kerr & McKay, 2014; Sulloway, 1997). The IMTD goes a long way toward its goal of providing a clear and straightforward path for the field of gifted education to follow.

The IMTD is also a developmental approach in the sense that it assumes that whatever "gifts" one is born with will not bear fruit without support, guidance, and expert teaching (called "catalysts" in the theory) over several years of the child's life. Nonuniversal Theory does not provide much detail about the actual process of how expertise is achieved, so Gagné's focus on the development process is a welcome complement to Nonuniversal Theory's emphasis on the nature and variety of domains.

The main way in which the two approaches differ is in the definitions of the key terms *gifts* and *talents* (Feldman, 2016). For Gagné, gifts are the natural abilities that children come into the world with, while talents are the outcomes that show mastery in specific fields that result from the successful development of the set of natural gifts a child possesses from birth. Although clear, this use of the key terms *gifts* and *talents* tends to obfuscate one of the deeper issues that divides the field of gifted education. This issue is the argument between those who see giftedness as one thing versus those who see it as one of several possible things (see the previous discussion of MI theory). By putting the label *gift* on natural, largely inborn abilities, and *talent* on largely developed expertise, Gagné does not directly address the critical issue of one versus many gifts and/or talents.

Based on a reading of primate evolution (Feldman, 1986), Nonuniversal Theory takes a different stance on the gifts/talents issue. It assumes that over evolutionary time, and in distinction from other primates, homo sapiens are the recipients of two kinds of natural abilities: gifts and talents. Gifts are defined as the more general capabilities associated with symbolic and abstract reasoning referenced typically by IQ, while talents are defined as more specific abilities associated with specific domains (physics, dance, culinary, veterinary, and numerous others). Gifts and talents are both natural, both vary from child to child, and both may be further developed, sharpened, and focused over time. This is in contrast with humans' closest primate relatives who tend to have either general adaptive ability *or* specific abilities matched to specific habits, but rarely both (Bruner, 1972).

This definitional difference notwithstanding, Gagné's theory—with its focus on the several dimensions of development of natural abilities; its appreciation of personal, emotional, as well as intellectual qualities; its recognition of the importance of available resources to support development; and its comprehensive structure for the field of gifted education—is a welcome complement to Nonuniversal Theory.

MI theory provides a good summary of the likely natural abilities that all people work with (albeit in varying strengths). Gagné's theory provides a good general framework within which to analyze the dimensions and contributions to talent development made by various influences. Nonuniversal Theory provides a good account of the range and variety of domains where expertise may be developed, as well as a general framework for understanding the process through which it may be developed.

Dai's Evolving Complexity Theory of Talent Development

Perhaps closest to Nonuniversal Theory in its stage sequential development emphasis is Dai's Evolving Complexity Theory (ECT; Dai, 2010, 2017). At the core of ECT is a sequence of stages and transitions from birth to maturity and beyond, organized around the extent to which natural talents emerge, are crystallized into adaptive form (called "Characteristic Adaptation"), and then shaped and further developed into the unique forms of expression achieved at the higher levels of all talent development areas (called "Maximal Adaptation").

The main difference between ECT and Nonuniversal Theory is the emphasis in the former on individual development from universal to unique; the latter emphasizes the nature of the many domains through which individuals can potentially express their natural gifts and talents and how these domains have developed. Dai used Nonuniversal Theory fairly extensively in constructing his domains and stages, so the similarity is not surprising.

The other distinct quality of ECT is its embrace of a dynamic systems framework to explain the emergence of gifts and talents, their development from more spontaneous to more intentional form (called the "push" and "sustain" aspects of development), and the ways in which natural, social, and cultural influences help "crystallize" the possible forms of talent into stable, focused, and goal-oriented systems under the control of the developing individual (Dai, 2017). The dynamic interplay of contributors to talent development found in ECT gives it a contemporary quality not found in other approaches, including Nonuniversal Theory.[3]

---

[3] Although not explicitly part of Nonuniversal Theory, I have used a version of dynamic systems to help explain the phenomenon of the child prodigy. The "co-incidence" framework proposes several interacting dimensions, including the child's talent and personal qualities, the target domain, teachers, material resources, family, and broader social and historical influences as jointly contributing to the process of prodigy development (Feldman, 1986, 2016).

Of the theories discussed here, Dai's comes down most solidly on the talent development side of the "talent versus giftedness" issue. There is no image of a gifted child in Dai's framework; rather there are many possible images of children developing their natural and evolved talents within existing domains of expertise, possibly extending their talent development into distinctive, even unique, forms over their life spans. This latter state may share some qualities of the "gifted child" growing into the "gifted adult" image, but Dai's account is very different from the traditional one: more diverse, more probabilistic, and more emergent (Dai, 2017).

Dai's purposes in developing the ECT are essentially twofold: (a) to bring more diversity into the field of developmental psychology by broadening its scope to include the many talents and abilities that children develop, in contrast with the traditional preoccupation of that field with developmental universals (see also Feldman, 1980, 1994); and (b) to provide the field of gifted education with a solidly grounded framework based on the best theory and research in developmental psychology, as well as gifted and creativity studies on which to build its future.

To a substantial degree, ECT succeeds in potentially achieving its goals. Developmental psychology has begun to embrace greater domain specificity in its core research programs, and gifted education has begun to recognize that a new paradigm is going to be necessary to guide the field into and beyond the 21st century (see, for example, the following discussion of the Talent Development Megamodel). Most likely, some combination of ECT, with its emphasis on individual development within talent domains; MI, with its emphasis on the natural talents and abilities that vary among people; IMTD, with its careful analysis of the many facets of general and specific talent development; and Nonuniversal Theory, with its emphasis on the nature and development of the vast landscape of domains of knowledge and skill to be mastered, will be adopted to guide programs and practices that meet the specific needs in a given locale. This leads to a broad framework proposed as a general guide for the field in the 21st century.

Subotnik, Olszewski-Kubilius, and Worrell's Talent Development Megamodel

Subotnik, Olszewski-Kubilius, and Worrell (2011, 2019; Olszewski-Kubilius et al., 2018) put forward a general framework—not a theory, but what they refer to as a "Megamodel"—that they hope will guide the field of gifted education through the next century. The framework emerged out of a distillation, synthesis, and integration of relevant research and policy within and outside the field of gifted education. The features of the model are largely consonant with the theories discussed in this chapter: a developmental emphasis, a domain-specific emphasis, emphasis on the development of expertise, general and specific intellectual and personal qualities that predict success in development of high-level achievement, and the vital roles of parents, peers, teachers, and coaches as guides to help manage the complex talent development process. Although there are some differences in emphasis, the Talent Development Megamodel hits most of the notes and produces the harmonies that many theorists can likely endorse.

The Megamodel explicitly places talent development at the core of the field, as contrasted with identification of general intellectual potential, which is the core of the traditional field. That said, the Megamodel acknowledges the importance of general as well as specific abilities as necessary (but not sufficient) for the optimal development of potential (Subotnik et al., 2011, 2019). The aim is not to eliminate the knowledge and wisdom gained from a century of research, theory, policy, and practice on general intelligence (g), but to integrate them into a more encompassing framework that includes specific subfields that seek to learn about the nature of specific talent domains, the personal qualities (such as motivation) other than intellectual that contribute to optimal talent development, distinctions between those who perform within a domain versus those who produce new works, the kinds of roles that other participants in the talent development process play, creativity, and how chance affects talent development (Subotnik et al., 2011, 2019).

Olszewski-Kubilius et al. (2018) also produced a volume, *Talent Development as a Framework for Gifted Education*, intended to guide the application of the Talent Development Megamodel. There are chapters on identification and assessment, programming, curriculum, and other topics to aid the practitioner in transitioning from traditional to talent development programming.

One feature of the Talent Development Megamodel that has been controversial is its proposed goal of eminence within talent domains (see, for example, Borland, 2012; Worrell et al., 2018). The reasons for choosing eminence as a goal are straightforward enough: It is a relatively clear criterion, it marks the highest achievements one can reach, and it places individual fulfillment of potential at the heart of the field (Subotnik et al., 2011).

But eminence is also problematic in several respects. Eminence is a label set by both professional and nonprofessional judges, including the general public. The man who likely was Jack the Ripper was at the time of his crimes one of the most eminent visual artists in Britain (Cornwell, 2002, 2017). Francis Galton's study of eminence was as much a study of class and wealth as it was of great achievement (Simonton, 1994). There is simply no way to disaggregate social judgments of eminence from the talents and abilities that made it possible. Over time, it is true, that the label of eminence may be withdrawn, earned posthumously, or achieved decades or even centuries after a person's work is done. It is not clear that a criterion that is changing and changeable after the fact serves well as the core outcome of talent development.

There is no doubt a positive correlation between achieved eminence and actual achievement, but the relationship is not straightforward. Many things may contribute to the status of eminence during a given period, including connections, promotion, timing, chance, and health. During most of his lifetime, Salieri was more eminent than Mozart (Feldman, 1986; Solomon, 1995). If eminence changes, as it often does, does that change the degree of success in the optimal development of talent?

A more appropriate goal for the field is optimal development of individual talent (Feldman, 1986). Granted, this goal may be more difficult to assess than eminence (which has its own challenges), but it is more consonant with the rest of the Megamodel and more consonant with the field. If, at the onset of the talent development process, each person has natural gifts and talents, personal qualities, and resources, and if the field of gifted education's purpose is to provide every child who shows promise in any valued domain with optimal conditions for the fulfillment of that promise, then wouldn't educators' goal be to assess the degree to which over that child's lifetime the child made the most of the gifts and talents they developed?

For some, to be sure, becoming eminent would be the only way to be confident that one's talents had been fully developed, but for others, eminence may seem more of a public label—possibly deserved, possibly not—

that is only partially a mark of optimal development of talent. An individual might achieve eminence but know that public recognition came at the cost of doing what was fashionable rather than what would have been the greatest challenge. Ervin Nyiregyházi was a music prodigy at the turn of the last century, often compared with Mozart, with a promising career. During his lifetime Nyiregyházi composed more than 600 works, none of which was performed regularly or became part of the classical repertoire (Bazzana, 2007). Yet by his own reckoning, he did exactly what he wanted to do without the constraints and demands of a public musical career (Bazzana, 2007). By his own standard, his potential was more fully expressed than if he had become famous or eminent by pursuing a traditional professional music career.

It is certainly reasonable to have eminence as one criterion of successful fulfillment of potential, but it should not be the only one. There are those whose gifts and talents may not be expressed within existing domains, or within domains of expertise at all. Extraordinary empathy, for example, need not manifest itself in Mother Teresa-level eminence. It could be just as importantly manifested in ways that fly under the radar but make important differences in the lives of those it touched.

In Nonuniversal Theory, the ultimate criterion for the fulfillment of the potential of one's gifts and talents is the personal judgment that a person did the very best they could with what they were given (Feldman, 2018). For many, doing one's best will not lead to outstanding performance in an existing domain. For the field of gifted education, as Subotnik et al. (2011) proposed, the goal should be to make it possible for all children to feel fulfilled in their efforts to make the most of their talents, especially when there are reasons to believe that in doing so they will contribute to what is known about the world and about each other and make positive contributions to their societies.

Ideally, the feeling that one has done the best they could is accompanied by contributions that are recognized as excellent or even among the best ever, but this outcome is a rare and multidetermined one. The Megamodel (Subotnik et al., 2011) is nonetheless a major step forward and, my comments about eminence notwithstanding, will guide the field of gifted education for decades to come.

A Few Words for Practitioners About Theory

Psychologist Kurt Lewin is quoted as saying, "There is nothing so practical as a good theory." As a theorist I hope that is true, but it is not obvious what makes a "good" theory, on the one hand, or how to use it to achieve applied goals, on the other. Here are a few tips on how to choose good theory and apply it to achieve practice goals.

- A theory is a set of general statements that aim to help explain something that is not well enough understood. As such it should be clear what the theory is trying to explain and how it proposes to explain it. It should also state its claims in clear enough terms that they can be put to empirical test. There is nothing magical about a theory, nor are theories sacrosanct. How good a theory is depends on how well it explains what it set out to explain. One of the big mistakes in using theory is to try to use it for purposes for which it was not constructed. A theory might be useful to explain animal learning, for example, but fail when applied to human learning. So the first rule of using theory is to find out why the theory was built. It is likely to be most useful when it is applied to similar situations as the ones it was built to explain.
- It is not necessary to "buy" the whole theory. Especially when a theory was built for different purposes from the ones needed, it may be that one or more aspects of a theory are useful, while others are not. To use theories in this partial way requires that a practitioner understand the theory well enough to make informed judgments about its usefulness in a particular applied situation. In other words, it should not be a pick-and-choose process, but rather a result of carefully studying a theory, its assumptions, claims, empirical support, and coherence, and then choosing components that best fit one's situation. If a practitioner is clear about what they are doing and why, they should be on solid ground.
- Good theorists know that the theories they construct are likely not complete (especially in areas dealing with human development and giftedness) or able to endure unchanged. Theories are, in this sense, the best currently available ways to explain something that is important to explain, like how to foster learning in specific domains or why some kids seem to be able learn so much more easily than

others. These concepts are not likely to be fully explained by any theory, but good theories may help explain one or more aspect.
- In order to apply theory well, one must be a serious student of theory. It is probably better not to try to use a theory unless one understands it well. There is nothing inherently wrong in not using theory; it is just more likely to be better if it is understood and used well. So I might add to Kurt Lewin's earlier quote, "There is nothing so practical as a good theory," that there is nothing so impractical as using a theory poorly.
- About applying Nonuniversal Theory in gifted education: Nonuniversal Theory is a broad, general theory of cognitive development, built to help move the field of developmental psychology beyond the universal milestones that were its preoccupation. It was not built for gifted education, but there are several features of the theory that may be used for applications in that field. The two that seem most promising are the regions of the universal to unique continuum and the levels of expertise proposed to provide a framework for development in nonuniversal domains. The regions of the universal to unique continuum help show the diversity of ways in which gifts and talents may be expressed, as well as the occasionally creative transformations that occur within domains as the result of the efforts of individuals who have found existing forms and functions inadequate. The levels of expertise found in most domains may have potential for helping organize curricula and establish criteria for degrees of mastery in talent domains, as well as point to the importance of building better knowledge of the talent domains themselves, something currently lacking in the field (Subotnik et al., 2011). In Subotnik et al.'s (2019) *The Psychology of High Performance: Developing Human Potential Into Domain Specific Talent*, one chapter uses Nonuniversal Theory (along with Subotnik & Jarvin's [2005] work on very high-level achievement) as a guide to studying two practice domains: medicine and software engineering. I recommend this chapter (McWilliams et al., 2019) as a thoughtful, sophisticated example of how to apply Nonuniversal Theory (and other theories) in gifted education.

Theory, research, policy, and practice in a field like gifted education should inform one another. Theory should guide but not control practice, practice should show where theory works and where it doesn't work, research should test the claims of both theory and practice, and policy should be based on the best theory, research, and practice that the field has produced. Each person has a role to play in this challenging but vital field of human endeavor. Working collaboratively is most likely to bring positive outcomes for the field.

DISCUSSION QUESTIONS

1. How is Nonuniversal Theory different from traditional theories of giftedness and talent with respect to its definitions of giftedness and talent?

2. How is Nonuniversal Theory complementary to theories such as multiple intelligences (Gardner, 1983/2011), the Integrative Model of Talent Development (Gagné, 2005), and the Evolving Complexity Theory of Talent Development (Dai, 2010, 2017)?

3. How does Nonuniversal Theory differ from the Talent Development Megamodel (Subotnik et al., 2011) for the field of gifted education?

4. How should theories be used when applied in policy and practice in gifted education?

References

Assouline, S. G., Colangelo, N., VanTassel-Baska, J., & Lupkowski-Shoplik, A. (Eds.). (2015). *A nation empowered: Evidence trumps the excuses that hold back America's brightest students* (Vol. 2). The University of Iowa, The Connie Belin & Jacqueline N. Blank International Center for Gifted Education and Talent Development.

Bazzana, K. (2007). *Lost genius: The curious and tragic story of an extraordinary musical prodigy.* Da Capo Press.

Benjamin, A. (1989). *Levels of expertise in early childhood teaching: An initial field test of a diagnostic instrument* [Doctoral dissertation]. Tufts University.

Bloom, B. S. (Ed.). (1985). *Developing talent in young people.* Ballantine Books.
Borland, J. H. (Ed.). (2003). *Rethinking gifted education.* Teachers College Press.
Borland, J. H. (2012). A landmark monograph in gifted education, and why I disagree with its major conclusion. *The Creativity Post.*
Bruner, J. S. (1972). Nature and uses of immaturity. *American Psychologist, 27*(8), 687–708. https://doi.org/10.1037/h0033144
Campbell, R., Brown, N. R., & DiBello, L. A. (1992). The programmer's burden: Developing expertise in programming. In R. R. Hoffman (Ed.), *The psychology of expertise: Cognitive research and empirical AI* (pp. 269–294). Springer.
Chase, W. G., & Simon, H. S. (1973). Perception in chess. *Cognitive Psychology, 4*(1), 55–81. https://doi.org/10.1016/0010-0285(73)90004-2
Cornwell, P. (2002). *Portrait of a killer: Jack the Ripper—Case closed.* Putnam.
Cornwell, P. (2017). *Ripper: The secret life of Walter Sickert.* Thomas & Mercer.
Dai, D. Y. (2010). *The nature and nurture of giftedness: A new framework for understanding gifted education.* Teachers College Press.
Dai, D. Y. (2017). Envisioning a new foundation for gifted education: Evolving Complexity Theory (ECT) of talent development. *Gifted Child Quarterly, 61*(3), 172–182. https://doi.org/10.1177/0016986217701837
Ericsson, K. A. (Ed.). (1996). *The road to excellence: The acquisition of expert performance in the arts and sciences, sports, and games.* Erlbaum.
Feldman, D. H. (1980). *Beyond universals in cognitive development.* Ablex.
Feldman, D. H. (with Goldsmith, L. T.). (1986). *Nature's gambit: Child prodigies and the development of human potential.* Basic Books.
Feldman, D. H. (1994). *Beyond universals in cognitive development* (2nd ed.). Greenwood Press.
Feldman, D. H. (2003). A developmental, evolutionary perspective on gifts and talents. In J. H. Borland (Ed.), *Rethinking gifted education* (pp. 9–33). Teachers College Press.
Feldman, D. H. (2004). Piaget's stages: The unfinished symphony of cognitive development. *New Ideas in Psychology, 22*(3), 175–231. https://doi.org/10.1016/j.newideapsych.2004.11.005
Feldman, D. H. (2016). Two roads diverged in the music wood: A co-incidence approach to the lives and careers of Nyiregyhazi and Menuhin. In G. McPherson (Ed.), *Musical prodigies: Interpretations from psychology, education, musicology, and ethnomusicology* (pp. 115–133). Oxford University Press.

Feldman, D. H. (2018). *CSHD 151: Cognitive development* [PowerPoint slides]. Tufts University.

Feldman, D. H., & Katzir, T. (1998). Natural talents: An argument from the extremes. *Behavioral and Brain Sciences, 21*(3), 415. https://doi.org/10.1017/S0140525X98301235

Feldman, D. H., & Morelock, M. J. (2020). Prodigies and savants. In R. J. Sternberg (Ed.), *The Cambridge handbook of intelligence* (2nd ed., pp. 258–290). Cambridge University Press.

Gagné, F. (2005). From gifts to talents: The DMGT as a developmental model. In R. J. Sternberg & J. E. Davidson (Eds.), *Conceptions of giftedness* (2nd ed., pp. 98–119). Cambridge University Press.

Gagné, F., & McPherson, G. (2016). Analyzing prodigiousness using Gagné's integrative model of talent development. In G. McPherson (Ed.), *Musical prodigies: Interpretations from psychology, education, musicology, and ethnomusicology* (pp. 3–114). Oxford University Press.

Gardner, H. (2006). *Multiple intelligences: New horizons* (Rev. ed.). Basic Books.

Gardner, H. (2011). *Frames of mind: The theory of multiple intelligences*. Basic Books. (Original work published 1983)

Gardner, H., Feldman, D. H., & Krechevsky, M. (Eds.). (1998). *Project Spectrum*. Teachers College Press.

Kerr, B., & McKay, R. (2014). *Smart girls in the 21st century: Understanding talented girls and women*. Great Potential Press.

Killas, H. (Director). (2019). *Superkids 2* [Film]. Cesarini Bros Entertainment.

McWilliams, M. A., Holding, E. Z., & Knotek, S. E. (2019). Talent development in medicine and software engineering. In R. F. Subotnik, P. Olszewski-Kubilius, & F. C. Worrell (Eds.), *The psychology of high performance: Developing human potential into domain-specific talent* (pp. 109–134). American Psychological Association. https://doi.org/10.1037/0000120-006

Olson, D. R. (1970). *Cognitive development: The child's acquisition of diagonality*. Elsevier.

Olson, D. R. (2003). *Psychological theory and educational reform: How school remakes mind and society*. Cambridge University Press.

Olszewski-Kubilius, P., Subotnik, R. F., & Worrell, F. C. (Eds.). (2018). *Talent development as a framework for gifted education: Implications for best practices and applications in schools*. Prufrock Press.

Simon, H. S., & Chase, W. G. (1973). Skill in chess. *American Scientist, 61*(4), 364–403.

Simonton, D. K. (1994). *Greatness: Who makes history and why*. Guilford Press.

Snyder, S. S., & Feldman, D. H. (1977). Internal and external influences on cognitive developmental change. *Child Development, 48*(3), 937–943. https://doi.org/10.2307/1128344

Solomon, M. (1995). *Mozart: A life*. HarperCollins.

Subotnik, R. F., & Jarvin, L. (2005). Beyond expertise: Conceptions of giftedness as great performance. In R. J. Sternberg & J. E. Davidson (Eds.), *Conceptions of giftedness* (2nd ed., pp. 343–357). Cambridge University Press.

Subotnik, R. F., Olszewski-Kubilius, P., & Worrell, F. C. (2011). Rethinking giftedness and gifted education: A proposed direction forward based on psychological science. *Psychological Science in the Public Interest, 12*(1), 3–54. https://doi.org/10.1177/1529100611418056

Subotnik, R. F., Olszewski-Kubilius, P., & Worrell, F. C. (Eds.). (2019). *The psychology of high performance: Developing human potential into domain specific talent*. American Psychological Association.

Sulloway, F. (1997). *Born to rebel: Birth order, family dynamics, and creative lives*. Pantheon.

Vygotsky, L. S. (1978). *Mind in society: The development of higher psychological processes*. Harvard University Press.

Walton, R. (1987). *Emotional concomitants of developmental transitions* [Unpublished master's thesis]. Tufts University.

Worrell, F. C., Subotnik, R. F., & Olszewski-Kubilius, P. (2018). Talent development: A path toward eminence. In S. I. Pfeiffer, E. Shaunessy-Dedrick, & M. Foley-Nicpon (Eds.), *APA handbook of giftedness and talent* (pp. 247–258). American Psychological Association. https://doi.org/10.1037/0000038-016

CHAPTER 7

Transformational Giftedness

ROBERT J. STERNBERG

Suppose that you desperately need someone who is an expert on brain surgery (neurosurgery). You want absolutely the most gifted individual you can find. Fortunately, you have resources and so can choose among five individuals:

1. A gifted brain surgeon who has successfully performed many operations for which the prognoses actually were not all that positive.
2. A gifted research professor of surgery who has written some of the most important and widely respected scientific research articles on brain surgery but does not actually do brain surgery himself.
3. A gifted professor of surgery who once was a brain surgeon and no longer does brain surgery, but now trains future brain surgeons and has trained some of the best brain surgeons in the world.

DOI: 10.4324/9781003233787-7

4. A gifted science writer/journalist who has never taken a single course on brain surgery but has written a popular best-seller on what actually happens to people when they undergo brain surgery.
5. A gifted student in a brain surgery residency program at the best residency program in the country who is described by mentors as the best resident they have ever produced but who has not, as of yet, led even a single brain-surgery operation in a high-stakes situation.

Which is the correct answer? Which one would you choose—1, 2, 3, 4, or 5?

This is obviously a poorly constructed multiple-choice item. There may be multiple reasons the item is poorly constructed, but certainly a major one is that there is no one-size-fits-all notion of giftedness that will provide you with the best expert on neurosurgery. If you have brain cancer, certainly you will choose #1. If you want to propel your university or institute up in national and international ratings for neurosurgery, for sure you will choose #2. If you want to study brain surgery and become a gifted surgeon yourself, then #3 is the obvious choice. If you are a layperson with no particular background in neurosurgery or even perhaps in medicine, #4 is your best choice by far. If you want to hire someone just starting out for your neurosurgery group practice, then no doubt you will select #5. All five individuals are gifted, but when it comes to identifying the right kind of giftedness, you simply must specify, "giftedness for what?"

The lesson of the test item described above seems, oddly enough, not to have been learned by the field of giftedness. Laypersons and experts alike speak of "giftedness" as though it is somehow a "thing"—that there is some kind of unified construction that constitutes giftedness that crosses all boundaries of the use or uses to which giftedness is put. Perhaps because of the origins of the field in the work of Lewis Terman (1925), the dominant focus of much of the field of giftedness has been on IQ and related constructs. That is not to say that there has been a dearth of broader conceptions of giftedness (e.g., Heller et al., 2000; Pfeiffer, 2019; Pfeiffer et al., 2018; Renzulli et al., 2009; Sternberg, 2004a; Sternberg & Davidson, 1986, 2005; Subotnik et al., 2011; see also the chapters in this volume). But the field of giftedness, as practiced in educational institutions, has shown remarkable resistance to change. Standardized cognitive tests and school grades (which measure constructs closely related to those measured by standardized tests) still seem to rule the day. For independent school and college admissions to elite schools for the gifted, for example, test scores and grades are the sine qua non except for a small number of test-optional schools.

The thesis of this chapter is that arguments about the "true nature" of giftedness are no more productive than arguments about how many angels can dance on the head of a pin. A single construct of giftedness is no more realistic. In the previous example, all five individuals are gifted but in different ways. There probably is some overlap in who might have become who, had their educations differed. But in terms of gifted societal contributions, they are nonoverlapping. One would not want someone who is a teacher of surgery but does not perform surgery to perform a life-saving surgical operation. And many top surgeons would be only mediocre as researchers. What four of the five individuals have in common is that they transform lives, and the fifth individual, the student, looks to be someone who someday will be in that category as well.

Rather than arguing for a particular definition of giftedness, I would instead like to define a new concept, *transformational giftedness*, as exceptional ability or talent that can enable or has enabled an individual to make one or more extraordinary and meaningful contributions that help to make the world a better place. Making the world a better place could involve an effort as large scale as reducing climate change, or as small scale as transforming a child's life in a classroom (as happened to me with my fourth-grade teacher, Mrs. Alexa). Transformational giftedness is idiographic, or individualized. What is transformational at one time may be trivial at another (see also Ziegler, 2005). For example, there is no single predictive formula that will enable educators or anyone else to foretell who, even among individuals identified as gifted, will become transformational in some way. Certainly, an IQ test is a poor excuse for predicting transformational giftedness. As shown in Terman and Oden's (1959) and Subotnik et al.'s (1989) studies, IQ and related constructs are modest to moderate predictors of various kinds of success, but that they are very weak predictors of what I call "transformational" success.

Measures of IQ and related constructs may be the best standardized and published tests available today for identifying the gifted, but they strongly resemble the tests of the early 20th century. A field that has not transformationally progressed in a century, but rather has developed only through cosmetic variations, is in need of rejuvenation. Compare medicine, biology, physics, astronomy, chemistry, or practically any other field to psychological measurement. Those fields have moved forward transformationally. Psychological measurement and underlying conceptions of giftedness, as used in schools, have not.

Kinds of Giftedness

It may help to place transformational giftedness into perspective by creating a taxonomy into which it fits. I present here for the first time such a taxonomy.

Latent Giftedness

I define *latent giftedness* as giftedness that exists in potential only but through circumstances cannot be observed. A potential musically gifted child who grows up in a religious culture that forbids music or a potentially gifted writer who grows up in a preliterate society are examples of latent giftedness. The circumstances of the environment leave the gifts unable to be observed or even discovered.

Inert Giftedness

I define *inert giftedness* as giftedness that is identified and thus observed, unlike latent giftedness, but that goes largely or even entirely unused. For example, a child might be identified as musically gifted, but because they have no interest in music—or because their parents or school steer them elsewhere—those gifts are never developed. Or a child might have a gift for art but be steered entirely away from art because the parents do not see art as leading to a viable career. Inert giftedness can be identified, but through lack of interest or motivation on the part of the child, parents, or school, it remains underdeveloped or even entirely undeveloped. Inertly gifted people may be high in abilities but lacking in motivation to direct their abilities (see Dai & Sternberg, 2004).

Reactive Giftedness

I define *reactive giftedness* as giftedness residing in a person who, when presented with a problem, will solve the problem in a way that reflects unusual skills, but who is simply reactive to what is presented. A child might do extremely well on standardized tests or in school when problems are presented to them but not actively seek out any way actively to express their giftedness. This child is *receptively gifted* but not motivated to go beyond what is given to them.

Proactive Giftedness

I define *proactive giftedness* as giftedness that actively seeks out problems to solve or products to create. The individual goes beyond the given. They do not just do well on presented problems but also seek to identify new problems and to go beyond. Proactive giftedness can be of two kinds:
- *Paradigm-preserving giftedness* moves the world forward, but in a way that preserves existing paradigms (see Sternberg et al., 2002). It could be a new work of art in a given artistic paradigm (e.g., Impressionism), a new scientific study within a given paradigm (e.g., cognitivism in psychology), or a new piece of music in an existing style (e.g., the classical style).
- *Transformational giftedness* is a form of proactive giftedness in which the individual not only acts, but also acts in a transformational way. Transformational giftedness goes beyond existing paradigms and either redirects or reinitiates ways of thinking (Sternberg et al., 2002).

There are other classification schemes related to those presented here. For example, Renzulli (1977, 1978) distinguished between schoolhouse giftedness and creative productive giftedness. This distinction is similar but not identical to that between reactive giftedness and proactive giftedness. The reason is that an individual could be reactively or proactively gifted in any environment, whether a school or an adult professional environment. The question is not whether one is doing school tasks or more career-related tasks but, rather, whether one is more passive in simply reacting to stimuli or more active in seeking out and creating stimuli. Someone could be passive or active—reactive or proactive—in any kind of setting or for any kind of task.

Transformational giftedness, of course, is also very different from profound giftedness, usually defined as an IQ of 180 or above. Someone could be profoundly gifted and yet in their life effect no serious transformations at all.

Why Transformational Giftedness?

A reasonable question to ask would be: Why is transformational giftedness so important or even important at all? There are so many domains of giftedness, such as mathematical, musical, verbal, artistic, and scientific. What makes transformational giftedness—which has not even previously been defined, to my knowledge—anything more than just another term in a sea of terms? For one thing, transformational giftedness crosses domains, rather than residing in any one of them or being itself a domain (see also Ambrose, 2015). But transformational giftedness is important for a more pressing reason.

A recent United Nations report stated that one million species around the world face extinction as a result of human activity (Fears, 2019). Humans will suffer as a result, according to the report's chair, because species diversity provides "the foundations of our economies, livelihoods, food security, health and quality of life worldwide" (para. 4). In a sense, therefore, one could propose that humans as a species (*Homo sapiens*) are not only taking down one million species that most could not name, but also, themselves. They are engaged in a maladaptive slow-motion attempt at mass suicide. The people doing this often are high in IQ, such as those who work in nonrenewable energy, those who manage factories that pollute the environment, or those who work on developing more sophisticated weapons of mass destruction.

Many people notice and want to do something; however, others notice but do nothing, and still others do not want to notice because, as is the case with smoking, they enjoy the seeming benefits and comforts of contemporary society too much, even as things fall apart. It used to be thought that people allowed this mass extinction to go on because the effects are largely delayed—they will be felt by people's children and grandchildren, much like the current $24 trillion national debt in the United States that will have to be paid off, but probably after most of the people who incur it die.

Species extinctions are being caused, in part, by another enormously pressing problem in the world—global climate change. As a result of climate change, temperatures are rising, weather is becoming more severe and volatile, forest fires are increasing in size and severity, and places that once were livable are no longer livable because they are literally underwater (see Climate Central, 2019; Harvey, 2018; National Climate Assessment, n.d.; Union of Concerned Scientists, 2018).

Greenland is disappearing, which might seem to those not in Greenland like no big deal, except that it is not land that is disappearing but rather water, and the water that is no longer in ice packs in Greenland needs somewhere to go. One place it goes is the Solomon Islands. Five islands in the Solomon Islands have disappeared, and six more are on the way to disappearing (Albert et al., 2016). These places may seem far away to many readers. Consider, then, the State of Louisiana, which for some readers may be closer to home. The state consists largely of land that is low-lying; some of that land is (or was) below sea level. On a map, Louisiana looks like a big boot, except that this image is wrong, or to be precise, out of date.

Much of the land that is shown on a map of Louisiana as land mass is now submerged underwater. The land mass of the state is disappearing at a rapid and probably accelerating rate. Each hour and a half, the equivalent of one football field of land disappears underwater (Kolbert, 2019). This rate of land submersion is not sustainable over many years, as eventually, there will be no land in the state left to become submerged. Strangely, perhaps, in the 2018 presidential election, 58% of Louisiana citizens who cast ballots voted for a candidate who denies human-caused climate change.

Sea levels are rising all over the world (University of Waterloo, 2018). Yet, in a recent survey, only Indonesia and Saudi Arabia had a higher proportion of climate change deniers than did the United States (Milman & Harvey, 2019). This is despite the fact that 95% of researchers of climate change and 80 national academies of science support the idea of human-induced climate change. Recently, in Finland, an ultra-right-wing political party that scolded other parties for wanting to take action on climate change watched its percentage of support double among the general Finnish public. What is perhaps ironic is that recent Programme for International Student Assessment (PISA) results show Finland as ranking an impressive #5 overall (Organisation for Economic Co-operation and Development, 2016).

If human-originated global climate change were the only problem the world was facing, things might not be so bleak. But global climate change is only one of several enormous problems, such as nuclear weapons, violence and terrorism, profound income inequality, growing antibiotic resistance of bacteria, and disappearing drinking water. Consider just one more enormous problem, air pollution.

Air pollution is responsible for roughly 4.2 million deaths each year, plus innumerable respiratory and other illnesses (World Health Organization, 2019). This figure of 4.2 million exceeds the population of Los Angeles, CA, the second largest city in the United States after New York City. (Los Angeles also happens to rank #1 among cities in the United States for ozone pollution [American Lung Association, n.d.]). Air pollution, of course, is annoying to everyone, but mere annoyance is the least of the issues. Air pollution kills people and also has harmful effects. For example, it stunts the cognitive growth of children (Williams, 2018). Some countries and cities have made visible progress in combating air pollution (Barone, 2017). But the fight against air pollution in major cities of the world (e.g., Mexico City, Jakarta, Beijing) has a long way to go (e.g., South China Morning Post, 2019). The city with the worst air pollution in the world is Delhi, India, where pollution is estimated to kill more than a million people per year and to damage the lungs of an additional more than 2 million children, which constitutes half of Delhi's juvenile population.

I wish to stress that although, to some readers, these issues might seem political, they really are not political at all. Climate change and air pollution do not care about whether the population they strike is Republican or Democrat, conservative or liberal. Their effects are immune to political party. Conservative Louisiana gets submerged; liberal California gets consumed by wildfires. The natural phenomena are indifferent to politics. To other readers, these issues may seem to have little or nothing to do with giftedness, but if the gifted are not going to solve these problems, who will?

I believe all kinds of giftedness can be potentially important. The world needs more great mathematical advances, musical compositions, exciting novels, and scientific discoveries. These are the kinds of advances that have created today's seemingly advanced civilization. I say "seemingly advanced" because there is an exceptionally large elephant in the room that seems perhaps to have eluded some in the field. That elephant is the convergence of world problems that have destroyed a million species and could take down humans—problems of humankind's own creation. The dinosaurs, at least, were not the cause of the meteorite or comet that struck the Earth and wiped them out. In contrast, humans have only themselves to blame if they join the million extinguished species.

Although transformationally gifted individuals are crucial in society, they are not necessarily transformational leaders (Bass & Avolio, 1994; Bass et al., 1996) and are not necessarily identified as leaders at all. For example, Rosa Parks was not looking for a leadership role when she refused to yield her seat on a bus to a White person. Marie Curie was transformationally gifted in her physics research, but she was not what one would usually identify as a "transformational leader." Transformationally gifted individuals may make a difference on their own or as team members exercising no particular leadership in their team. They are not necessarily famous—they may make a positive difference in their family or community rather than on any larger stage. Nor are they necessarily particularly high in IQ. Rather, they have a broader set of skills, which I refer to collectively as successful intelligence. To make a transformational difference, these broader skills all are essential in some significant degree.

The Augmented Theory of Successful Intelligence

Although I have not written or spoken before of the concept of transformational giftedness, I have proposed previously a theory designed to predict it, at least at some level. The model for selection is called ACCEL—selection for Active Concerned Citizenship and Ethical Leadership (Sternberg, 2017). This model can be used to identify gifted children with the attributes for exhibiting transformational behavior. The underlying theory is the augmented theory of successful intelligence (Sternberg, 2018b). The theory originally was designed to characterize what I call *successful intelligence—* one's ability to formulate, reformulate as necessary, and, within environmental constraints, achieve one's prosocial goals in life (see also Forgeard & Mecklenburg, 2013, for further discussion of the importance of prosocial motivation). That is, people are successfully intelligent to the extent that they can use their cognitive and other skills to make prosocial, personally meaningful plans, modify those plans as needed, and execute and evaluate those plans throughout one's life. I am now arguing that very high levels of successful intelligence are a necessary but not sufficient condition for transformational giftedness.

Successfully intelligent people identify their strengths and weaknesses and then figure out, one way or another, how to capitalize on their strengths and to compensate for or correct their weaknesses. They are experts in adapting to environments. To the extent that they are transformationally gifted, they also are experts in *shaping* those environments so that the environments are transformed for the better, not just with respect to themselves, but with respect to the world, at some level. In terms of the theory of successful intelligence, shaping is a key to transformational giftedness. Transformationally gifted individuals are not content just to adapt to whatever environment they happen to find themselves in. Nor are they content, if the environment is not perfectly suited to them, merely to look elsewhere—to select another environment. Rather, they attempt to shape the environment—to make wherever they are a better place, not just for them, but for everyone.

Transformationally gifted people draw especially upon four kinds of skills and attitudes: creative, analytical, practical, and wisdom-based. Basically, one needs creative skills and attitudes to generate novel and viable ideas; one needs analytical skills and attitudes to ascertain whether the ideas are good ideas; one needs practical skills and attitudes to implement one's ideas and to persuade others to accept those ideas; and one needs wisdom-based skills and attitudes to ensure that one's ideas help to achieve a common good, not just for one's allies and friends, but also for all stakeholders.

Creative Skills and Attitudes

Creative skills and attitudes are used to generate ideas that are novel and, in some way, useful (Kaufman, 2016; Kaufman & Sternberg, 2019). That is, to be creative, an idea needs to be high in quality, not just original (Sternberg, 2018c). People who are creatively gifted are well able to create, design, invent, suppose, and imagine. IQ tests, of course, do not measure creative skills and attitudes, nor were they designed to. Most creativity tests, including the Torrance tests, measure an aspect of creativity—divergent thinking—but at the same time trivialize creativity. Creativity involves far more than divergent thinking (Sternberg, 2018a, 2018c). It involves skills and attitudes involved in three kinds of defiance—*defying the crowd*, or being willing to stand up, ultimately successfully, to whatever most other people are thinking and doing; *defying oneself*, or being willing and able to let go of and go beyond one's past ways of thinking; and *defying the zeitgeist*, or being willing to identify and then challenge a society's or field's conventional ways of thinking, many of which are ingrained and hardly conscious. Creative people are willing and able to redefine problems, ask whether their solutions to problems are truly high-quality, sell their ideas, persist in the face of obstacles, believe in themselves even when no one else seems to, have the courage to stand up to falsehoods and misleading assumptions, and tolerate the ambiguity that creative people always encounter. At the same time, creativity can be used for good ends but also for bad or even disastrous ends (Cropley & Cropley, 2019; Cropley et al., 2010; Sternberg, 2010b).

In a way, the traditional creativity tests (e.g., the Torrance Tests of Creative Thinking) do for creativity what intelligence tests have done for intelligence—they narrow and trivialize it so that what they measure bears only a faint resemblance to the underlying construct. If users of tests acknowledged these limitations, scores at least could be used with full understanding of their limitations. But unfortunately, many users engage in the fallacy of pseudo-quantitative precision, believing that if something is quantified, it must be valid (Sternberg, 1997).

Transformationally gifted individuals must be creatively oriented. They need to be willing and able to defy the crowd, themselves, and the zeitgeist. To change the world for the better, one needs to be able to envision a better world and then have ideas that are both original and useful so as to make these transformations occur.

Analytical Skills and Attitudes

Analytical skills and attitudes are used to evaluate one's own and others' ideas. People who are analytically gifted are well able to analyze, critique, compare and contrast, and evaluate ideas and products. IQ tests and related tests, such as the SAT, SSAT, ACT, GRE, and other proxies for IQ tests (Sackett et al., 2020) measure primarily analytical skills as well as the knowledge base to which they are applied. But, as I will show later in this chapter, these tests measure some generalized kind of abstracted analysis, not necessarily the analytical skills that are applied to solving concrete problems in any particular field.

Transformational giftedness requires high levels of analytical skills and attitudes, because without them, one cannot distinguish good from not so good or even mediocre ideas and products. Some people have the implicit theory (folk conception) that creative and analytical skills are somehow negatively correlated—that those who are creative are idea generators rather than idea critics. But that implicit theory has no basis in fact. Creative ideas are not only original but also high in quality, and recognizing quality requires analytical skills. Thus, transformationally gifted individuals need to excel in analytical as well as creative skills and attitudes. Indeed, analysis is part of the creative process (Sternberg & Lubart, 1992). However, someone can be highly analytical without being creative (Sternberg, 1997).

Practical Skills and Attitudes

To make an outstanding positive and meaningful, as well as transformational, difference to the world, one needs to excel in practical (commonsense) skills and attitudes, or at the very least, know how to recruit as collaborators people who do excel in these skills. Individuals who are strong in practical skills are those who are effective in putting ideas into practice, implementing ideas, and persuading others of their point of view. Creative individuals who lack high levels of practical skills are often frustrated—they have the ideas but cannot get others to implement them and often cannot implement them by themselves. Research has shown that "practical intelligence," or common sense, is only very weakly correlated with IQ and related cognitive abilities (Sternberg et al., 2000; Sternberg & Hedlund, 2002). Of course, these correlations can be increased by correcting for attenuation and restriction of range, but such corrected correlations show a hypothetical state of the world, not a real one.

Transformational giftedness requires high levels of practical, commonsense skills because to make changes in the real world almost always requires one to deal with everyday obstacles to the implementation of one's ideas—lack of resources, opposition, an unsupportive environment, and so forth. People who are creative may get nowhere with their ideas because they do not know how to make their ideas work in practice as well as in theory.

Wisdom-Based Skills and Attitudes

Perhaps most important for transformational giftedness, at least in current times, are wisdom-based skills and attitudes. Wisdom is represented by using one's knowledge, skills, and attitudes to achieve a common good, by balancing one's own with others' and larger interests, over the long as well as the short term, through the infusion of positive ethical values (Sternberg, 2000, 2004b, 2019). This emphasis on positive ethical values is reflected not just in my own work, but in that of other leading theorists in the field (e.g., Ambrose & Cross, 2009). The wise individual, therefore, looks out for others, not just for themselves. Moreover, the wise individual knows not only what they know, but also what they do not know, and even what they cannot know—what is unknowable. Thus, the wise individual excels in metacognitive skills (Weststrate, 2019).

What is notable, and perhaps startling, is that the increase around the world of IQs in the 20th century by 30 points (Flynn, 2016) seems to have done little or nothing to increase the wisdom of the population. If one looks at leaders today, or at the voters who elect them, whatever their IQs, some of them seem astonishingly foolish, for example, encouraging use of scientifically disproven cures for COVID-19 or encouraging people to congregate in groups that will put them all at risk for transmission of the disease. Any number of countries have elected or sham-elected dictators or would-be dictators, including countries in Asia, Europe, South America, and, arguably, North America. What could be seen as depressing is that whereas dictators used to need coups d'état to get into power, today they simply get themselves elected. And then, predictably, they govern in a way that looks out for their own interests and the interests of those around them, not for the common good (Sternberg, 2017).

Why Use the Augmented Theory of Successful Intelligence for Identifying Transformationally Gifted Individuals?

The augmented theory of successful intelligence may be useful for selecting possible future transformationally gifted individuals because it takes into account skills and attitudes that are crucial for making a positive difference but that are not measured by traditional measures. The added advantage is that use of the theory reduces group differences and hence helps to achieve a measure of social justice that has been largely missing from U.S. society and many other societies. Most standardized test measures, in contrast, increase prediction at the expense of also increasing group differences (see discussion in Sternberg, 2010a).

I have spent much of my career validating various versions of the augmented theory of successful intelligence (which evolved from the theory of successful intelligence, which evolved from the triarchic theory of intelligence, which evolved from a componential theory of intelligence; see Sternberg, 2020). I will describe here only those data that I view as most relevant for present purposes.

Skill-Instructional Interactions

In an early work, we selected high school students who were gifted only in creative skills, only in analytical skills, only in practical skills, in all three kinds of skills, or in none of these skills (Sternberg & Clinkenbeard, 1995; Sternberg et al., 1999). The students were selected by means of an early version of a test that measured creative, analytical, and practical skills (Sternberg, 1993). The earlier test had primarily multiple-choice items measuring each of the three kinds of skills plus essay items. The test had been shown previously to measure these distinct abilities. But at the same time, the use of multiple-choice format severely reduced the differential validity of tests of creative and practical skills (Sternberg et al., 2001). The students were brought to Yale University to take a summer college-level course in psychology that was taught either to emphasize memory (standard course), analytical thinking, creative thinking, or practical thinking. Students were randomly assigned to instructional groups, so that some were a match in their ability pattern to the group to which they were assigned and others were not. All students were assessed for memory, analytical, creative, and practical applications of knowledge. The key outcome was that students who were assigned to an instructional condition that better matched their pattern of abilities performed better in the course than did students who ended up in a nonmatching condition. The results suggested that some students who were gifted, at least in analytical, creative, or practical skills, might underperform in a course (in this case in psychology) because the way the course was taught did not well match the way they learned best. Students might be gifted, but it might not show through when giftedness is only conceptualized and operationalized in terms of a narrow definition, such as in terms of a high level of analytical (IQ-like) skills.

The Rainbow Project

In a later study, we devised a more comprehensive test of creative, analytical, and practical skills for what we referred to as the Rainbow Project (Sternberg & the Rainbow Project Collaborators, 2006). The test we used was administered to approximately 1,000 students around the United States, varying widely in levels of academic skills, ethnicity, and socioeconomic status. This test deemphasized multiple choice. For example, one could show creative skills through short stories, cartoon captioning, and drawing a creative picture. One could show practical skills by reading about or viewing movies of students facing practical problems, and then by stating how the students should solve the problems they face. And one could show analytical skills through multiple-choice items. As previously (Sternberg et al., 2001), we found that multiple-choice items were poor measures of creative and practical skills: Multiple-choice items that were supposed to measure creative and practical skills primarily ended up measuring analytical skills. However, we also found in the hierarchical regressions of the Rainbow Project that we could roughly double prediction, relative to SAT alone, of first-year GPA by adding creative and practical tests to the SAT. In other words, just using a test of academic analytical skills to predict success would have given a highly incomplete picture of what the students were capable of. Equally importantly, our tests showed far smaller ethnic-group differences than did the SAT. So, at the same time that they *decreased* ethnic-group differences, they *increased* levels of prediction. From a social justice standpoint, the results suggested that using analytical tests alone failed to give students a "fair shake." Those who were gifted in other ways could succeed in college, if only they were given a chance.

The Kaleidoscope Project

After the Rainbow Project was completed, I moved to Tufts University as Dean of Arts and Sciences. There we conducted a project called Kaleidoscope (Sternberg, 2009, 2010a). Because Tufts University is a very highly selective school, by traditional definitions, almost all of the students who are admitted and many who apply but are not admitted would be considered to be "gifted" as the word is traditionally defined. Tufts had been using so-called holistic admissions, meaning that the university tried to look at the whole person in making an admissions decision. At Tufts, we started using an assessment based on the augmented theory of successful intelligence, measuring wisdom as well as creative, analytical, and practical thinking. The creative assessments gave options such as drawing a creative picture, designing a scientific experiment, writing a short story, and speculating about what the world would be like today if some major historical even had come out differently. The analytical assessments asked for analysis, such as of one's favorite book. The practical assessments asked for essays, such as of how one may have persuaded a friend of an idea that the friend did not initially accept. The wisdom-based assessments were also essay-based, asking, for example, how an applicant might someday turn a personal interest toward achieving a common good.

The assessment has now been used on tens of thousands of students applying to Tufts University. The results for the first couple of admitted classes (all of those which were analyzed while I was there) were extremely encouraging. We improved prediction not only of academic success, but also of extracurricular success. Moreover, ethnic differences were essentially eliminated (although raters of Kaleidoscope were not blind to applicants' ethnicities, so that it is possible that the raters were biased in their ratings—we just had no way of knowing; see Sternberg, 2010a). The project lasted for many years, even after I left Tufts.

The Panorama Project

After Tufts, I went to Oklahoma State as provost and senior vice president. When I arrived, the ways in which an undergraduate could be admitted to Oklahoma State were through schools grades, ACT scores, or a combination of the two. At Oklahoma State, we initiated a project called Panorama. It was similar in concept to Kaleidoscope, but for a different population. As one would expect, in terms of measures of academic preparation, the applicants were not as strong, on average, as those at Tufts. But if one looked at giftedness more broadly, there were many outstanding applicants, and many students came to be admitted through Panorama to Oklahoma State who otherwise would have been rejected. I left before we formally analyzed the data, but the system provided opportunity for broadly gifted students who otherwise would have been excluded.

Scientific Reasoning

In more recent research (Sternberg & Sternberg, 2017; Sternberg et al., 2017, 2019), we followed up on the work of Sternberg and Williams (1997), which found the Graduate Record Examination (GRE) to be a poor predictor of success in a graduate psychology Ph.D. program for gifted students (at Yale). Sternberg and Williams found the GRE to be ineffective, but they did not suggest a replacement.

In the newer research, we devised problems that measured skills in scientific reasoning, including generating alternative hypotheses to explain data; generating experiments to test hypotheses; and drawing conclusions from data, reviewing scientific articles, and editing reviews of scientific articles. The last task, reviewing, proved to be too challenging for our undergraduate sample at Cornell University, despite its consisting of traditionally gifted students with average reported SAT scores in the low 700s (compared with a national mean originally set at 500 with a standard deviation of 100). In one study, we also had students evaluate faulty teaching: Professors taught lessons and purposely made major pedagogical mistakes. The participants had to identify what they were.

The results across the series of studies was quite clear. The various tests of scientific reasoning, including the test of reasoning about teaching, were generally significantly correlated with each other. The tests also factored together, either in a single factor or in two factors. Psychometric tests, such as the SAT, ACT, number series, and letter sets, also generally correlated significantly with each other and formed a separate factor. Thus, the scientific reasoning tests and the psychometric tests formed separate factors. As can be inferred from these data, the scientific reasoning tests generally did *not* correlate significantly with the psychometric tests. Sometimes they correlated, but some of the correlations were negative, and others were positive. These results suggested that scientific reasoning, which has creative, analytical, and practical aspects, is rather distinct from the kind of analytic reasoning measured by psychometric tests, at least in our gifted sample. More importantly, the results show that analytical reasoning is not just of the kind measured by standardized tests. These tests do not appear to be effectively measuring analytical reasoning as it applies to scientific research.

The failure of the tests to measure scientific reasoning cannot help but recall the PISA results discussed previously. The U.S. did not come out in the top 10 in scientific reasoning (it came in 25th), and Finland, which did come out in the top 10, just bolstered support for a political party that consists of many climate change deniers. Clearly, many countries are educating and assessing students in ways that are not likely to produce transformationally gifted individuals, at least in the sciences, and perhaps not in any field at all. What should educators do, in educating gifted children, to help develop transformationally gifted individuals?

Education for Transformational Giftedness

Of course, children are not born transformationally gifted. It is not clear they are gifted in any other way, either, from the moment of birth. Gifts have to be developed. Mozart was a child prodigy and later a gifted composer, but if he had grown up in a home without music and with a father who discouraged rather than encouraged his musical efforts, Mozart might have become someone else entirely, at least with regard to his profession. What can school teachers and parents do to develop transformational giftedness? I list here a dozen steps teachers of the gifted (or really, teachers of anyone) can take to develop transformational giftedness.

Teaching That Anyone and Everyone Can Make a Difference

One has to start with the belief that anyone and everyone can make a difference. This is not easy to do in a world in which individual efforts at change often seem to be so little rewarded. A recent article described the career-long efforts of a transformationally gifted individual, Lloyd Thacker, to change college admissions in the United States (Hoover, 2019). The system is notoriously influenced (some would say, corrupted) by special interests—parental wealth, alumni connections, political influence, demands of athletic coaches, to name just a few. Recently, a major admissions scandal made clear just how easily the system could be corrupted to lead to the admission of children who had others take standardized tests for them and whose applications made the pretense of their having athletic skills they never had (Ellis, 2019). Lloyd Thacker himself had no special connections to ensure that anything would change. He was a lone man on a mission. He was able, over the course of a career, to make some headway, but not to change the system as a whole. Nevertheless, he never gave up hope and was able to effect small changes that improved admissions procedures, at least at some colleges. He made a positive, meaningful, and hopefully enduring difference, and that is what transformational giftedness is about.

Everyone would rather make a bigger difference than a smaller difference. Sometimes that is possible; often it is not. Even when it is possible, one never knows exactly what effect one's work will have, when viewed over a period of many years. For example, Henry Chauncey was the first president of the Educational Testing Service (ETS) and by any standard, unlike Lloyd Thacker, has had an enormous influence on college admissions through the test his organization developed, the SAT. But was the SAT a good innovation, a bad innovation, or a little of each? At the time, Chauncey wanted to break the stranglehold that socioeconomic status (SES) had on college admissions, and he viewed the test as a way to help do that. But he could not have known, when ETS was founded in 1947, that the pool of college applicants would become much more diverse than it was at the time, and that test scores would prove to be moderately to highly correlated with SES (Sackett et al., 2012). This is not to say that SES is all that matters. But students who grow up in well-resourced communities and who go to well-resourced schools have an edge in testing and, of course, in gifted identification over those who grow up in poverty (Ambrose, 2013; Olszewski-Kubilius & Thomson, 2010). Those who come from poverty can overcome these obstacles, but only if parents and schools provide the resources and the programs to enable them to do so (e.g., Cross & Burney, 2005). Chauncey wanted to do a good thing—to help young people achieve their potential—but in his case, as with all people, one's ultimate performance is for history to decide.

The Importance of Persistence in the Face of Obstacles

Both Thacker and Chauncey faced enormous obstacles to changing admissions. In Chauncey's case, the obstacle was that many people, including educators, did not want to give up a system that favored already privileged children, some of whom were of dubious merit. In Thacker's case, the obstacle was that the system Chauncey and others introduced had become so embedded in the admissions system that it was now as entrenched as (and, unfortunately, not much better than) the system it replaced. But the point is that, if one wants to achieve creative transformation, then one inevitably will encounter stiff opposition (Sternberg, 2018c). To become transformationally gifted, one must learn to combat and, hopefully, conquer the opposition.

Emphasis on Making the World a Better Place

Anyone and everyone can make a difference, but what kind of difference will they make? Teachers and parents can help encourage students to seek to make the world a better place. They can seek jobs that help fight climate change rather than ones that promote it. They can work in industries that combat pollution rather than cause it. They can work for antismoking campaigns rather than for tobacco companies or other companies that manufacture vaping products. Endeavors and jobs are a matter of choice. Gifted students can choose to make the world better, or they can be indifferent, or they can enter jobs, perhaps high-paying, that harm the people of the world (and other species as well). Teachers and parents need to emphasize that one's endeavors are a choice; even if one does not pose them as a choice, they nevertheless are.

Emphasis on the Common Good, Not Just the Individual Good

The individualistic orientation of much of education—the focus on individual success—can steer young gifted students into careers that maximize only their own individual success, often defined by society in financial terms. A program to develop transformational giftedness must emphasize not only making one's own life better, but also improving the lives of people throughout the world.

Emphasis on Questions Asked, Not Just Questions Answered

Schools and classes, even for the gifted, emphasize answering questions. Standardized tests used to identify the gifted are usually 100% about answering questions. But transformationally gifted individuals are not merely better at answering questions than are other individuals; they also are better at asking important questions—questions whose answers have the potential to transform the world. These individuals not only defy the crowd; they also question the zeitgeist, or the assumptions almost everyone else makes and therefore does not question (Sternberg, 2018c). Education for transformational giftedness needs to emphasize teaching students to ask questions of importance, not merely to answer questions of little or no importance, such as those found on most standardized tests used to identify the gifted. Transformationally gifted individuals are not merely good problem solvers; they are excellent problem finders—they find the problems that matter to the betterment of the world.

Ill-structured Rather Than Well-Structured Problems

One of the biggest problems with most identification and instruction of the gifted is the overuse of well-structured problems—problems that have a clear definition and a clear path to solution. So, what is measured is one's ability to find that solution. In the case of my own triplets' experience in second-grade math, this mentality is taken to the extreme. They have to not only get the right answer, but also show their work and show that they got the answer the way they were told to get it—not some other way, even if that other way yields the right answer. Important problems in the world are almost all ill-structured. How does one counter global warming, pollution, bacterial resistance to antibiotics, income disparities, hunger, or violence? And how does solving trivial well-structured problems tell anything about how people will go about solving ill-structured but important problems?

Creative, Analytical, Practical, and Wise Thinking

The emphasis in most schooling, including of the gifted (especially accelerated classes), is on memory and analytical thinking. What can a student remember, and how well can they analyze it, whatever it is? But analytical thinking, as discussed earlier in this chapter, is only a small part of what is required for an individual to become transformationally gifted. The individual also needs to be creative, practical, and wise. Because of society's overemphasis on analytical thinking, many fields are training individuals who are analytically precocious but lacking in creative ideas, common sense, and wisdom. The result is, I believe, societally disastrous, leading to, for example, politicians who merely propose and implement failed ideas from the past, scientists who work well within existing paradigms but are incapable of going outside them, and novelists who write successful novels not because they find their own formulas, but because they adhere to tried-and-true formulas. Schools need to teach much more broadly if they are to produce transformationally gifted individuals (Sternberg & Grigorenko, 2007; Sternberg et al., 2009).

Emphasis on What One Does Not Know (and Perhaps Cannot Know) as Well as What One Does Know

I have suggested that foolish people—those utterly lacking in wisdom—show an "omniscience fallacy" in their thinking: They think they know everything (Sternberg, 2004b). Unfortunately, experiences of getting very high grades in school and very high scores on standardized tests may inadvertently lead to foolishness—the belief that one truly knows everything, or at least everything worth one's knowing. According to the legend, the Oracle at Delphi informed Socrates that he was the wisest man in Athens, precisely because Socrates realized how very little he knew. Wise people have a sense of what they do not know. For transformationally gifted individuals to effect change, they have to be willing to push the frontiers of knowledge—to realize that their knowledge is insignificant compared with what they do not know. Few schools and teachers teach that way, however. Transformationally gifted individuals are special in part because they appreciate their own lack of knowledge and seek to remedy that lack.

Emphasis on the Need to Balance Competing Interests

Transformational giftedness involves making not just significant changes, but also positive and meaningful changes at some level. In a social system, ranging upward from a family to a nation or even the world, such a change always involves balancing competing interests—one's own interests, others' interests, and often, larger systemic interests. Transformationally gifted individuals need the wisdom to balance competing interests to ensure that the changes they effect are ones that will be beneficial, on the whole, to those affected by the changes.

Emphasis on Positive Ethical Values

Transformationally gifted individuals also take into account the ethical dimensions of the transformations they effect or at least try to effect. Many of the transformational technological innovations of current times—Facebook, Twitter, and the like—seem to have been created without much consideration of ethical issues, such as privacy, handling of hateful content, and sharing of data.

Role-Modeling Transformational Giftedness

Finally, and perhaps most importantly, transformational giftedness is learned from role-modeling. Of course, this can mean learning from great transformationally gifted individuals of the past—Leonardo da Vinci, Charles Darwin, Geoffrey Chaucer, Albert Einstein, Marie Curie, Nelson Mandela—but even more so from teachers who themselves show the way toward transformational giftedness. To teach in a way that encourages transformational giftedness requires in the teacher transformational giftedness with regard to methods of teaching. It is doubtful there are many, if any, schools that encourage teaching in this way. Thus, teachers, by role-modeling transformational giftedness, can encourage it in their students. Students are most likely to behave as adults act, not as adults wish they would act. Teachers thus can be role models for how students can change the world, as the teachers are through their teaching.

Summary

Transformational giftedness is exceptional ability or talent that can enable or has enabled an individual to make one or more extraordinary and meaningful contributions to the world that help to make the world a better place. It is not inborn; it is acquired through an interaction of a person with the environment, especially with one's parents and the teachers in one's environment. It is different from other forms of giftedness in that it concerns the realization and utilization of potential, not merely the possession of potential.

Transformationally gifted people make a difference; there might be people who possess the skills and attitudes to be transformationally gifted, but they are not transformationally gifted unless they actually utilize these skills and talents in a positive, meaningful, and potentially enduring way that somehow transforms the way things are.

Transformational giftedness is one of several forms or levels of giftedness. Latent giftedness is a form of giftedness in which the giftedness cannot be identified because of societal or possibly individual constraints. For example, a prescientific society cannot well support scientifically gifted individuals. Inert giftedness is identifiable but is not developed because the individual or the people in this environment choose to leave the gifts largely unexplored and unnurtured. Reactive giftedness is giftedness in response to presented stimuli, such as the stimuli of a test. And proactive giftedness is giftedness in which an individual finds and defines problems on their own terms. Transformational giftedness is a form of proactive giftedness in which the individual is not only proactive, but also proactive in a way that makes the world, in one way or another, a better place.

There are no surefire predictors of transformational giftedness. But my colleagues and I have used tests based on an augmented theory of successful intelligence to attempt to make predictions. The idea is that transformationally gifted people, at the very least, need high levels of creative skills and attitudes to generate ideas that are novel and useful, analytical skills and attitudes to ascertain whether the ideas are good ones, practical skills in order to implement their ideas and persuade others of their usefulness, and wisdom-based skills and attitudes to help to ensure that the ideas work toward the achievement of a common good. If people are not strong in all of these skills and attitudes, they still can be transformationally gifted by compensating for their weakness(es), seeking out others to assist them in those areas that are challenging for them.

Education for transformational giftedness looks quite different from the education most children, including gifted children, receive today. It emphasizes ill-structured rather than well-structured problems, and, especially, it emphasizes problem finding (Csikszentmihalyi, 2013) and problem definition in addition to problem solving. It is project-based rather than narrowly content-based and seeks to apply knowledge to problems of true consequence beyond the individual. Educators who want to develop transformational giftedness in their students must model it and show how they as teachers hope to contribute toward making the world a better place in which to live.

The multiple-choice problem at the beginning of this chapter showed five individuals gifted in different aspects of neurosurgical expertise. They are all experts of some kind (Ericsson & Pool, 2017; Hambrick et al., 2017), but they share relatively little in common. They show how giftedness is not a single thing. But is any of them transformationally gifted? They all could be. What they show is that transformational giftedness is not a matter of genes or education—it's a matter of what one does with one's genes and education. It's a matter of making the most of one's skills and attitudes to make the world a better place in which to live.

DISCUSSION QUESTIONS

1. What is transformational giftedness?
2. Why is transformational giftedness important?
3. How does transformational giftedness differ from other kinds of giftedness, such as verbal or mathematical giftedness?
4. What kinds of assessments administered to young people might predict transformational giftedness in adulthood?
5. How can schools and parents develop transformational giftedness in children?

References

Albert, S., Leon, J. X., Grinham, A. R., Church, J. A,. Gibbes, B. R., & Woodroffe, C. D. (2016, May 6). Interactions between sea-level rise and wave exposure on reef island dynamics in the Solomon Islands. *Environmental Research Letters, 11*(5). https://doi.org/10.1088/1748-9326/11/5/054011

Ambrose, D. (2013). Socioeconomic inequality and giftedness: Suppression and distortion of high ability. *Roeper Review, 35*(2), 81–92. https://doi.org/10.1080/02783193.2013.766960

Ambrose, D. (2015). Borrowing insights from other disciplines to strengthen the conceptual foundations for gifted education. *International Journal of Talent Development and Creativity, 3*(2), 32–57.

Ambrose, D., & Cross, T. L. (Eds.). (2009). *Morality, ethics, and gifted minds.* Springer.

American Lung Association. (n.d.). *Most polluted cities.* https://www.lung.org/our-initiatives/healthy-air/sota/city-rankings/most-polluted-cities.html

Barone, J. (2017). *Is air pollution getting worse or better?* Berkeley Wellness. https://www.berkeleywellness.com/healthy-community/environmental-health/article/air-pollution-getting-worse-or-better

Bass, B. M., & Avolio, B. J. (Eds.). (1994). *Improving organizational effectiveness through transformational leadership.* SAGE.

Bass, B. M., Avolio, B. J., & Atwater, L. (1996). The transformational and transactional leadership of men and women. *International Review of Applied Psychology, 45*(1), 5–34. https://doi.org/10.1111/j.1464-0597.1996.tb00847.x

Climate Central. (2019). *The 10 hottest global years on record.* https://www.climatecentral.org/gallery/graphics/the-10-hottest-global-years-on-record

Cropley, D. H., & Cropley, A. J. (2019). Creativity and malevolence: Past, present, and future. In J. C. Kaufman & R. J. Sternberg (Eds.), *Cambridge handbook of creativity* (2nd ed., pp. 677–690). Cambridge University Press.

Cropley, D. H., Cropley, A. J., Kaufman, J. C., & Runco, M. A. (Eds.). (2010). *The dark side of creativity.* Cambridge University Press.

Cross, T. L., & Burney, V. (2005). High ability, rural and poor: Lessons from Project Aspire and implications for school counsellors. *Journal for Secondary Gifted Education, 16*(4), 148–156. https://doi.org/10.4219/jsge-2005-483

Csikszentmihalyi, M. (2013). *Creativity: Flow and the psychology of discovery and invention.* Harper Perennial.

Dai, D. Y., & Sternberg, R. J. (Eds.). (2004). *Motivation, emotion, and cognition: Integrative perspectives on intellectual functioning and development.* Erlbaum.

Ellis, L. (2019). *We asked 20 elite-college admissions deans about the bribery scandal. Here's what they said.* Chronicle of Higher Education. https://www.chronicle.com/article/We-Asked-20-Elite-College/245920

Ericsson, A., & Pool, R. (2017). *Peak: Secrets from the new science of expertise.* Houghton Mifflin Harcourt.

Fears, D. (2019). *One million species face extinction, UN report says. And humans will suffer as a result.* The Washington Post. https://www.washingtonpost.com/climate-environment/2019/05/06/one-million-species-face-extinction-un-panel-says-humans-will-suffer-result

Flynn, J. R. (2016). *Does your family make you smarter?: Nature, nurture, and human autonomy.* Cambridge University Press.

Forgeard, M. J. C., & Mecklenburg, A. C. (2013). The two dimensions of motivation and a reciprocal model of the creative process. *Review of General Psychology, 17*(3), 255–266. https://doi.org/10.1037/a0032104

Hambrick, D. Z., Campitelli, G., & Macnamara, B. N. (Eds.). (2017). *The science of expertise: Behavioral, neural, and genetic approaches to complex skill.* Routledge.

Harvey, C. (2018). CO_2 *emissions reached an all-time high in 2018.* Scientific American. https://www.scientificamerican.com/article/co2-emissions-reached-an-all-time-high-in-2018

Heller, K. A., Mönks, F. J., Sternberg, R. J., & Subotnik, R. F. (Eds.). (2000). *International handbook of giftedness and talent* (2nd ed.). Elsevier.

Hoover, E. (2019). *An idealist set out to change college admissions. It was a long, lonely quest.* Chronicle of Higher Education. https://www.chronicle.com/article/An-Idealist-Set-Out-to-Change/246247

Kaufman, J. C. (2016). *Creativity 101* (2nd ed.). Springer.

Kaufman, J. C., & Sternberg, R. J. (Eds.). (2019). *Cambridge handbook of creativity.* Cambridge University Press.

Kolbert, E. (2019). *Louisiana's disappearing coast.* The New Yorker. https://www.newyorker.com/magazine/2019/04/01/louisianas-disappearing-coast

Milman, O., & Harvey, F. (2019). *US is hotbed of climate change denial, major global survey finds.* The Guardian. https://www.theguardian.com/environment/2019/may/07/us-hotbed-climate-change-denial-international-poll

National Climate Assessment. (n.d.). *Extreme weather.* https://nca2014.globalchange.gov/highlights/report-findings/extreme-weather

Olszewski-Kubilius, P., & Thomson, D. (2010). Gifted programming for poor or minority urban students: Issues and lessons learned. *Gifted Child Today, 33*(4), 58–64. https://doi.org/10.1177/107621751003300413

Organisation for Economic Co-operation and Development. (2016). *PISA 2015: PISA results in focus.* https://www.oecd.org/pisa/pisa-2015-results-in-focus.pdf

Pfeiffer, S. I. (Ed.). (2019). *Handbook of giftedness in children: Psychoeducational theory, research, and best practices.* Springer.

Pfeiffer, S. I., Shaunessy-Dedrick, E., & Foley-Nicpon, M. (Eds.). (2018). *APA handbook of giftedness and talent*. American Psychological Association.

Renzulli, J. S. (1977). *The Enrichment Triad Model: A guide for developing defensible programs for the gifted and talented*. Creative Learning Press.

Renzulli, J. S. (1978). What makes giftedness? Reexamining a definition. *Phi Delta Kappan, 60*(3), 180–184, 261.

Renzulli, J. S., Gubbins, E. J., McMillen, K. S., Eckert, R. D., & Little, C. A. (Eds.). (2009). *Systems and models for developing gifted programs for the gifted and talented* (2nd ed.). Prufrock Press.

Sackett, P. R., Kuncel, N. R., Beatty, A. S., Rigdon, J. L., Shen, W., & Kiger, T. B. (2012). The role of socioeconomic status in SAT-grade relationships and in college admissions decisions. *Psychological Science, 23*(9), 1000–1007. https://doi.org/10.1177/0956797612438732

Sackett, P. R., Shewach, O. R., & Dahlke, J. A. (2020). The predictive value of general intelligence. In R. J. Sternberg (Ed.), *Human intelligence: An introduction* (pp. 381–414). Cambridge University Press.

South China Morning Post. (2019). *China's air quality worsens as national PM2.5 level rises 5.2% in January and February*. https://www.scmp.com/news/china/politics/article/3002655/chinas-air-quality-worsens-national-pm25-level-rises-52pc

Sternberg, R. J. (1993). *Sternberg triarchic abilities test* [Unpublished test]. Department of Education, Yale University.

Sternberg, R. J. (1997). *Successful intelligence*. Plume.

Sternberg, R. J. (2000). Wisdom as a form of giftedness. *Gifted Child Quarterly, 44*(4), 252–260. https://doi.org/10.1177/001698620004400406

Sternberg, R. J. (Ed.). (2004a). *Definitions and conceptions of giftedness*. Corwin.

Sternberg, R. J. (2004b). Wisdom and giftedness. In L. V. Shavinina & M. Ferrari (Eds.), *Beyond knowledge: Extracognitive aspects of developing high ability* (pp. 169–186). Erlbaum.

Sternberg, R. J. (2009). The Rainbow and Kaleidoscope Projects: A new psychological approach to undergraduate admissions. *European Psychologist, 14*(4), 279–287. https://doi.org/10.1027/1016-9040.14.4.279

Sternberg, R. J. (2010a). *College admissions for the 21st century*. Harvard University Press.

Sternberg, R. J. (2010b). The dark side of creativity and how to combat it. In D. H. Cropley, A. J. Cropley, J. C. Kaufman, & M. A. Runco (Eds.), *The dark side of creativity* (pp. 316–328). Cambridge University Press.

Sternberg, R. J. (2017). ACCEL: A new model for identifying the gifted. *Roeper Review, 39*(3), 139–152. https://doi.org/10.1080/02783193.2017.1318658

Sternberg, R. J. (2018a). Creative giftedness is not just what creativity tests test: Implications of a triangular theory of creativity for understanding creative giftedness. *Roeper Review, 40*(3), 158–165. https://doi.org/10.1080/02783193.2018.1467248

Sternberg, R. J. (2018b). Teaching and assessing gifted students in STEM disciplines through the augmented theory of successful intelligence. *High Ability Studies, 30*(1–2). https://doi.org/10.1080/13598139.2018.1528847

Sternberg, R. J. (2018c). A triangular theory of creativity. *Psychology of Aesthetics, Creativity, and the Arts, 12*(1), 50–67. https://doi.org/10.1037/aca0000095

Sternberg, R. J. (2019). Why people often prefer wise guys to guys who are wise: An augmented balance theory of the production and reception of wisdom. In R. J. Sternberg & J. Glück (Eds.), *Cambridge handbook of wisdom* (pp. 162–181). Cambridge University Press.

Sternberg, R. J. (2020). The augmented theory of successful intelligence. In R. J. Sternberg (Ed.), *Cambridge handbook of intelligence* (2nd ed., pp. 679–708). Cambridge University Press.

Sternberg, R. J., Castejón, J. L., Prieto, M. D., Hautamäki, J., & Grigorenko, E. L. (2001). Confirmatory factor analysis of the Sternberg triarchic abilities test in three international samples: An empirical test of the triarchic theory of intelligence. *European Journal of Psychological Assessment, 17*(1) 1–16. https://doi.org/10.1027//1015-5759.17.1.1

Sternberg, R. J., & Clinkenbeard, P. R. (1995). The triarchic model applied to identifying, teaching, and assessing gifted children. *Roeper Review, 17*(4), 255–260. https://doi.org/10.1080/02783199509553677

Sternberg, R. J., & Davidson, J. E. (Eds.). (1986). *Conceptions of giftedness.* Cambridge University Press.

Sternberg, R. J., & Davidson, J. E. (Eds.). (2005). *Conceptions of giftedness* (2nd ed.). Cambridge University Press.

Sternberg, R. J., Forsythe, G. B., Hedlund, J., Horvath, J., Snook, S., Williams, W. M., Wagner, R. K., & Grigorenko, E. L. (2000). *Practical intelligence in everyday life.* Cambridge University Press.

Sternberg, R. J., & Grigorenko, E. L. (2007). *Teaching for successful intelligence* (2nd ed.). Corwin.

Sternberg, R. J., Grigorenko, E. L., Ferrari, M., & Clinkenbeard, P. (1999). A triarchic analysis of an aptitude–treatment interaction. *European Journal of Psychological Assessment, 15*(1), 1–11. https://doi.org/10.1027//1015-5759.15.1.3

Sternberg, R. J., & Hedlund, J. (2002). Practical intelligence, g, and work psychology. *Human Performance, 15*(1–2), 143–160. https://doi.org/10.1080/08959285.2002.9668088

Sternberg, R. J., Jarvin, L., & Grigorenko, E. L. (2009). *Teaching for wisdom, intelligence, creativity, and success.* Corwin.

Sternberg, R. J., Kaufman, J. C., & Pretz, J. E. (2002). *The creativity conundrum: A propulsion model of kinds of creative contributions.* Psychology Press.

Sternberg, R. J., & Lubart, T. I. (1992). Creative giftedness in children. In P. Klein & A. Tannenbaum (Eds.), *To be young and gifted* (pp. 33–51). Ablex.

Sternberg, R. J., & The Rainbow Project Collaborators (2006). The Rainbow Project: Enhancing the SAT through assessments of analytical, practical and creative skills. *Intelligence, 34*(4), 321–350. https://doi.org/10.1016/j.intell.2006.01.002

Sternberg, R. J., & Sternberg, K. (2017). Measuring scientific reasoning for graduate admissions in psychology and related disciplines. *Journal of Intelligence, 5*(3), Article 29. https://doi.org/10.3390/jintelligence5030029

Sternberg, R. J., Sternberg, K., & Todhunter, R. J. E. (2017). Measuring reasoning about teaching for graduate admissions in psychology and related disciplines. *Journal of Intelligence, 5*(4), Article 34. https://doi.org/10.3390/jintelligence5040034

Sternberg, R. J., & Williams, W. M. (1997). Does the Graduate Record Examination predict meaningful success in the graduate training of psychologists? A case study. *American Psychologist, 52*(6), 630–641. https://doi.org/10.1037/0003-066X.52.6.630

Sternberg, R. J., Wong, C. H., & Sternberg, K. (2019). The relation of tests of scientific reasoning to each other and to tests of general intelligence. *Journal of Intelligence, 7*(3), Article e20. https://doi.org/10.3390/jintelligence7030020

Subotnik, R. F., Karp, D. E., & Morgan, E. R. (1989). High IQ children at midlife. *Roeper Review, 11*(3), 139–144. https://doi.org/10.1080/02783198909553190

Subotnik, R. F., Olszewski-Kubilius, P., & Worrell, F. C. (2011). Rethinking giftedness and gifted education: A proposed direction forward based on psychological science. *Psychological Science in the Public Interest, 12*(1), 3–54. https://doi.org/10.1177/1529100611418056

Terman, L. M. (1925). *Genetic studies of genius: Vol. 1. Mental and physical traits of a thousand gifted children.* Stanford University Press.

Terman, L. M., & Oden, M. H. (1959). *Genetic studies of genius: Vol. 5. The gifted group at mid-life: 35 years' follow-up of the superior child.* Stanford University Press.

Union of Concerned Scientists. (2018). *The science connecting extreme weather to climate change.* https://www.ucsusa.org/our-work/global-warming/science-and-impacts/climate-attribution-science

University of Waterloo. (2018). *Climate change accelerating rise in sea levels.* ScienceDaily. https://www.sciencedaily.com/releases/2018/06/180613163025.htm

Weststrate, N. (2019). The mirror of wisdom: Self-reflection as a developmental precursor and core competency of wise people. In R. J. Sternberg & J. Glück (Eds.), *Cambridge handbook of wisdom* (pp. 500–518). Cambridge University Press.

Williams, S. (2018). *Air pollution linked to decline in cognitive performance.* The Scientist. https://www.the-scientist.com/news-opinion/air-pollution-linked-to-decline-in-cognitive-performance-64725

World Health Organization. (2019). *Air pollution.* https://www.who.int/airpollution/en

Ziegler, A. (2005). The actiotope model of giftedness. In R. J. Sternberg & J. E. Davidson (Eds.), *Conceptions of giftedness* (2nd ed., pp. 411–436). Cambridge University Press. https://doi.org/10.1017/CBO9780511610455.024

CHAPTER 8

The Talent Search Model for Identifying and Developing Academic Talent

LINDA E. BRODY

The Talent Search model of talent development consists of a conceptual framework for discovering talent potential and a pragmatic approach to providing each student with appropriately challenging opportunities that match their need for differentiated academic services. Supported by decades of research (e.g., Benbow & Lubinski, 1996; Benbow & Stanley, 1983; Brody & Mills, 2005; Keating, 1976; Olszewski-Kubilius, 2015), the assumption underlying this model is that individuals vary in their specific cognitive abilities, in their skills and knowledge, and in their personality traits, interests, and motivation. Consequently, these differences result in differing academic, social, and emotional needs that must be addressed if students are to achieve their full potential.

Three principles from developmental psychology support the educational recommendations behind this model: that learning is sequential and developmental (Hilgard & Bower, 1974), that children learn at different rates (Bayley, 1955, 1970), and that effective teaching involves an optimal match between the child's readiness to learn and the level of content presented (Hunt, 1961; Robinson & Robinson, 1982). The implication is that the level, pace, and nature of educational programs must be adapted to the capacities and knowledge of individual children, and a variety of options is needed from which to choose those that are appropriate for meeting individual needs.

Since Julian Stanley and the Study of Mathematically Precocious Youth (SMPY) launched the ideas that underlie the Talent Search model in the 1970s, its implementation has been centered at a number of university-based Talent Search centers where millions of students have directly benefitted from the services they continue to provide today. As the centers have expanded the nature and reach of their programmatic initiatives, the model has proven to be flexible in responding to change yet true to the core principles that SMPY established.

The Talent Search programs were established in response to certain demonstrated unfulfilled needs among students, and they can be an important part of the solution for those who participate in them. However, the model is broader than the centers' programs; it encourages educators, counselors, and parents to identify the particular academic, social, and emotional needs of their students, and to utilize whatever combination of in- and out-of-school educational resources can meet those needs. To expand options for students, SMPY and the Talent Search centers have supported the establishment of such offerings as magnet and residential high schools, early college programs, summer programs, academic competitions, and other challenging extracurricular activities. Their endorsement of these initiatives, along with increased student participation, has arguably fueled the development and expansion of the initiatives, making them more available to more students. Talent Search research on acceleration has also contributed to making it more acceptable and common to place students at appropriately challenging instructional levels in schools.

Despite evidence of the widespread influence of the Talent Search model, critics often fail to see its applicability to school-based services for gifted students, most likely because so much of the Talent Search centers' work does focus on providing direct services that supplement school programs. Critics also question its relevance for students today and its ability to attend to future needs, possibly because of the historic nature of the development of this model, or they may question the value of assessment, which is a core component. In fact, the Talent Search model has stood the test of time. It has grown and responded to changing needs, and it has been shown effective for students who come from many different types of schools, settings, and locales. As the world becomes more global in its orientation, and schools more diverse in their representation, the appreciation of individual differences in human characteristics and the recognition of unique needs that are inherent in the Talent Search model seem to be more relevant than ever.

The Beginnings

The Talent Search story, as it is often told, began in the late 1960s when Johns Hopkins University professor Julian Stanley met Joe Bates, an encounter that led Stanley on a path toward establishing the Study of Mathematically Precocious Youth and developing the components that underlie the Talent Search model today (Stanley, 2005; Stanley et al., 1974). However, it can be argued that the roots of the ideas underlying the model came from Stanley's own experiences growing up as an intellectually precocious child in a working class community in the suburbs of Atlanta during the Depression. So the story starts there.

School was never challenging for Stanley, and he did not grow up with intellectual aspirations. Seeing that Stanley was achieving ahead of his peers, a teacher finally suggested that he skip the fourth grade, but the next grade wasn't particularly stimulating either, and he wasn't happy about leaving friends behind. In middle school, Stanley tested at a high school level in math, but no accommodations were made to advance him in math in any way. In high school, after missing several months of school for health reasons, Stanley was able to make up the work he had missed in little time with little effort. In retrospect, these experiences gave Stanley much insight into the amount of educational time many gifted students waste when limited to age-in-grade educational programs.

College was not particularly challenging for Stanley either, but he took a summer tests and measurements course after college, through which he came to appreciate the value of assessments, and he subsequently proceeded to administer tests to any family members and friends who would cooperate. His interest in testing continued while he served in World War II. Stanley managed to gain access to the military entrance exams of his fellow soldiers, and he discovered that some very bright people were underachieving significantly in their occupational achievements, which he saw as a serious waste of talent. Later, as a graduate student at Harvard, Stanley excelled despite his modest educational background thanks to a stimulating curriculum and positive mentors. These experiences all reinforced his growing belief that talent potential can be identified through assessments and that the right educational opportunities can increase one's aspirations and spur high achievement.

Stanley's career path did not lead him immediately to working with gifted students. Instead, his interest in tests and measurements led to significant work in experimental design and psychometrics. By the time he met Joe Bates, Stanley was a professor at Johns Hopkins and a world-renowned methodologist. However, with his own educational experiences influencing him, and a strong belief in the value of assessment, Stanley was apparently ready for his career to go in a new direction.

The Study of Mathematically Precocious Youth

In the summer of 1968, Joe Bates was a 12-year-old middle school student excelling in a computer class with college students on the Johns Hopkins campus. The instructor turned to Stanley for advice because of Bates's young age. In an effort to determine the full extent of Bates's knowledge and abilities, Stanley administered the SAT and other above-grade-level tests to Bates, who scored at or above the level of high school seniors enrolling in selective universities. When Stanley could not find a high school willing to accommodate Bates's advanced academic needs in any way, he helped Bates enroll as a full-time student at Johns Hopkins. Bates earned a master's degree before his 18th birthday and went on to obtain a Ph.D. in computer science. Soon other exceptional students approached Stanley for help, and they also succeeded as young entrants to Johns Hopkins, further validating the use of the above-level SAT to predict an intellectually precocious young student's readiness to master content well above their grade level. These experiences inspired Stanley to want to discover and help more students with exceptional mathematical abilities. Stanley founded the Study of Mathematically Precocious Youth in 1971 to "find youths who reason exceptionally well mathematically and to provide them the special, supplemental, accelerative 'smorgasbord' of educational opportunities they sorely need and... richly deserve for their own optimal development and the good of society" (Stanley, 2005, p. 9).

Stanley and the SMPY staff had many ideas about how to proceed, but much was unproven, so they dove into the research literature on acceleration and gifted education (Daurio, 1979) and launched a period of experimentation and evaluation. They were influenced by Hollingworth's (1942) use of above-grade-level assessments and by Terman's (1925) longitudinal study design. Zuckerman's (1977) work identifying the cumulative advantage of opportunities that Nobel Prize recipients had experienced and Lehman's (1953) findings that mathematicians made their greatest discoveries at relatively young ages supported the urgency of SMPY's mission: to provide brilliant young people with opportunities to gain a knowledge base at early ages so that they will be prepared to achieve at high levels in mathematics and math-related fields. In order to cast a wide net to find students with the potential to excel in mathematics, SMPY sponsored a Talent Search in which middle school students came to the Johns Hopkins campus to take the SAT. The success of the first Talent Search set the stage for SMPY to sponsor Talent Searches throughout the 1970s and for the university-based Talent Search centers that followed to adopt this method for identifying students with above-grade-level reasoning abilities.

Additional cognitive, achievement, and affective assessments were administered to the high-scoring students by SMPY in an effort to learn more about these students. Perhaps the most important finding was the discovery of how much the students varied in these traits, in their content knowledge, and in their home and school environments. These results reinforced the need to identify and/or develop a variety of options for meeting the needs of advanced students and to work with students individually to find the right fit for each.

There was much experimentation with, and evaluation of, accelerative program models. Newsletters informed students about the acceleration strategies they validated, as well as about out-of-school programs and resources, and individual students received help finding those opportunities that might best serve their needs. With few students identified by SMPY attending any one school, the staff did not immediately try to influence school programs but hoped that students would put demands on schools to meet their needs and that the schools would respond. Stanley recalled that SMPY "meant to be 'benignly insidious,' i.e., to burrow up under school systems to coerce changes there in curricular flexibility and articulation of in-school with out-of-school experiences" (Stanley, 2005, p. 11).

SMPY summarized its early efforts in its first book, *Mathematical Talent: Discovery, Description, and Development* (Stanley et al., 1974). Widely referred to as MTD³, this acronym describes the stages and core components in the Talent Search model as initially designed: (1) Discovery (finding students with exceptional abilities), (2) Description (describing other characteristics in order to determine their needs), and (3) Development (providing the educational opportunities to develop their talents). It was soon understood that in order to influence others, the results must be shared, so a fourth D was added for Dissemination. As the program model expanded to serve students with exceptional verbal ability, a V was added to the acronym as well. These elements are now referred to in the literature as the MVTD⁴ model (e.g., Brody, 2009; Brody & Stanley, 2005), a way of depicting the Talent Search model that emphasizes the components involved in its implementation.

The Talent Search Centers

By 1979, the SMPY program had grown considerably, middle school students were coming from neighboring states to Baltimore to take the above-grade-level SAT test, and the demand for programs to meet the needs of the participating students was huge, including students with high verbal reasoning abilities who were emerging from the Talent Searches. The program could no longer be restricted to finding exceptional math-talented students, which was SMPY's initial vision; rather it was clear that a much broader group of students was in need of services.

Consequently, the Center for Talented Youth (CTY) was established at Johns Hopkins to serve this broader mission: to sponsor Talent Searches beyond the Baltimore area and to offer programs for the students it hoped to serve, including courses for verbally talented students and residential summer programs that allowed students who did not live locally to participate. Soon thereafter, the Talent Identification Program (TIP) at Duke University, the Center for Talent Development (CTD) at Northwestern University, and (what is now) the Center for Bright Kids in Denver were founded as regional centers to expand the model into their service areas. In addition, the University of Washington, Sacramento State University, the University of Iowa, and Vanderbilt University are among an expanding list of other universities that have adopted elements of the Talent Search model, with these centers introducing a number of their own initiatives, such as the early college entrance programs at the Universities of Washington and Iowa. With students having access to Talent Search centers around the country, the programs became truly national in their reach. Today they are international, as students from around the world participate each year in Talent Search programs in the United States, and Talent Search centers have also emerged in other countries, notably the Irish Centre for Talented Youth at Dublin City University and CTY Greece at Anatolia College.

The Talent Search centers' services have expanded, and they now utilize a number of above-grade-level tests for identification and serve a wider age and ability group. Participation in the popular Talent Search residential summer programs has grown exponentially, and other services have been introduced to support an increasingly diverse student body, including, depending on the center, online courses, service learning opportunities, diagnostic assessments and accommodations for twice-exceptional students, outreach programs for students from low-income backgrounds, and numerous scholarship and counseling programs. Efforts to encourage widespread application of the components of the model beyond the centers' offerings have continued as staff members maintain an active presence in the gifted education community, conduct research, consult with schools and families, and share information about a variety of programs and opportunities through websites, webinars, and newsletters.

One challenge the Talent Search centers have faced is a lack of adequate representation of students who are traditionally underserved or from low-income backgrounds in many of their programs. In particular, Black and Latino/Hispanic students are underrepresented compared to the general population, as are, to a lesser extent, White students, while Asian students are overrepresented; students from low-income backgrounds are also underrepresented (Lee et al., 2008). Significant outreach by the centers to low-income communities and scholarship support for students have been implemented to combat this trend, but barriers of cost, logistics, and cultural backgrounds appear to persist. However, the Talent Search centers have achieved significant success reaching underrepresented groups with special program initiatives that aim to help close the opportunity/excellence gap that exists between income and racial groups in the United States. See Plucker and Peters (2016) for more information on the excellence gap.

The Talent Search centers worked with the Jack Kent Cooke Foundation to develop its prestigious Young Scholars program, and the centers continue to market this opportunity to Talent Search participants from low-income backgrounds who might qualify. Duke TIP has also partnered with the Jack

Kent Cooke Foundation on another outreach program, Project Launch, which provides elementary school-age students from low-income backgrounds with access to TIP's academic programming and other services, including offering advice to parents on how to support their children's efforts in school. Evaluation of the impact of Project Launch continues, but, notably, many of the participants in this program have enrolled in TIP's programs for middle and high school students (Young et al., 2019).

CTY currently offers two programs specifically aimed at traditionally underserved populations. The Baltimore Emerging Scholars initiative provides STEM (science, technology, engineering, and mathematics) enrichment courses to Baltimore city public school students with the goal of helping them develop their potential (Bowman, 2018), and the CTY Scholars program offers scholarships for CTY courses, as well as academic, college, and career counseling throughout the high school years, to selected students from low-income backgrounds. Many graduates of the CTY Scholars program have gone on to enroll in the nation's most selective colleges and universities (Bowman, 2019).

Another intervention that has shown much success is CTD's Project EXCITE, which offers supplemental STEM learning experiences to underrepresented gifted students from partnering school districts. In follow-up studies on a variety of achievement measures, participants in this program have been shown to outperform their nonparticipating Black, Latino, and low-income peers and to come close to the performance levels of White, Asian, and higher income peers, thus contributing to closing the opportunity gap between racial/ethnic minority and nonminority students (Olszewski-Kubilius & Steenbergen-Hu, 2017; Olszewski-Kubilius et al., 2017). At the University of Iowa, the Belin-Blank Center has made students from rural areas, another underserved population, a special focus. The Belin-Blank Center has shown that systematic identification of students using above-level tests and STEM enrichment programming can contribute to students achieving at higher levels (Assouline et al., 2017).

Meanwhile, CTY's Study of Exceptional Talent (SET) continues SMPY's work by offering individualized counseling to exceptionally advanced students, specifically to students who score 700 or above on the verbal or mathematical parts of the SAT before age 13. The SET staff works to identify each student's strengths, weaknesses, and interests; advocates for school accommodations; and recommends a variety of in- and out-of-school supplemental options to meet individual needs. In addition to helping these students find the resources they need to achieve their full potential, SET aims to be a prototype of the approach the Talent Search model advocates for all parents, counselors, and educators to use as they seek to address the academic, social, and emotional needs of their students and to advance their talent development (Brody, 2007, 2017). The assumption is that if educators can utilize existing strategies and programs to meet the needs of their most exceptional students, finding the resources to serve a broader group of students should not be difficult.

Core Components and Supporting Research

Since its earliest days, SMPY validated its work with a huge body of research that resulted in seven books and hundreds of articles. Today, SMPY at Vanderbilt is conducting a 50-year longitudinal study of more than 5,000 intellectually talented individuals in five cohorts, four of which were from SMPY Talent Searches. In addition, researchers at the other university-based Talent Search centers continue to contribute to the knowledge base by publishing research findings that offer current insights into the characteristics and needs of academically advanced students and that support the effectiveness of Talent Search programs (e.g., Lee et al., 2015).

The Talent Search model incorporates many programmatic elements, but four components stand out as essential features of its implementation. These include: (a) using assessments to identify abilities and academic needs, including above-grade-level assessments; (b) adjusting the level and pace of instruction to meet individual needs; (c) extending learning beyond the classroom through supplemental opportunities; and (d) addressing the psychosocial needs of students, particularly by providing access to intellectual peers.

Using Assessments to Identify Needs

To discover talents that may otherwise go unrecognized and to guide educational decision making, the Talent Search model advocates ongoing assessments for all students, not just those who are likely to be identified as highly gifted. However, what most sets the Talent Search model apart from other efforts to identify gifted students is the use of above-grade-level tests to distinguish among students who all "hit the ceiling" on in-grade tests. Performance on the above-level SAT is what gave Julian Stanley the confidence to enroll Joe Bates as a young college student at Johns Hopkins, and many years of Talent Search data since then support the value of above-grade-level tests being able to differentiate within the group tested (e.g., Barnett et al., 2005; Olszewski-Kubilius, 2015; Stanley, 1977–1978). The results suggest that students who earn high scores on the above-grade-level tests may be ready to master more accelerated and advanced content, while those with the lower scorers may need challenging and enriching opportunities with grade-level content.

For identification purposes, the Talent Search tests are domain-specific and, to the extent possible, are reasoning tests. When SMPY began its work, general intelligence tests were common tools for identifying students for gifted programs, but Stanley knew that a general IQ measure would not be helpful for identifying the students with the most potential to move ahead, specifically in math. Talent Search tests are also intended to assess reasoning abilities rather than learned content knowledge because the latter is less predictive of a student's cognitive readiness to master more advanced, and potentially abstract, content. When the questions on an above-level test include topics to which the students have not been formally exposed, this enhances its credibility as a reasoning test.

Research supports both the short- and long-term effectiveness of Talent Search tests to predict achievement. For example, numerous studies have shown how Talent Search scores predict a student's ability to learn content at a faster pace than lower scorers or average classmates (Bartkovich & Mezynski, 1981; Gustin & Corazza, 1994; Olszewski-Kubilius et al., 1989) and show that high scorers can achieve at high levels in accelerated programs (e.g., Kolitch & Brody, 1992). Research has also linked high performance in the Talent Searches to patterns of taking advanced courses in high school, more honors and awards in high school, and higher educational aspirations (Barnett & Durden, 1993; Lupkowski-Shoplik et al., 2003; Mills & Ablard, 1993; Olszewski-Kubilius, 1998).

Follow-up studies of subjects years after participating in Talent Searches have also shown their test scores in middle school to be highly predictive of later achievements (Bernstein et al., 2019; Lubinski et al., 2014). In particular, the accomplishments of some of the highest scoring Talent Search participants (top 1 in 10,000) have been outstanding, with them, as a group, earning advanced degrees at rates well beyond what might be expected, receiving accolades and awards in their chosen professions, and producing exceptionally creative products and published papers (Kell et al., 2013).

Notably, a recent replication of SMPY's research with another group of equally talented Talent Search participants confirmed the predictability of Talent Search scores for achievement later in life (Makel et al., 2016).

The value of domain-specific identification was shown by studies that linked ability "tilt" (i.e., whether a student's verbal or math SAT score in middle school was higher) with whether adult achievement was more likely to be in the humanities or in STEM fields and with the level of their achievements (Park et al., 2007). Spatial ability has also been found to predict success in relevant courses in summer programs (Stumpf et al., 2013) and adult achievement in STEM fields (Wai et al., 2009; Webb et al., 2007).

Although high performance on the above-level tests spotlights a student's potential for high achievement in a talent area, more information is necessary for educational decision making. Students with similar aptitude scores may have quite different cognitive and personal profiles, and their content knowledge may vary, resulting in differing educational needs. For example, students with comparable scores on SAT-Math may have quite different levels of actual math knowledge, so a math achievement measure can help with placement. To assist with this, Stanley developed the Diagnostic Testing-Prescriptive Instruction (DT-PI) model, an approach that includes testing students to determine what they already know and focusing the instructional program on what they don't know, with posttests applied to assess mastery after each topic is completed (Assouline & Lupkowski-Shoplik, 2011; Stanley, 2000).

Students who exhibit high abilities in math may also differ in the level of their abilities in other domains, which has consequences for educational decision making. For example, a student who exhibits advanced mathematical and verbal reasoning abilities might warrant a grade skip to move ahead in all subjects, while a mathematically talented student whose verbal abilities are more age-typical might opt to accelerate in math but remain with age peers for other subjects. In addition, students differ in their interests and motivation, as well as their eagerness to seek learning opportunities outside of school. Such affective traits should be assessed, whether with formal inventories or informally in an interview. Longitudinal follow-up studies of Talent Search students have affirmed the relevance of personality traits, values, interests, and preferences to predicting career choice and level of achievement among high-ability students over time (Achter et al., 1999; Bernstein et al., 2019; Lubinski et al., 1995; Lubinski & Benbow, 2000; Wai et al., 2005). Overall, this body of research suggests that, although ability may predict a student's potential to achieve in a domain, personality traits and interests clearly influence one's choices and possibly eagerness to work hard on something, and these factors also affect achievement. Therefore, assessment of these characteristics can enhance the reliability of decisions that affect talent development.

With its emphasis on individual differences and recognition of discrepancies between domains of talent, the Talent Search approach is useful when applied to meeting the needs of students who might be diagnosed as twice-exceptional, or 2e (i.e., students with co-existing talents and disabilities). A symposium at Johns Hopkins in 1981 followed by relevant publications set the stage for more work in this area by Talent Search researchers (e.g., Brody & Mills, 1997; Foley-Nicpon et al., 2013; Fox et al., 1983). To determine the needs of 2e students, assessment is particularly important, if possible with a full psychoeducational evaluation, to identify strengths and weaknesses and to delineate the underlying causes of any weaknesses. CTY and the Belin-Blank Center at the University of Iowa offer diagnostic assessment services with a focus on 2e students, and all Talent Search programs offer needed accommodations and support to 2e program participants.

Adjusting the Level and Pace of Instruction

From the beginning, SMPY staff knew that it was not enough to identify talent; it must be developed through appropriate educational experiences and opportunities. Although it soon became clear that the diversity of students' characteristics required a "smorgasbord" of options to meet their individual needs, the staff recognized that, by identifying students with above-level reasoning abilities and content knowledge, some degree of acceleration was likely to be needed for many of the students served. Yet, educators at the time were fearful of acceleration, fearful that students would not retain knowledge that was gained quickly, and fearful of negative social and emotional effects.

Consequently, much research was undertaken to evaluate acceleration in various forms, including fast-paced math classes (e.g., Stanley, 1976a), accelerated summer programs (e.g., Stanley & Stanley, 1986), early entrance to college (e.g., Brody et al., 1988), and grade skipping and other forms of acceleration (e.g., Brody & Benbow, 1987). The results were extremely positive, demonstrating that, for groups of students, acceleration was a highly effective form of intervention for developing academic talents and not causing social or emotional difficulties (e.g., Pollins, 1983; Richardson & Benbow, 1990). Many of the studies resulted in specific recommendations that could be helpful. For example, a study of young entrants to a highly selective university found that completion of Advanced Placement courses prior to enrolling in college was highly predictive of their achievement in college, suggesting that students contemplating early entrance into a selective university should be sure they have adequate content knowledge before enrolling (Brody et al., 1990).

Eventually, at least 17 different ways to accelerate one's education were recognized, including those that accelerate grade placement in different ways and those that provide acceleration within a domain (Southern & Jones, 2015; Southern et al., 1993). A student accelerating in math, for example, might take a more advanced class in a different format or place, such as online, in the summer, in a higher grade in school, or at a local college. A student accelerating in grade placement might do so by entering kindergarten early, skipping a year or more at any time, and/or entering college early. Grade skips at transition points when students change schools (e.g., the last year of middle school before entering high school) are often advocated for their relative ease of adjustment. The Iowa Acceleration Scale helps parents and educators make informed decisions about the suitability of having their children skip grades.

Follow-up research of Talent Search participants also supports acceleration as an effective intervention that fosters talent development. For example, Park et al. (2013) compared grade skippers to students who progressed through school at the typical pace and found the grade skippers to be more likely to pursue advanced degrees in STEM fields than other students. Another study, which tracked top-scoring Talent Search participants (top 1 in 10,000) over a 10-year period, reported that 95% of them had used some form of acceleration to individualize their education (Lubinski et al., 2001). The truly exceptional achievements of this group testify to the value of acceleration for meeting their educational needs.

Today acceleration is viewed more favorably than in the past, and much of the change can be credited to the large body of Talent Search research that supports its efficacy. Still, there were individuals within the groups studied whose accelerative experiences were less positive; other interventions might have been more appropriate for meeting their needs. This finding reinforces the view that decisions about adjusting the level and pace of instruction should consider each student's characteristics, needs, and relevant opportunities. See Assouline et al. (2015) for a review of acceleration research.

Utilizing Supplemental Opportunities

When educators talk about acceleration in any form, it is about speeding a student's progress through the regular curriculum in some way. Students who process information more quickly than other students do, and/or who have mastered content at a more advanced level than age peers, should have access to accelerated programming that is appropriately challenging for them. However, there is also value in expanding students' learning opportunities through extracurricular activities and supplemental out-of-school programs—opportunities that may also have psychosocial benefits if they deepen a student's passion for a subject or provide access to intellectual peers who share their interests.

An illustration of the value of supplemental programs comes from what has been learned from the students who participate in the Talent Search residential summer programs. For example, CTY evaluations over many years have shown positive short-term and long-term effects, with program participants reporting that the program helped them experience academic rigor, enhanced their desire to learn, increased their academic confidence, and prepared them well for college. The social benefits may be even more important, as CTY students have suggested that the program gave them a sense of belonging because they were able to interact with other students who are more like themselves than they typically find in school (Mickenberg & Wood, 2009a, 2009b). Evaluations of other Talent Search summer programs have found similar results, leading to the conclusion that "summer programs, particularly residential ones, may play a significant role in fostering the healthy social and emotional development of participants" (Lee et al., 2015, p. 275).

In addition to summer programs, participation in competitions and other extracurricular activities that bring students together with peers who share their love for a particular subject can be beneficial for enhancing learning and providing social and emotional support (Stanley, 1987). In fact, early entrance into college at a young age may be less necessary for exceptionally talented students if they take full advantage of the growing number of rigorous extracurricular opportunities available for academically advanced students during their high school years. This was true for mathematician Lenny Ng, who was well prepared intellectually and academically to enroll in college at a younger-than-typical age, but instead chose to stay in high school while he participated in several summer programs and engaged in math competitions. Lenny earned a silver and two gold medals representing the United States in International Mathematical Olympiad competitions, and he later reported that "It was the competitions that really introduced the fun side of math to me. [They] also contributed quite a bit to my social life. . . . I could hang out with kids with similar interests" (Muratori et al., 2006, pp. 316–317).

Follow-up studies of Talent Search participants found that "special educational opportunities can . . . markedly enhance the development of talent" (Lubinski & Benbow, 2006, p. 316). In fact, the number of such activities in which a student participates can make a difference, according to research by Wai et al. (2010). They found that those students with the greatest STEM accomplishments as adults, in their educational and career attainments and quality of creative outputs, had experienced a richer level of precollege educational experiences and opportunities—what the researchers called a higher "STEM dose." This result recalls Zuckerman's (1977) finding that, among Nobel Prize winners, one special opportunity led to another and contributed to success, a phenomenon she referred to as cumulative educational advantage. Her work definitely had an impact on the thinking behind the Talent Search model.

Providing Psychosocial Support

No matter how appropriate or excellent the academic opportunities are for academically talented students, their talents are unlikely to fully develop if their psychosocial needs are not also met. The important role of psychosocial factors in the development of talent has been emphasized in the work of Subotnik et al. (2011; see also Olszewski-Kubilius et al., 2015), and others, and addressing students' social and emotional needs is a vital part of the Talent Search model.

In Stanley's early work, psychological health was among the variables studied (e.g., Haier & Denham, 1976), and it remained an ongoing focus as the staff interacted with and counseled students. Increasingly, concerns centered on students' lack of access to peers who share their abilities and interests, leaving many feeling isolated and unhappy in school. Stanley recalled his own experiences, where his achievement motivation was ultimately fueled by interaction with peers in graduate school, something he didn't have when he was young. He believed in the importance of peer support for achieving one's goals, and he was concerned that, without ongoing interaction with peers, students' social skills might not develop adequately for them to be prepared to interact with confidence in the adult world.

Consequently, much focus turned toward finding ways for students to interact with intellectual peers who are also age peers. This was much of the impetus behind the creation of the residential summer programs, as well as magnet high schools and early college programs, and it remains a concern today. Counseling activities of the Study of Exceptional Talent focus heavily on finding environments where students can interact with like-minded peers (Brody, 2007), and Talent Search residential summer programs continue to make the social environments they offer supportive of students' needs (Lee et al., 2015). Some students, of course, may face serious psychological problems, problems that must be addressed with professional intervention. But for many gifted students, it is the sense of belonging that they crave, and being with peers who share their interests and abilities can help to provide this.

Comparison to Other Conceptions of Giftedness

Anyone new to the field of gifted education is likely to be confused and perhaps a bit overwhelmed by the fact that the field can't seem to agree on how to define, identify, or serve gifted students. Although theorists and educators agree that the goal is to help students with potential develop their talents to the fullest extent possible so that they will be prepared to make important contributions to society as adults, there is a lack of consensus on how to achieve this. The complexity of human development and the many pathways that eminent individuals have taken to achieve their accomplishments make it difficult to predict optimal pathways for others. Questions persist like: What role do inborn traits versus educational experiences play in the development of talent? How relevant is general ability versus domain-specific talents in determining the level an individual achieves? In seeking to encourage problem-solving abilities and innovation in gifted students, is it best to focus on providing students with advanced content or more creative pursuits? How do educators identify talent potential in a student who is not currently achieving at a high level? Attempts to answer such questions have contributed to the differing responses represented in various theories of intelligence and conceptions of giftedness.

Nonetheless, there is also much commonality and overlap among the most respected theories today. The field has notably seen a shift over time toward theories that focus more on domain-specific talents and less on giftedness as high general ability. Most theories also include some acknowledgement that psychosocial traits play a role in talent development, although some may suggest that they be part of an identification strategy, while others focus on cultivating psychosocial skills as part of the talent development process. Creativity is another common theme, although there is variability as to whether educators should try to identify students' creative potential or if creative output is a product of talent development.

What perhaps sets the Talent Search model apart from many others is that it is primarily pragmatic, focusing much less on answering the theoretical question "What is giftedness?" and more on asking educators to respond to the educational needs of individual students. Stanley referred to his prodigies as "youths who reason extremely well mathematically" (e.g., Stanley, 1976b, p. 237), not as gifted students, because it described what he knew about them at the time. He did not want to imply that they had gifts in areas other than mathematics, nor did he necessarily want to predict that their ultimate achievements might qualify them to be considered gifted as adults.

The Talent Search model has much in common with most of the other theories presented in this book, and areas of disagreement are relatively subtle. For example, the approach that perhaps comes closest to the Talent Search model is the Talent Development Megamodel offered by Subotnik, Olszewski-Kubilius, and Worrell (see Chapter 2). Both are domain-specific, incorporate recognition of the importance of psychosocial as well as cognitive characteristics in their understanding of relevant student profiles, and incorporate a variety of programmatic options to develop talents. There is, perhaps, more emphasis in the Talent Development Megamodel on preparing students to achieve eminence in their domain as adults than there is in the Talent Search model as it has evolved, although Stanley did aim for that outcome when he worked with the earliest prodigies.

The Talent Search model's emphasis on providing appropriately challenging academic opportunities also has much in common with Peters's Advanced Academics perspective (see Chapter 10). Using educational need as a guide, when students exhibit exceptional reasoning abilities, advanced achievement, and/or passion to explore a subject in depth, schools should be expected to respond with appropriately challenging opportunities to fulfill the demonstrated needs. If there is a difference between the Advanced Academics and the Talent Search approaches, it may be that the Talent

Search model focuses much more on utilizing outside-of-school supplemental opportunities as educational resources.

The Talent Search model also shares an emphasis with the many theorists who recognize the role psychosocial skills play in the development of talent. Tannenbaum's psychosocial conception of giftedness and Renzulli's Three-Ring Conception of Giftedness, in particular, had huge impacts on the field when they broadened many people's view of giftedness to include components beyond ability (see Chapters 4 and 5). The difference between their theories and the Talent Search view is that the Talent Search model, although valuing enrichment opportunities, is much more domain-specific in its orientation, calling for the identification of domain-specific abilities and for providing specific rigorous, accelerative, and enriching opportunities to cultivate learning within that domain.

Implications of the Talent Search Model for Schools

It has always been the hope that the support for curricular flexibility and for supplemental programs that is embodied in the Talent Search model would move beyond the university-based Talent Search centers and into the schools. As early as 1974, Lynn Fox, who worked with Stanley to establish SMPY, wrote: "We must consider how to create a more flexible educational system in which individuals would be provided with the opportunities and encouragement needed for them to perform at their highest level and at their own rate" (p. 67). Stanley suggested that K–12 school-based longitudinal teaching teams within content areas such as mathematics might facilitate students moving at their own pace through a subject. He also recommended that schools employ special coordinators whose role would be to assess students' strengths and weaknesses, identify needs, and coordinate providing the resources necessary to meet those needs (Stanley, 1980).

To implement the Talent Search model in schools, educators need to move away from the emphasis on age-in-grade instruction because the assumption that all students of the same age are ready to learn the same thing at the same time is faulty. The fact that a grade spans a full 12 months, resulting in the oldest and youngest students in a grade being a full year apart in age, is a problem if age matters at all. In reality, age may matter less than many other factors that affect learning, including one's cognitive abilities, prior knowledge, rate of learning, learning styles, and interests. There are times when grouping students in school by age makes sense, but not in all subjects all day.

In an effort to address the special needs of gifted students, many school systems offer special classes and/or enrichment opportunities for students who qualify on some criterion; some districts even have magnet schools for gifted students. Clearly, such offerings present more opportunities than typical classes do to students who are ready to learn at a faster pace or higher level, but admission to them may depend on criteria that are hard to defend: Is the last student admitted to the program really qualitatively different from the first on the list who was turned away? Among students who fail to be admitted to these programs, how often is it because they have never been given the opportunity to do more than grade-level work but might have the talent to excel in a more challenging program if given the chance? And do those programs actually serve the full need for differentiation for all participants? For example, enrichment programs that are not domain-specific in their orientation are unlikely to address the needs of students who are ready to study a particular subject at a more accelerated pace, on a more advanced level, and in greater depth. And when a program is domain-specific, such as an advanced math class for fourth graders with a curriculum on a sixth-grade level, it may still fail to meet the needs of all of its participants, such as the student who is well beyond the sixth-grade level in her math skills and knowledge.

To implement the Talent Search model in schools, the four elements described earlier are essential. The schools must embrace the value of assessment to identify students' needs, be willing to adjust the pace and level of instruction for students in response to demonstrated readiness for advanced content, encourage involvement in supplemental opportunities and activities for enrichment and talent development, and be consciously aware of students' social and emotional needs, especially their need to interact with intellectual peers.

Testing is a hugely important part of this model; there needs to be more testing, not less, as the trend seems to be going. However, a focus on assessment should not drive the curriculum toward becoming a test-prep curriculum; nor should tests be used for high-stakes decision making about qualifying students as gifted or not gifted as is commonly done in many schools. The purpose of assessment should be to learn about a student, to identify strengths, weaknesses, and learning needs, not to worry about passing some arbitrary cutoff score. If a high-achieving student scores near the top on an in-level test, more assessment is needed, specifically an above-grade-level test to determine the full extent of their abilities and readiness for more advanced content. Students' content knowledge and noncognitive traits, including interests, should also be assessed and factored into educational decision making.

The movement toward universal screening of all students in an effort to identify students for gifted programming is helpful for identifying those whose advanced abilities might not otherwise be recognized, and the Talent Search model fully supports it. Too often, however, screening for gifted programs consists of a single assessment (sometimes as early as kindergarten) and is not repeated for students who fail to qualify on that round. With much evidence that students' cognitive abilities and learning develop at different rates, reassessment should occur at regular intervals, as well as whenever new opportunities emerge that require evidence of academic readiness for participation.

In response to what is learned about each student's cognitive abilities, content knowledge, interests, and other factors, a combination of in- and out-of-school opportunities should be utilized to develop a program that meets their individual academic, social, and emotional needs. A knowledgeable counselor should help identify options. If there is evidence of content already mastered, credit should be awarded and students given the flexibility to move ahead in their placement. Online learning, independent study, and academic programs outside of school can supplement school options, while dual enrollment with a local college or university and internship programs can meet the needs of accelerated students who complete the high school curriculum in a particular subject before they are ready to graduate from high school. When the need for an advanced program pertains to just a few advanced students and/or teaching staff is limited in its knowledge of advanced content, schools might consider developing collaborative programs with other schools and/or universities. See McCarthy (1998) for an example of a long-standing multidistrict/university collaboration in Michigan that provides courses to mathematically talented students; there is a similar program affiliated with the University of Minnesota (Keynes & Rogness, 2011).

The Talent Search model also calls for students to have access to supplemental opportunities beyond the classroom to explore their interests, extend their learning in greater depth, and interact with intellectual peers who share their interests. Fortunately, such opportunities have greatly increased in number in recent years, with schools offering students access to more clubs and academic competitions than in the past, and parents enrolling their children in summer programs, internships, and a variety of out-of-school activities that develop specific talents in academic subjects, music, art, athletics, and other areas. The problem is that access to these opportunities is uneven. More affluent schools typically offer many more activities than do schools in lower income neighborhoods, and parents who lack knowledge of out-of-school programs or who believe that the logistical and financial barriers to participating are insurmountable are unlikely to seek them out. There is little doubt that the widening of the opportunity/excellence gap that educators have witnessed can be at least partially attributed to differential access to extracurricular out-of-school programs and informal learning opportunities (Olszewski-Kubilius & Corwith, 2018).

Schools need to expand their extracurricular offerings so that they are available to all students, and counselors need to view it as part of their role to help students find a way to participate in the out-of-school programs that will advance their talent development needs. Schools also need to take more responsibility for helping students find summer opportunities that extend their learning, especially as it has been well-documented that students from low-income backgrounds experience significant learning loss if they do not have access to stimulating academic and extracurricular experiences during the summer break (e.g., Alexander et al., 2007). If educators want to reduce the opportunity gaps that are defined by income and differential access to resources, they need to make summer learning opportunities, as well as accelerated learning options and out-of-school supplemental programs during the school year, available to more students.

Conclusion

The Talent Search model evolved from a demonstrated need to help advanced students achieve their full potential. Research supports the effectiveness of this approach, as there is much evidence that adults whose talents were identified by the Talent Searches when they were in middle school and who pursued appropriately challenging learning opportunities are now achieving at high levels and contributing to society in important and creative ways.

Today, many more students are pursuing the pathways that the Talent Search model recommends. Some even arrive for Talent Search testing already accelerated in math and other subjects and involved in a wide variety of supplemental activities, and they go on to pursue more exciting opportunities to develop their talents. Significant numbers of high school students graduate with transcripts that list the completion of several years of college-level work, and the award winners of high school science competitions present projects that might have been the work of graduate students a generation ago. For most of these students, however, their accomplishments would not have been possible without parental involvement—that is, without parents who make the effort to get their children tested, who learn about educational opportunities, and who pave the way for their children to participate in them.

Too many other students are less fortunate. Their parents lack knowledge of such opportunities and/or lack the resources to pursue them. These students have exceptional abilities that no one is aware of, sit in classes frustrated by a pace of instruction that is too slow or too repetitive for their quick minds, and face barriers to involvement in out-of-school learning opportunities that might contribute to the development of their talents. The result is a widening gap in achievement between those who have access to accelerative opportunities and enriching programs and those who do not. With the many challenges facing society today, educators cannot afford to leave so many talents untapped, and so many students frustrated and unfulfilled. Schools must get involved in expanding the talent development opportunities for all of the students they serve. Embracing the principles and practices of the Talent Search model can show them the way.

DISCUSSION QUESTIONS

1. Discuss the pros and cons of using above-level tests in your setting. Is it logistically possible? Who would you test? What tests might you use?

2. If you wanted to incorporate an accelerated continuous progress program in your school in core subjects, how would that work? How could you assure students who accelerate in content that they will not have to repeat work in a subsequent school year that they will have already mastered?

3. The Talent Search model encourages active participation in out-of-school learning opportunities and activities. How can your school play a role in supporting this? Will access be a problem for students from low-income backgrounds in your school?

DISCUSSION QUESTIONS, continued

4. If your school already has a gifted program in place, to what degree is it compatible with the components of the Talent Search model as outlined? Would any modifications to the existing program be necessary in order to introduce the elements of domain-specific talent identification, flexible placement, and support for supplemental learning options as described in the Talent Search model?

5. What implications are there from this model for students who will not qualify as needing advanced courses? Describe how their educational experiences might still benefit by adopting components of the Talent Search model.

References

Achter, J. A., Lubinski, D., Benbow, C. P., & Eftekhari-Sanjani, H. (1999). Assessing vocational preferences among gifted adolescents adds incremental validity to abilities: A discriminant analysis of educational outcomes over a 10-year interval. *Journal of Educational Psychology, 91*(4), 777–786. https://doi.org/10.1037/0022-0663.91.4.777

Alexander, K. L., Entwisle, D. R., & Olson, L. S. (2007). Summer learning and its implications: Insights from the beginning school study. *New Directions for Youth Development, 114,* 11–32. https://doi.org/10.1002/yd.210

Assouline, S. G., Colangelo, N., VanTassel-Baska, J., & Lupkowski-Shoplik, A. (Eds.). (2015). *A nation empowered: Evidence trumps the excuses that hold back America's brightest students* (Vol. 2). The University of Iowa, The Connie Belin & Jacqueline N. Blank International Center for Gifted Education and Talent Development.

Assouline, S. G., Ihrig, L. M., & Mahatmya, D. (2017). Closing the excellence gap: Investigation of an expanded talent search model for student selection into an extracurricular STEM program in rural middle schools. *Gifted Child Quarterly, 61*(3), 250–261. https://doi.org/10.1177/0016986217701833

Assouline, S. G., & Lupkowski-Shoplik, A. (2011). *Developing math talent: A comprehensive guide to math education for gifted students in elementary and middle school* (2nd ed.). Prufrock Press.

Bartkovich, K. G., & Mezynski, K. (1981). Fast-paced precalculus mathematics for talented junior-high students: Two recent SMPY programs. *Gifted Child Quarterly, 25*(2), 73–80. https://doi.org/10.1177/001698628102500206

Barnett, L. B., Albert, M. E., & Brody, L. E. (2005). The Center for Talented Youth talent search and academic programs. *High Ability Studies, 16*(1), 27–40. https://doi.org/10.1080/13598130500115197

Barnett, L. B., & Durden, W. G. (1993). Education patterns of academically talented youth. *Gifted Child Quarterly, 37*(4), 161–168. https://doi.org/10.1177/001698629303700405

Bayley, N. (1955). On the growth of intelligence. *American Psychologist, 10*(12), 805–818. https://doi.org/10.1037/h0043803

Bayley, N. (1970). Development of mental abilities. In P. H. Mussen (Ed.), *Carmichael's manual of child psychology* (3rd ed., Vol. 1, pp. 1163–2109). Wiley.

Benbow, C. P., & Lubinski, D. (Eds.). (1996). *Intellectual talent: Psychometric and social issues.* Johns Hopkins University Press.

Benbow, C. P., & Stanley, J. C. (Eds.). (1983). *Academic precocity: Aspects of its development.* Johns Hopkins University Press.

Bernstein, B. O., Lubinski, D., & Benbow, C. P. (2019). Psychological constellations assessed at age 13 predict distinct forms of eminence 35 years later. *Psychological Science, 30*(3), 444–454. https://doi.org/10.1177/0956797618822524

Bowman, K. (2018). *CTY expands efforts to connect with Baltimore's brightest students.* Johns Hopkins University. https://hub.jhu.edu/2018/01/31/cty-baltimore-advanced-learning-efforts

Bowman, K. (2019). *Program helps prepare low-income students for success at some of the nation's top colleges.* Johns Hopkins University. https://hub.jhu.edu/2019/04/04/cty-scholars-head-to-college

Brody, L. E. (2007). Counseling highly gifted students to utilize supplemental educational opportunities: Using the SET program as a model. In J. L. VanTassel-Baska (Ed.), *Serving gifted learners beyond the traditional classroom* (pp. 123–143). Prufrock Press.

Brody, L. E. (2009). The Johns Hopkins talent search model for identifying and developing exceptional mathematical and verbal abilities. In L. V. Shavinina (Ed.), *International handbook on giftedness* (pp. 999–1016). Springer.

Brody, L. E. (2017). Meeting the educational needs of students by applying talent search principles to school settings. In J. A. Plucker, A. N. Rinn, & M. C. Makel (Eds.), *From giftedness to gifted education: Reflecting theory in practice* (pp. 43–63). Prufrock Press.

Brody, L. E., Assouline, S. G., & Stanley, J. C. (1990). Five years of early entrants: Predicting successful achievement in college. *Gifted Child Quarterly, 34*(4), 138–142. https://doi.org/10.1177/001698629003400402

Brody, L. E., & Benbow, C. P. (1987). Accelerative strategies: How effective are they for the gifted? *Gifted Child Quarterly, 31*(3), 105–110. https://doi.org/10.1177/001698628703100302

Brody, L. E., Lupkowski, A. E., & Stanley, J. C. (1988). Early entrance to college: A study of academic and social adjustment during freshman year. *College and University, 63*(4), 347–359.

Brody, L. E., & Mills, C. J. (1997). Gifted children with learning disabilities: A review of the issues. *Journal of Learning Disabilities, 30*(3), 282–296. https://doi.org/10.1177/002221949703000304

Brody, L. E., & Mills, C. J. (2005). Talent search research: What have we learned? *High Ability Studies, 16*(1), 97–111. https://doi.org/10.1080/13598130500115320

Brody, L. E., & Stanley, J. C. (2005). Youths who reason exceptionally well mathematically and/or verbally: Using the MVT:D^4 model to develop their talents. In R. J. Sternberg & J. E. Davidson (Eds.), *Conceptions of giftedness* (2nd ed., pp. 20–37). Cambridge University Press.

Daurio, S. P. (1979). Educational enrichment versus acceleration: A review of the literature. In W. C. George, S. J. Cohn, & J. C. Stanley (Eds.), *Educating the gifted: Acceleration and enrichment* (pp. 13–63). Johns Hopkins University Press.

Foley-Nicpon, M., Assouline, S. G., & Colangelo, N. (2013). Twice-exceptional learners: Who needs to know what? *Gifted Child Quarterly, 57*(3), 169–180. https://doi.org/10.1177/0016986213490021

Fox, L. H. (1974). Facilitating the educational development of mathematically precocious youth. In J. C. Stanley, D. P. Keating, & L. H. Fox, (Eds.). *Mathematical talent: Discovery, description, and development* (pp. 47–69). Johns Hopkins University Press.

Fox, L. H., Brody, L., & Tobin, D. (1983). *Learning-disabled/gifted children: Identification and programming*. PRO-ED.

Gustin, W. C., & Corazza, L. (1994). Mathematical and verbal reasoning as predictors of science achievement. *Roeper Review, 16*(3), 160–162. https://doi.org/10.1080/02783199409553564

Haier, R. J., & Denham, S. A. (1976). A summary profile of the nonintellectual correlates of mathematical precocity in boys and girls. In D. P. Keating (Ed.), *Intellectual talent: Research and development* (pp. 225–241). Johns Hopkins University Press.

Hilgard, E. R., & Bower, G. H. (1974). *Theories of learning* (4th ed.). Prentice Hall.

Hollingworth, L. S. (1942). *Children above 180 IQ Stanford-Binet: Origin and development*. World Book.

Hunt, J. M. (1961). *Intelligence and experience*. Ronald Press.

Keating, D. P. (Ed.). (1976). *Intellectual talent: Research and development*. Johns Hopkins University Press.

Kell, H. J., Lubinski, D., & Benbow, C. P. (2013). Who rises to the top? Early indicators. *Psychological Science, 24*(5), 648–659. https://doi.org/10.1177/0956797612457784

Keynes, H. B., & Rogness, J. (2011). Historical perspectives on a program for mathematically talented students. *The Mathematics Enthusiast, 8*(1).

Kolitch, E. R., & Brody, L. E. (1992). Mathematics acceleration of highly talented students: An evaluation. *Gifted Child Quarterly, 36*(2), 78–86. https://doi.org/10.1177/001698629203600205

Lee, S.-Y., Matthews, M. S., & Olszewski-Kubilius, P. (2008). A national picture of talent search and talent search educational programs. *Gifted Child Quarterly, 52*(1), 55–69. https://doi.org/10.1177/0016986207311152

Lee, S.-Y., Olszewski-Kubilius, P., Makel, M. C., & Putallaz, M. (2015). Gifted students' perceptions of an accelerated summer program and social support. *Gifted Child Quarterly, 59*(4), 265–282. https://doi.org/10.1177/0016986215599205

Lehman, H. C. (1953). *Age and achievement*. Princeton University Press.

Lubinski, D., & Benbow, C. P. (2000). States of excellence. *American Psychologist, 55*(1), 137–150. https://doi.org/10.1037/0003-066X.55.1.137

Lubinski, D., & Benbow, C. P. (2006). Study of Mathematically Precocious Youth after 35 years: Uncovering antecedents for the development of math-science expertise. *Perspectives on Psychological Science, 1*(4), 316–345. https://doi.org/10.1111/j.1745-6916.2006.00019.x

Lubinski, D., Benbow, C. P., & Kell, H. J. (2014). Life paths and accomplishments of mathematically precocious males and females four decades later. *Psychological Science, 25*(12), 2217–2232. https://doi.org/10.1177/0956797614551371

Lubinski, D., Benbow, C. P., & Ryan, J. (1995). Stability of vocational interests among the intellectually gifted from adolescence to adulthood:

A 15-year longitudinal study. *Journal of Applied Psychology, 80*(1), 196–200.

Lubinski, D., Webb, R. M., Morelock, M. J., & Benbow, C. P. (2001). Top 1 in 10,000: A 10-year follow-up of the profoundly gifted. *Journal of Applied Psychology, 86*(4), 718–729. https://doi.org/10.1037/0021-9010.86.4.718

Lupkowski-Shoplik, S., Benbow, C. P., Assouline, S. G., & Brody, L. E. (2003). Talent searches: Meeting the needs of academically talented youth. In N. Colangelo & G. A. Davis (Eds.), *Handbook of gifted education* (pp. 204–218). Allyn & Bacon.

Makel, M. C., Kell, H. J., Lubinski, D., Putallaz, M., & Benbow, C. P. (2016). When lightning strikes twice: Profoundly gifted, profoundly accomplished. *Psychological Science, 27*(7), 1004–1018. https://doi.org/10.1177/0956797616644735

McCarthy, C. R. (1998). Assimilating the talent search model into the school day. *The Journal of Secondary Gifted Education, 9*(3), 114–123. https://doi.org/10.1177/1932202X9800900304

Mickenberg, K. E., & Wood, J. (2009a). *Alumni program satisfaction and benefits of CTY summer programs* (Technical Report No. 29). Johns Hopkins Center for Talented Youth.

Mickenberg, K. E., & Wood, J. (2009b). *Short-term benefits of CTY summer programs* (Technical Report No. 30). Johns Hopkins University Center for Talented Youth.

Mills, C. J., & Ablard, K. E. (1993). Credit and placement for academically talented students following special summer courses in math and science. *Journal for the Education of the Gifted, 17*(1), 4–25. https://doi.org/10.1177/016235329301700103

Muratori, M., Stanley, J. C., Gross, M. U. M., Ng, L., Tao, T., Ng, J, & Tao, B. (2006). Insights from SMPY's former child prodigies: Drs. Terrence ("Terry") Tao and Lenhard ("Lenny") Ng reflect on their talent development. *Gifted Child Quarterly, 50*(4), 307–324. https://doi.org/10.1177/001698620605000404

Olszewski-Kubilius, P. (1998). Research evidence regarding the validity and effects of talent search educational programs. *Journal of Secondary Gifted Education, 9*(3), 134–138. https://doi.org/10.1177/1932202X9800900306

Olszewski-Kubilius, P. (2015). Talent searches and accelerated programming for gifted students. In S. G. Assouline, N. Colangelo, J. VanTassel-Baska, & A. Lupkowski-Shoplik (Eds.), *A nation empowered: Evidence trumps the excuses holding back America's brightest students* (Vol. 2, pp. 111–

121). The University of Iowa, The Connie Belin & Jacqueline N. Blank International Center for Gifted Education and Talent Development.

Olszewski-Kubilius, P., & Corwith, S. (2018). Poverty, academic achievement, and giftedness: A literature review. *Gifted Child Quarterly, 62*(1), 37–55. https://doi.org/10.1177/0016986217738015

Olszewski-Kubilius, P., Kulieke, M. J., Willis, G. B., & Krasney, N. (1989). An analysis of the validity of SAT entrance scores for accelerated classes. *Journal for the Education of the Gifted, 13*(1), 37–54. https://doi.org/10.1177/016235328901300104

Olszewski-Kubilius, P., & Steenbergen-Hu, S. (2017). Blending research-based practices and practice-embedded research: Project Excite closes achievement and excellence gaps for underrepresented gifted minority students. *Gifted Child Quarterly, 61*(3), 202–209. https://doi.org/10.1177/0016986217701836

Olszewski-Kubilius, P., Steenbergen-Hu, S., Thomson, D., & Rosen, R. (2017). Minority achievement gaps in STEM: Findings of a longitudinal study of project Excite. *Gifted Child Quarterly, 61*(1), 20–39. https://doi.org/10.1177/0016986216673449

Olszewski-Kubilius, P., Subotnik, R. F., & Worrell, F. C. (2015). Antecedent and concurrent psychosocial skills that support high levels of achievement within talent domains. *High Ability Studies, 26*(2), 195–210. https://doi.org/10.1080/13598139.2015.1095077

Park, G., Lubinski, D., & Benbow, C. P. (2007). Contrasting intellectual patterns predict creativity in the arts and sciences. *Psychological Science, 18*(11), 948–952. https://doi.org/10.1111/j.1467-9280.2007.02007.x

Park, G., Lubinski, D., & Benbow, C. P. (2013). When less is more: Effects of grade skipping on adult STEM productivity among mathematically precocious adolescents. *Journal of Educational Psychology, 105*(1), 176–198. https://doi.org/10.1037/a0029481

Plucker, J. A., & Peters, S. J. (2016). *Excellence gaps in education: Expanding opportunities for talented students*. Harvard Education Press.

Pollins, L. D. (1983). The effects of acceleration on the social and emotional development of gifted students. In C. P. Benbow & J. C. Stanley (Eds.), *Academic precocity: Aspects of its development* (pp. 160–178). Johns Hopkins University Press.

Richardson, T. M., & Benbow, C. P. (1990). Long-term effects of acceleration on the social-emotional adjustment of mathematically precocious youths. *Journal of Educational Psychology, 82*(3), 464–470. https://doi.org/10.1037/0022-0663.82.3.464

Robinson, N. M., & Robinson, H. B. (1982). The optimal match: Devising the best compromise for the highly gifted student. In D. Feldman (Ed.), *New directions for child development: Developmental approaches to giftedness and creativity* (pp. 79–94). Jossey-Bass.

Southern, W. T., & Jones, E. D. (2015). Types of acceleration: Dimensions and issues. In S. G. Assouline, N. Colangelo, J. VanTassel-Baska, & A. Lupkowski-Shoplik (Eds.), *A nation empowered: Evidence trumps the excuses holding back America's brightest students* (Vol. 2, pp. 9–18). The University of Iowa, The Connie Belin & Jacqueline N. Blank International Center for Gifted Education and Talent Development.

Southern, W. T., Jones, E. D., & Stanley, J. C. (1993). Acceleration and enrichment: The context and development of program options. In K. A. Heller, F. J. Monks, & A. H. Passow (Eds.), *International handbook of research and development of giftedness and talent* (pp. 387–409). Pergamon.

Stanley, J. C. (1976a). Special fast-mathematics classes taught by college professors to fourth- through twelfth-graders. In D. P. Keating (Ed.), *Intellectual talent, research, and development* (pp. 132–159). Johns Hopkins University Press.

Stanley, J. C. (1976b). Youths who reason extremely well mathematically: SMPY's accelerative approach. *Gifted Child Quarterly, 20*(3), 237–238. https://doi.org/10.1177/001698627602000301

Stanley, J. C. (1977–1978, Winter). The predictive value of the SAT for brilliant seventh and eighth graders. *College Board Review, 106*, 30–37.

Stanley, J. C. (1980). On educating the gifted. *Educational Researcher, 9*(3), 8–12. https://doi.org/10.3102/0013189X009003008

Stanley, J. C. (1987). Making the IMO team: The power of early identification and encouragement. *Gifted Child Today, 10*(2), 22–23. https://doi.org/10.1177/107621758701000208

Stanley, J. C. (2000). Helping students learn only what they don't already know. *Psychology, Public Policy, and Law, 6*(1), 216–222. https://doi.org/10.1037/1076-8971.6.1.216

Stanley, J. C. (2005). A quiet revolution: Finding boys and girls who reason exceptionally well mathematically and/or verbally and helping them get the supplemental educational opportunities they need. *High Ability Studies, 16*(1), 5–14. https://doi.org/10.1080/13598130500115114

Stanley, J. C., Keating, D. P., & Fox, L. H. (Eds.). (1974). *Mathematical talent: Discovery, description, and development.* Johns Hopkins University Press.

Stanley, J. C., & Stanley, B. S. K. (1986). High-school biology, chemistry, or physics learned well in three weeks. *Journal of Research in Science Teaching, 23*(3), 237–250. https://doi.org/10.1002/tea.3660230308

Stumpf, H., Mills, C. J., Brody, L. E., & Baxley, P. G. (2013). Expanding talent search procedures by including measures of spatial ability: CTY's Spatial Test Battery. *Roeper Review, 35*(4), 254–264. https://doi.org/10.1080/02783193.2013.829548

Subotnik, R. F., Olszewski-Kubilius, P., & Worrell, F. C. (2011). Rethinking giftedness and gifted education: A proposed direction forward based on psychological science. *Psychological Science in the Public Interest, 12*(1), 3–54. https://doi.org/10.1177/1529100611418056

Terman, L. M. (1925). *Genetic studies of genius: Vol. 1. Mental and physical traits of a thousand gifted children.* Stanford University Press.

Wai, J., Lubinski, D., & Benbow, C. P. (2005). Creativity and occupational accomplishments among intellectually precocious youths: An age 13 to age 33 longitudinal study. *Journal of Educational Psychology, 97*(3), 484–492. https://doi.org/10.1037/0022-0663.97.3.484

Wai, J., Lubinski, D., & Benbow, C. P. (2009). Spatial ability for STEM domains: Aligning over 50 years of cumulative psychological knowledge solidifies its importance. *Journal of Educational Psychology, 101*(4), 817–835. https://doi.org/10.1037/a0016127

Wai, J., Lubinski, D., Benbow, C. P., & Steiger, J. H. (2010). Accomplishment in science, technology, engineering, and mathematics (STEM) and its relation to STEM educational dose: A 25-year longitudinal study. *Journal of Educational Psychology, 102*(4), 860–871. https://doi.org/10.1037/a0019454

Webb, R. M., Lubinski, D., & Benbow, C. P. (2007). Spatial ability: A neglected dimension in talent searches for intellectually precocious youth. *Journal of Educational Psychology, 99*(2), 397–420. https://doi.org/10.1037/0022-0663.99.2.397

Young, S., Andrew, P., Cerrato-Amador, T., Cooper, B., Makel, M. (2019, November 9). *Achieving lift off: Using Project Launch interventions to serve gifted, low-income students* [Paper presentation]. National Association for Gifted Children 66th Annual Convention, Albuquerque, NM, United States.

Zuckerman, H. (1977). *Scientific elite: Nobel laureates in the United States.* Free Press.

CHAPTER 9

An Enhanced School-Based Conception of Giftedness

TRACY L. CROSS AND JENNIFER RIEDL CROSS

> "Until you folks in gifted education can get your act together and offer a consistent model of gifted education, we cannot help you!"—Quote from the leader of a state association of superintendents, expressed during a meeting of the state legislature

This school superintendent perfectly expressed the frustration felt among those most likely to be ultimately responsible for the recommendations of members of gifted education in schools. School leaders cannot be expected to act on ambiguous or contradictory conceptions of giftedness or identification schemes that create advantages for some groups at the expense of others. Giftedness, the ability or potential to achieve at an exceptional (i.e., superior) level (T. L. Cross & Cross, 2019), had been defined in many ways. There are numerous categories of conceptions of giftedness (Coleman & Cross, 2005), with some being created in an omnibus fashion (giftedness in all talent domains and across all contexts), and others focused on more specific topics, such as creativity. Some conceptions are IQ-based and others *de facto*, meaning that true giftedness is identified by post-school outcomes without reliance on special educational opportunities. In another example (kinesthetic giftedness), middle and high school athletic teams often select players on the basis of perceived ability or previous achievement. Only these students are given the opportunity to develop their abilities and interests.

In essence, the field has described numerous reasonable and thoughtful conceptions of giftedness, with the boom years being between 1971 and 1986 (e.g., Bloom, 1985; Gardner, 1983/2011; Marland, 1972; Renzulli, 1977; Sternberg, 1985). Gagné, who originally published his Differentiated Model of Giftedness and Talent (DMGT) in the late 1990s (Gagné, 1998), attempted to distinguish between gifts—naturally occurring abilities—and talents—outcomes of systematic development. A smaller, but important, second contemporary wave began in 2005 and has yielded increasing numbers of talent development conceptions of giftedness (e.g., School-Based Conception of Giftedness, T. L. Cross & Coleman, 2005; Talent Development Megamodel, Subotnik et al., 2011; Actiotope Model of Giftedness, Ziegler, 2005). Between the two waves, Borland (2003, 2005) actively challenged the need for a conception of giftedness, proposing that gifted education be provided without identification of students with gifts and talents (SWGT[1]), thus offering a radical departure from traditional practice. Despite the many thoughtful published conceptions of giftedness, traditional practices have largely continued.

In 1984, while I (Tracy Cross) was a doctoral student late in my program, I had the great fortune of working with Dr. Laurence J. Coleman as he wrote his important textbook *Schooling the Gifted* (Coleman, 1985). Over that year, we had many fascinating conversations. I did not know how prophetic some of the ideas he shared would end up being. For example, at the end of a 67-page chapter on identification methods, he offered the field two not so "whimsical suggestions" (p. 117) for identifying SWGT. These were, in effect, examples of schools offering gifted education without the trappings and shortcomings of the traditional identification systems (see Figure 9.1).

---

[1] This acronym allows the authors to use preferred people-first language, avoiding the entity framing of the term *gifted student*.

School-Based Conception of Giftedness

FIGURE 9.1
Examples of Gifted Education Systems Without Nontraditional Identification Methods

System I: A school system constructs a large sign:

Gifted Program: Apply Here

The program will consist of special activities in _____

Sign here: _____

Names
1. _____
2. _____
3. _____
4. _____

System II: A school opens a classroom one day a week for 50% of the students for half a year. In the class, they are challenged by a rigorous curriculum as if they were in a gifted program. Those children who seem to thrive in this environment are selected for the formal program.

Note. Adapted from *Being Gifted in School: An Introduction to Development, Guidance, and Teaching* (2nd ed., pp. 126–127), by L. J. Coleman and T. L. Cross, 2005, Taylor & Francis. Copyright 2005 by Taylor & Francis. Adapted with permission.

The School-Based Conception of Giftedness (SCG; T. L. Cross & Coleman, 2005) was originally created to focus on giftedness in school settings. It was the primary interest of the originators (Coleman & Cross, 2001; T. L. Cross & Coleman, 2005) to assist schools as they serve millions of students. We determined that traditional gifted education approaches have struggled with issues of underrepresentation, identification, budget, and inconsistencies in philosophy, definition, identification, and services. Other issues such as underachievement and moving students into and out of programs were also problematic. Plus, it was determined that an omnibus conception might not fit the specific needs of the contexts of schools, and a narrow conception, such as a creativity-focused one, would not be adequate for the task. Finally, with many years of direct experience in a public residential academy for SWGT, plus having worked with the state legislatures for years and in teacher training programs for decades, we (Coleman & Cross, 2001; T. L. Cross & Coleman, 2005) decided to focus on trying to reimagine gifted education and talent development within the current architecture of schools in a manner that could be feasibly implemented nationwide. Strengths of the SCG include its applicability and ease of implementation.

The purpose of gifted education is to support the development of talent among students capable of achieving at levels beyond that of their peers' capabilities. As schools have attempted to implement the recommendations of researchers and theorists in the field, only rarely is this accomplished to the satisfaction of all members of a community. Exclusive identification practices mistakenly exclude students who could be successful (a Type 1 error; see Table 9.1) or include students with no interest in performing at advanced levels in school. Reliance on test scores with limited predictive validity for success in school-related domains has led to problems in schools (T. L. Cross & Cross, 2017a). In the most egregious example, the combination of efforts to this point has led to gross underrepresentation of some community members (e.g., ethnic or racial minorities, students from low-income backgrounds, those culturally and/or linguistically different from the dominant group). In an era when most people value inclusivity, such a system is untenable.

The SCG was designed to resolve problems faced by schools that are exacerbated by differing conceptions of giftedness with associated inadequate approaches to identification, each of which leads to different requirements of schools. The Gifted Child Paradigm (Dai & Chen, 2013) works well for those who wish to explain the phenomenon of giftedness. For institutions, however, boundaries must be put in place. For the SCG, those boundaries are placed around the types of giftedness that matter in school-related domains.

Describing the Model

Three components are at the core of the SCG: (a) domains of talent development, (b) schools' responsibilities, and (c) students' responsibilities. Note that a student's giftedness is not at the core. Rather than taking an entity perspective of giftedness, which schools are expected to nurture, the SCG conceptualizes giftedness as developing from an interaction of abilities and context. The tenets of the model are described in the following sections.

TABLE 9.1
Possible Gifted Identification Errors

	Reject gifted identification	Accept gifted identification
Child is capable of performing at advanced levels	**Type I error**	Correct
Child is not capable of performing at advanced levels	Correct	**Type II error**

- **Tenet 1:** Giftedness exists at the intersection of the child and their context.

The *gifted child model* conception of giftedness has been the dominant paradigm within gifted education since the early 20th century (Dai & Chen, 2013). This paradigm built upon the research of Terman (1925) and, later, Hollingworth (1942), who focused on intelligence testing as a means of identifying the giftedness that existed within a child. The child who performed at the highest level on a test of IQ would necessarily be qualitatively different from their peers, not only cognitively, but also emotionally. Under the Gifted Child Paradigm, schools are responsible for recognizing these qualitative differences within the child and providing specialized services to cater to their unique needs in developing their abilities. Schools have attempted to meet the expectations of the Gifted Child Paradigm by identifying students through standardized testing and offering special programs for identified students.

The expansion of this paradigm to include multiple areas in which giftedness could be acknowledged (e.g., Marland, 1972) provided freedom from the limitations of a single indicator of exceptional ability. With this expansion, however, the possibility of a mismatch between identification of exceptional potential and what schools offered increased substantially. The SCG resolves this problematic issue by conceptualizing giftedness as a confluence of students' abilities and schools' offerings. Each party—school and child—brings important components to the development of exceptional talent.

- **Tenet 2:** Schools are a unique context, charged with the development of specific, societally valued knowledge and skills, and bounded by cultural, environmental, and temporal limitations.

Schools reflect the values of society. As such, the domains within their purview are societally determined. In the U.S., schools generally teach students from ages 5 to 18. Preschools are increasingly being recognized for their importance to later academic performance and, even, adult outcomes (Ramey & Ramey, 2004), suggesting earlier ages will be included in the expected age range schools must be prepared to teach. An academic focus on language skills, mathematics, science, and history is common. The arts and physical education are sometimes included. In the past, homemaker and agricultural skills, civics, business, and a wide variety of societally relevant domains have been included in the curriculum. The interests of dominant groups in a society often drive the curriculum (Goodson, 2013). There are no domains that should be uniquely taught to students capable of exceptional performance. All societally valued domains offer the possibility of exceptional achievement. The ones that are selected to be taught in schools are the ones for which they have a responsibility to offer advanced training. The fact that students are capable of advanced development in other domains does not mean schools have a responsibility to provide training in them.

- **Tenet 3:** In schools, giftedness is conceptualized as a context-limited, age-related phenomenon.

In the early grades, children who are gifted show "high general cognitive ability, either through potential (ability), actions (performance), or rapid learning in school-related domains" (T. L. Cross & Coleman, 2005, p. 59).

The use of an ability (e.g., IQ, creativity, etc.) test to identify giftedness can be a source of frustration to school leaders, who carry out programs of instruction in which success may or may not be accurately measured or predicted by that test. It is not always possible to transfer skills that enable a high score on a test of creativity to classroom activities. What, then, is the purpose of identifying a student who has high creativity scores, for example? Some might argue that classroom activities should change to allow for the expression of greater creativity. We would not disagree.

Ability tests can indicate potential and are, therefore, a useful tool for locating young students who may be capable of advanced development. This does not mean that students who do not perform at a specified level will not be capable of equally advanced development. The prediction of academic outcomes from psychometrically sound ability tests is correlated, but not perfectly. This means a measure of ability would necessarily miss some students who could achieve at an advanced level and would incorrectly predict that some students would be capable of such achievement (see Table 9.1).

The development of abilities students bring to school may be limited by outside forces. The nonmodal gifted, those whose "attributes are viewed as being inconsistent with those of the [stereotypical] gifted" (Coleman & Cross, 2005, p. 61) may be subject to biases that interfere with their achievement opportunities (Gilliam et al., 2016; Harvey et al., 2016; Okonofua & Eberhardt, 2015). Impoverished environments can inhibit development, through an inability to access resources or by diverting attention from academic pursuits. When the potential to achieve in school has been restricted by external factors, assessments of ability may offer a window into a student's potential. With the application of greater resources in these cases, the likelihood of the advanced development of which individuals are capable increases.

The problems of imperfect correlations (of tests and outcomes) and impoverished environments can be resolved by applying ability tests to identify potential but allowing all students to have access to advanced opportunities. At early ages, particularly, schools should be providing opportunities to all students, offering additional resources to students who show potential via ability tests or other criteria but who are unable to achieve due to external factors (e.g., English language learners [ELLs], students from poverty, etc.). Given the degree of heterogeneity across students and the intersections of individual students with numerous meaningful characteristics and/or experiences, educators need to recognize the idiosyncratic nature of each child when planning instruction.

- **Tenet 4:** In later grades (i.e., secondary), giftedness is the expression of potential in the form of advanced development in a foundational domain or production of creative works in some societally valued area, with consistent engagement in activities associated with either type. Without such expression, the secondary student should not be considered gifted in school.

In the dominant paradigm of giftedness, the Gifted Child Paradigm (Dai & Chen, 2013), the entity of giftedness is found within a child, through testing or evidence of potential. As the gifted child moves through school, their giftedness moves with them, regardless of academic success. A gifted child who does not work at the level of their previously identified potential, is considered to be *underachieving* (Reis & McCoach, 2000). The school is seen to be at fault, then, and must take steps to ameliorate this problem (T.

L. Cross & Coleman, 2005). In some cases, the school will be at fault, as discussed in Tenet 9. When development of talent has been adequately supported, however, and secondary students once identified with gifted potential are not performing (achieving) at an advanced level, the school should not be required to continue making efforts to elicit that identified potential. The student should no longer be considered gifted in school.

- **Tenet 5:** Assessments should reflect differences in age and context. Ability testing should be used for identifying potential among young and nonmodal students who may not have had opportunities to develop through achievement. Subsequent assessment should be based on achievement.

Assessments of ability (e.g., IQ, creativity, nonverbal abilities, etc.) can effectively be used to identify potential, but the utility of such measures is limited in schools, in part because the distinction between foundational domains and performance domains has not been firmly established. T. L. Cross and Coleman (2005) described foundational domains as those most often found in schools—the school subjects of math, language arts, science, and the like, that build a foundation for later use in a performance domain that applies aspects or combinations of these in adult-level occupations. Math knowledge is foundational to architecture (a performance domain), for example. The potential for exceptional achievement in a foundational domain is identified by an ability or achievement test. The potential for exceptional achievement in a performance domain is identified by a test of achievement or one's performance.

Problems ensue when tests of ability continue to be used as an assessment of success in a domain of either type. Although tests of ability may be predictive of achievement in foundational domains, because of the fundamental level of each (test and domain), this is not always the case. There is a greater mismatch between a student's performance and ability test scores than between performance and achievement measures (T. L. Cross & Coleman, 2005). This distinction becomes clear with the recognition of the differences between foundational and performance domains. The SCG proposes that achievement is a more effective basis of assessment for activities in either foundational or performance domains. Ability tests can be helpful in identifying potential, but not for evaluating achievement.

- **Tenet 6:** Education should be in the form of planned, progressive acceleration in a domain, as opposed to dispersed forms of enrichment.

Talent domains are a critical component of the SCG. Educators must have a deep understanding of the domains in which they plan to develop talent. The ultimate goal of gifted education is to prepare students for advanced or creative production in the adult world. This requires an in-depth knowledge of achievement domains and what factors lead to exceptional performance in them. Little research in high performance has focused on the school's role in the development of talent in academic domains. Retrospective studies of mathematicians (Leiken, 2019) and academic psychologists (Simonton, 2019) provide little advice for elementary educators. Gifted education that supports the SCG requires an analysis of the foundations that feed into successful talent in adult domains. Acceleration of learning is the most effective means of developing talent, because it "more closely parallels the natural progression of learning in a domain, that is, the movement from simple to complex, from concrete to abstract, from unfocused creativity to focused creativity" (T. L. Cross & Coleman, 2005, p. 61). Other, less targeted educational experiences, such as enrichment, although enjoyable, are less conducive to the development of talent in a domain.

- **Tenet 7:** Schools are responsible for providing opportunities for the development of exceptional talent, offering scaffolding in foundational domains at early ages and increasingly sophisticated challenges in performance domains at secondary school ages.

For the SCG to be an effective framework for the development of exceptional talent, schools must be willing to bear the burden of offering opportunities to students. At the elementary level, rather than being a separate program for an exclusive group of students, gifted education should be a variety of offerings in school-related domains for all students. These should be more advanced for students who already have shown potential for mastery in the domain. As students attempt and succeed in each domain, they should be given more focused opportunities, allowing for development within the domain. Clustering similarly advanced students for lessons can provide flexible groups based on speed of learning, depth of knowledge, and so forth. Average-level achievement should be a requirement for all students, but as any show exceptional ability in any domain, they should have opportunities to advance to the level of which they are capable. Vygotsky's

(1978) zone of proximal development (ZPD) is the zone in which students can work with guidance from a more knowledgeable person. Working below the ZPD will be boring, as that content is easily mastered. Assignments above the ZPD may be frustrating, as students do not have the foundational knowledge to be successful. The ZPD will differ for students, and all students should be working at the level of their ZPD with scaffolded support of a teacher or more experienced peer.

Schools will need to be prepared for greater scaffolding needs among some students, such as students from low-income backgrounds, ELLs, or twice-exceptional students. On the other end of the spectrum, the school must be prepared for students who are able to do more than the average curriculum. Waiting for others to catch up to their level is a common, sometimes painful experience, as Peine and Coleman (2010) found. Although students may consider this to be a "fair" situation (Peine & Coleman, 2010), especially when they are young, boredom is the opposite of learning (Kanevsky & Keighley, 2003) and can be the death of students' motivation. As students become more proficient in a domain, the school should be responsive to their needs for additional opportunities such as mentors, advanced training, competitions, and highly qualified teachers. To thrive, advanced students also need to spend time with peers who share their interest in a domain and who can challenge them. Schools that undertake a talent development model should commit to being responsive when a few students are able to work far beyond the average curriculum.

- **Tenet 8:** Schools are responsible for eliminating systemic impediments to the development of talent in school-related domains. For example, the domains should not be presented in a boring manner. Students should not be inhibited in the development of their abilities by untrained teachers or gatekeepers who can subvert their pursuits, based on behavior or other non-domain-related assessments.

In being responsive to their students with high ability, schools must maintain an awareness of systemic issues that create barriers to students' maximization of potential. It is impossible for students to sustain interest in a domain when it is presented to them by an untrained, unenthusiastic teacher or when its relevance to them is not obvious. Kanevsky and Keighley (2003) found that the gifted students in their study who dropped out of high school did so because they were missing one or more of the "Five Cs": Control, Choice, Challenge, Complexity, and Caring. These fit within the components of Deci and Ryan's (2000) self-determination theory of motivation: autonomy, competence, and relatedness. Without control over the way they were able to approach the material and choices in what they were learning, they lacked the autonomy they desired. Without challenge that came from complexity in the material presented, they were unable to experience a sense of their true competence: "They sought novel, authentic, abstract, open-ended experiences and felt the familiar, artificial, concrete, decontextualized, simplistic nature of most assigned work contributed to their boredom" (Kanevsky & Keighley, 2003, p. 24). Caring teachers provided for their needs to feel related to others in school. When this need was fully met, students could overlook deficiencies in other areas, but a truly caring environment was evident in the way it provided them with control, choice, challenge, and complexity.

Other systemic impediments to talent development include the acceptance of teacher biases. Teachers who have not been challenged to recognize their implicit biases may inappropriately assume that their students from underrepresented backgrounds are not capable of advanced-level work (McBee, 2006, 2010; Siegle & Powell, 2004) or that misbehavior should exclude students from such opportunities (e.g., Okonofua & Eberhardt, 2015). When schools include behavior as a determinant in access to opportunities, many students who are capable, but bored or actively seeking companionship, may be excluded. Gatekeepers who are unaware of the impact of their decisions on students' future opportunities can create systemic impediments. For example, students discouraged from or unable to take advanced math in middle school are often unable to complete a sequence of math courses required for some majors in college. Such missed opportunities can have lifelong consequences. Schools have a responsibility to recognize and eliminate systemic impediments to students' development of talent.

- **Tenet 9:** Students are responsible for pursuing domains of interest to them, exhibiting early potential and showing increasing commitment as they move through school. SWGT are those who perform at a significantly higher level than peers in a school-related domain.

The SCG is unique in its proposal that secondary students who do not perform, regardless of their early identification of potential, should not be considered gifted in school. This contention stands in stark contrast to the Gifted Child Paradigm (Dai & Chen, 2013), but it acknowledges the limitations within which schools operate. When schools offer opportunities for talent development, students must be willing to not only take them, but also apply themselves. Developing talent in a school-related domain can be very difficult, requiring hours of study and practice. Accepting the mantle of "scholar" can lead to rejection by peers who are less serious in their academic pursuits (J. R. Cross et al., 2016, 2018, 2019; T. L. Cross et al., 1995). In an atmosphere that respects all students, those with exceptional ability should not be fearful of the threat they present to their peers (Exline et al., 2004, 2013).

Students must be willing to make sacrifices in the development of their talent, but this should not come at the cost of their psychological well-being. Students with exceptional potential can be motivated by models presented by peers also willing to take a challenge. As their identity develops through the acceptance of challenging opportunities in a community of scholars, their motivation to achieve more will develop simultaneously (Oyserman, 2007). Those students who have a passion for learning in a domain (Coleman & Guo, 2013) will welcome the opportunity to advance their abilities within it.

In schools where the SCG is the framework for talent development, there will be no such thing as an underachiever (T. L. Cross & Coleman, 2005). Students will not be measured as deficient according to their scores on an ability test. Instead, all students will be achieving at the level of their ability, according to their interests and commitment to the task. Underachievement will only occur when the school does not provide opportunity at an appropriately challenging level. The SCG places great responsibility on both schools and students for the development of talent.

- **Tenet 10:** Psychosocial skills training should be part of the school's curriculum to foster students' abilities to pursue talent development opportunities.

Although some may consider schools to be responsible solely for students' academic development, a talent development paradigm requires schools to attend to their nonacademic needs, as well. Over time, schools have incorporated more nonacademic supports for their students. The National School Lunch Program (NSLP) was developed, at least in part, to ensure that learners would not be hungry in school (Levine, 2008). In a similar response to student needs, the role of the school counselor has evolved from academic guidance to one of developmental support to foster achievement (American School Counselor Association, 2014). The importance of psychological support to academic success has become increasingly apparent. Subotnik et al. (2011) claimed, "psychosocial variables are determining factors in the successful development of talent" (p. 4). To ensure students' success, it is clear that schools will be required to attend to this "determining factor" as part of a planned program of support.

As Tenet 9 indicates, developing talent requires the students' active involvement. Commitment to talent development requires resolve, strategies for dealing with setbacks, fortitude in the face of challenge, and motivation to resist attractive options competing for one's time. As T. L. Cross and Cross (2017b) stated:

> Optimal talent development can only occur when high ability students are willing to take opportunities for growth in a domain and are able to persist when presented with challenges that accompany performance or production at the highest levels. (p. 43)

Elementary and secondary students experience more physical, emotional, and social changes more rapidly than any other age group. To layer demands for exceptional talent development on top of these common challenges can be overwhelming. The stressors of high academic achievement can have negative psychological outcomes (Suldo et al., 2009). Empirical evidence of the vulnerability of SWGT to psychological distress is mixed (Neihart, 1999), but there is greater evidence for the conclusion that they are not significantly more vulnerable than peers (J. R. Cross & Cross, 2015; Martin et al., 2010). This does not mean that SWGT are invulnerable. Mental health topics such as anxiety, depression, and even suicide appear regularly in the gifted education literature (e.g., Neihart et al., 2015; Pfeiffer et al., 2017). Schools should be concerned about the impact mental health has on the achievement of any student, but it is generally not within their purview to resolve mental health issues.

Schools can, however, address environmental issues that produce or contribute to negative outcomes for students, taking proactive approaches, rather than ameliorative. In a review of research on the lived experience of SWGT, Coleman et al. (2015) described settings in which schools are unprepared for them, requiring them to wait or to be unchallenged. The label of giftedness can draw unwanted attention from peers (J. R. Cross, 2015), leading to threatening social comparisons (Exline et al., 2013). Students may experience excessive pressure from parents, teachers, and peers (J. R. Cross et al., 2019). Effective programming, qualified teachers, reasonable class sizes, and other accommodations can relieve stress among all students, including SWGT, contributing to their successful talent development.

Over the years, psychosocial variables that have been concerning to those in the field (e.g., motivation, self-concept, perfectionism, resilience, etc.) have been approached in a piecemeal fashion. Without a guiding framework, schools have been challenged to address these issues individually, as they emerge as problems among their SWGT. Building from the goal of the SCG to solve a problem that occurs within schools, T. L. Cross and Cross (2017b; T. L. Cross et al., 2017) proposed a theory-driven, school-based solution. Based on Erikson's (1961, 1963, 1968) theory of psychosocial development, the school-based psychosocial curriculum model (SPCM) offers a plan for schools to develop the ego strength of students, enabling them to take full advantage of the opportunities presented to them by the school.

The SPCM (T. L. Cross & Cross, 2017b; T. L. Cross et al., 2017) emphasizes student learning about themselves (their psychology) and their relationship to others (social). The essential strengths that result from the navigation of Erikson's (1963) developmental crises provide a focal point for lessons. Erikson's theory is a stage theory, suggesting that individuals will pass through certain crises that will be met during approximate age ranges. There are elements of his theory and its application, however, that suggest that the learning that occurred during these crises can be revisited in service of building ego strength (T. L. Cross & Cross, 2017b). The objective of the SPCM is to help students develop or fortify their essential strengths of Hope, Willpower, Purpose, Competence, Fidelity, and Love. Lessons based on the SPCM are created by identifying intrapersonal and contrasting interpersonal knowledge that can be useful to the developing SWGT. For example, to encourage a student's developing sense of Purpose, a lesson in self-advocacy addresses their intrapersonal need to know themselves and what they want. A contrasting interpersonal need would be a lesson in considering others in achieving their goals, by avoiding egocentrism or narcissism. Learning about both encourages what Erikson called a *favorable ratio*, an understanding of the balance between intrapersonal and interpersonal tensions that leads to a healthy sense of Purpose.

The SPCM offers one option to schools for meeting the requirement of the SCG to provide psychosocial skills training. Whatever method is used, attention must be paid to students' nonacademic needs in school. SWGT may need direct instruction to be successful in maintaining motivation, responding to feedback, and being resilient when failure is inevitably met in an environment dedicated to increasing challenge. Students must be willing participants in the development of their talents. When they are, the sacrifices required to be truly exceptional in any domain will be acceptable.

Distinguishing the SCG From Other Models

The SCG proposes that schools should be making opportunities for advanced development in domains available to students (e.g., advanced curriculum, mentorships, specialized training). As students show promise, either through ability or achievement testing, they should be given greater opportunities for advancement in a domain. These are school-related domains, not every talent domain possible. Schools should also provide training in psychosocial skills for all students to foster their ability to take advantage of opportunities. Schools should not limit students' opportunities, especially for reasons of convenience, such as discipline. Schools should ensure the opportunities are attractive and motivating. Students are responsible for pursuing their areas of interest, putting forth the effort required to be successful at the advanced opportunities presented. Where they are disinterested or not capable of performing, they should be offered opportunities to achieve at an average level. Psychosocial training for all students is necessary to ensure they have the nonacademic skills needed to be successful at exceptional levels, if they have the interest and ability.

Figure 9.2 depicts the components of the SCG. Development in a domain occurs generally in the elementary years, as students build foundational skills. These become more focused as training emphasizes performance and specialization in secondary school. Development in a domain will continue after graduation, becoming even more specialized and narrow. Along the Y-axis, a students' level of performance will be high or low depending on both school and student inputs. Schools must offer resources, academic supports, psychosocial support, and, most importantly, opportunities, to underpin optimal performance, raising the level to exceptional achievement. Student ability, interest, psychosocial skills, and commitment to development in a domain are required for an exceptional level of development in a domain. Without the combination of all of these components, maximum performance will not be achieved in school.

The SCG is within the family of talent development models of gifted education. In this way, it differs from other models that describe giftedness as an innate characteristic (e.g., IQ-based). A student's inborn abilities can support their talent development if they are given the opportunity and commit themselves to the work required in a domain. The SCG does not claim that gifted abilities do not exist, simply that they are relevant to schools when

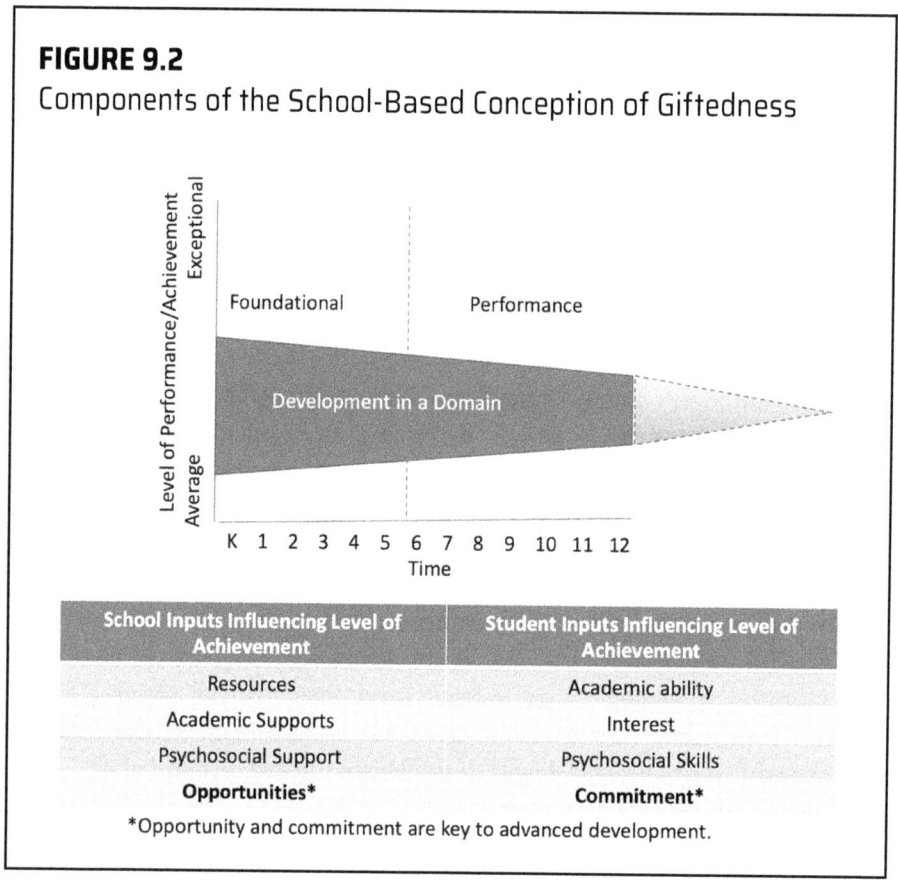

FIGURE 9.2
Components of the School-Based Conception of Giftedness

School Inputs Influencing Level of Achievement	Student Inputs Influencing Level of Achievement
Resources	Academic ability
Academic Supports	Interest
Psychosocial Support	Psychosocial Skills
Opportunities*	Commitment*

*Opportunity and commitment are key to advanced development.

offerings must be made to support their advanced development. Ideally, all students in a school will be positively affected when the SCG is the chosen framework for gifted education. All will have access to opportunities, in a fashion similar to Renzulli's (1977) Three-Ring Conception. What differs is the emphasis on advanced development. Enrichment does not have a role in the SCG. The Advanced Academics model (Peters et al., 2014) is similar to the SCG in its focus on schools and advanced curriculum, but it differs in its avoidance of the construct of giftedness and the lack of attention to psychosocial variables. There is overlap with Subotnik et al.'s (2011) Talent Development Megamodel, which was developed from a synthesis of research and early models of talent development, including the original SCG (T. L. Cross & Coleman, 2015). Both focus on talent domains, but the Megamodel extends beyond the walls of school into all areas of talent.

Practical Issues

According to the U.S. Census Bureau (2017), in 2014 there were 13,490 school districts in the U.S. The system of decentralized, local control of public education in the U.S. means that nearly 14,000 school boards can make decisions regarding gifted education. The SCG provides flexibility in what is offered, so long as districts accept the responsibilities outlined in the tenets listed previously. Social justice goals are served when identification of exceptional ability is no longer based on a test score or teacher recommendation, but on actual achievement in a domain. All students should be presented with opportunities to achieve to the level of their potential. With the proper scaffolding of students who have not had the same economic or educational advantages as advantaged peers, those with exceptional potential will be apparent.

One of the most difficult components of the SCG for those who hold an entity view of giftedness—who consider it to be part of the person—is Tenet 4. Freeing schools of the responsibility to maximize the potential of students who are not achieving may seem wrong-minded to those who believe the giftedness can be coaxed into expression. In making such a dramatic assertion, T. L. Cross and Coleman (2005) proposed an entirely new perspective. If schools claim to be supporting the development of talent through the SCG, they must undergo dramatic changes from the current typical design. One can imagine schools redesigning their gifted services, shelving identification procedures, and taking a few steps to improve instruction in the domains already being taught, then claiming to be focused on talent development. This is not an acceptable response. The SCG is an entire package. No single or multiple tenets can be accepted without the others. A school that expects students to be responsible for their own achievement (Tenet 9), but does not offer opportunities at the level of which students are capable (Tenet 7) or places systemic barriers to their achievement (Tenet 8), has not committed to the SCG.

Conclusion

In this chapter, using the SCG, we described how schools can become environments wherein all students develop their potential into varying degrees of talent, moving from foundational abilities to achievement in performance domains, by emphasizing schools' responsibilities and students' responsibilities. To assist the reader, we discussed the 10 tenets of the SCG in a refinement of the conception first proposed by Coleman and Cross (2001) and described in greater depth by T. L. Cross and Coleman (2005). Rather than taking an entity perspective of giftedness, the SCG conceptualizes giftedness as developing at the intersection of abilities and context. It assumes a limited curricular purview of schools, relative to academic responsibilities. The SCG does not attempt to plan for and develop all forms of talent. Consequently, the SCG can be tailored to the particular curriculum identified and supported by local school boards and the peculiarities of school districts.

The SCG greatly reduces any cost associated with the implementation of identification procedures, thus making the money previously spent on identification available for the educational components appropriate for developing talent. Successful forms of effective gifted education practices, such as curriculum compacting, flexible ability grouping, and multiple acceleration approaches, can be utilized. One of the greatest outcomes of employing the SCG will be the elimination of the longstanding problem of underrepresentation of certain groups of SWGT. Improvement will be realized by the successful interaction of hardworking students of high ability, with schools that are ready for them. Combined, the SCG will enable all SWGT to develop their talents, without influence from the prejudices and assessment errors long associated with identification procedures (T. L. Cross & Cross, 2017a).

DISCUSSION QUESTIONS

1. What are benefits to having a school-based conception of giftedness? What are disadvantages?

2. What does it mean for the conception of giftedness to change as a student matures?

3. How do schools need to change to adopt a school-based conception of giftedness?

DISCUSSION QUESTIONS, continued

4. Will implementing the SCG in schools change attitudes about giftedness?
5. Discuss the role of effort in the SCG. Is it any different than in other gifted education paradigms?
6. How is accelerated education different from enrichment?
7. What organizational structures or expectations in schools can impede students' talent development?
8. How can a program of psychosocial skills training be effectively implemented in schools?

References

American School Counselor Association. (2014). *Mindsets and behaviors for student success: K–12 college- and career-readiness standards for every student.*

Bloom, B. S. (Ed.). (1985). *Developing talent in young people.* Ballantine Books.

Borland, J. H. (2003). The death of giftedness. In J. H. Borland (Ed.), *Rethinking gifted education* (pp. 105–124). Teachers College Press.

Borland, J. H. (2005). Gifted education without gifted children: The case for no conception of giftedness. In R. J. Sternberg & J. Davidson. (Eds.), *Conceptions of giftedness* (2nd ed., pp. 1–19). Cambridge University Press.

Coleman, L. (1985). *Schooling the gifted.* Addison-Wesley.

Coleman, L. J., & Cross, T. L. (2001). *Being gifted in school: An introduction to development, guidance, and teaching.* Prufrock Press.

Coleman, L. J., & Cross, T. L. (2005). *Being gifted in school: An introduction to development, guidance, and teaching* (2nd ed.). Prufrock Press.

Coleman, L. J., & Guo, A. (2013). Exploring children's passion for learning in six domains. *Journal for the Education of the Gifted, 36*(2), 155–175. https://doi.org/10.1177/0162353213480432

Coleman, L. J., Micko, K. J., & Cross, T. L. (2015). Twenty-five years of research on the lived experience of being gifted in school: Capturing the students' voices. *Journal for the Education of the Gifted, 38*(4), 358–376. https://doi.org/10.1177/0162353215607322

Cross, J. R. (2015). Gifted children and peer relationships. In M. Neihart, S. I. Pfeiffer, & T. L. Cross (Eds.). *The social and emotional development of gifted children: What do we know?* (2nd ed., pp. 41–54). Prufrock Press.

Cross, J. R., Bugaj, S. J., & Mammadov, S. (2016). Accepting a scholarly identity: Gifted students, academic crowd membership, and identification with school. *Journal for the Education of the Gifted, 39*(1), 23–48. https://doi.org/10.1177/0162353215624162

Cross, J. R., & Cross, T. L. (2015). Clinical and mental health issues in counseling the gifted individual. *Journal of Counseling & Development, 93*(2), 163–172. https://doi.org/10.1002/j.1556-6676.2015.00192.x

Cross, J. R., Frazier, A. D., Kim, M., & Cross, T. L. (2018). A comparison of perceptions of barriers to academic success among high-ability students from high- and low-income groups: Exposing poverty of a different kind. *Gifted Child Quarterly, 62*(1), 111–129. https://doi.org/10.1177/0016986217738050

Cross, J. R., Vaughn, C. T., Mammadov, S., Cross, T. L., Kim, M., O'Reilly, C., Spielhagen, F., Pereira Da Costa, M., & Hymer, B. (2019). A cross-cultural study of the social experience of giftedness. *Roeper Review, 41*(1), 224–242. https://doi.org/10.1080/02783193.2019.1661052

Cross, T. L., & Coleman, L. J. (2005). School-based conception of giftedness. In R. J. Sternberg & J. E. Davidson (Eds.), *Conceptions of giftedness* (2nd ed., pp. 52–63). Cambridge University Press.

Cross, T. L., Coleman, L. J., & Stewart, R. S. (1995). Psychosocial diversity among gifted adolescents: An exploratory study of two groups. *Roeper Review, 17*(3), 181–185. https://doi.org/10.1080/02783199509553655

Cross, T. L., & Cross, J. R. (2017a). Challenging an idea whose time has gone. *Roeper Review, 39*(3), 191–194. https://doi.org/10.1080/02783193.2017.1319000

Cross, T. L., & Cross, J. R. (2017b). Maximizing potential: A school-based conception of psychosocial development. *High Ability Studies, 28*(1), 43–58. https://doi.org/10.1080/13598139.2017.1292896

Cross, T. L., & Cross, J. R. (2019). *Conceptions of giftedness and gifted students*. Oxford Research Encyclopedia of Education. https://doi.org/10.1093/acrefore/9780190264093.013.922

Cross, T. L., Cross, J. R., & Andersen, L. (2017). The school-based psychosocial curriculum model. In J. VanTassel-Baska & C. A. Little (Eds.),

Content-based curriculum for high-ability learners (3rd ed., pp. 383–407). Prufrock Press.

Dai, D. Y., & Chen, F. (2013). Three paradigms of gifted education: In search of conceptual clarity in research and practice. *Gifted Child Quarterly, 57*(3), 151–168. https://doi.org/10.1177/0016986213490020

Deci, E. L., & Ryan, R. M. (2000). The "what" and "why" of goal pursuits: Human needs and the self-determination of behavior. *Psychological Inquiry, 11*(4), 227–268. https://doi.org/10.1207/S15327965PLI1104_01

Erikson, E. H. (1961). The roots of virtue. In J. S. Huxley (Ed.), *The humanist frame* (pp. 147–165). Harper & Brothers.

Erikson, E. H. (1963). *Childhood and society* (2nd ed.). Norton.

Erikson, E. H. (1968). *Identity: Youth and crisis*. Norton.

Exline, J. J., Single, P. B., Lobel, M., & Geyer, A. L. (2004). Glowing praise and the envious gaze: Social dilemmas surrounding the public recognition of achievement. *Basic and Applied Social Psychology, 26*(2–3), 119–130.

Exline, J. J., Zell, A. L., & Lobel, M. (2013). Sidestepping awkward encounters: Avoidance as a response to outperformance-related discomfort. *Journal of Applied Social Psychology, 43*(4), 706–720. https://doi.org/10.1111/j.1559-1816.2013.01047.x

Gagné, F. (1998). A proposal for subcategories within the gifted or talented populations. *Gifted Child Quarterly, 42*(2), 87–95. https://doi.org/10.1177/001698629804200203

Gardner, H. (2011). *Frames of mind: The theory of multiple intelligences*. Basic Books. (Original work published 1983)

Gilliam, W. S., Maupin, A. N., Reyes, C. R., Accavitti, M., & Shic, F. (2016). *Do early educators' implicit biases regarding sex and race relate to behavior expectations and recommendations of preschool expulsions and suspensions?* Yale Child Study Center. https://medicine.yale.edu/childstudy/zigler/publications/Preschool%20Implicit%20Bias%20Policy%20Brief_final_9_26_276766_5379_v1.pdf

Goodson, I. F. (2013). *School subjects and curriculum change*. Routledge.

Harvey, K. E., Suizzo, M., & Jackson, K. M. (2016). Predicting the grades of low-income–ethnic-minority students from teacher-student discrepancies in reported motivation. *The Journal of Experimental Education, 84*(3), 510–528. https://doi.org/10.1080/00220973.2015.1054332

Hollingworth, L. S. (1942). *Children above 180 IQ Stanford-Binet: Origin and development*. World Book.

Kanevsky, L., & Keighley, T. (2003). To produce or not to produce? Understanding boredom and the honor in underachievement. *Roeper Review, 26*(1), 20–28. https://doi.org/10.1080/02783190309554235

Leiken, R. (2019). Developing mathematical talent in schoolchildren: Who, what, and how? In R. F. Subotnik, P. Olszewski-Kubilius, & F. C. Worrell (Eds.), *The psychology of high performance: Developing human potential into domain-specific talent* (pp. 173–192). American Psychological Association.

Levine, S. (2008). *School lunch politics: The surprising history of America's favorite welfare program.* Princeton University Press.

Marland, S. P., Jr. (1972). *Education of the gifted and talented: Report to the Congress of the United States by the U.S. Commissioner of Education.* U.S. Government Printing Office.

Martin, L. T., Burns, R. M., & Schonlau, M. (2010). Mental disorders among gifted and nongifted youth: A selected review of the epidemiologic literature. *Gifted Child Quarterly, 54*(1), 31–41. https://doi.org/10.1177/0016986209352684

McBee, M. T. (2006). A descriptive analysis of referral sources for gifted identification screening by race and socioeconomic status. *Journal of Secondary Gifted Education, 17*(2), 103–111. https://doi.org/10.4219/jsge-2006-686

McBee, M. T. (2010). Examining the probability of identification for gifted programs for students in Georgia elementary schools: A multilevel path analysis study. *Gifted Child Quarterly, 54*(4), 283–297. https://doi.org/10.1177/0016986210377927

Neihart, M. (1999). The impact of giftedness on psychological well-being: What does the empirical literature say? *Roeper Review, 22*(1), 10–17. https://doi.org/10.1080/02783199909553991

Neihart, M., Pfeiffer, S. I., & Cross, T. L. (Eds.). (2015). *The social and emotional development of gifted children: What do we know?* (2nd ed.). Prufrock Press.

Okonofua, J. A., & Eberhardt, J. L. (2015). Two strikes: Race and the disciplining of young students. *Psychological Science, 26*(5), 617–624. https://doi.org/10.1177/0956797615570365

Oyserman, D. (2007). Social identity and self-regulation. In A. Kruglanski & T. Higgins (Eds.), *Handbook of social psychology* (2nd ed., pp. 432–453). Guilford Press.

Peine, M., & Coleman, L. (2010). The phenomenon of waiting in class. *Journal for the Education of the Gifted, 34*(2), 220–244.

Peters, S. J., Matthews, M. S., McBee, M. T., & McCoach, D. B. (2014). *Beyond gifted education: Designing and implementing advanced academic programs.* Prufrock Press.

Pfeiffer, S. I., Foley-Nicpon, M., & Shaunessy-Dedrick, E. (Eds.). (2017). *APA handbook of giftedness and talent*. American Psychological Association.

Ramey, C. T., & Ramey, S. L. (2004). Early learning and school readiness: Can early intervention make a difference? *Merrill-Palmer Quarterly, 50*(4), 471–491. https://doi.org/10.1353/mpq.2004.0034

Reis, S. M., & McCoach, D. B. (2000). The underachievement of gifted students: What do we know and where do we go? *Gifted Child Quarterly, 44*(3), 152–170. https://doi.org/10.1177/001698620004400302

Renzulli, J. S. (1977). *The enrichment triad model: A guide for developing defensible programs for the gifted and talented*. Creative Learning Press.

Siegle, D., & Powell, T. (2004). Exploring teacher biases when nominating students for gifted programs. *Gifted Child Quarterly, 48*(1), 21–29. https://doi.org/10.1177/001698620404800103

Simonton, D. K. (2019). Talent development in the domain of academic psychology. In R. F. Subotnik, P. Olszewski-Kubilius, & F. C. Worrell (Eds.), *The psychology of high performance: Developing human potential into domain-specific talent* (pp. 201–218). American Psychological Association.

Sternberg, R. J. (1985). *Beyond IQ*. Cambridge University Press.

Subotnik, R. F., Olszewski-Kubilius, P., & Worrell, F. C. (2011). Rethinking giftedness and gifted education: A proposed direction forward based on psychological science. *Psychological Science in the Public Interest, 12*(1), 3–54. https://doi.org/10.1177/1529100611418056

Suldo, S. M., Shaunessy, E., Thalji, A., Michalowski, J., & Shaffer, E. (2009). Sources of stress for students in high school college preparatory and general education programs: group differences and associations with adjustment. *Adolescence, 44*(176), 925–948.

Terman, L. M. (1925). *Genetic studies of genius: Vol. 1. Mental and physical traits of a thousand gifted children*. Stanford University Press.

United States Census Bureau. (2017). *School district estimates for 2014*. U.S. Department of Commerce. https://www.census.gov/data/datasets/2014/demo/saipe/2014-school-districts.html

Vygotsky, L. S. (1978). *Mind and society: The development of higher mental processes*. Harvard University Press.

Ziegler, A. (2005). The actiotope model of giftedness. In R. J. Sternberg & J. Davidson (Eds.), *Conceptions of giftedness* (2nd ed., pp. 411–434). Cambridge University Press.

CHAPTER 10

Advanced Academics

A Model for Gifted Education Without Gifted Students

SCOTT J. PETERS AND JAMES H. BORLAND

What's in a Paradigm?

The term *paradigm* owes its ubiquity in academic discourse to Thomas Kuhn, the historian of science whose book *The Structure of Scientific Revolutions* (1962/1996) was one of the most influential scholarly works of the 20th century. According to Kuhn, a paradigm comprises of the theories, methods, important questions, jargon, and human relationships within a scientific discipline. A paradigm defines a discipline, guides the activities of scholars working within the discipline, and delineates the boundaries of what Kuhn called *normal science* at any particular time. By *normal science*,

Kuhn meant the regular, everyday work carried out by scientists under the term of a settled, dominant paradigm.

Dai and Chen (2013, 2014) identified three gifted education paradigms that guide the work of the field's scholars and practitioners. We are going to discuss one of these, which Dai and Chen called the *Gifted Child Paradigm*, and explain why we believe it is lacking as a guiding paradigm for the field, before outlining our vision for a better replacement. The Gifted Child Paradigm was a product of the early 20th century, and it was the source of the ideas and educational practices that shaped the field of gifted education at its birth. As Dai and Chen pointed out, even 100 years later, the Gifted Child Paradigm still dominates thinking and practice in the field. It has given rise to the field's analog of Kuhn's (1962/1996) notion of normal science, which we refer to as *normal practice*. Normal practice governs what educators believe about gifted students, the manner in which they attempt to provide gifted students with differentiated curriculum and instruction, and the manner in which they strive to understand the construct of giftedness.

Normal practice in gifted education incorporates the following basic, foundational beliefs, derived from the Gifted Child Paradigm:

- There exists in the school-age population a distinct group of students, known as "gifted students," who possess certain defining traits and characteristics that are educationally relevant and distinguish them from other students.
- Gifted students constitute a small percentage of the school-age population.
- A clear, widely accepted definition of this population can lead to accurate identification of the "truly gifted."
- "Truly gifted" students, by virtue of having the trait of giftedness, require specialized services different from what they are already receiving in school.
- Providing these services to gifted students requires the creation of full-time or part-time segregated programs in which students identified as gifted receive differentiated curriculum and instruction, thereby ensuring that they will receive an effective and appropriate education.

We suspect that the majority of individuals involved in the field of gifted education would regard these propositions as unexceptionable, even axiomatic. However, we have come to question and, ultimately, to reject these beliefs as misguided, an incorrect representation of the truth, and counterproductive to the goal of challenging a wider range of learners in school.

This seeming apostasy does not mean that we are indifferent to the needs of gifted students—quite the opposite. Rather, we believe that the Gifted Child Paradigm is not just ineffective but is actually counterproductive and an active barrier to a larger number of students being challenged in K–12 school.

We now believe that the Gifted Child Paradigm, and the beliefs and practices derived from it, has outlived whatever usefulness it once had and will become more and more of a liability to the field. Almost weekly, there are news alerts of a person in a school district calling for the end of the gifted label or gifted services entirely. We, therefore, believe that it is essential to the well-being of the field, and more importantly to that of the students, that educators seek another way of thinking about and practicing gifted education. We believe there are ways to have the benefits of "gifted education" without all of the baggage that comes with giftedness as a concept or the common practices stemming from the Gifted Child Paradigm.

But why do we believe that the normal practice derived from the Gifted Child Paradigm is no longer defensible, if it ever was? That requires stepping back a bit and asking some basic questions.

Problematizing Gifted Education

There is considerable benefit to be gained by thinking radically—in the original sense of *radical* as meaning "going to the root or origin"—about what educators ought to be doing and how they ought to be doing it. Put another way, we are suggesting there is considerable benefit to be gained by *problematizing* gifted education and the Gifted Child Paradigm. What does this mean? According to Gallagher (1999), "problematizing [is] the process of grasping an assumption, that is, a taken-for-granted way of thinking, and turning it into a question" (p. 70). It involves surfacing and identifying certain, often implicit, assumptions and beliefs and asking whether they really make sense. We think that practitioners in the field would benefit from problematizing many beliefs and practices because, we believe, educators have grown too comfortable with certain "taken-for-granted" ways of thinking, and this has limited the vision effectiveness of educators.

We will address three issues that could be usefully and profitably problematized. We will start by examining our *raison d'etre*—why gifted education exists as a field. We will then question the notion that "gifted" programs are necessary to accomplish the shared goals of the field. Finally, we will problematize the construct of the gifted student itself. After all of this, we will provide our own ideas for how to best move forward as a field.

Why Does the Field of Gifted Education Exist?: Untangling Means and Ends

One of the most basic questions, and perhaps the most important one the field of gifted education can ask, is, "Why does gifted education exist as a field?" What is the problem the field seeks to solve, or the student need the field exists to address? Many people who count themselves among the ranks of gifted educators believe that the answer to this question is obvious: The field exists in order to create, operate, and perpetuate gifted programs in order to serve *gifted* students. Gifted educators do this so that certain students can be identified as gifted and benefit from differentiated curriculum and instruction in these programs. This is consistent with the axioms of the Gifted Child Paradigm, and it constitutes normal practice. However, we submit that this is a myopic view of the field's purpose and that it represents a confusion of means with ends.

It is the proper education of gifted students, not the creation or preservation of gifted programs, that should be the field's ultimate goal. If one views the purpose of the field as advocating for and working toward appropriate education for capable students, which is consistent with the larger goal of providing every student with an appropriate education, it becomes clear that creating and operating gifted programs is a means—only *one* means, and conceivably not the best means—toward achieving the larger goal. Reflective practitioners should all be open to the idea that there might be better ways to accomplish goals and should continuously experiment with alternative approaches or practices.

Problematizing Gifted Programs

A number of years ago, Borland (1996) suggested that it might be a useful thought experiment to consider whether effective gifted education could be achieved without gifted-specific programs. Coleman (1985) made a similar point in his book *Schooling the Gifted*, suggesting that typical gifted programs should be open to any students, thereby negating the challenges associated with "identifying" the gifted. We (the authors) have since come to see this less as a useful thought experiment and more as sound educational policy. Returning to the means-ends issue raised previously, educators must question the extent to which the most common means (typical gifted programs) achieve the desired end (effective education for students typically identified as gifted). We submit that, in this respect, typical gifted programs fall short.

The most frequently encountered type of gifted program is the part-time, enrichment-based pull-out program. Although, over the years, a considerable amount of money, time, effort, and hope has been invested in this sort of program, there is very little evidence on the programs' efficacy. A number of scholars (e.g., Adelson et al., 2012; Colangelo et al., 2004; Coleman & Cross, 2005; George et al., 1977; Shore et al., 1991; Slavin, 1990; Southern & Jones, 1991) have questioned whether enrichment programs are as effective as their proponents contend.[1] Contrast this with the mountain of studies, dating back to Terman's (1925) landmark longitudinal study, showing that acceleration does work (Colangelo et al., 2004; Steenbergen-Hu et al., 2016).

Having a Program in Order to Have a Program

It is interesting to ask school administrators why they have gifted programs. Usually, this proves to be a surprisingly difficult question for them to answer. When the boilerplate responses and the hemming and hawing are finished, probing further almost always reveals that administrators have a program in order to have a program. Educators assume that a gifted program is something they ought to have, often to please parents, but when pressed to delineate the specific educational needs the program attempts to address, they often are at a loss.

Although educators can adduce sound educational reasons for the existence of the English language arts curriculum, the social studies curriculum, the music curriculum, and other parts of the K–12 curriculum, edu-

---

1 A fairly recent, methodologically sound meta-analysis by Kim (2016) does lend support to the contention that pull-out programs can be associated with desirable academic and other outcomes. However, other studies reporting positive effects (e.g., Delcourt et al., 1994; Vaughn et al., 1991) have serious methodological problems. Kim's study aside, the evidence for the efficacy of enrichment program is quite exiguous.

cators frequently have difficulty delineating reasons—educationally based reasons—for the existence of their gifted programs. This is why it is so rare to find a sound scope and sequence in most gifted enrichment programs. No one has taken the time to determine what certain students need that is not found in the core curriculum and then used that knowledge to structure a defensible curriculum. This is an essential component of the effective education of advanced students for which we are advocating—one that is designed to challenge and meet the needs of students who would otherwise go underchallenged. This should be the field's reason for being. What's more, even when there is this logical rationale for gifted programs, at best they are a part-time solution to a full-time, identified need (Cox et al., 1985). No matter how exemplary a pull-out gifted program might be, gifted students will spend a small (often very small) percentage of their school time in it. The rest of the time, they are in heterogeneously grouped classrooms where instruction is tied to age-based, grade-level standards. This suggests that even the best gifted programs are bandages, not comprehensive educational programs.

Problematizing Giftedness

We want to take this line of reasoning a significant step further. If we problematize gifted enrichment programs sufficiently to bring us to the point of questioning their axiomatic necessity, why not go further and trouble the notion of giftedness itself, at least as it plays out in schools? In other words, can we consider the possibility of gifted education without gifted students (see also Borland 2003, 2005, 2009, 2013, 2018; McBee et al., 2012; Peters, Kaufman, et al., 2014; Peters, Matthews, et al., 2014)? After all, in a world of perfectly differentiated or personalized learning for every child, would labels and specialized programs and services, such as special education or gifted education, be necessary? This is rhetorical, of course, and unlikely to ever happen, but it gets at the question of whether or not typical gifted education practices are both necessary and sufficient to accomplish their stated purpose.

Giftedness as a Social Construct

It is our contention that giftedness, as it is understood in an educational context, is a social construct. That is to say, it is something that was not discovered but invented. Take, for example, the planet Uranus, which has existed much longer than humans have as a species. That Uranus exists is an undeniable fact of nature, although the planet remained undiscovered until William Herschel observed it in 1781 (see Holmes, 2008, for a fascinating account). Gifted students as a distinct school subpopulation, however, only came into existence in the second decade of the 20th century when certain historical forces (including compulsory education laws, increased immigration, and especially the advent and widespread adoption of mental testing in schools) created a situation in which educators and psychologists felt a need for an organizing principle, a construct, that allowed them to make sense of observed phenomena (e.g., variance in scores on mental tests and in school performance in general). Someone saw the label as instructionally useful, just like any other label in education (e.g., learning disabled, exceeds standards).

According to this way of thinking, there were no gifted students in schools in the 19th century because the construct had not come into being. Of course, there have always been students who were remarkably precocious, unusually clever, or academically able, but the belief that students of that sort were representative of a group of students with certain defining characteristics that set them apart from other students (i.e., they had the "trait" of giftedness) and defined them as a discrete subpopulation was not widely accepted among educators of that time. Therefore, gifted students, as they are understood today, did not exist. It was not until educators and psychologists felt the need for the construct that it was created, and gifted students came into existence.

Now, to state that giftedness among school students is a social construct is not, *ipso facto*, to deny its importance or legitimacy. Many of the important things educators deal with in education and the social sciences are social constructs, such as intelligence, creativity, disability, depression, and countless others. In schools, constructs serve some useful instructional purpose. All labels come with unintended consequences and side effects. For example, it could be argued that labeling students as having a learning disability[2] has a negative effect on their academic self-efficacy or even

---

[2] The label "learning disabled," which has been applied to countless students in the past, has now generally been replaced by the phrase "students with learning disabilities," which is less stigmatizing.

sense of self-worth. However, even if this is the case, we think most special education scholars and teachers would argue that the benefits of labeling some students outweigh the negatives—that the range of specialized services make any negative side effects "worth it" in the end. Can the same be said for giftedness and gifted education?

Consequences of Labeling Students as Gifted

For about a century, the field of education's response to the fact that children differ in the ways in which they interact with the school curriculum (or curriculums, including the informal and hidden curriculums; see Martin, 1983) has been to attribute this difference to the existence of distinct groups of children, including gifted children, who possess characteristics that separate them from "average students." This has led to the practice of labeling some students as "gifted" and implicitly labeling the rest "ungifted." This sort of existential triage[3] is simplistic on its face, and it has resulted in beliefs and practices that are difficult to defend. Among these are treating students labeled "gifted" as a monolithic group whose members have the same educational needs, assuming that all students with this label are academically strong in all areas, and not differentiating the curriculum of the gifted program (even after arguing for the need for differentiation).

Even a casual examination of the field of gifted education illustrates how inadequate this gifted/ungifted dichotomy is as a basis for defensible practice. Take the semifacetious phenomenon of "geographical giftedness" (Borland, 1989, 2005) or "gifted today but not tomorrow" (Lohman & Korb, 2006), the not-uncommon phenomenon whereby a gifted child, so-labeled by their school district, finds themselves no longer gifted after moving to another school system that uses a different definition of giftedness. Prior to a certain date, the student was a gifted child; after that date, the student reverts to being "average." This is not unreasonable in a world where gifted services are provided to a student if and when other services are insufficient. But in a world where gifted is seen as a something a person is (i.e., a trait), this cannot be defended.

---

3 Underlying our argument is the belief that gifted education should be an educational, not an existential, undertaking.

Giftedness as a Floating Signifier

Is there a "correct" definition of giftedness, and, if so, what is it? The field's failure to answer that question is reflected in the multiplicity of definitions that have been proposed over the years. Sternberg and Davidson's (2005) anthology, *Conceptions of Giftedness*, contains 24 chapters, 23 of which set forth definitions of giftedness, which are remarkable for their variety and divergence. McBee and Makel (2019) outlined that, depending on how various terms in common definitions of giftedness are operationalized, 75% or more students would meet published criteria for giftedness. Claiming that 75% of people are gifted would likely outrage followers of the Gifted Child Paradigm and would be concerning from the perspective of giftedness as denoting unmet educational needs.

All of this strongly suggests that "the gifted" and "the average," rather than being preexisting human genera, are labels for socially constructed groups that are constituted, in both theory and practice, in ways that are far from consistent and, in many cases, anything but logical, systematic, or scientific. Giftedness has become what Stuart Hall (e.g., 1997), writing about race, has called a *floating signifier*, a semiotic term referring to a signifier that denotes vague or shifting meanings. Floating signifiers mean different things to different people, and they may mean whatever their interpreters want them to mean. This makes it difficult for such terms to serve useful purposes in or out of school. So it is with giftedness. This has practical implications as well, given, for example, the prevalence of teacher ratings or nominations in gifted child identification procedures. If everyone operationalizes the term differently, how can an educational system ever find and serve those students who require additional challenge?

Giftedness and Equity

From the beginning, the practice of gifted education has been criticized on the grounds that it is at odds with education in a democracy and that it violates principles of equity that are, or ought to be, paramount in society.[4] Gifted programs and their proponents have been called "elitist" and worse, and advocates of gifted education have been seen as the last-ditch defenders of tracking and other damaging educational practices (Oakes, 1985).

---

4 See the debates between Lewis M. Terman and Walter Lippmann in the pages of *The New Republic* in 1922.

Educators in this field have vigorously countered these charges, denying both that their goals are antiegalitarian and that gifted programs are necessarily antidemocratic.

These defenses of the field are, we believe, sincere in that educators in the field of gifted education see gifted education as redressing a wrong—as a way of making the educational system meet the legitimate needs of an underserved population of K–12 students. Moreover, professionals in gifted education believe that appropriate educational programs for students identified as gifted can be implemented without being elitist, racist, sexist, or blighted by socioeconomic inequities. If, as we believe, the intentions of educators in the field of gifted education are unexceptionable, it is also the case that the results of educators' efforts far too often betray the purity of their intentions. Sufficient evidence exists to suggest that the practice of gifted education is rife with inequities that have proven to be extremely difficult to eliminate (Peters, Gentry, et al., 2019).

Take what is probably the most egregious example of preventable, policy-driven inequality in gifted educational practice. The New York City Department of Education, which serves 1.1 million students, operates Gifted and Talented (G&T) programs across the five boroughs that serve thousands of identified students. Admission to these self-contained classes is based on the combined scores on two standardized tests administered, for the most part, to preschoolers and kindergarteners. Predictably, the results are distressing. Whereas roughly 70% of New York City public school students are Black or Latinx, only about 25% of the students in G&T classes fall into those two groups (see Borland, 2012).

Despite decades of efforts to eliminate racial and socioeconomic imbalances in how gifted students are identified and educated, gifted programs have continued to serve middle- and upper-middle-class children to a degree disproportionate to their numbers in the population while underserving children living in poverty and children from racial/ethnic minority populations. It is worth repeating that this fact has nearly always been seen, within the professional field, as wrong and requiring redress. It may be that the inequities that plague the field are an ineluctable consequence of the dominance of the Gifted Child Paradigm (see Borland & Wright, 2001, for a pessimistic speculation).

Moreover, there have been instances in which gifted programs have served purposes that few, if any, within the gifted education field could countenance. According to Sapon-Shevin (1994),

> Within large urban districts, particularly those characterized by impoverished, struggling schools and large, ethnically diverse populations, gifted programs (including gifted magnet programs) have served (and sometimes been promoted) as a way of stemming *white flight*; by providing segregated programming for "gifted students," some white parents—whose children are in the gifted program—will remain within the district (and the tax assessment area). (p. 35)

Two things are indisputably true. The first is that professionals in the field of gifted education, no less than any other group of educators, are opposed to racial and other forms of inequity and are committed to fairness in access to education. Indeed, most would argue that educational equity is what brought them to the field in the first place. The second is that, despite the best of intentions, gifted education, as historically and currently practiced, mirrors and perhaps perpetuates vicious inequities in society. If this isn't a reason to reflect on and reconsider the status quo, we don't know what is.

The Advanced Academic Approach

The Advanced Academic model sees the goal of "gifted education" as challenging students who have progressed beyond typical levels of readiness and who, without additional intervention, would go underchallenged. In this way, Advanced Academics wants the same thing for every student—an appropriately challenging education. For this reason, Advanced Academics fits well with other efforts such as Response to Intervention or personalized learning. This underlying philosophy serves as a framework under which to judge existing models and practices of gifted education in schools. Is gifted education, as implemented, assuring that all advanced learners are appropriately challenged? Is it both necessary and sufficient to accomplish this goal? That is the end goal from which educators should evaluate the means.

One of the ways that the Advanced Academic framework differs from the Gifted Child Paradigm is that it is focused on a far larger and more local service population. Challenging the underchallenged, as a service population, is always an inherently local task. Schools are concerned with challenging the kids who attend them right now. This has implications for identification that we will discuss later. Whereas typical models of gifted education are focused on the top 2%, 5%, or 10% of students, Advanced Academics is interested in whichever students are currently underchallenged by existing services. This could be 2%, but it could also be 0% or 50% of a given grade level.

There is no way to apply a universal criterion to all schools because whether or not a child is currently being challenged right here and right now depends on many local factors. For example, what skills has the student already mastered? How do those skills compare to the local school curriculum? How much can (or will) the classroom teacher differentiate the curriculum in order to challenge that child? This final point means that every classroom is different. Some teachers can (or will) differentiate more than others. Some are skilled at remediating and scaffolding for students who are struggling, while others are better at extension lessons. The key factor is that a child's current level of ability, achievement, or giftedness is not enough information to determine if they require supplementary services. It is a necessary data point, but not sufficient to make that educational determination.

The average American classroom has a wide range of learners in terms of academic readiness. In a 2017 paper, Peters et al. found that approximately 10% of American fifth-grade students scored 4 or more years above grade level in reading. Two percent were 4 or more years advanced in math. Even more important is that the vast majority of the diversity in academic readiness is at the school level. This means there is no such thing as "diverse schools" and "homogenous" schools in terms of within-grade variation. In the 2017 analysis of Measure of Academic Progress data, 86% of the variance in achievement was at the school level. This means that most schools are very diverse places and have as many as six to eight grade levels of readiness in any given age-based, grade-level classroom. Is the standard, grade-level curriculum enough to challenge all of those students? That is the question that the Gifted Child Paradigm never asks. And why would it? In the Gifted Child Paradigm, the goal is to diagnose students as having the trait of giftedness. Their current educational placement or what they are currently being taught in school is irrelevant.

What Does This Mean for Services?

First, it should be emphasized that the Advanced Academic framework is focused on K–12 education. This means it is not interested in "gifted" adults or students who are gifted, advanced, or underchallenged in domains that are not served by a particular school. This focus does not mean that humans cannot be gifted in other areas, just that Advanced Academics is a model of advanced learning in the context of K–12 schools. Schools cannot possibly address every area, domain, or talent. Instead, we suggest a three-tier process for making decisions about what services to offer in which domains or content areas: philosophical, cultural, and practical.

Philosophical Considerations

Although most educators or policymakers might not think about this very often, offering mathematics, science, and history in school is not sacrosanct. There is no eleventh commandment that says, "Thou shalt teach American literature in schools." Instead, these are philosophical, values choices based on what a community sees as important. Time and resources are finite. At some point, someone decided that mathematics is more worthy of inclusion in the school curriculum than is dance. This does not mean that dance is not valuable, just that mathematics was judged more important to a particular constituency (e.g., a school board or state legislature). The same is true with respect to the domains or content areas covered by a school's Advanced Academic services.

Unlike the Gifted Child Paradigm, the Advanced Academic approach has no content area or domain. Whereas many traditional gifted programs focus on creative thinking, critical thinking, or enriched/greater depth approaches to curriculum, the Advanced Academic approach is only concerned about students who are underchallenged in areas that the school or district has decided to serve. If a school offers agriculture programs, then provisions must be made for what will happen if a child is ready for more. If the school has a robotics class, what about that student who has already mastered the material on day one? The same should be applied to seventh-grade math. If a middle school has decided that math is an important content area to offer, what if some students are ready for high school math? These are the philosophical questions that Advanced Academics is concerned with in any and all domains offered by a school. The skills taught, dispositions fostered, or content areas covered by a school and by Advanced Academic services are foremost a philosophical values decision.

Cultural Considerations

Once philosophical decisions are made, factors unique to the culture of the specific school or district should be considered. Services of all types should be responsive to the students enrolled in the particular school or district. Following the philosophical consideration, every school might offer mathematics and history, but after that some services should be locally determined. For example, schools in rural areas might focus more heavily on agriculture. Schools located near major science hubs or research labs (e.g., Boeing in Seattle or Los Alamos National Laboratory in New Mexico) might offer greater depth of content in the STEM areas because of local interest—it is part of the local culture. There is nothing wrong with this. There is some baseline for what all students should be able to access regardless of where they live (this was the point of the Common Core State Standards), but the local values of the culture and community should also play a role in both grade-level, Tier I, universal instruction as well as what is offered to advanced learners. Another example of this will be discussed later and relates to equity. Many districts in urban areas (e.g., Elgin, IL; Baltimore, MD; Fairfax County, VA) have implemented early talent development programs designed to increase the number of advanced learners among their students from lower income, racial, or ethnic minority populations. These are services based on the local culture and values of the district that would not make sense in some other districts because of their particular service population.

Practical Considerations

Finally, there are always practical considerations for what services to offer and in what areas. Sometimes there is not sufficient need in a school to offer a particular course or program. Instead, perhaps the school connects the student to an online learning option. Similarly, there are some domains that are just outside the scope of what the school has to offer. A school might not have the resources to offer an advanced pottery or Advanced Placement European History class. Again, this does not mean these are not valuable domains. But schools need to make tough decisions about how to use limited resources.

In principle, in any area or domain for which the school offers instruction or "grade-level" content, the school should also make provisions for students who are ready for more. This does not mean there need be a gifted mathematics program at every grade level. Instead, the school might proactively implement subject acceleration identification policies to make sure that any student who would be better served in seventh-grade math instead of sixth-grade math is able to access that content. A stand-alone "program" is not needed. The goal is proactively planning for what will happen for a given student who has already mastered the content about to be delivered. What is the plan for the child who is about to start kindergarten but is already reading chapter books? What about the 7% of kindergarteners who enter kindergarten already able to perform addition and subtraction (Engel et al., 2013)? Once a school or community decides what to offer (based on philosophical, cultural, and practical criteria), it must decide what needs to be put in place to assure what will happen for those students who have already mastered the skills taught in a particular course or intervention and who, without additional intervention, would go underchallenged. A visual can help explain this model.

Figure 10.1 shows the continuum of services that need to be available and proactively planned for in every school. The universal, grade-level offerings of a particular school (or grade-level curriculum) are represented by Tier I. This tier should be planned with state standards and local learning objectives in mind (philosophical and cultural considerations), but also with consideration for student readiness. After all, the point of Tier I curriculum and instruction is to challenge the largest percentage of students. If it is too easy or too hard for the majority of students, it needs to change. In concept, Advanced Academic services are those that kick in when the student's needs fall outside what can be met by the Tier I interventions offered. This is represented by the dotted line between Tiers I and II.

What Does Identification Look Like?

The lines between Tiers I and II and Tiers II and III concern identification (see Figure 10.1). However, unlike in the Gifted Child Paradigm, the goal is not to identify students as gifted. Instead, identification is used

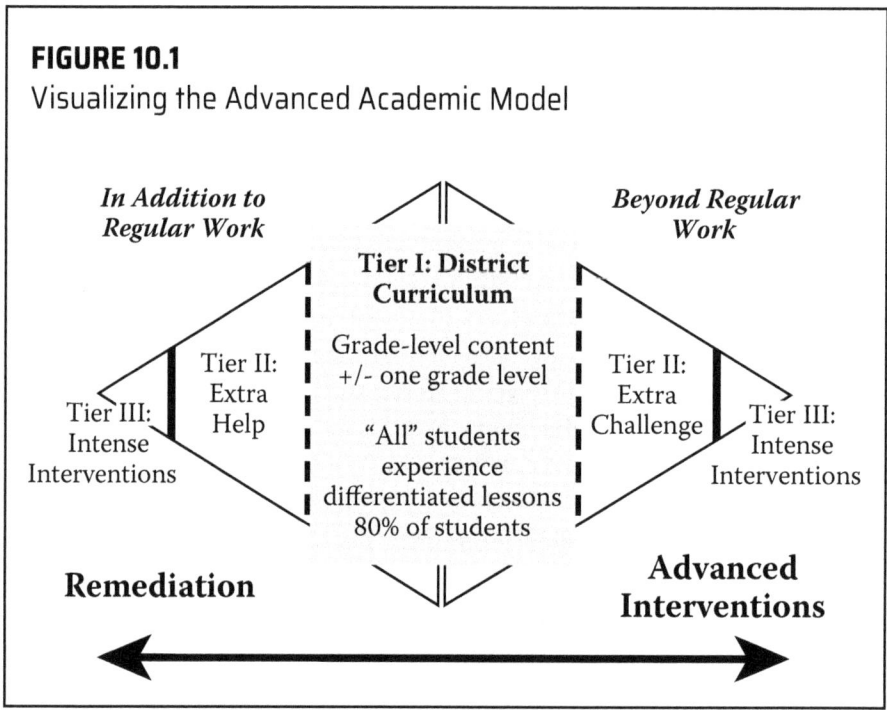

FIGURE 10.1
Visualizing the Advanced Academic Model

to determine who has a need that cannot be met by a lower-tier service and/or who would benefit from the higher-tier service. This means that the first step in identification is to understand what skills and range of needs can be addressed in the Tier I, "regular" education classroom. Can a sixth-grade student who is ready for algebra be effectively challenged in a Tier I, grade-level classroom? Is this a reasonable expectation given all of the other forms of diversity one teacher needs to support in a class of 30? If the answer is yes, all else being equal, then the student is being appropriately challenged, and no further intervention is necessary. Similarly, if a 4-year-old child is already reading independently, then it is unlikely that waiting another year to start kindergarten will be sufficiently challenging. Again, ignoring many other factors such as the child's maturity, it is likely that early entrance to kindergarten is a necessary intervention for that child.

So how does one operationalize the lines between the tiers? This is one of the least appealing parts of the Advanced Academic model because of how subjective and imperfect this process is. Whereas under the Gifted Child model, a child is gifted if, for example, they have an IQ of 130 or more, in the Advanced Academic model, a child is placed in a service or receives an intervention if they have a need for it and will benefit from it. The first step in identification is talking to grade-level teachers and looking at the grade-level, Tier I curriculum to understand what level of needs can be addressed therein. Teachers know what skills they address, and how often and how able they are to tweak or extend lessons for students who need more support or additional challenge. Although inherently a subjective process, when applied to each domain or content area, this can help operationalize the boundaries of a grade level's Tier I instruction. Each grade-level "core" curriculum should have a scope and sequence in place so that everyone involved knows what skills are taught where, when they are reviewed and assessed, etc.

There is also a less precise, but more efficient way to operationalize the lines between the tiers. Instead of basing those lines on what content the student needs to have mastered in order to require additional intervention, the school can set expectations for the grade-level teacher that determine when additional supports kick in. For example, a school could mandate that the middle 80% of students are the responsibility of the grade-level, Tier I teacher. The teacher is expected to utilize technology, preassessment, and differentiation to challenge the middle 24 of their 30 students.

On the remediation end and advanced end of the continuum, supplementary staff and services are available. If a student in third grade cannot read and is too far behind for the regular education teacher to support on their own, then additional, more intensive services kick in. The same should be true on the advanced end of the learning continuum. Hopefully it is obvious why this is less preferable to the first option; it has logistical appeal but is less precise. The teacher in the second option might only be able to effectively challenge 10 of her 30 students, and yet nothing else is available for the other 14; only the top three and bottom three receive additional intervention. Hopefully the percentage of students assigned to Tier I is based on actual experience and data. Perhaps in past years, teachers felt that the middle 70% (and the content mastery associated with that group) was a more reasonable expectation. This is fine, but it does make for a larger caseload for the Tier II and Tier III services. Every student needs to be challenged somewhere. Advanced Academics is focused on the question, "Where is the student most likely to be challenged?" Is the Tier I "regular" grade-level curriculum enough, or is additional intervention necessary?

Once the line between Tiers I and II has been operationalized, the next step is to translate that line into measurable identification criteria. For example, if a school decides that the third-grade teachers need to be able to differentiate up and down 2 years each, or if they decide that students at that level can no longer be challenged by the standard grade 3 content, then the point at which a student requires an Advanced Academic service is when they have mastered the grade 5 content. In Wisconsin, on the Northwest Evaluation Association Measures of Academic Progress, a student who scores a 226 in math in the spring is proficient in grade 5 math content. This student would then qualify for an advanced academic intervention in math—likely some form of subject acceleration or compacted math instruction. These criteria need not be based on a single standardized test score. Perhaps some above-level language mastery is also needed for a student to be successful in a Tier II intervention in math. This means both a 226 in math as well as a 204 in reading (on level for grade 4) would be required. We make no claim that such criteria are appropriate for any particular intervention. The important takeaway is that once the conceptual criteria are established for who needs something beyond Tier I, those criteria must be translated into formal identification policies and procedures.

The example just described makes the most sense for elementary grades. Luckily, secondary-level Advanced Academic interventions and identification are slightly easier due to the constant rotation across different rooms and subjects. Whereas it might be difficult for a third-grade student to arrange to move across the school to participate in advanced math with the fifth- or sixth-grade students, it should be easier for a sixth-grade student to attend the math class meant for Tier I eighth-grade students. Just as in special education, the goal is placement in the least-restrictive environment; the goal of Advanced Academics, and for all K–12 education, should be curriculum and instruction that is aligned to the students' zone of proximal development (Vygotsky, 1978).

Proactive identification criteria need to be in place at two levels—between Tiers I and II and between Tiers II and III (and in all domains of service). Conceptually, these two identification levels ask the questions: (a) Which students need more than Tier I can provide in order to be challenged? and (b) For which students are the Tier II options still going to be insufficient? Operationalizing the line between Tiers II and III is the same process as was applied between Tiers I and II. Again, it is important to ask: For whom will the Tier II interventions still be insufficient to place students in their zone of proximal development? Once a student exhausts Tier I and II options, what remains is a personalized plan. Some students are so different from their same-age peers that no amount of differentiation, compacting, or even subject acceleration is enough. For example, a 10th-grade student who has completed all of the available AP classes and dual-enrollment options, and is simply out of courses to take, should be graduated early and enrolled in higher education. Obviously, that would require a personalized learning plan or differentiated education plan similar to the Individualized

Education Programs often used for students with disabilities. Students like these are so atypical that no existing services will meet their needs. They need a personalized education.

All of this should make clear that Advanced Academics is focused on identifying students for services that they need and will benefit from. This perspective is not trying to identify students as gifted. The first step is to try to work within existing courses, units, and interventions even if they are atypical for students of that age. For example, a school might be able to challenge a larger number of fourth-grade students with existing services and instruction if students can go across the hall for the math block. If that is not possible, then there is no Tier II math intervention, and such a child would need a Tier III personalized intervention. The first step is breaking down the barriers between existing courses or the places where different levels of content are taught. On one extreme, students are only exposed to content when they are a certain age—that is the concept behind age-based grade levels. This is why the first step in Advanced Academics is blurring those lines to make it so the students who would be better off learning in a different classroom—part- or full-time—can do so. Of course, this will not meet all existing needs.

Why Is the Advanced Academic Model More Equitable?

First, as noted, decisions about services and identification under the Advanced Academic model are inherently local. Every school has students who are underchallenged by their current placement and the instruction they are receiving. Even schools with 100% of student who are below grade-level standards have kids who could do more. In 2016, approximately 42% of American schools had zero students identified as gifted (Peters, Gentry, et al., 2019). In the Advanced Academic model, this makes no sense. Unless a school can demonstrate how existing Tier I services place every student in their zone of proximal development (Vygotsky, 1978), then Tier II and Tier III services need to be in place. This approach means there will be identified students in every building.

Such an inherently local focus also means that students can and will move in and out of services as needed. Although some students might require a Tier II service every year for their entire K–12 career, others might only need such a service one time. This has equity implications because it means identification is ongoing and that there are multiple opportunities to be identified as gifted. Those students who had fewer early learning experiences need not be high achieving by second grade because that is when the district's identification happens. If they do not qualify for an Advanced Academic service until fifth grade, that is fine. Because of the local focus and the emphasis on challenging any underchallenged students, there are multiple opportunities to be identified and served. This supports greater equity, as it allows for those students on a different developmental trajectory to have opportunities to be placed in advanced learning opportunities.[5]

Another way the emphasis on local student needs and services is applied is with the application of local building norms for identification. As noted previously, students should be placed in an intervention if there is evidence they have a need for it and will benefit from it. Building norms work much better in finding such students than do national norms because the former tells a school which students are the furthest away from what is the typical level of readiness in a particular learning context. The child at the 98th percentile in their school's third-grade class is more likely to be underchallenged than a child at the 50th percentile (in that building's third grade). Also, this will be a better indicator of who needs additional challenge than will knowing which child is at the 95th percentile nationally. Knowing where a child stands compared to same-age peers across the country just is not instructionally useful. Building norms provide a much better indicator of who is likely to be underchallenged in the Tier I environment and will also yield greater aggregate diversity of the identified gifted population.

Building norms will not increase the diversity of the identified gifted or advanced academic service population of every building. Instead, they work on the aggregate. In large districts, building norms will make the district's gifted program more diverse and will also make every state's gifted population more diverse on the whole. Put simply, building norms are a statement that gifted students exist in every building and that every building must proactively plan for those students who need something more. A recent study on building norms showed 157% to 300% increases in Black and Latinx student representation in gifted populations when building norms were applied as opposed to national norms (Peters, Rambo-Hernandez, et al., 2019). This is an obvious equity victory, but building norms also make

---

[5] It is not reasonable to expect Advanced Academics to lead to completely equitable schooling. The goal should be to try to fashion programs that are as equitable as possible in an inequitable society.

more sense from the standpoint of gifted education as a special education service. Borland made this point in 2005:

> The only justification for gifted programs is a special educational one grounded in a belief [evidence] that the regular curriculum designed to meet the needs of most students, is inappropriate for some students who, by virtue of disability or ability, are exceptional and will not receive the education to which they are entitled unless the curriculum is modified. (p. 13)

Building norms yield better information about who is most likely to need a special service in order to meet a need that is not being met by local educational services. Between this better logical foundation and the equity benefits, building norms are a win-win.

One thing worth noting with regard to building norms is that they are only possible when students are universally evaluated for gifted program eligibility. After all, if the identification assessments are only administered to those students who are referred for testing, then there is no way to calculate a building norm because not everyone in the building was tested. This is a limitation because building norms can only be utilized in that context, but it is also a positive because it means that universal consideration and building norms should be used together. Universally evaluating all students for program eligibility will always result in fewer students missed than if a two-phase identification system is used (McBee et al., 2016).

Advanced Academics as a framework is also more equitable than practice rooted in the traditional Gifted Child Paradigm because it is much more focused on talent development as opposed to only working to challenge students who are already advanced according to traditional standards. Traditional gifted education seeks to challenge students who are more able or have achieved at higher levels than their same-age peers. Advanced Academics is concerned with every student who is underchallenged in the local learning context. This means that a student need not have already had extensive educational opportunities in order to be eligible. It is not just how much a student knows that determines program eligibility, but rather what a student already knows compared to what is being taught. Whereas in traditional gifted education, most of the gifted kids are in the higher income suburbs where students have had extensive educational opportunities, in the Advanced Academic model, students who are underchallenged are more likely to be in underresourced schools or those focusing heavily on remediation. If the entire focus of a school is on remediating students up to "grade-level standards," then even students who are "only" at that level might require a Tier II service due to insufficient challenge in the Tier I classroom. The implication here is that far more students will be identified as "gifted" or for Tier II/III services in underresourced, overall lower performing schools than under the Gifted Child Paradigm. We admit this is a radical way to conceive of gifted education, but we believe it is far more likely to challenge a larger number of students in a larger number of schools and to do so with fewer of the negative externalities that often come with traditional gifted programs.

Conclusion

A key component of Advanced Academics is that it approaches "giftedness," gifted services, or advanced learning opportunities within the context of K–12 schools. This is critical. We hope it is obvious that the model we describe would make little sense outside of the K–12 structure. We do not see this as a limitation, but some have taken issue with this somewhat narrow focus. Our goal in the Advanced Academic model is to challenge a larger number of students as they move through K–12 school in as practical a way as possible. To accomplish this, a range of interventions should be made available for students who are unlikely to be challenged in the existing, typical, or grade-level Tier I services. What schools offer in terms of their Tier I "regular" or "grade level" classroom will vary. For this reason, what needs to be offered at the Tiers II and III levels will also vary based on the needs of the students in that particular school.

We have attempted in this chapter to undermine some of the most fundamental articles of faith in the field of gifted education that derive from what Dai and Chen (2013, 2014) identified as the Gifted Child Paradigm. Among these are the belief that enrichment works, the belief that gifted education requires gifted-specific programs, and the belief that the notion of giftedness among school students makes sense and results in positive outcomes. Many, if not most, people in the field of gifted education, we suspect, would reject our arguments out of hand because, for them, gifted education is contained within the boundaries of the Gifted Child Paradigm. If some or most readers of this chapter find much to disagree with, that is well and good. Intellectual disagreement and informed debate are healthy signs in any discipline or field of practice. What we would find disturbing, however, would be a dismissal of the value of problematizing cherished notions. Progress in any field requires rationale, evidence-based discourse.

More than 2 decades ago, Borland (1996) wrote an article entitled "Gifted Education and the Threat of Irrelevance" in which he suggested that the field has a "fear of the big questions." By this he meant that educators let others explore questions they find to be too controversial, even dangerous or taboo. By avoiding such fundamental questions as whether the construct of the gifted student makes sense, they cede to others important intellectual territory that ought to be theirs. Educators need to reclaim those "big questions" that others, including some not so friendly to the purposes of gifted education, have laid claim to. Problematizing the most fundamental beliefs would be a good step in that direction. We do not claim to be right or in any way divine in our views, but we do hope to have problematized many of the common practices in the field in such a way as to provoke debate and further radical thinking.

MAJOR POINTS

- The Advanced Academic model sees "gifted" students as those who are underchallenged in their current educational environment. The goal of Advanced Academic services is to alleviate that lack of challenge through a range of increasingly intensive services.
- Services are "good" or effective if they successfully alleviate a lack of challenge.
- Students should receive an Advanced Academic intervention if they have a need for and would benefit from it. Similarly, students should not be denied participation in a service unless there is evidence they will not benefit or be successful.
- The only justification for gifted programs is a special educational one grounded in a belief (evidence) that the regular curriculum designed to meet the needs of most students, is inappropriate for some students who, by virtue of disability or ability, are exceptional and will not receive the education to which they are entitled unless the curriculum is modified (Borland, 2005).

- The services to be offered should be a local decision based on philosophical, cultural, and practical criteria.
- Traditional models of gifted education (vis-à-vis the Gifted Child Paradigm) will always be inequitable in their service populations because they are only focused on children who come into school high achieving.

DISCUSSION QUESTIONS

1. Do you agree with Peters and Borland's critique of the Gifted Child Paradigm?
2. What do you think of the argument that the goal of gifted education should be to challenge students who would otherwise go underchallenged? Is that the basis by which educators should judge effectiveness?
3. How would the Advanced Academic framework work with existing policy mandates and state funding in your state?
4. What do you see as the major barriers to implementing the Advanced Academic framework in schools?
5. Do you buy the arguments that the Advanced Academic perspective is more equitable than traditional models of gifted education?

References

Adelson, J. L., McCoach, D. B., Gavin, M. K. (2012). Examining the effects of gifted programming in mathematics and reading using the ECLS-K. *Gifted Child Quarterly*, 56(1), 25–39. https://doi.org/10.1177/0016986 211431487

Borland, J. H. (1989). *Planning and implementing programs for the gifted.* Teachers College Press.

Borland, J. H. (1996). Gifted education and the threat of irrelevance. *Journal for the Education of the Gifted, 19*(2), 129–147. https://doi.org/10.1177/016235329601900202

Borland, J. H. (2003). The death of giftedness. In J. H. Borland (Ed.), *Rethinking gifted education* (pp. 105–124). Teachers College Press.

Borland, J. H. (2005). Gifted education without gifted children: The case for no conception of giftedness. In R. J. Sternberg & J. Davidson (Eds.), *Conceptions of giftedness* (2nd ed., pp. 1–19). Cambridge University Press.

Borland, J. H. (2009). Gifted education without gifted programs or gifted students: Differentiation of curriculum and instruction as an instructional model for gifted students. In J. S. Renzulli, E. J. Gubbins, K. S. McMillen, R. D. Eckert, & C. A. Little (Eds.), *Systems and models for developing programs for the gifted and talented* (2nd ed., pp. 105–118). Prufrock Press.

Borland, J. H. (2012). *New York City gets it wrong again.* The Creativity Post. https://www.creativitypost.com/education/new_york_city_gets_it_wrong_again

Borland, J. H. (2013). Problematizing gifted education. In C. M. Callahan & H. Hertberg-Davis (Eds.), *Fundamentals of gifted education: Considering multiple perspectives* (pp. 69–80). Routledge.

Borland, J. H. (2018). Problematizing gifted education: Thinking radically about our beliefs and practices. In C. M. Callahan & H. L. Hertberg-Davis (Eds.), *Fundamentals of gifted education: Considering multiple perspectives* (2nd ed., pp. 71–82). Routledge.

Borland, J. H., & Wright, L. (2001). Identifying and educating poor and under-represented gifted students. In K. A. Heller, F. J. Mönks, R. J. Sternberg, & R. F. Subotnik (Eds.), *International handbook of research and development of giftedness and talent.* Pergamon Press.

Colangelo, N., Assouline, S. G., & Gross, M. U. M. (2004). *A nation deceived: How schools hold back America's brightest students* (Vol. 1). The University of Iowa, The Connie Belin & Jacqueline N. Blank International Center for Gifted Education and Talent Development.

Coleman, L. J. (1985). *Schooling the gifted.* Addison-Wesley.

Coleman, L. J., & Cross, T. L. (2005). *Being gifted in school: An introduction to development, guidance, and teaching* (2nd ed.). Prufrock Press.

Cox, J., Daniel, N., & Boston, B. (1985). *Educating able learners: Programs and promising practices.* University of Texas Press.

Dai, D. Y., & Chen, F. (2013). Three paradigms of gifted education: In search of conceptual clarity in research and practice. *Gifted Child Quarterly, 57*(3), 151–168. https://doi.org/10.1177/0016986213490020

Dai, D. Y., & Chen, F. (2014). *Paradigms of gifted education: A guide for theory-based, practice-focused research.* Prufrock Press.

Delcourt, M. A. B., Loyd, B. H., Cornell, D. G., & Goldberg, M. D. (1994). *Evaluation of the effects of programming arrangements on student learning outcomes* (RM94108). University of Connecticut. The National Research Center on the Gifted and Talented.

Engel, M., Claessens, A., & Finch, M. A. (2013). Teaching students what they already know? The (mis)alignment between mathematics instructional content and student knowledge in kindergarten. *Educational Evaluation and Policy Analysis, 35*(2), 157–178. https://doi.org/10.3102/0162373712461850

Gallagher, S. (1999). An exchange of gazes. In J. L. Kincheloe, S. R. Steinberg, & L. E. Villeverde (Eds.), *Rethinking intelligence: Confronting psychological assumptions about teaching and learning* (pp. 69–84). Routledge.

George, W. C., Cohn, S. J., & Stanley, J. C. (1977). *Educating the gifted: Acceleration and enrichment: Proceedings of the ninth annual Hyman Blumberg symposium on research in early childhood education.* Johns Hopkins University Press.

Hall, S. (Ed.). (1997). *Representation: Cultural representations and signifying practices* (Vol. 2). SAGE.

Holmes, R. (2008). *The age of wonder: How the romantic generation discovered the beauty and terror of science.* HarperPress.

Kim, M. (2016). A meta-analysis of the effects of enrichment programs on gifted students. *Gifted Child Quarterly, 60*(2), 102–116. https://doi.org/10.1177/0016986216630607

Kuhn, T. S. (1996). *The structure of scientific revolutions.* University of Chicago Press. (Original work published 1962)

Lohman, D. F., & Korb, K. A. (2006). Gifted today but not tomorrow? Longitudinal changes in ability and achievement during elementary school. *Journal for the Education of the Gifted, 29*(4), 451–484. https://doi.org/10.4219/jeg-2006-245

Martin, J. (1983). What should we do with a hidden curriculum when we find one? In H. Giroux & D. Purpel (Eds.), *The hidden curriculum and moral education* (pp. 122–139). McCutchan.

McBee, M. T., & Makel, M. C. (2019). The quantitative implications of definitions of giftedness. *AERA Open, 5*(1). https://doi.org/10.1177/2332858419831007

McBee, M. T., McCoach, D. B., Peters, S. J., & Matthews, M. S. (2012). The case for a schism: Commentary on Subotnik, Olszewski-Kubilius, and Worrell (2011). *Gifted Child Quarterly, 56*(4), 210–214. https://doi.org/10.1177/0016986212456075

McBee, M. T., & Peters, S. J., & Miller, E. M. (2016). The impact of the nomination stage on gifted program identification: A comprehensive psychometric analysis. *Gifted Child Quarterly, 60*(4), 258–278. https://doi.org/10.1177/0016986216656256

Oakes, J. (1985). *Keeping track: How schools structure inequality.* Yale University Press.

Peters, S. J., Gentry, M., Whiting, G. W., & McBee, M. T. (2019). Who gets served in gifted education? Demographic representation and a call for action. *Gifted Child Quarterly, 63*(4), 273–287. https://doi.org/10.1177/0016986219833738

Peters, S. J., Kaufman, S. B., Matthews, M., McBee, M. T., & McCoach, D. B. (2014). Gifted ed. is crucial, but the label isn't. *Education Week, 33*(28), 40, 34.

Peters, S. J., Matthews, M. S., McBee, M. T., & McCoach, D. B. (2014). *Beyond gifted education: Designing and implementing advanced academic programs.* Prufrock Press.

Peters, S. J., Rambo-Hernandez, K., Makel, M. C., Matthews, M. S., & Plucker, J. A. (2017). Should millions of students take a gap year? Large numbers of students start the school year above grade level. *Gifted Child Quarterly, 61*(3), 229–238. https://doi.org/10.1177/0016986217701834

Peters, S. J., Rambo-Hernandez, K., Makel, M. C., Matthews, M. S., & Plucker, J. A., (2019). Effect of local norms on racial and ethnic representation in gifted education. *AERA Open, 5*(2), 1–18. https://doi.org/10.1177/2332858419848446

Sapon-Shevin, M. (1994). *Playing favorites: Gifted education and the disruption of community.* State University of New York Press.

Shore, B. M., Cornell, D. G., Robinson, A., & Ward, V. S. (1991). *Recommended practices in gifted education: A critical analysis.* Teachers College Press.

Slavin, R. E. (1990). Achievement effects of ability grouping in secondary schools; A best-evidence synthesis. *Review of Educational Research, 60*(3), 471–499. https://doi.org/10.3102/00346543060003471

Southern, W. T., & Jones, E. D. (Eds.). (1991). *The academic acceleration of gifted children.* Teachers College Press.

Steenbergen-Hu, S., Makel, M. C., & Olszewski-Kubilius, P. (2016). What one hundred years of research says about the effects of ability grouping and acceleration on K–12 students' academic achievement: Findings of two second-order meta-analyses. *Review of Educational Research, 86*(4), 849–899. https://doi.org/10.3102/0034654316675417

Sternberg, R. J., & Davidson, J. (Eds.). (2005). *Conceptions of giftedness* (2nd ed.). Cambridge University Press.

Terman, L. M. (1925). *Genetic studies of genius: Vol. 1. Mental and physical traits of a thousand gifted children*. Stanford University Press.

Vaughn, V. L., Feldhusen, J. F., & Asher, W. J. (1991). Meta-analyses and review of research on pull-out programs in gifted education. *Gifted Child Quarterly, 35*, 92–98. https://doi.org/10.1177/001698629103500208

Vygotsky, L. S. (1978). *Mind in society: The development of higher psychological processes*. Harvard University Press.

CHAPTER 11

Giftedness as IQ

JOHN D. WASSERMAN

Now we see the case of another type of student who does not profit from the school program for a truly paradoxical reason: he is too intelligent. We sometimes meet brilliant children whose intellectual development is very superior to that of children their own age. They are not the last ones to find this out. In class a minimum of effort gets them the best grade. Their vanity is kindled, their work is whimsical. They learn their lessons at the last minute and readily become insubordinate. They do homework which was not assigned to them just to attract attention. During study periods they prevent other students from working. They are resented and punished but they are always forgiven come examination time. Classes for the gifted should be created. . . . A child of superior intelligence is an asset not to be wasted. (Binet, 1909/1975, p. 85–86)

The beginning of the 20th century saw a new, scientifically grounded psychology applied to measuring the abilities of children, with the 1905 publication of Alfred Binet and Théodore Simon's *La mesure de l'intelligence*. The 1905 test, which had a good floor but no ceiling (in terms of the relative difficulty of content) was improved with an age-scaled format in 1908 that was revised to extend upward through adulthood in 1911. Then called "The Measuring Scale of Intelligence" (*L'échelle métrique de l'intelligence*), the Binet-Simon Scale offered an objective, norm-referenced form of ability measurement, necessary because neither teachers nor anyone else could reliably identify low- or high-ability students (Binet, 1911/1916; Terman et al., 1917). It was through the 1908 and 1911 editions of the Binet-Simon Scale that modern gifted assessment first became possible.

If Spearman's (1904) derivation of the general ability factor g is added to the mix, then there exists the foundations of the IQ-based psychometric framework to understanding giftedness in place: a *guiding theory* (Spearman's two-factor theory, particularly his identification of general cognitive ability, or the g factor) and a *working test of general ability* (the Binet-Simon Intelligence Scale). Galton (1879) had already introduced *psychometry* as "the art of imposing measurement and number upon operations of the mind" (p. 149), opening the door to norm-referenced test construction. The potential of the 1908 Binet-Simon Scale to detect intellectual giftedness on a large scale became evident in the United States in 1910, when Henry H. Goddard had five assistants from his Vineland research laboratory test all of the primary school students in one school system. Goddard (1911) reported that 4.2% of students could be considered "gifted" (p. 235), as defined by *two or more grades advanced* in mental level. With a working measurement tool in place, the needs and education of intellectually advanced students became the focus of serious scholarship (e.g., Stern, 1911a, 1911b; Whipple, 1913, 1919), and comprehensive systems of educational exceptionality including giftedness were proposed by educators in U. S. Bureau of Education publications (Van Sickle et al., 1911). Although many labels were applied to describe high-ability students, including *bright, elite, exceptional, select, superior, supernormal,* and *surnormal,* Whipple's (1911) proposed term *gifted* has proved most enduring.

Now, more than 100 years later, the concept of giftedness and its primary method of measurement, psychometric testing, are being critically reexamined. Over time, the ability or intelligence test, whether given individually or in groups, has become the cornerstone of methods for objective identification of gifted students. Gifted education programs tend to serve students identified with high ability/intelligence test performance, so much of what educators understand about the qualities of gifted students stems directly or indirectly from the measurement tools used to identify them. In this chapter, the *g* factor and what it predicts is explained, and contemporary tests of intelligence are briefly discussed. Some strengths and limitations of testing and psychometric *g* are presented.

Composite IQ and Psychometric *g*

In contemporary assessment, the intelligence test summary score, usually an IQ, is almost always an estimate of psychometric *g*, the general ability factor that saturates test batteries. Psychometric *g* is also known as the *g factor*, *Spearman's g*, *general mental ability*, and *general cognitive ability*. Summary or composite scores that serve as proxies for *g* include the Full Scale IQ (Wechsler and Stanford-Binet intelligence scales), the General Ability Index (a purer index of *g* from the Wechsler scales), General Intellectual Ability (from the Woodcock-Johnson IV Tests of Cognitive Abilities), and General Conceptual Ability (from the Differential Ability Scales). The degree to which these composite scores accurately measure *g*, and their usefulness for decision making relative to giftedness, continues to be the subject of research (e.g., Rowe et al., 2010).

David Wechsler, the developer of the industry-leading Wechsler intelligence scales, called the psychometric *g* "one of the great discoveries of psychology" (Wechsler, 1939, p. 6). The *g* factor was first conceptualized by Charles Spearman in 1904 and is derived statistically from positive intercorrelations between individual scores in batteries of mental measures. After correcting correlation coefficients for the effects of measurement error and restriction of range, Spearman (1904) extracted a single factor and demonstrated that "all branches of intellectual activity have in common one fundamental function" (p. 284).

Although there are dissenters (some represented in this volume), recognition of the importance of *g* appears to represent consensus thought in intelligence. Reeve and Charles (2008) surveyed 36 experts in intelligence and found agreement that *g* is an important, nontrivial determinant of important real-world outcomes without substitute. The *g* factor was affirmed in the "Mainstream Science on Intelligence" professional consensus statement (Gottfredson, 1997a), but the "Intelligence: Knowns and Unknowns" statement by an APA task force was slightly more equivocal on *g*, concluding that "while the *g*-based factor hierarchy is the most widely accepted current view of the structure of abilities, some theorists regard it as misleading" (Neisser et al., 1996, p. 81).

The place of *g* as the highest order factor with the greatest *generality* (i.e., breadth of application) in the structure of human cognitive abilities was affirmed by Carroll (1993) in his landmark factor analytic survey. Carroll, who spent 10 years amassing and reanalyzing more than 460 datasets of cognitive abilities, used hierarchical exploratory factor analysis to formulate a three-stratum organization of cognitive abilities with *g* at the apex (Stratum III), approximately eight independent broad abilities at a lower level (Stratum II), and 50 or more narrow abilities at the lowest level (Stratum I). Carroll (1993) specified that *g* was most strongly associated with fluid reasoning—a finding consistent with earlier studies by Gustafsson (1984) and Undheim (1981)—and that *g* was most weakly associated with processing speed. In his last publication, Carroll (2003) reaffirmed the general ability factor, which he described as "almost universally accepted" (p. 5). A more recent adaptation of Carroll's work, Cattell-Horn-Carroll (CHC) theory, deemphasizes *g* in favor of lower order broad cognitive abilities (Schneider & McGrew, 2018).

The Meaning of Psychometric *g*

The meaning of general intelligence has long been a subject of concern, as a mathematically derived *g* was hard to translate into applied practice. In the famous 1921 *Journal of Educational Psychology* print symposium, 17 leading psychologists were asked to define intelligence, producing wildly divergent responses. Spearman (1927) despaired: "Chaos itself can go no further! . . . In truth, 'intelligence' has become a mere vocal sound, a word with so many meanings that it finally has none" (p. 14). More recently, Sternberg and Detterman (1986) repeated the exercise with 25 authorities, reaching the same endpoint. A list of nearly all of these definitions, along with others, may be found in Wasserman (2018). The most practical definition of general intelligence can probably be found in Gottfredson's (1997a) consensus statement:

A very general capacity that, among other things, involves the ability to reason, plan, solve problems, think abstractly, comprehend complex ideas, learn quickly and learn from experience. It is not merely book learning, a narrow academic skill, or test-taking smarts. Rather, it reflects a broader and deeper capability for comprehending our surroundings—"catching on," "making sense" of things, or "figuring out what to do." (p. 13)

Charles Spearman (1923, 1927, 1930) sought to explain how *g* works by articulating three deceptively simple cognitive-intellectual processes by which people can draw meaning from their experiences:

- **Principle of Apprehension of Experience:** "A person tends to know his own sensations, feelings, and strivings" (Spearman, 1930, p. 15).
- **Principle of Relations:** "When two or more items (percepts or ideas) are given, a person may perceive them to be in various ways related" (Spearman, 1930, p. 18).
- **Principle of Correlates:** "When any item and a relation to it are present to mind, then the mind can generate in itself another item so related" (Spearman, 1930, p. 23).

Spearman saw the capacity to understand how two or more separate ideas might be connected ("eduction of relations") as a form of abstract reasoning, and the use of an idea and a relation to generate another idea ("eduction of correlates") as a form of reasoning and creativity. The term *eduction* refers to drawing the "essence or nature" from two or more things (Spearman, 1930, p. 34).

As for the functional, everyday qualities that constitute *g*, one can find no better descriptors that those reported by Arvey (1986), who listed the following job performance appraisal items emerging as a first factor from a performance appraisal instrument with some 65 task and ability job analysis statements collected for more than 140 jobs. Correlations with the mathematically derived *g* factor appear in parentheses:

- Deal with unexpected situations (.75).
- Able to learn and recall job-related information (.71).
- Able to reason and make judgments (.69).
- Able to identify problem situations quickly (.69).
- React swiftly when unexpected problems occur (.67).
- Able to apply common sense to solve problems (.66).

- Able to learn new procedures quickly (.66).
- Alert and quick to understand things (.55).
- Able to compare information from two or more sources to reach a conclusion (.49).

Although these descriptors were generated for adults in the working world, they also serve exceptionally well as descriptors of *g* for children and adolescents at school. For further in-depth discussion of *g*, the interested reader is referred to the writings of Linda S. Gottfredson (begin with Gottfredson, 1997b, where Arvey's 1986 work was first brought to my attention).

Two Test Illustrations of Psychometric *g*

One more step to understand the *g* factor and its associated eductive principles is today called *fluid reasoning* or *fluid intelligence*. Spearman authored two separate intelligence tests, one completely verbal and one almost entirely nonverbal. Neither of these tests remains in use at present, but both provide very helpful illustrations of how *g* might be translated into ability and intelligence tests. Moreover, they are each quite representative of contemporaneous ability/intelligence testing procedures.

Spearman's (1925) "A Measure of 'Intelligence' for Use in Schools" was the highly verbal test that required the examinee to educe relations in different ways on seven tests. The test required some basal English language word knowledge but was intended to measure abstract thinking. Figure 11.1 contains sample items.

In stark contrast to his verbal measure, Spearman also authored a nonverbal measure of general ability, the Spearman Visual Perception Test (SVPT; Spearman, 1933). It also consisted of seven tests and initially had oral directions, although pantomimed directions were later developed, along with norms. Through its requirements that examinees derive and understand relations between and among geometric figures, it was designed to minimize any semantic or pictorial meanings. Sample items for the SVPT appear in Figure 11.2.

The SVPT may be considered an antecedent to the Raven's Progressive Matrices (Penrose & Raven, 1936; Raven, 1938), Cattell's (1940) Culture-Free Intelligence Test, and more recently, the Naglieri Nonverbal Ability Test (NNAT; Naglieri, 2003). The popularizer of the nonverbal matrix reasoning task, Raven sought a measure that was equally applicable to all ages and

FIGURE 11.1
Sample Items From Spearman's (1925) "A Measure of 'Intelligence' for Use in Schools"

Test I. Same or Opposite (30 items)
1. Are "small" and "little" nearly the *same,* or about as *different* as possible?
2. Are "good" and "bad" nearly the *same* or about as *different* as possible?

Test II. Synonyms (24 items)
1. *To strike* means most nearly the same as what?
   To fool? To hit? To hurt? To break?

2. *Wealth* means most nearly the same as what?
   Purse? Bank? Riches? Wages?

Test III. Classification (28 items)
1. I am going to read you some sets of four words each. Look which means something most unlike the other three.

   Ring. Stick. Wheel. Circle.
   Which word means something most like the rest?

   Skipping-rope. Ball. Ink. Doll.
   Which word means something most like the rest?

Test IV. Questions (12 items)
Which of the four words answers the question best?
1. What was it that made him eat?
   Thirst? Hunger? Pain? Joy?

2. On what account did he put up his umbrella?
   Wind? Sun? Rain? Frost?

> **FIGURE 11.1,** continued
>
> **Test V. Completion (24 items)**
> 1. I am going to read you some incomplete sentences. Look which of the four words completes it best.
>
>   Stamps are put on —?
>   *Tables? Letters? Pictures? Trees?*
>
>   Heat turns ice into —?
>   *Ink? Beer? Water? Cream?*
>
> **Test VI. Analogies (28 items)**
> 1. *White* is to *Black* as Yes is to —?
>   *No? Perhaps? If? When?*
>
> 2. *Head* is to *Mouth* as Room is to —?
>   *Chair? Chimney? Door? Table?*
>
> **Test VII. Inferences (17 items)**
> 1. If "A" is larger than "B" and "B" is larger than "C", how is "A" compared with "C"?
>   *Smaller? Larger? Better? Equal?*
>
> *Note.* From *A Measure of "Intelligence" for Use in Schools*, by C. Spearman, 1925, Methuen. In the public domain.

abilities, independent of previous experience, and on a scale of increasing difficulty and complexity. Raven specified that the ideal test should be consistent, novel, and interesting; easy to administer and demonstrate; readily grasped by examinees; and accurately scored. Most importantly, Raven specified that an intelligence test should remove the scholastic bias often found in other tests (see Watt, 1998, for a historical account).

What IQ Predicts

In this section, I address the predictive capacity of IQ and the *g* factor. To avoid the limitations of reporting individual investigations, I am

Giftedness as IQ

> **FIGURE 11.2**
> Sample Items From the Spearman Visual Perception Test
>
> **Instructions:** "Look at the drawings in the first row under A and B. In what way is B different from A? Now look at the 3 pairs of drawings that come after A and B. Find which pair contains the drawings that are as different from each other as B is different from A."
>
>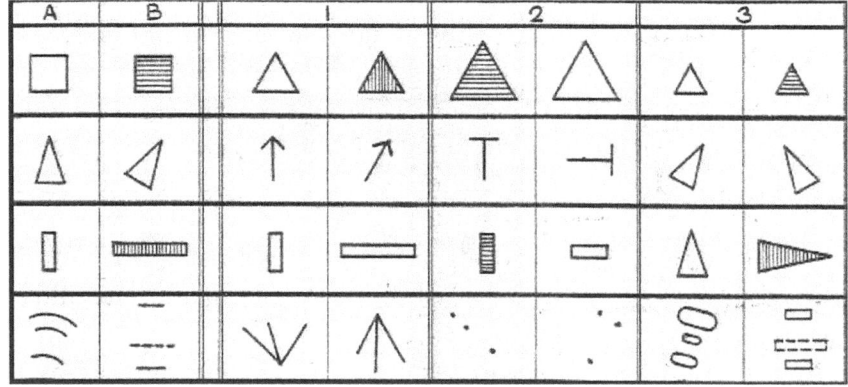
>
> *Note.* From *The Spearman Visual Perception Test,* by C. Spearman, 1933. Reprinted with permission of the History of Psychology Centre, British Psychological Society.

mainly citing the quantitative research reviews known as meta-analyses, which permit results from many primary studies to be aggregated on a single topic. Longitudinal studies, such as the Terman Study of the Gifted (formerly *Genetic Studies of Genius*) and other post-Terman investigations, are also cited. In addition, large-scale population studies, principally the Scottish Mental Surveys of 1932 (87,498 children tested) and 1947 (70,805 children tested) with the follow-up Lothian Birth Cohort studies, are also referenced. Here I report aggregate predictions, using IQ and general cognitive ability g interchangeably, as they tend to be indistinguishable on correlational studies.

Each predictive methodology has its strengths and limitations. Meta-analyses are generally considered to offer a higher level of evidential support than individual studies, and they are available here because of the size and scope of the IQ research literature. Some of the alternative approaches described elsewhere in this book have not yet been studied enough to support a meta-analysis. The advent of meta-analyses is said to have improved the quality of research in gifted education (Steenbergen-Hu & Olszewski-Kubilius, 2016). At the same time, the emphasis in meta-analyses upon the magnitudes of effect sizes (*ES*) can obscure findings of small magnitude differences that can be quite meaningful in real life (e.g., Abelson, 1985). Following Cohen's (1988) guidance for interpreting effect sizes, a correlation of $r = .10$ may be considered *small*, $r = .30$ may be considered *medium*, and $r = .50$ may be considered *large*. Effect sizes of .20 may be considered *small*, .50 may be considered *medium*, and .80 may be considered *large*. Through their forward-looking design, longitudinal research methodologies also offer unparalleled predictive insights, while also carrying significant limitations (e.g., participant attrition and generalizability across time, cohorts, and populations). Longitudinal investigations have proven instrumental in dispelling myths about gifted children (e.g., Subotnik & Arnold, 1994). Finally, large-scale population studies like the Scottish Mental Surveys (conducted when participants had a mean age of 11 years) with their follow-ups (when participants had mean ages ranging from 70 years to 90 years) offer unprecedented insights into long-term outcomes directly or indirectly associated with childhood intelligence.

By way of preview, the predictive capacity of IQ/psychometric *g* has been described as "one of the most central phenomena in all of behavioral science, with broad explanatory powers" (Jensen, 1998, p. xii) and as "one of the most replicated results in psychology" (Deary, 2012, p. 146). Schmidt and Hunter (2000) concluded that intelligence is "the most important trait or construct in all of psychology, and the most 'successful' trait in applied psychology" (p. 4). As 52 prominent signatories agreed, general cognitive ability is "strongly related, probably more so than any other single measurable human trait, to many important educational, occupational, economic, and social outcomes" (Gottfredson, 1997a, p. 14). At the same time, however impressive the predictive capacity of IQ, it must be understood as only a partial predictor of outcome and a probability of sorts. There are many pathways to success in life (and many different forms of success), and they do not all require high IQ. High IQ does not guarantee successful outcome in any area, except perhaps IQ tests.

Educability, Occupational Achievement, and Adaptive Behaviors

In examining predictive capacity, it is helpful to begin with Leta S. Hollingworth's (1931) observation that the "gifted child" (as defined by high

IQ) is far more *educable* than most children. The association of IQ with educability extends to teacher-assigned grades, achievement test scores, and years of education completed. Selected meta-analyses and large-scale/longitudinal findings pertaining to education and IQ report show the following:

- A large population correlation of $\rho = .54$ between g and *school grades*, after correction for measurement error and indirect range restriction (Roth et al., 2015) derived from 162 primary studies and 240 independent samples, with an overall sample size of $N = 105,185$.
- An aggregated correlation of $r = .74$ between g and Basic Reading ($N = 5,873$), aggregated $r = .76$ with Reading Comprehension ($N = 10,041$), and aggregated $r = .72$ with Basic Math ($N = 5,357$) on *standardized achievement tests* (Zaboski et al., 2018; average ES between psychometric g and reading/math achievement test skills was $r^2 = .54$; derived from 37 primary studies covering ages 6–19 years, most involving large standardization samples). In related large-scale findings, Deary and his colleagues (2007) reported a .81 correlation between intelligence at the age of 11 and achievement test results at the age of 16. This 5-year prospective longitudinal study of more than 70,000 English students examined the association between psychometric intelligence and educational achievement in national examinations in 25 academic subjects.
- Much higher long-term *educational attainment* (based on highest level of education completed) for gifted than for nongifted students: Findings with gifted participants (IQ > 140) in psychology's first longitudinal study, Terman's Study of the Gifted, showed that 99% (1,516 of the 1,528 participants) graduated from high school; approximately 70% of the males and 67% of the females graduated from college (compared to 8% normative expectations in California at the time); and almost 40% of males and 22% of the females completed some postgraduate work (Tomlinson-Keasey & Little, 1990). More recent meta-analytic investigations of the association of IQ with educational attainment have reported reciprocal causation, finding that education has a small but beneficial effect on intelligence (Ritchie & Tucker-Drob, 2018).

As Deary and Johnson (2010) observed, "Bright people tend to get more schooling, and the longer-schooled tend to be brighter" (p. 1362).

In terms of occupational achievement, meta-analyses have also shown that general cognitive ability g also plays an integral role (consistently with high *r* > .50 correlations) at predicting occupational attainment, occupational training success, and occupational performance (e.g., Ree & Earles, 1992, Salgado et al., 2003). In a 2004 review of meta-analytic studies, Schmidt and Hunter reported that general cognitive ability "predicts both occupational level attained and performance within one's chosen occupation and does so better than any other ability, trait, or disposition" (p. 162). Across job positions, they reported the following unweighted average correlations with IQ or its equivalent:

- .72 with level of *occupational attainment* (corrected for measurement error, with both cross-sectional and longitudinal variation as a person ages and takes new jobs);
- .63 with *performance on job training* programs; and
- .55 for *job performance*, ranging from to .23 (lowest complexity jobs) to .58 (highest complexity jobs, including professional, scientific, and upper management jobs).

Finally, high intelligence has long been understood as a protective factor, supporting individual resilience to sociocultural adversity, as initially proposed in the Kauai Longitudinal Study (Werner & Smith, 1982). Meta-analyses have shown IQ to predict adaptive behaviors, reduced emotional distress, and better health, including the following:

- A high population correlation between IQ and *adaptive behavior* of $\rho=.51$ (Alexander, 2017; 148 samples, with 16,468 participants); although this meta-analysis is restricted to lower ability samples, other investigations suggest that the association between IQ and adaptive behavior may also hold for high-ability samples (e.g., Douthitt, 1992; Kane & Oakland, 2015).
- Significantly lower levels of *anxiety* in gifted compared to nongifted children (*ES* = -0.72, 4 studies) and no difference in *depressive symptomatology* (*ES* = -0.17, 6 studies; Martin et al., 2010).
- A 24% lower *risk of early death* during adulthood, from a +1 standard deviation (*SD*) advantage in childhood cognitive test scores, independent of childhood socioeconomic status (Calvin et al., 2011; 16 prospect cohort studies with a 17- to 69-year follow-up, comprising 22,453 deaths across 1,107,022 participants). In a large-scale population study with follow-up, Čukić and her colleagues (2017) reported that higher childhood IQ is associated with lower risk of all-cause mortality across most of the human life span (based on findings from the 1947 Scottish Mental Survey, in which students

in an entire country were tested with an IQ test at age 11 and then followed longitudinally for more than 60 years).

Gottfredson and Deary (2004) explained the health benefits of high intelligence as coming through acquisition of knowledge and skills that prove helpful in preventing chronic disease and injury, as well as complying with complex treatment regimens.

Limits to IQ's Predictive Capacity

What does IQ *not* predict? A great deal, it turns out. Square all of the correlations provided in the meta-analyses in the previous section, and you will get the proportion of variance that has been explained (or more accurately, shared between variables). Multiply this number by 100 to convert to percent, and then subtract from 100%, and you have computed the percent of unexplained variance. It is always large. IQ's predictive power is considerable, but what is left unexplained is also considerable. Wechsler spent most of his life trying unsuccessfully to develop tests of what he called the "non-intellective factors" that explain the variance in real-life performance that intelligence tests cannot explain (e.g., Wechsler, 1950).

Of the areas specified in the Marland Report's (1972) federal definition of giftedness, IQ does not appear to predict creativity or leadership. Kim (2005) reported meta-analytic findings of a small correlation ($r = .17$) between intelligence and creativity (derived from 21 studies and 45,880 participants), with little support for a higher correlation with creativity being found above a 120 IQ threshold. Similarly, Judge et al. (2004) reported meta-analytic findings showing that the relationship between intelligence and leadership is small (uncorrected $r = .21$; when corrected for range restriction, $r = .27$). Their meta-analysis was derived from 96 sources, 151 samples, and $N = 40,652$ participants. As a point of reference, McClain and Pfeiffer (2012) reported that 90% of state definitions of giftedness include intelligence, 78% include high achievement, 54% include creativity, 56% include a specific talent (e.g., artistic talent), and 30% include leadership.

The self-report of gifted individuals also confirms the limits in IQ's predictive power. When asked directly in midlife, about one-third of the adult participants (32.0% of males; 35.3% of females) in Terman's Study of the Gifted reported they had fallen short of living up to their intellectual capabilities. A small 1.1% of men considered themselves "largely a failure," compared to 1.0% of women. Some 67.3% of men and 63.4% of women rated themselves as having fulfilled their early intellectual capabilities (Oden, 1968; Shurkin, 1992). Clearly, more than IQ is necessary for success in life.

Contemporary Cognitive-Intellectual Tests

Modern psychometric measures of cognitive-intellectual ability tend to share some common characteristics. In perhaps the first important insight about essential content, Sharp (1899) concluded that measures need to require *complex* rather than *elementary* mental processes for successful performance (see also Gottfredson, 1997b). Phrased differently, cognitive-intellectual tasks should ideally involve mental transformation or manipulation of stimuli. Second, they need to sample a wide range of mental abilities, avoiding overreliance on a single cognitive domain (e.g., acquired knowledge). Third, they need to use multiple and varied testing methods, avoiding dependency on a single method (e.g., matrix reasoning). Fourth, they need to sample abilities with performances that vary widely between people and across ages, recognizing that age-sensitive growth in normative performance is a natural way of accessing low and high ability levels. Fifth, they should be careful to avoid construct-irrelevant testing requirements (e.g., performance speed) that may detract from valid measurement of the targeted ability. Sixth, contemporary tests need to be standardized and constructed using age-stratified, representative normative samples, closely paralleling U. S. Census findings. Based on normative findings, item difficulties and corresponding ability scores are extracted. Moreover, an examinee's performance may be ranked relative to those of age peers. Seventh, they need to be validated through multiple methodologies for their intended application. Eighth, they need to be shown to yield temporally stable and internally consistent scores. And finally, they need to use a variety of statistical and expert review methods to minimize sex, racial, or ethnic group biases. Existing professional standards provide further guidance in the areas of test score reliability, validity, and fairness (American Educational Research Association et al., 2014).

Robertson et al. (2011) surveyed school psychologists and reported that tests endorsed by at least 10% of practitioners for identification of giftedness included the Wechsler intelligence scales (endorsed by 51%),

Woodcock-Johnson Tests of Cognitive Abilities (24%), Stanford-Binet Intelligence Scales (17%), and the Differential Ability Scales (13%). To these might be added popular group ability tests like the Cognitive Abilities Test (CogAT) and the Otis-Lennon School Abilities Test (OLSAT), both used widely by educators and school systems across the nation. Most identification of gifted and talented students is no longer done by psychologists.

Evolution of Composite IQ

For better or worse, the summary/composite score generated by intelligence tests is often one of the criteria used for eligibility determination for gifted education programs. The acronym *IQ* is still used by several tests, but Intelligence Quotient is a misnomer because no contemporary intelligence tests use the ratio (*quotient*) method of deriving a composite. As originally formulated by William Stern (1912/1914), the Intelligence Quotient was a ratio of *mental age* (in months) to *chronological age* (in months). The IQ was later multiplied by 100 to eliminate the decimals. From the start, however, psychologists recognized that reduction of any person's performance to a single number was a betrayal of the intent of intelligence tests (see Wolf, 1973, p. 203, for Théodore Simon's reaction to the IQ score, and Lamiell, 2012, for a description of Stern's regret at how the IQ summary score was used). The original IQ also provided misleading results beyond a certain age, because although chronological age continues to increase in a linear manner, mental age does not.

For more than 75 years, the preferred IQ summary score has been a deviation standard score that describes an examinee's test performance relative to their age peers, based upon normative expectations. Most intelligence tests set a normative *mean* of 100 ($SD = 15$), although some group ability tests use a *SD* of 16. Assuming a normal bell-curve distribution of scores, the deviation method means that an IQ of 100 ranks at the 50th percentile for age, 120 at the 91st percentile, 125 at the 95th percentile, 130 at the 98th percentile, and 135 at the 99th percentile. Because psychometrics show that test scores are imprecise due to measurement error and other statistical effects, it is considered optimal in practice to report a probability-based confidence interval surrounding the obtained score. Descriptive labels that vary from test to test are commonly attached to IQ, with the relatively neutral Wechsler intelligence scale descriptions being widely used for varying test scores (i.e., *extremely low, very low, low average, average, high average,* and *very high*). It should be noted that there are many other classes of scores beyond deviation standard scores by which test performance may be understood (e.g., Woodcock, 1999).

Some 82.6% of school psychologists consider the IQ test score as being "Important or Very Important" in determining gifted eligibility (Robertson et al., 2011, p. 792), although as a matter of educational policy, a majority of states currently do not stipulate specific IQ test or cut scores for gifted eligibility decisions (McClain & Pfeiffer, 2012). The Marland Report (1972) included a statement that a minimum of 3% to 5% of the school population would be found to be gifted according to its definition. Historically, Terman (1931) suggested setting an arbitrary IQ of 130 or 140 to identify gifted students, while Hollingworth (1931) considered an IQ of 130 or more (then at the 99th percentile on the Stanford-Binet) as a reasonable demarcation for identifying gifted children. It is most accurate to state that both saw the IQ score as a *necessary but not sufficient* criterion for gifted placement.

How Different Composite IQs Fare With Gifted Samples

Intelligence test results have historically been considered largely interchangeable, thanks in part to Spearman's (1927) theorem of the *indifference of the indicator*, which stated that "for the purpose of indicating the amount of g possessed by a person, any test will do just as well as any other, provided only that its correlation with g is equally high" (p. 197). In practical terms, this has meant that as long as intelligence tests remain saturated with g, one test may be reasonably substituted for another without expectations of significant score changes. Table 11.1 provides preliminary evidence that non-g measures yield lower scores. This finding is not new; McCallum et al. (1984) reported that cognitive processing measures yielded significantly lower scores than either the Stanford-Binet or Wechsler scales, likely resulting in fewer positive eligibility decisions for gifted education placement. The implication is that school districts expecting gifted students to approach the +2 *SD* score level may reduce the number of eligible students by requiring a CHC or cognitive processing test to be administered. Of course, there may also be advantages in using nontraditional tests to select different types of students for gifted education placement.

Table 11.1 reports the mean (*SD*) composite IQs for research samples of gifted students for several major intelligence tests. Convenience samples of students who have been found to be eligible for gifted education place-

TABLE 11.1
Mean (SD) Overall Composite Scores for Gifted Student Samples on Major Tests

Test	Gifted Sample	Composite Score
WISC-V	$n = 95$	FSIQ = 127.5 (*8.8*)
WISC-V	$n = 95$	GAI = 127.1 (*9.6*)
DAS-II	$n = 68$	GCA = 125.4 (*10.3*)
SB5	$n = 96$	FSIQ = 123.7 (*9.0*)
KABC-II	$n = 95$	FCI = 120.1 (*11.8*)
WJ IV Cog	$n = 53$	Gf-Gc Comp. = 119.2 (*9.6*)
KABC-II	$n = 95$	MPI = 118.7 (*11.9*)
CAS	$n = 118$	FS = 118.2 (*10.0*)
WJ III Cog NU	$n = 124$	GIA Standard = 116 (*10*)

Note. These composite score values are listed in descending order and are derived from validity studies in test technical manuals. FSIQ = Full Scale IQ; GAI = General Ability Index; GCA = General Conceptual Ability; FCI = CHC Global Fluid-Crystallized Index; Gf-Gc Composite = Fluid-Crystallized Composite; MPI = Luria's Global Mental Processing Index; FS = Full Scale Standard Score; and GIA = General Intellectual Ability. For tests, WISC-V = *Wechsler Intelligence Scale for Children, Fifth Edition* (Wechsler et al., 2014); DAS-II = *Differential Ability Scales, Second Edition* (Elliott, 2007); SB5 = *Stanford-Binet Intelligence Scales, Fifth Edition* (Roid, 2003); KABC-II = *Kaufman Assessment Battery for Children, Second Edition* (Kaufman & Kaufman, 2004); WJ IV Cog = *Woodcock-Johnson IV Tests of Cognitive Abilities* (McGrew et al., 2014); CAS = *Das-Naglieri Cognitive Assessment System* (Naglieri & Das, 1997); WJ III Cog NU = *Woodcock-Johnson III Tests of Cognitive Abilities, Normative Update* (McGrew et al., 2007).

ment are routinely gathered as part of the special population studies each time a new test is published. The criteria for identification are variable but usually include gifted eligibility and an individual or group cognitive ability score that is two standard deviations or more above the normative mean. Unexpectedly, the most recent edition of the Woodcock-Johnson (WJ IV Cog; McGrew et al., 2014) does not report a mean GIA for its gifted sample, so the table has defaulted to the mean GIA reported for the immediate previous edition.

The composite mean scores listed in Table 11.1 are derived from seven independent gifted samples. Ideally, these scores could be compared across tests administered to a single rigorously identified sample. Intelligence test scores lower than an IQ of 130 may be partially explained by criterion contamination (unreliability in how students were initially placed), regression to the mean (lower IQs on retest), and the Flynn effect (increases in population intelligence and norms over time, thereby lowering individual scores).

In general, Table 11.1 shows that different intelligence tests can yield surprising variability in test scores, with more traditional *g* tests (WISC-V and DAS-II) yielding higher mean scores and tests derived from different theoretical models (i.e., CHC and cognitive processing theories) yielding lower mean scores. The SB5, WJ IV Cog, and WJ III NU Cog are derived from the Cattell-Horn-Carroll (CHC) model, which emphasizes broad second-order ability factors, while the KABC-II and the CAS are derived from a Lurian model of cognitive processing.

Specific Forms of Giftedness and the Broad Ability Factors

Intelligence tests have long performed best as measures of general intellectual giftedness, but they also are of value in identifying students with more specific or circumscribed gifts, such as those in mathematical reasoning (e.g., Sowell et al., 1990) or visual-spatial ability (e.g., Wai et al., 2009). The most recent editions of the Wechsler and Stanford-Binet intelligence scales, for example, contain composite indices of both quantitative reasoning and visual-spatial processing (Roid, 2003; Wechsler et al., 2014). Domain-specific giftedness has been emphasized over general ability by some scholars in giftedness because of its potential to lead to specialization and, presumably, eventual eminence (e.g., Subotnik et al., 2011).

Although the higher order general cognitive ability factor *g* is derived from test variance common to *all* tests in a given cognitive battery, lower order broad (or group) ability factors are derived from variance shared by just two or more cognitive tests. Broad ability scores tend to be narrower in focus and easier to describe, with less generality and less predictive capacity than *g*. The broad ability factors generated by Carroll (1993) are summarized as follows:
- **Fluid intelligence:** Facility in reasoning, particularly where adaptation to new situations is required and previously acquired knowledge and learning assemblies are of limited utility. Ability is said to be *fluid* when it takes different forms or utilizes different cognitive

skill sets according to the unique demands of the problem requiring solution.
- **Crystallized intelligence:** Depth and breadth of accessible stores of culture-specific knowledge and skills, as well as the capacity to acquire further knowledge via familiar learning strategies. Ability is said to be *crystallized* when it has taken a definitive form through practice, repetition, and frequent use. Crystallized ability is most synonymous with verbal intelligence, including word knowledge and factual knowledge.
- **Visual-spatial processing:** Analysis, synthesis, transformation, and retention of visual-spatial stimuli, including images (pictorial and figural), perspectives, and locations.
- **Auditory processing:** Analysis, discrimination, closure, and synthesis of auditory stimuli, including speech sounds, environmental sounds, and prosody; related to phonological awareness.
- **Processing speed:** Rate of performance when completing low-difficulty cognitive tasks, including reaction time, thinking speed, and performance speed.
- **Retrieval ability:** Accuracy and efficiency of mental retrieval from long-term and remote memory storage.
- **Memory and learning:** Ability to hold, transform, and act on material in immediate awareness; related to working memory and short-term memory.

In an expanded conceptual framework, Schneider and McGrew (2018) offered the Cattell-Horn-Carroll model as a synthesis of the contributions of Raymond B. Cattell, John L. Horn, and John B. Carroll. Some 20 broad ability factors are proposed, including a domain-free reasoning factor of fluid reasoning (*Gf*); several acquired knowledge capacities, including comprehension knowledge (*Gc*), domain-specific knowledge (*Gkn*), reading and writing (*Grw*), and quantitative knowledge (*Gq*); several factors related to memory, including working memory capacity (*Gwm*), learning efficiency (*Gl*), and retrieval fluency (*Gr*); at least six domain-specific sensory and motor abilities, including visual (*Gv*), auditory (*Ga*), olfactory (*Go*), tactile (*Gh*), kinesthetic (*Gk*), and psychomotor ability (*Gp*); and several speed factors including reaction/decision time (*Gt*), processing speed (*Gs*), and psychomotor speed (*Gps*). Although there is much to commend in the CHC model, there are some serious limitations documented in Wasserman (2019).

The possibility that some individuals may demonstrate high performance on measures of these broad abilities opens up possibilities for many new subtypes of specific giftedness, but it should be cautioned that there is not much of a research foundation for the educational implications of these abilities (see Wai et al., 2009, for a remarkable example of broad ability research that moves the field beyond g). Moreover, research has not convincingly demonstrated the stability and validity of ability profiles (e.g., Borsuk et al., 2006; Watkins, 2003), and the predictive capacity of the broad ability factors has not been consistently demonstrated after the contributions of g have been statistically controlled or partialled out (Canivez & Youngstrom, 2019; McGill, 2017). As Zaboski et al. (2018) reported in their meta-analyses, "Psychometric g explained more variance in academic outcomes than all broad abilities combined" (p. 42).

One possible value of broad ability measures is generating modal profiles of gifted samples. Table 11.2 contains mean (*SD*) standard scores for four independent gifted samples, groups of students already placed in gifted education (usually after having obtained a composite IQ ≥ 130 in previous testing), on four major ability/intelligence tests. Due to missing data, the Woodcock-Johnson IV Tests of Cognitive Abilities reported only two cluster scores, so the table defaults to the previous edition, the WJ III Cog NU. The table includes data from the WISC-V (Wechsler et al., 2014), the DAS-II (Elliott, 2007), the SB5 (Roid, 2003), and the WJ III Cog NU (Woodcock et al., 2001).

As shown in Table 11.2, scores reflecting verbal or crystallized knowledge tend to consistently rank among the highest scores generated by students previously identified as gifted. Fluid reasoning, including mathematical reasoning, ranks high. Scores tapping information processing speed tend to consistently rank among the lowest scores generated by gifted students, consistent with observations that many gifted students are more thoughtful or contemplative than fast in their work.

Best Practices for Gifted Assessment

"We don't read your reports," I was told by the county gifted education coordinator, commenting on the gifted assessment program I ran at the local university. "We just look at the scores."

TABLE 11.2
Mean (SD) Broad Ability Scores for Gifted Student Samples

	WISC-V (n = 90–95)	DAS-II (n = 69)	SB5 (n = 96)	WJ III Cog NU (n = 40–125)
Knowledge/Verbal	127.7 (12.3)	125.4 (12.2)	121.7 (9.7)	116 (10)
Quantitative	122.1 (11.8)	--	121.6 (13.5)	--
Visual Spatial	121.2 (11.5)	117.8 (12.3)	123.0 (11.3)	107 (11)
Reasoning/Nonverbal	120.3 (12.0)	121.4 (12.8)	121.0 (10.3)	115 (9)
Working Memory	117.9 (11.7)	116.7 (12.0)	115.8 (10.1)	109 (13)
Processing Speed	112.9 (13.5)	112.0 (13.3)	--	114 (17)

Note. For tests, WISC-V = Wechsler Intelligence Scale for Children, Fifth Edition (Wechsler et al., 2014); DAS-II = *Differential Ability Scales, Second Edition* (Elliott, 2007); SB5 = *Stanford-Binet Intelligence Scales, Fifth Edition* (Roid, 2003); and WJ III Cog NU = *Woodcock-Johnson III Tests of Cognitive Abilities, Normative Update* (McGrew et al., 2007).

I was stunned by this sobering disclosure and did not share it with my graduate students, who were taught that intelligence test scores should never be interpreted blindly and without context. Intelligence test scores provide a snapshot of an individual's cognitive abilities at a fixed point in time and in a specific environment, relative to one's background and history. Although this chapter has focused on the high predictive value of IQ, it is best understood in context in conjunction with other relevant information about the examinee. As Wechsler (1939, p. 48) advised, when the background history is incongruent with the IQ, trust the life history.

Several Tenets of Best Practice

There is no single best practice for gifted assessment, because gifted assessments may be done for a variety of reasons—eligibility determination, academic underachievement, twice-exceptionality, and eligibility for radical acceleration—and each assessment may take different forms, depending upon the referral questions, the needs of the student, and the educational decision to be made. Here, however, I will offer some best practice generalizations for typical gifted education programs.

First, make sure that you understand the purpose of the assessment. If program eligibility determination is the goal, then make sure that you understand basics about the curriculum's pace, breadth, and depth. Most curriculums for gifted learners include provisions for acceleration, complexity, depth, challenge, creativity, and abstraction (e.g., VanTassel-Baska & Stambaugh, 2006). A fast moving, accelerated program will require students to learn more quickly than regular education students. A useful rule of thumb is that gifted students can learn at roughly twice the speed of regular education students (e.g., Gray & Hollingworth, 1931). Students who are slow to grasp complex abstract concepts may struggle to keep up.

Second, always begin by taking a history from a parent and the student, as well as reviewing teacher-assigned academic grades and any previous standardized or criterion-referenced test results. The best predictor of future behavior is past behavior, so the student with a history of successful academic performance is more likely to make the transition to a more demanding gifted curriculum than, perhaps, the student who has never established good work and study habits. Many gifted students thrive in a challenging, stimulating academic environment after having faltered in a poorly fitting environment, so some consideration needs to be given to the possibility that a teacher-student mismatch or other problems with educational fit can obfuscate the identification process. Formal teacher input needs to be interpreted with caution, given published concerns about the validity and technical adequacy of teacher-completed gifted behavior rating scales (Cleveland, 2017; Jarosewich et al., 2002).

Third, explain the purpose of the assessment and build rapport with the examinee. I sometimes say, "We want to understand what is easiest and hardest for you, so we can help you be at your best in school." It may be helpful to present subtests using respected scholar-practitioner Nancy Robinson's suggested introduction, "Here are some tasks that I think you will find interesting" (as opposed to representing the IQ subtests as "games"). During test administration, the examiner should endeavor to "bring out the best" in the examinee, while still respecting standardization procedures. Silverman (2013) and Gilman (2008) offered some exceptionally helpful guidance for test administration and interpretation, to which I might add: Be prepared for your highly gifted examinees to surprise you with correct responses that the test developers never envisioned.

Select an intelligence test that will make it possible to highlight any reported strengths or specific talents, to the extent possible. My default measures are generally the WISC-V or DAS-II, both exceptionally well-developed norm-referenced tests. If a student is mathematically precocious, then there is value in selecting a measure that explicitly measures mathematical reasoning. Students who are bilingual or English language learners, for example, will commonly perform lower on measures of verbal knowledge and abstraction, simply because they may know fewer English language words. Such a performance pattern (verbal < nonverbal) will need to be discussed and contextually explained in the report. Instead of administering an English language intelligence measure, it may be wiser to select and administer a test in the student's native language, such as the WISC-V Spanish (Wechsler, 2017) or the Batería IV Woodcock-Muñoz (Woodcock et al., 2019), or a multidimensional nonverbal measure, such as the UNIT2 (Bracken & McCallum, 2016).

Note that an assessment conducted specifically to support eligibility for gifted education may *not* be ideal to understand the strengths and weaknesses of gifted learners. A comprehensive assessment can transcend information from the intelligence test to include formal measurement of academic skills, learning style, Dabrowski's intensities, motivation, and social and emotional adjustment. Most often, a comprehensive assessment is requested when a gifted student is underachieving educationally.

Cautions About Nonverbal Testing

Unidimensional, group-administered, nonverbal tests, particularly matrix reasoning measures (e.g., Raven's Progressive Matrices, Naglieri Nonverbal Ability Test), have seen a surge in popularity in recent years, mostly in the hope of improving the underrepresentation of ethnic, racial, and socioeconomic minorities in gifted education, but some caution is recommended. Gifted education as it currently stands is extremely verbal, saturated with meaning and spoken communication. The matrix reasoning measures use geometric figures without inherent meaning to examine problem-solving processes that include matching visual patterns, reasoning by analogy, serial reasoning, and spatial visualization (e.g., mentally rotating and folding), among others. These forms of reasoning may not be the kinds of reasoning that are most predictive of success in gifted placements. In 1966, David Wechsler anticipated this problem in one of the last articles he wrote for the general public when he explicitly argued against the use of nonverbal tests to predict academic performance:

> It is now two years since the New York City school system eliminated the I.Q. from pupils' records. Banned under the pressure of groups that claimed the I.Q. was unfair to the culturally deprived, it has been replaced by achievement tests. Meanwhile, a great deal of effort is being put into developing new, nonverbal scales to measure schoolchildren's abilities while eliminating the troublesome factor of language.... Neither of these substitutes is an adequate replacement for the I.Q.... The substitutes simply do not test enough of the abilities that go to make up individual intelligence.... Contrary to claims, the results of [nonverbal] performance tests have been generally disappointing. The findings indicate that while they may be useful in certain situations, and for certain diagnostic groups, they prove quite unsatisfactory as alternates for verbal scales. They correlate poorly with verbal aptitudes and are poor prognosticators of over-all learning ability as well as school achievement. Above all, they have turned out to be neither culture-free nor culture-fair. (Wechsler, 1966, pp. SM12, 63)

Other concerns with overreliance on nonverbal testing may be found in Lohman (2005) and Lakin and Lohman (2011). It is possible that use of nonverbal measures intended to improve diversity in gifted education may have the unintended consequence of identifying some students who struggle to succeed in the language-intensive accelerated gifted classroom. There need to be multiple pathways to gifted education eligibility, with careful follow-up of students identified in every pathway.

Strengths and Limitations of the Psychometric Approach

The IQ-based psychometric approach to intelligence testing has much to recommend it. First, it has more than 100 years of research support behind it, marking *intelligence* as the most researched construct in the entire field of psychology. At the time this chapter is being written, more than 160,000 citations are generated from "intelligence" on the American Psychological Association PsycNet database, with more than 30,000 specifically for "IQ." Intelligence testing made possible the oldest longitudinal study, the Terman Study of the Gifted, followed by many other longitudinal studies of gifted individuals (e.g., Subotnik & Arnold, 1994). Intelligence testing is also the subject of unprecedented large-scale studies, such as the Scottish Mental Surveys of 1932 and 1947. While considering alternative ways to think about serving the needs of gifted students, it would be a mistake to overlook the massive body of research undergirding IQ testing.

Second, intelligence tests provided the scientifically grounded foundation not only for IQ but also for gifted education and its practices in acceleration, enrichment, and differentiation. Research into the use of intelligence tests for efficient academic student grouping began in 1916, when Elisabeth A. Irwin, the founder of the Little Red Schoolhouse in Manhattan, set a goal of creating "a school environment in which the child himself could feel that he belonged" (Irwin & Marks, 1924, p. v). A larger scale approach for grouping students was launched in the Oakland experiment of 1917–1918, when Terman's student Virgil E. Dickson organized the intelligence testing of some 6,500 students in each of Oakland, CA's 45 elementary schools. As recounted in Chapman's (1988) *Schools as Sorters*, Dickson concluded that low-ability students struggle to master the standard curriculum, while high-ability students need accelerated curriculums. Dickson called for segregation of students into special classes based on their ability levels. Receiving enthusiastic endorsements from administrators and teachers, Dickson (1919) concluded:

> Standard tests, both psychological and pedagogical—group and individual—should be of great assistance in classification of pupils according to ability and capacity to do the work. They should inspire better teaching and better educational guidance through a more intimate knowledge of the individual child. (p. 225)

By 1932, Hollingworth optimistically (and perhaps naively) predicted that in the future, education would be differentiated for all students, based on their individual learning differences:

> It will become inconceivable that once upon a time the American people forcibly seized the children of the nation, and subjected them from seven to fourteen or sixteen years of age indiscriminately to undifferentiated education, without knowledge of their abilities, their mental contents, or their emotional problems.
> By means of scientific psychological service, education will become differentiated on the rational basis of individual differences in biological nature. The school will be fitted to the child. (Hollingworth, 1940, p. 48)

Ability grouping became widely practiced in school systems, until Oakes (1985) and Slavin (1987) published criticisms of educational tracking, especially its contribution to racial and ethnic inequality through early-age placement and difficulty changing tracks once placed. In the last decade or two, however, ability grouping has seen a resurgence. In a recent second-order meta-analysis of six meta-analyses, Steenbergen-Hu et al. (2016) reported findings that gifted students consistently benefit from being placed in special groups or programs designed for high-ability/achieving students (Hedges's $g = 0.37$, a medium effect size ranging from 0.32 to 0.47). Outcomes of multiple ability group meta-analyses showed that students benefited from within-class groupings and cross-grade subject groupings, but not between-class groupings. Three meta-analyses on acceleration showed that accelerated students significantly outperformed their nonaccelerated same-age peers (Hedges's g = 0.70, a large effect size).

Third, intelligence testing is *objectively* based on the child's responses to a wide array of problem-solving behaviors, determined through standardized inquiry in the testing situation, and statistically evaluated relative to expectations from a nationally representative normative sample. Teacher, parent, and institutional input do not count—only the child's test performance. In this way, every child has an equal opportunity. At the same time, any person's test performance, especially on measures of acquired knowledge, may reflect shortcomings in prior learning opportunities stemming from an economically disadvantaged background. The same disadvantages may find expression in suboptimal classroom academic performance. The test that can predict academic performance while compensating for a disadvantaged environment has not yet been developed. Robinson (2003) confronted the unfortunate reality:

> It is argued that children who have had a less facilitative upbringing or come from poorer educational backgrounds should not be penalized for their history. . . . But this argument ignores the fact that it is those very experiences, in addition to whatever genetic elements may be at work, that develop academic outcomes. That some children have been deprived of needed cognitive and academic sustenance all their lives is a monumental tragedy, but we cannot correct the situation by placing them in ill-fitting programs nor denying program access to children who need them. (p. 257)

In identification and education of gifted and talented students, Benbow and Stanley (1996) recommended that educators promote *both* equity and excellence, rather than pitting equity against excellence.

Several limitations are prominent with gifted and talented intelligence testing, beginning with the comparatively impoverished interpretive yield from these tests. IQ tests yield scores that permit a student's performance to be ranked relative to normative age expectations, thereby helping with eligibility decisions. In some cases, they help to specify performance ranks in specific areas of giftedness (i.e., verbal, mathematical, spatial). What they do *not* do but could do is:

- examine different forms of reasoning proficiency across different academic contents (i.e., language, figures, numbers);

- measure capacity for rote learning of different types, required in education but often intensely disliked by gifted learners;
- specify how a student learns best and under what conditions;
- sample meta-cognitive processes, especially proficiency with study skills and problem-solving strategies selection and implementation; and
- measure motivation and need for achievement.

If there is a market, intelligence tests could be designed to yield considerably more information about student learning characteristics that are relevant to gifted education.

A second shortcoming is related to reporting standards, or what I call *application-centered psychometrics*. There is reasonably high agreement among psychometricians that tests are not themselves inherently valid, reliable, or fair, but their scores may be valid, reliable, and fair for specific applications and special populations. As articulated by Wilkinson and the American Psychological Association's Task Force on Statistical Inference (1999), for example, "Reliability is a property of the scores on a test for a particular population of examinees" (p. 596). For educators' purposes, reporting of test score psychometrics should include explicit and specific focus on validity, reliability, and fairness with respect to gifted and talented applications. For example, the factor structure of a test should remain robust in high-ability examinees, the test-retest stability over time should remain high in gifted samples, and the classification frequencies (i.e., IQ ≥ 130) across different racial and ethnic groups should be reported. Moreover, if a test is intended for use with intellectually gifted students, then its capacity to discriminate between different levels and subtypes of giftedness should be established. Although reporting application-centered psychometrics for high-ability students would probably require that more cases be collected and more efforts be expended by test developers, it becomes a way of rigorously supporting the use of the test among gifted students. The complacency with which test developers expect that all intelligence tests can be used to identify gifted students was first evident to me when a new intelligence test promoted its value for gifted assessment *without* having actually gathered a gifted sample (Brueggemann et al., 2006).

A third shortcoming of intelligence tests is their often inadequate *ceilings* (i.e., when the uppermost limits of tests are inadequate to capture true student capabilities). In their book on giftedness research, Thompson and Subotnik (2010) conveyed concern about the abundance of test score ceilings that are "too low to measure progress or growth" (p. 3). It is an industry-wide problem. When developing the Wechsler intelligence scales, Wechsler (1958) went on record as deliberately keeping test score ceilings artificially low:

> The lower ceiling of the W-B [Wechsler-Bellevue] and the WAIS [Wechsler Adult Intelligence Scale] is no accident but represents the author's deliberate attempt to eschew measuring abilities beyond points at which he feels they no longer serve as valid measures of a subject's general intelligence. IQ's of 150 or more may have some discriminative value in certain fields, such as professional aptitude, but only as measures of unusual intellectual capacity. Intellectual ability, however, is only partially related to general intelligence. Exceptional intellectual ability is itself a kind of special ability. (p. 110)

Wechsler's decision was ideological rather than scientific and has effectively made it difficult to study individuals who are highly and profoundly gifted (e.g., Gross, 2004; Hollingworth, 1942; Lubinski et al., 2001). Fortunately, the publisher of the WISC-IV extended the norms upwards (Zhu et al., 2008), and there is reason to hope the same will be done with succeeding editions.

Perhaps the most pressing perceived shortcoming of intelligence testing stems from proportional underrepresentation of ethnic, racial, and socioeconomic minorities in gifted education programs (e.g., Ford, 2014; National Research Council, 2002). Although Ford (1998) reported that ethnic, racial, and socioeconomic minorities are underrepresented in every phase of the gifted eligibility process, from recruitment and referral through retention, Cross and Cross (2017) indicted the IQ test "as a gatekeeper that continues to perpetuate the underrepresentation of some groups" (p. 191). Although intelligence tests may yield scores that produce a disproportionate impact for various racial or ethnic groups, test developers use a number of psychometric procedures to reduce or eliminate potential biases (e.g., Wasserman & Bracken, 2013). Moreover, modifications in testing, such as nonverbal testing, multilingual testing, and some of the methods described elsewhere in this book continue to be developed and refined in efforts to reduce minority-majority intelligence score gaps, as well as to offer alternative pathways to identification of gifted students. Concerns about the effects of socioeconomic status upon intelligence test performance are as old as the tests themselves; Binet (1911/1916) reviewed several datasets comparing the test performances of students from rich neighborhoods to those from poor neighborhoods, tentatively concluding that higher socioeconomic class tends to benefit language development. That children from lower income backgrounds are educationally disadvantaged in ways reflected on the intelligence tests is not a fault of the tests. As Robinson (2003) wisely observed, intelligence tests cannot reasonably be expected to solve the problems of society.

I close this chapter with an idea and a recommendation. The idea is that the intelligence test is *just a technology*—a powerful and predictive technology, but still just a technology to serve the needs of exceptional children. Educators should continue to refine technologies and create new technologies, but should not throw away the old technologies until they have developed a new one that is equally useful and without the limitations. However intelligence tests have been misused, there is evidence that they can perform some tasks quite well. As Frank L. Schmidt, a leading developer of meta-analytic methods, concluded in 2002: "If we want to remain a science-based field, we cannot reject what we know to be true in favor of what we would like to be true."

DISCUSSION QUESTIONS

1. Spearman identified a statistically derived general ability factor. What qualities do you think best define the general intellectual ability?
2. What outcomes can be predicted by IQ?
3. What current role do IQ and ability scores have in eligibility decisions for gifted placement? What is the role in your region?
4. What broad abilities do you think are most essential to academic and professional success, and why?
5. What are some strengths and limitations of the psychometric approach in gifted and talented identification?
6. What alternatives to intelligence in gifted and talented identification do you most value, and why?

DISCUSSION QUESTIONS, continued

7. Which do you think is more important for gifted education—a curriculum matched to student cognitive and academic characteristics, or a curriculum developed for equity and social justice?

References

Abelson, R. P. (1985). A variance explanation paradox: When a little is a lot. *Psychological Bulletin, 97*(1), 129–133. https://doi.org/10.1037/0033-2909.97.1.129

Alexander, R. M. (2017). *The relation between intelligence and adaptive behavior: A meta-analysis* (Publication No. 10287961) [Doctoral dissertation, University of Kansas]. ProQuest Dissertations and Theses Global.

American Educational Research Association, American Psychological Association, & National Council on Measurement in Education. (2014). *Standards for educational and psychological testing.* American Educational Research Association.

Arvey, R. D. (1986). General ability in employment: A discussion. *Journal of Vocational behavior, 29*(3), 415–420. https://doi.org/10.1016/0001-8791(86)90017-5

Binet, A. (1916). New investigation upon the measure of the intellectual level among school children. In H. H. Goddard (Ed.) & E. S. Kite (Trans.), *The development of intelligence in children* (pp. 274–329). Williams & Wilkins. (Original work published 1911)

Binet, A. (1975). *Modern ideas about children* (S. Heisler, Trans.). Heisler. (Original work published 1909)

Benbow, C. P., & Stanley, J. C. (1996). Inequity in equity: How "equity" can lead to inequity for high-potential students. *Psychology, Public Policy, and Law, 2*(2), 249–292. https://doi.org/10.1037/1076-8971.2.2.249

Borsuk, E. R., Watkins, M. W., & Canivez, G. L. (2006). Long-term stability of membership in a Wechsler Intelligence Scale for Children—Third Edition (WISC-III) subtest core profile taxonomy. *Journal of Psychoeducational Assessment, 24*(1), 52–68. https://doi.org/10.1177/0734282905285225

Bracken, B. A., & McCallum, R. S. (2016). *Universal nonverbal intelligence test* (2nd ed.). PRO-ED.

Brueggemann, A. E., Reynolds, C. R., & Kamphaus, R. W. (2006). The Reynolds Intellectual Assessment Scales (RIAS) and assessment of intellectual giftedness. *Gifted Education International, 21*(2–3), 127–136. https://doi.org/10.1177/026142940602100305

Calvin, C. M., Deary, I. J., Fenton, C., Roberts, B. A., Der, G., Leckenby, N., & Batty, G. E. (2011). Intelligence in youth and all-cause-mortality: Systematic review with meta-analysis. *International Journal of Epidemiology, 40*(3), 626–644. https://doi.org/10.1093/ije/dyq190

Canivez, G. L., & Youngstrom, E. A. (2019). Challenges to the Cattell-Horn-Carroll theory: Empirical, clinical, and policy implications. *Applied Measurement in Education, 32*(3), 232–248. https://doi.org/10.1080/08957347.2019.1619562

Carroll, J. B. (1993). *Human cognitive abilities: A survey of factor-analytic studies*. Cambridge University Press.

Carroll, J. B. (2003). The higher-stratum structure of cognitive abilities: Current evidence supports g and about ten broad factors. In H. Nyborg (Ed.), *The scientific study of general intelligence* (pp. 5–21). Pergamon.

Cattell, R. B. (1940). A culture-free intelligence test. I. *Journal of Educational Psychology, 31*(3), 161–179. https://doi.org/10.1037/h0059043

Chapman, P. D. (1988). *Schools as sorters: Lewis M. Terman, applied psychology, and the intelligence testing movement, 1890–1930*. New York University Press.

Cleveland, L. M. (2017). *Examining the relationship between gifted behavior rating scores and student academic performance* (Publication No. 10280435) [Doctoral dissertation, Concordia University-Portland]. ProQuest Dissertations and Theses Global.

Cohen, J. (1988). *Statistical power analysis for the behavioral sciences* (2nd ed.). Erlbaum.

Cross, T. L., & Cross, J. R. (2017). Challenging an idea whose time has gone. *Roeper Review, 39*(3), 191–194. https://doi.org/10.1080/02783193.2017.1319000

Čukić, I., Brett, C. E., Calvin, C. M., Batty, G. D., & Deary, I. J. (2017). Childhood IQ and survival to 79: Follow-up of 94% of the Scottish Mental Survey 1947. *Intelligence, 63*, 45–50. https://doi.org/10.1016/j.intell.2017.05.002

Deary, I. J. (2012). 125 years of intelligence in The American Journal of Psychology. *American Journal of Psychology, 125*(2), 145–154. https://doi.org/10.5406/amerjpsyc.125.2.0145

Deary, I. J., & Johnson, W. (2010). Intelligence and education: Causal perceptions drive analytic processes and therefore conclusions. *International Journal of Epidemiology, 39*(5), 1362–1369. https://doi.org/10.1093/ije/dyq072

Deary, I. J., Strand, S., Smith, P., & Fernandes, C. (2007). Intelligence and educational achievement. *Intelligence, 35*(1), 13–21. https://doi.org/10.1016/j.intell.2006.02.001

Dickson, V. E. (1919). Report of the Department of Research. In *Report of the Superintendent of Schools, 1917–1918* (pp. 173–225). Board of Education.

Douthitt, V. L. (1992). A comparison of adaptive behavior in gifted and nongifted children. *Roeper Review, 14*(3), 149–151. https://doi.org/10.1080/02783199209553410

Elliott, C. D. (2007). *Differential ability scales—second edition: Introductory and technical handbook*. Pearson.

Ford, D. Y. (1998). The underrepresentation of minority students in gifted education: Problems and promises in recruitment and retention. *Journal of Special Education, 32*(1), 4–14. https://doi.org/10.1177/002246699803200102

Ford, D. Y. (2014). Segregation and the underrepresentation of Blacks and Hispanics in gifted education: Social inequality and deficit paradigms. *Roeper Review, 36*(3), 143–154. https://doi.org/10.1080/02783193.2014.919563

Galton, F. (1879). Psychometric experiments. *Brain: A Journal of Neurology, 2*(2), 149–162. https://doi.org/10.1093/brain/2.2.149

Gilman, B. J. (2008). *Academic advocacy for gifted children: A parent's complete guide*. Great Potential Press.

Goddard, H. H. (1911). Two thousand normal children measured by the Binet Measuring Scale of Intelligence. *Pedagogical Seminary, 18*(2), 232–259. https://doi.org/10.1080/08919402.1911.10532788

Gottfredson, L. S. (1997a). Mainstream science on intelligence: An editorial with 52 signatories, history, and bibliography. *Intelligence, 24*(1), 13–23. https://doi.org/10.1016/S0160-2896(97)90011-8

Gottfredson, L. S. (1997b). Why g matters: The complexity of everyday life. *Intelligence, 24*(1), 79–132. https://doi.org/10.1016/S0160-2896(97)90014-3

Gottfredson, L. S., & Deary, I. J. (2004). Intelligence predicts health and longevity, but why? *Current Directions in Psychological Science, 13*(1), 1–4. https://doi.org/10.1111/j.0963-7214.2004.01301001.x

Gray, H. A., & Hollingworth, L. S. (1931). The achievement of gifted children enrolled and not enrolled in special opportunity classes. *Journal of Educational Research, 24*(4), 255–261. https://doi.org/10.1080/00220671.1931.10880207

Gross, M. U. M. (2004). *Exceptionally gifted children* (2nd ed.). Routledge.

Gustafsson, J.-E. (1984). A unifying model for the structure of intellectual abilities. *Intelligence, 8*(3), 179–203. https://doi.org/10.1016/0160-2896(84)90008-4

Hollingworth, L. S. (1931). How should gifted children be educated? *Baltimore Bulletin of Education, 9*(9), 195–198.

Hollingworth, L. S. (1940). Psychological service for public schools. In H. L. Hollingworth (Ed.), *Public addresses by Leta S. Hollingworth* (pp. 37–48). Science Press.

Hollingworth, L. S. (1942). *Children above 180 IQ Stanford-Binet: Origin and development*. World Book.

Irwin, E. A., & Marks, L. A. (1924). *Fitting the school to the child: An experiment in public education*. Macmillan.

Jarosewich, T., Pfeiffer, S. I., & Morris, J. (2002). Identifying gifted students using teacher rating scales: A review of existing instruments. *Journal of Psychoeducational Assessment, 20*(4), 322–336. https://doi.org/10.1177/073428290202000401

Jensen, A. R. (1998). *The g factor: The science of mental ability*. Praeger.

Judge, T. A., Colbert, A. E., & Ilies, R. (2004). Intelligence and leadership: A quantitative review and test of theoretical propositions. *Journal of Applied Psychology, 89*(3), 542–552. https://doi.org/10.1037/0021-9010.89.3.542

Kane, H., & Oakland, T. D. (2015) The differentiation of adaptive behaviours: Evidence from high and low performers. *Educational Psychology 35*(6), 675–688. https://doi.org/10.1080/01443410.2014.893558

Kaufman, A. S., & Kaufman, N. L. (2004). *Manual. Kaufman assessment battery for children* (2nd ed.). Pearson.

Kim, K. H. (2005). Can only intelligent people be creative? *Journal of Secondary Gifted Education, 16*(2–3), 57–66. https://doi.org/10.4219/jsge-2005-473

Lakin, J. M., & Lohman, D. F. (2011). The predictive accuracy of verbal, quantitative, and nonverbal reasoning tests: Consequences for talent identification and program diversity. *Journal for the Education of the Gifted, 34*(4), 595–623. https://doi.org/10.1177/016235321103400404

Lamiell, J. T. (2012). Introducing William Stern (1871–1938). *History of Psychology, 15*(4), 379–384. https://doi.org/10.1037/a0027439

Lohman, D. F. (2005). The role of nonverbal ability tests in identifying academically gifted students: An aptitude perspective. *Gifted Child Quarterly, 49*(2), 111–138. https://doi.org/10.1177/001698620504900203

Lubinski, D. Webb, R. M., Morelock, M. J., & Benbow, C. P. (2001). Top 1 in 10,000: A 10-year follow-up of the profoundly gifted. *Journal of Applied Psychology, 86*(4), 718–729. https://doi.org/10.1037/0021-9010.86.4.718

Marland, S. P., Jr. (1972). *Education of the gifted and talented: Report to the Congress of the United States by the U.S. Commissioner of Education*. U.S. Government Printing Office.

Martin, L. T., Burns, R. M., & Schonlau, M. (2010). Mental disorders among gifted and nongifted youth: A selected review of the epidemiologic literature. *Gifted Child Quarterly, 54*(1), 31–41. https://doi.org/10.1177/0016986209352684

McCallum, R. S., Karnes, F. A., & Edwards, R. P. (1984). The test of choice for assessment of gifted children: A comparison of the K-ABC, WISC-R, and Stanford-Binet. *Journal of Psychoeducational Assessment, 2*(1), 57–63. https://doi.org/10.1177/073428298400200107

McClain, M.-C., & Pfeiffer, S. (2012). Identification of gifted students in the United States today: A look at state definitions, policies, and practices. *Journal of Applied School Psychology, 28*(1), 59–88. https://doi.org/10.1080/15377903.2012.643757

McGill, R. J. (2017). Re-(examining) relations between CHC broad and narrow cognitive abilities and reading achievement. *Journal of Educational and Developmental Psychology, 7*(1), 265–282. https://doi.org/10.5539/jedp.v7n1p265

McGrew, K. S., LaForte, E. M., & Schrank, F. A. (2014). *Woodcock-Johnson IV technical manual*. Riverside.

McGrew, K. S., Schrank, F. A., & Woodcock, R. W. (2007). *Woodcock-Johnson III Normative Update: Technical manual*. Riverside.

Naglieri, J. A. (2003). *Naglieri nonverbal ability test: Individual administration manual*. The Psychological Corporation.

Naglieri, J.A., & Das, J. P. (1997). *Cognitive assessment system: Interpretive handbook*. Riverside.

National Research Council. (2002). *Minority students in special and gifted education*. National Academies Press.

Neisser, U., Boodoo, G., Bouchard, T. J., Jr., Boykin, A. W., Brody, N., Ceci, S. J., Halpern, D. F., Loehlin, J. C., Perloff, R., Sternberg, R. J., & Urbina, S. (1996). Intelligence: Knowns and unknowns. *American Psychologist, 51*(2), 77–101. https://doi.org/10.1037/0003-066X.51.2.77

Oakes, J. (1985). *Keeping track: How schools structure inequality.* Yale University Press.

Oden, M. H. (1968). The fulfillment of promise: 40-year follow-up of the Terman Gifted Group. Stanford University Press. *Genetic Psychology Monographs, 77*(1), 3–93.

Penrose, L. S., & Raven, J. C. (1936). A new series of perceptual tests: Preliminary communication. *British Journal of Medical Psychology, 16*(2), 97–104. https://doi.org/10.1111/j.2044-8341.1936.tb00690.x

Raven, J. C. (1938). *Progressive matrices: A perceptual test of intelligence: Individual form.* Lewis.

Ree, M. J., & Earles, J. A. (1992). Intelligence is the best predictor of job performance. *Current Directions in Psychological Science, 1*(3), 86–89. https://doi.org/10.1111/1467-8721.ep10768746

Reeve, C. L., & Charles, J. E. (2008). Survey of opinions on the primacy of *g* and social consequences of ability testing: A comparison of expert and non-expert views. *Intelligence, 36*(6), 681–688. https://doi.org/10.1016/j.intell.2008.03.007

Ritchie, S. J., & Tucker-Drob, E. M. (2018). How much does education improve intelligence? A meta-analysis. *Psychological Science, 29*(8), 1358–1369. https://doi.org/10.1177/0956797618774253

Robertson, S. G., Pfeiffer, S. I., & Taylor, N. (2011). Serving the gifted: A national survey of school psychologists. *Psychology in the Schools, 48*(8), 786–799. https://doi.org/10.1002/pits.20590

Robinson, N. M. (2003). Two wrongs do not make a right: Sacrificing the needs of gifted students does not solve society's unsolved problems. *Journal for the Education of the Gifted, 26*(4), 251–273. https://doi.org/10.4219/jeg-2003-307

Roid, G. H. (2003). *Stanford-Binet intelligence scales: Technical manual* (5th ed.). Riverside.

Roth, B., Becker, N., Romeyke, S., Schäfer, S., & Spinath, F. M. (2015). Intelligence and school grades: A meta-analysis. *Intelligence, 53,* 118–137. https://doi.org/10.1016/j.intell.2015.09.002

Rowe, E. W., Kingsley, J. M., & Thompson, D. F. (2010). Predictive ability of the General Ability Index (GAI) versus the Full Scale IQ among gifted referrals. *School Psychology Quarterly, 25*(2), 119–128. https://doi.org/10.1037/a0020148

Salgado, J. F., Anderson, N., Moscoso, S., Bertua, C., de Fruyt, F., & Rolland, J. P. (2003). A meta-analytic study of general mental ability validity for different occupations in the European community. *Journal of*

Applied Psychology, 88(6), 1068–1081. https://doi.org/10.1037/0021-9010.88.6.1068

Schmidt, F. L. (2002). The role of general cognitive ability and job performance: Why there cannot be a debate. *Human Performance, 15*(1–2), 187–210. https://doi.org/10.1080/08959285.2002.9668091

Schmidt, F. L., & Hunter, J. E. (2000). Select on intelligence. In E. A. Locke (Ed.), *Handbook of principles or organization behavior* (pp. 3–14). Blackwell.

Schmidt, F. L., & Hunter, J. E. (2004). General mental ability in the world of work: Occupational attainment and job performance. *Journal of Personality and Social Psychology, 86*(1), 162–173. https://doi.org/10.1037/0022-3514.86.1.162

Schneider, W. J., & McGrew, K. S. (2018). The Cattell-Horn-Carroll theory of cognitive abilities. In D. P. Flanagan & E. M. McDonough (Eds.), *Contemporary intellectual assessment: Theories, tests, and issues* (4th ed., pp. 73–163). Guilford Press.

Schrank, F. A., McGrew, K. S., & Mather, N. (2014). *Woodcock-Johnson IV tests of cognitive abilities.* Riverside.

Sharp, S. E. (1899). Individual psychology: A study in psychological method. *American Journal of Psychology, 10*(3), 329–391. https://doi.org/10.2307/1412140

Shurkin, J. N. (1992). *Terman's kids: The groundbreaking study of how the gifted grow up.* Little, Brown.

Silverman, L. K. (2013). *Giftedness 101.* Springer.

Slavin, R. E. (1987). Ability grouping and student achievement in elementary schools: A best-evidence synthesis. *Review of Educational Research, 57*(3), 293–336. https://doi.org/10.3102/00346543057003293

Sowell, E. J., Zeigler, A. J., Bergwall, L., & Cartwright, R. M. (1990). Identification and description of mathematically gifted students: A review of empirical research. *Gifted Child Quarterly, 34*(4), 147–154. https://doi.org/10.1177/001698629003400404

Spearman, C. (1904). "General intelligence," objectively determined and measured. *American Journal of Psychology, 15*(2), 201–292. https://doi.org/10.2307/1412107

Spearman, C. (1923). *The nature of "intelligence" and principles of cognition.* Macmillan.

Spearman, C. (1925). *A measure of "intelligence" for use in schools.* Methuen.

Spearman, C. (1927). *The abilities of man: Their nature and measurement.* Macmillan.

Spearman, C. (1930). *Creative mind.* Nisbet & Co.

Spearman, C. (1933). *The Spearman visual perception test* [Unpublished test].

Steenbergen-Hu, S., Makel, M. C., & Olszewski-Kubilius, P. (2016). What one hundred years of research says about the effects of ability grouping and acceleration on K–12 students' academic achievement: Findings of two second-order meta-analyses. *Review of Educational Research, 86*(4), 849–899. https://doi.org/10.3102/0034654316675417

Steenbergen-Hu, S., & Olszewski-Kubilius, P. (2016). How to conduct a good meta-analysis in gifted education. *Gifted Child Quarterly, 60*(2), 134–154. https://doi.org/10.1177/0016986216629545

Stern, W. (1911a). The supernormal child. *Journal of Educational Psychology, 2*(3), 143–148.

Stern, W. (1911b). The supernormal child. II. *Journal of Educational Psychology, 2*(4), 181–190.

Stern, W. (1914). *The psychological methods of testing intelligence* (Educational Psychology Monographs, No. 13; G. M. Whipple, Trans.). Warwick & York. (Original work published 1912)

Sternberg, R. J., & Detterman, D. K. (Eds.). (1986). *What is intelligence? Contemporary viewpoints on its nature and definition*. Ablex.

Subotnik, R. F., & Arnold, K. D. (Eds.). (1994). *Beyond Terman: Contemporary longitudinal studies of giftedness and talent*. Ablex.

Subotnik, R. F., Olszewski-Kubilius, P., & Worrell, F. C. (2011). Rethinking giftedness and gifted education: A proposed direction forward based on psychological science. *Psychological Science in the Public Interest, 12*(1), 3–54. https://doi.org/10.1177/1529100611418056

Terman, L. M. (1931). The gifted child. In C. Murchison (Ed.), *A handbook of child psychology* (pp. 568–584). Clark University Press. https://doi.org/10.1037/13524-018

Terman, L. M., Lyman, G., Ordahl, G., Ordahl, L. E., Galbreath, N., & Talbert, W. (1917). *The Stanford revision and extension of the Binet-Simon Scale for measuring intelligence*. Warwick & York.

Thompson, B., & Subotnik, R. F. (Eds.). (2010). *Methodologies for conducting research on giftedness*. American Psychological Association.

Tomlinson-Keasey, C., & Little, T. D. (1990). Predicting educational attainment, occupational achievement, intellectual skill, and personal adjustment among gifted men and women. *Journal of Educational Psychology, 82*(3), 442–455. https://doi.org/10.1037/0022-0663.82.3.442

Undheim, J. O. (1981). On intelligence IV: Toward a restoration of general intelligence. *Scandinavian Journal of Psychology, 22*(1), 251–265. https://doi.org/10.1111/j.1467-9450.1981.tb00401.x

Van Sickle, J. H., Witmer, L., & Ayres, L. P. (1911). Provision for exceptional children in public schools. In *United States Bureau of Education, Bulletin No. 14, Whole No. 461* (pp. 7–92). United States Bureau of Education.

VanTassel-Baska, J., & Stambaugh, T. (2006). *Comprehensive curriculum for gifted learners* (3rd ed.). Allyn & Bacon.

Wai, J., Lubinski, D., & Benbow, C. P. (2009). Spatial ability for STEM domains: Aligning over 50 years of cumulative psychological knowledge solidifies its importance. *Journal of Educational Psychology, 101*(4), 817–835. https://doi.org/10.1037/a0016127

Wasserman, J. D. (2018). A history of intelligence assessment: The unfinished tapestry. In D. P. Flanagan & E. M. McDonough (Eds.), *Contemporary intellectual assessment: Theories, tests, and issues* (4th ed., pp. 3–55). Guilford Press.

Wasserman, J. D. (2019). Deconstructing CHC. *Applied Measurement in Education, 32*(3), 249–268. https://doi.org/10.1080/08957347.2019.1619563

Wasserman, J. D., & Bracken, B. A. (2013). Fundamental psychometric considerations in assessment. In J. R. Graham & J. A. Naglieri (Eds.), *Handbook of psychology, Vol. 10. Assessment psychology* (2nd ed., pp. 50–81). Wiley.

Watkins, M. W. (2003). IQ subtest analysis: Clinical acumen or clinical illusion? *The Scientific Review of Mental Health Practice, 2*(2), 118–141.

Watt, D. C. (1998). Lionel Penrose, F.R.S. (1898–1972) and eugenics: Part one. *Notes and Records of the Royal Society of London, 52*(1), 137–151. https://doi.org/10.1098/rsnr.1998.0041

Wechsler, D. (1939). *The measurement of adult intelligence*. Williams & Wilkins. https://doi.org/10.1037/10020-000

Wechsler, D. (1950). Cognitive, conative, and non-intellective intelligence. *American Psychologist, 5*(3), 78–83. https://doi.org/10.1037/h0063112

Wechsler, D. (1958). *The measurement and appraisal of adult intelligence* (4th ed.). Williams & Wilkins.

Wechsler, D. (1966, June 26). The I.Q. is an intelligent test. *The New York Times*, SM12–13, 63–66.

Wechsler, D. (2017). *Wechsler intelligence scale for children—Fifth edition: Spanish*. Pearson.

Wechsler, D., Raiford, S. E., & Holdnack, J. A. (2014). *WISC-V technical and interpretive manual*. Pearson.

Werner, E. E., & Smith, R. S. (1982). *Vulnerable but invincible: A longitudinal study of resilient children and youth*. McGraw-Hill.

Whipple, G. M. (1911). The supernormal child: A correction. *Journal of Educational Psychology, 2*(5), 287–288.

Whipple, G. M. (1913). Supernormal children. In P. Monroe (Ed.), *A Cyclopedia of Education* (Vol. 5; pp. 464–467). Macmillan.

Whipple, G. M. (1919). *Classes for gifted children: An experimental study of methods of selection and instruction*. Public School Publishing Company.

Wilkinson, L., & Task Force on Statistical Inference, American Psychological Association, Science Directorate. (1999). Statistical methods in psychology journals: Guidelines and explanations. *American Psychologist, 54*(8), 594–604. https://doi.org/10.1037/0003-066X.54.8.594

Wolf, T. H. (1973). *Alfred Binet*. University of Chicago Press.

Woodcock, R. W. (1999). What can Rasch-based scores convey about a person's test performance? In S. E. Embretson & S. L. Hershberger (Eds.), *The new rules of measurement: What every psychologist and educator should know* (pp. 105–127). Erlbaum.

Woodcock, R. W., Alvarado, C. G., Schrank, F. A., McGrew, K. S., Mather, N., & Muñoz-Sandoval, A. F. (2019). *Batería IV Woodcock-Muñoz*. Riverside Insights.

Woodcock, R. W., McGrew, K. S., & Mather, N. (2001). *Woodcock-Johnson III Tests of Achievement*. Riverside.

Zaboski, B. A., Kranzler, J. H., & Gage, N. A. (2018). Meta-analysis of the relationship between academic achievement and broad abilities of the Cattell-Horn-Carroll theory. *Journal of School Psychology, 71*, 42–56. https://doi.org/10.1016/j.jsp.2018.10.001

Zhu, J. J., Cayton, T., Weiss, L., & Gabel, A. (2008). *WISC-IV extended norms: WISC-IV Technical report #7*. Pearson.

CHAPTER 12

Charting a Course for the Future

PAULA OLSZEWSKI-KUBILIUS AND TRACY L. CROSS

The field of gifted education does not lack for conceptual frameworks or theories about giftedness and talent. There is a great deal of interest in understanding talent and what is needed to develop it from multiple sectors—educators who want to develop the potential of all of their students, domain specialists and professionals who seek to increase the number of individuals who become experts and contribute to their field, and psychologists who want to understand the nature of intelligence and abilities. Irrespective of the motivation, all would agree that developing talent requires an early, continuous, and synergistic investment on the part of families, schools and communities.

Educators who seek to identify their students' talents and provide appropriate opportunities for them are often overwhelmed with the numerous perspectives on giftedness. Some perspectives may resonate with their own beliefs and values more than others. Often, school personnel feel they must choose one perspective over others—one that is consistent with their school mission and culture and their community of students. Our goal with this last chapter is to help readers synthesize the various models, frameworks, and theories by discussing where they are similar, different, overlapping, and compatible (see Figure 12.1).

Similarities Among Models

Giftedness Is Not a Person Variable

Some of the authors refer to their work as theories, and others as models, conceptions, or frameworks. It is clear to us that there is more agreement than disagreement among the various frameworks presented in this book. One common theme across the frameworks is that giftedness is not viewed by the authors as an immutable aspect of an individual or as a person variable, but rather a malleable, acquired characteristic that is developed over time. This is in direct contrast to the typical and historical view of giftedness that emphasizes innate ability and dominates current school practice. Renzulli (Three-Ring Conception of Giftedness) is the most direct on this issue, preferring to label behaviors and products, not individuals, as gifted. This is very different from a traditional view of giftedness as an inborn trait (an entity) that characterizes a person regardless of actual achievement (i.e., giftedness as "being").

Giftedness Can Be Developed

If giftedness is not immutable, then consequently, it can be developed. The frameworks vary in the extent to which they focus on the critical elements involved in developing talent, such as the roles of environment and other personal qualities, but all agree that giftedness is multifaceted, requiring multiple supports and inputs. Subotnik et al. (Talent Development Megamodel) are the most explicit in stating that giftedness starts as potential in all domains and, with opportunity and psychosocial skills, can be

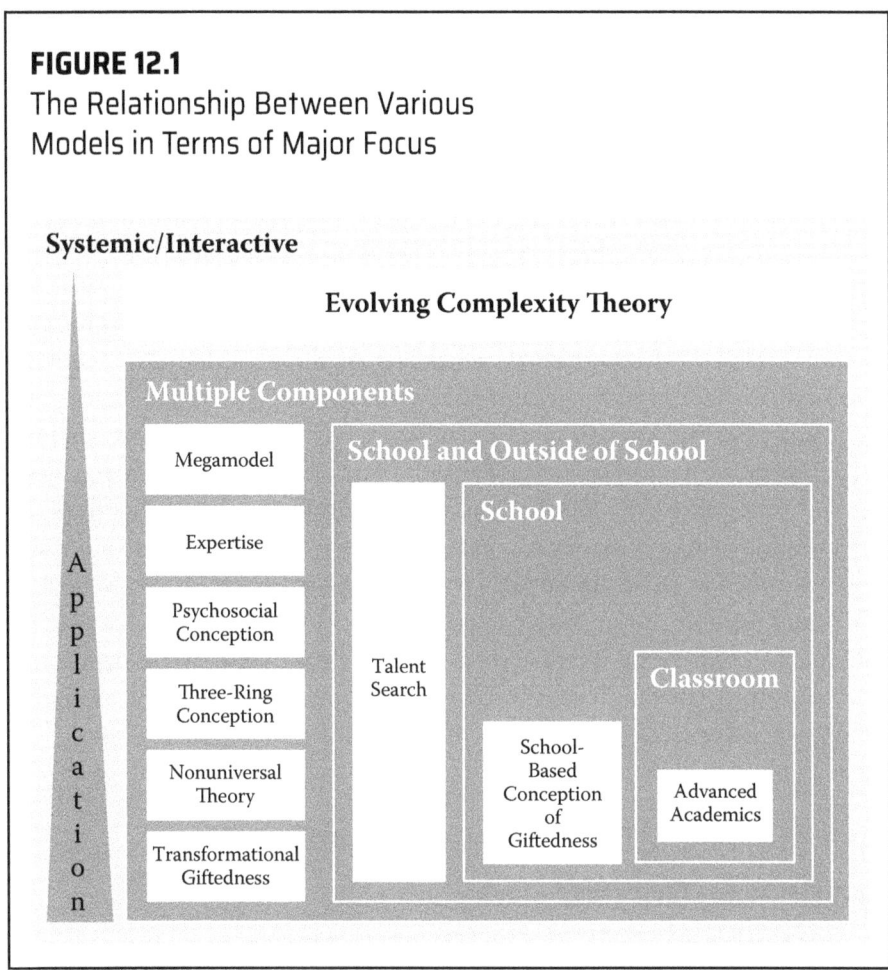

FIGURE 12.1
The Relationship Between Various Models in Terms of Major Focus

developed into competencies, expertise, and eminence. Cross and Cross (School-Based Conception) and Peters and Borland (Advanced Academics) put a primary focus on the role of the school environment in developing talent, while Brody (Talent Search) emphasizes the role of outside-of-school opportunities, including Talent Search assessment and programs. In this understanding, giftedness is "doing."

Giftedness Involves Personal Qualities

Although all of the models recognize the importance of other personal attributes of an individual, particularly motivation, in developing talent, Subotnik et al. (Talent Development Megamodel) and Renzulli (Three-Ring

Conception of Giftedness) are the most explicit about defining these and emphasizing their importance. Subotnik et al. cast these attributes as malleable psychosocial skills that can and must be cultivated via the right kinds of opportunities within and outside of school—a view echoed by the Talent Search model, with different skills being needed at different points in development and the importance of specific skills varying by domain of talent. Cross and Cross (School-Based Conception) claim that psychosocial skills training is necessary to support the motivation and commitment that are required for demonstrated achievement. These become more important as students move through K–12 schooling in their model. Dai (Evolving Complexity Theory) puts a great deal of emphasis on contextual factors and the role of the affordances and opportunities in the environment in shaping both important domain-general characteristics and domain-specific abilities and characteristics. Sternberg asserts the importance of understanding one's unique profile of strengths and weaknesses, using these to shape and select supportive environments, as well as personal characteristics such as ethics and wisdom. At an extreme and rare level involving child prodigies, Feldman (Nonuniversal Theory) recognizes the confluence of multiple family, community, and individual factors that must come together to enable prodigious achievement, which is why it is so infrequent and unique.

Giftedness and Talent Development Are Domain Specific

Another common endorsement among the frameworks within this book is that giftedness is domain specific and should be studied and developed within domains. Many of the authors reject the field's historical focus on IQ and general reasoning ability as the primary or only indicator of giftedness. Sternberg is probably the loudest critic of this limited conception of intelligence and has long argued for a broader conception of intelligence—one that acknowledges that individuals have different patterns of strengths and weaknesses across different types of abilities (creative, practical, and analytical) and that intelligent behavior involves capitalizing on strengths and minimizing weaknesses through careful selection of optimal environments, including domains of specialization. Over time, benefits to societies have come more from accomplishments within specific talent domains than from touting people with assessments of high levels of perceived generic abilities.

The Importance of Domain-Specific Abilities

The Talent Search Model, along with others, emphasizes the importance of patterns ("tilt") of more specific cognitive reasoning abilities, such as verbal, mathematical, and spatial reasoning, which research supports is a better predictor of areas of adult creative accomplishments. The Talent Development Megamodel and the Three-Ring Conception acknowledge the importance of both general IQ and domain-specific abilities to achievement in different domains, the balance and specific nature of which likely varies by domain and changes with development—with domain-specific abilities becoming more important as individuals progress. Cross and Cross, in their School-Based Conception, also acknowledge that general ability or IQ may be the hallmark of advanced potential in younger children, but specialization, domain-specific abilities, and commitment to a domain, along with actual achievement, are the features that define giftedness in school for older students. Similarly, the Advanced Academics model recognizes that students may excel in and only need advanced instruction in particular subject areas, suggesting that giftedness is not general. The canalization of general reasoning ability into specific abilities and interest through experiences within many different contexts in one's environment is at the crux of the ECT framework.

The Importance of the Match Between Abilities and Environmental Supports

Finally, there is agreement among the frameworks that talent flourishes when there is a good match between the propensities of the individual, including interest, ability areas, opportunities, and the affordances in the environment. Parents, educators, and community members can assist in recognizing children's abilities and providing them with the needed supports and resources to move childhood potential into adult achievement. Cross and Cross speak to this point by declaring that for high-ability students to thrive, the schools must be ready for them. Being ready includes a comprehensive plan involving appropriate instructional strategies, classroom and grouping organizations, flexible schedules, accelerative options, and so forth that are understood and supported by the educators, counselors, parents, and role models for the talent domains being emphasized in the particular school context.

Difference Across Models: Where They Focus

One of our goals for this book was to help readers see the connections between the various frameworks—how they intersect and how they can be used simultaneously. As discussed previously, there are many important tenets that they share. Some of the major differences across frameworks are not differences in fundamental beliefs, but in areas of focus or emphasis. See Figure 12.1 for a pictorial representation of where the models primarily focus. For example, the ECT model takes a very broad view, emphasizing that talent development occurs within a system that includes family, school, community, and society. This approach highlights the role of the interaction between person and environment in talent development; the proactive as opposed to passive role of the individual in shaping their environment, choosing opportunities, and recognizing and taking advantage of affordances; and the role of contexts, from the immediate to the distal, and their interactive influences. Understanding talent development from this framework requires looking deeply into the almost moment-by-moment interactions of the individual with their surroundings.

The Talent Development Megamodel emphasizes multiple contributors to talent development with special emphasis on opportunities, which must be offered and taken, and psychosocial skills, which are the levers to transitions to higher stages of talent development. The Three-Ring Conception similarly addresses the role of multiple components in developing potential into talent and has put the most effort into developing applications that enable schools to function as talent development entities. These frameworks provide a long-term perspective of talent development from early childhood to adulthood, with specific adult outcomes, and strive to address all talent domains.

In contrast, Cross and Cross (School-Based Conception) focus most on the K–12 years and on the role of the school in developing school-related talents as a foundation for the development of individual talent trajectories beyond high school. The Advanced Academics model includes an even narrower focus on what occurs at the classroom level. Talent Search really begins its focus in middle school with above-grade-level assessment and accelerative options, particularly those outside of school. Advanced Academics and Talent Search share a focus on programming that is based on educational need and adjustments in pacing and level of content to ensure maximal challenge. Sternberg is mainly concerned with adult manifestations of giftedness. Deliberate practice is applicable throughout the lifespan, more important in some domains than others and more important at particular phases of talent development (see Figure 12.2).

As noted previously, differences across models include where they start their focus (early childhood, middle school), the primacy of particular components (e.g., psychosocial skills, school programs, outside of school programs), and the proposed goal or ultimate purpose of gifted programming. As one might expect, goals mirror the focus of the framework. For example, in Advanced Academics, the goal is to provide the appropriate pacing and level of content within a particular subject at a particular point in time. For Talent Search, the goal is to identify exceptional reasoning abilities and provide acceleration and enrichment within and outside of school that will develop it. For the Three-Ring Conception, the ultimate goal is creative productivity, but this can be defined by the individual and does not necessarily have to be at the level of influencing society or advancing a field. For the Talent Development Megamodel and Transformational Giftedness Model, the goal is to provide the opportunities, training, and support to enable more individuals to make creative, eminent, field-altering contributions that help society.

Nuanced, but important differences exist even within the cases of the School-Based Conception of Giftedness and the Advanced Academics model. Although both are focused in school contexts, the SCG encourages a school-by-school contextual lens, while Advanced Academics offers a prescription for all school contexts.

Conclusion

This book offers descriptions of some of the state-of-the-art and most widely used and respected conceptions, theories, models, and frameworks about developing talent among highly able students. It offers models that are exceptionally broad and encompassing (Evolving Complexity Theory), those that are encompassing yet applied (Talent Development Model), and those that are more narrowly focused on school practice (School-Based Conception and Advanced Academics).

The book also offers domain-specific examples, like conceptions of giftedness within the sports talent domain and Feldman's essential break-

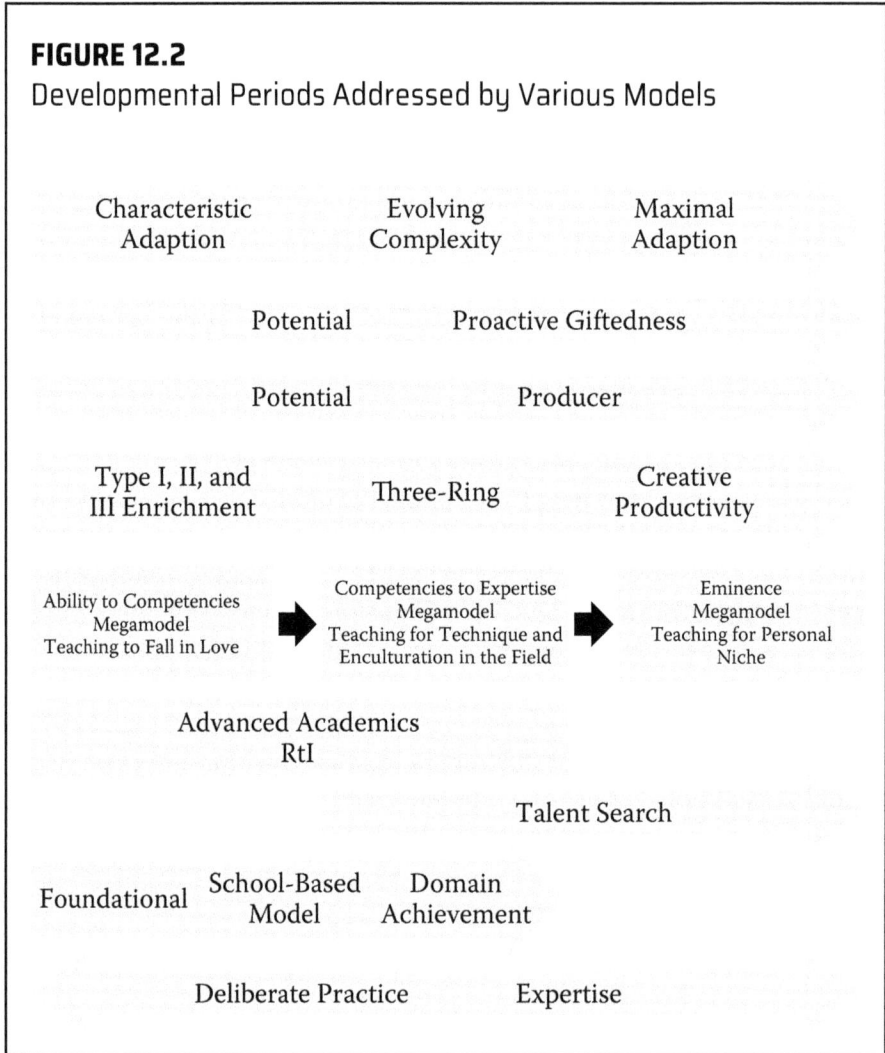

FIGURE 12.2
Developmental Periods Addressed by Various Models

through of Nonuniversal Theory of development. Individually, the chapters offer thoughtful ideas for developing talent in the 21st century. As a collective, the chapters reveal a strong case that promotes several aspects of the talent development philosophy that benefits from years of experimentation and rethinking of educator biases and prejudices. The overall content of the book suggests the arrival of a new halcyon period of gifted education.

ABOUT THE EDITORS

Tracy L. Cross, Ph.D., holds an endowed chair, Jody and Layton Smith Professor of Psychology and Gifted Education, and is the executive director of the Center for Gifted Education and the Institute for Research on the Suicide of Gifted Students at William & Mary. Previously he served Ball State University as the George and Frances Ball Distinguished Professor of Psychology and Gifted Studies, the executive director of the Center for Gifted Studies and Talent Development, and the Institute for Research on the Psychology of Gifted Students.

Paula Olszewski-Kubilius, Ph.D., is director of the Center for Talent Development and professor in the School of Education and Social Policy at

Northwestern University. For 37 years she has developed enrichment and accelerated program models for diverse gifted learners. She writes extensively on issues of talent development. She has served as editor of *Gifted Child Quarterly* and is currently a trustee of the Illinois Mathematics and Science Academy and past-president of the Illinois Association for Gifted Children. She is past-president of the National Association for Gifted Children and received the Distinguished Scholar Award in 2009.

ABOUT THE AUTHORS

James H. Borland, Ph.D., is professor of education at Teachers College, Columbia University, where he directs the programs in the education of gifted students. He has lectured on the education of gifted students across the U.S. and abroad, and he has consulted with numerous school districts, primarily as an evaluator of programs for gifted students. Dr. Borland is the author of numerous books, journal articles, and book chapters. Dr. Borland was awarded the *Gifted Child Quarterly* Paper of the Year Award for 1994 and 2000 and the Award for Excellence in Research from the Mensa Education and Research Foundation in 1989–1990 and 1999–2000.

Linda E. Brody, Ed.D., directs the Study of Exceptional Talent (SET) at the Johns Hopkins Center for Talented Youth. SET offers academic advising and counseling to exceptionally advanced students identified through talent searches and studies their progress over time. Dr. Brody's research focuses on evaluating strategies that facilitate talent development, especially acceleration, and on studying special populations of gifted students, including the highly gifted, gifted females, and twice-exceptional students. She was a recipient of the National Association for Gifted Children's Distinguished Service Award and was inducted into Bridges 2e Hall of Fame for her work on twice-exceptional students.

Jennifer Riedl Cross, Ph.D., is the director of research at the Center for Gifted Education at William & Mary. She is coeditor, with Tracy L. Cross, of *Handbook for Counselors Serving Students With Gifts and Talents* and coauthor, also with Tracy L. Cross, of the second edition of *Suicide Among Gifted Children and Adolescents*. As a social psychologist, Dr. Cross has studied peer relationships, with a particular focus on adolescent crowds. Her research in the field of gifted education emphasizes its social aspects, including attitudes toward giftedness and gifted education.

David Yun Dai, Ph.D., is Professor of Educational Psychology and Methodology at University at Albany, State University of New York. He received his doctoral degree in psychology from Purdue University and worked at a postdoctoral fellow at the National Research Center on the Gifted and Talented at the University of Connecticut. He is currently on the editorial boards of *Gifted Child Quarterly*, *Journal for the Education of the Gifted*, *Roeper Review*, and *Academic Journal of Special Education* (Taiwan).

David Henry Feldman, Ph.D., is a professor in the Eliot-Pearson Department of Child Study and Human Development at Tufts University. He has also served on the faculties of the University of Minnesota and Yale University, and had visiting appointments at Tel Aviv University; the University of California, San Diego; Harvard University; and the University of California, Berkeley. He is the author of *Nature's Gambit: Child Prodigies and the Development of Human Potential* (with Lynn Goldsmith) and *Changing the World: A Framework for the Study of Creativity* (with Mihaly Csikszentmihalyi and Howard Gardner). He has been a Fullbright Scholar and Distinguished Scholar of the National Assocation for Gifted Children. Dr. Feldman was trained at Rochester (B.A.), Harvard (M.Ed.) and Stanford University (M.A., Ph.D.).

About the Authors

David Z. (Zach) Hambrick, Ph.D., is a professor in the Department of Psychology at Michigan State University. His research focuses on the origins of individual differences in expertise. Dr. Hambrick is director of the Expertise Lab at Michigan State and cofounding editor of the *Journal of Expertise*. He is author of more than 100 scientific articles and chapters, and has written for *The New York Times, Slate, Politico,* and *Scientific American*.

Lannie Kanevsky, Ph.D., is an associate professor in the faculty of education at Simon Fraser University (British Columbia, Canada). Abraham J. Tannenbaum supervised her doctoral research in the late 1980s at Teachers College, Columbia University, NY. Her research has focused on the nature and extent of similarities and differences in students' learning processes and preferences. She is the author of the *Tool Kit for Curriculum Differentiation*, on which Possibilities for Learning (http://possibilitiesforlearning.com) is based.

Brooke N. Macnamara, Ph.D., received her doctorate in psychology from Princeton University and is currently an associate professor in the Department of Psychological Sciences at Case Western Reserve University. Her research focuses on predictors of performance variance within multiple domains (e.g., sports, academics, jobs). Specifically, she investigates individual differences in cognitive abilities, beliefs, and training and how well these factors predict achievement and expertise. She is a proponent of replication studies, meta-analyses, and transparency in research.

Scott J. Peters, Ph.D., is a professor of educational foundations and the Richard and Veronica Telfer Endowed Faculty Fellow of Education at the University of Wisconsin–Whitewater. His research work focuses on educational assessment, research design, gifted and talented student identification, equity within advanced educational programs and services, and educational policy.

Sally M. Reis, Ph.D., holds the Letitia Neag Chair in Educational Psychology and is a Board of Trustees Distinguished Professor, teaching fellow, and the former Vice Provost for Academic Affairs at the University of Connecticut. She was a classroom teacher in public education as well as an administrator before her work at UConn. She has authored and coauthored more than 270 articles, books, book chapters, monographs, and technical reports. She worked in a research team that has generated more than $50 million in grants in the last 15 years.

Joseph S. Renzulli, Ed.D., is a Distinguished Professor at the University of Connecticut and an international leader in gifted education and talent development for all students. His Schoolwide Enrichment Model focuses on total school improvement and is widely used throughout the world. He has obtained more than $50 million in research grants, and the American Psychological Association named him among the 25 most influential psychologists in the world. He lists Confratute, a summer program that began in 1978 and has served more than 30,000 educators, as his most important practical contribution.

Robert J. Sternberg, Ph.D., is professor of human development at Cornell University and honorary professor of psychology at the University of Heidelberg, Germany. His Ph.D. is from Stanford, and he holds 13 honorary doctorates. Sternberg's main work is in intelligence, creativity, wisdom, and giftedness. He has won the Grawemeyer Award in Psychology and the William James and James McKeen Cattell Awards from the Association for Psychological Science. He is a member of the National Academy of Education and the American Academy of Arts and Sciences. His work has been cited in the scholarly literature more than 185,000 times.

Rena F. Subotnik, Ph.D., is Director of the Center for Psychology in Schools and Education at the American Psychological Association. The Center promotes high-quality application of psychology to programs and policies for schools and education. One of the Center's missions is to generate public awareness, advocacy, clinical applications, and cutting-edge research ideas that enhance the achievement and performance of children and adolescents with gifts and talents in all domains.

John D. Wasserman, Ph.D., is a practicing child neuropsychologist in Northern Virginia where he specializes in working with twice-exceptional gifted learners. From 2001 to 2007, he developed and directed the Gifted Assessment Program at George Mason University. Previously he worked in psychological and educational test publishing at Riverside Publishing and The Psychological Corporation. He earned his doctorate in 1990 in clinical psychology from the University of Miami, FL, and he completed a 2-year fellowship in clinical neuropsychology at Louisiana State University and Tulane University Medical Centers in New Orleans, LA.

Frank C. Worrell, Ph.D., is a professor of school psychology at the University of California, Berkeley. His areas of expertise include talent development/gifted education, at-risk youth, cultural identities, scale development and validation, teacher effectiveness, time perspective, and the translation of psychological research findings into practice. Dr. Worrell is a fellow of the Association for Psychological Science, the American Educational Research Association, and five divisions of the American Psychological Association; a member of the National Academy of Education; and a former editor of *Review of Educational Research*.

Lightning Source UK Ltd.
Milton Keynes UK
UKHW032312130222
398531UK00016B/272